TEACH YOURSELF BOOKS

CONCISE
GERMAN AND ENGLISH
DICTIONARY

This dictionary contains both German into
English and English into German printed in
the modern Roman type which is clear and
easy to read. Its chief point is its simplicity,
as in nearly every case only one meaning is
given to each word.

The Schoolmaster

TEACH YOURSELF BOOKS

CONCISE GERMAN AND ENGLISH DICTIONARY

German-English/English-German

TEACH YOURSELF BOOKS

ST PAUL'S HOUSE WARWICK LANE LONDON E C 4

First Published 1945
New Edition with Grammar 1946
Revised Edition 1962
This Impression 1972

ISBN 0 340 05789 0

PRINTED AND BOUND IN ENGLAND
FOR THE ENGLISH UNIVERSITIES PRESS LTD
BY HAZELL WATSON AND VINEY LTD AYLESBURY

PREFACE

No dictionary can ever be complete, for language is a living thing that is constantly changing. No sooner is a dictionary compiled—and that may take twenty years—and printing started, than new words are created to meet the ever-changing needs of the day and the dictionary is partly out-of-date before it leaves the presses.

This is especially true in modern times when our life is constantly being altered to meet new conditions, and hosts of words and abbreviations appear, like mushrooms, overnight! Some of the words are ephemeral and will disappear as did "Blighty" after the First World War; others which appear equally transient will remain. What will be the fate of current colloquialisms? We cannot tell, and the dictionary maker must leave such words to future generations to handle: they may remain in the language as slang, they may disappear, or they may become respectable members of linguistic society, just as "pluck" and "guts"—both originally low slang words —are now mere synonyms of "courage."

If the dictionary is bilingual the task is complicated by the fact that both languages have been and are changing. But difficulties are made to be surmounted, and this Concise German Dictionary is a bold attempt to surmount them.

Now a Concise Dictionary has to face all the difficulties enumerated above in the case of full-sized works, together with two others peculiar to itself: (a) the compiler must make a choice of the words most frequently used in each language, and (b) he must give only the most general meanings in each language. Words are kittle cattle and refuse to behave as the dictionary maker would wish. Thus, for example, there are words which can be dismissed easily: *Frechheit* is "insolence," and there is no need to add "impudence" or "sauciness " or other synonyms. *Zug*, however, has a very great number of meanings such as : " drawing, train, march, draught (of air or of liquid), procession, range (of mountains), stroke, expedition, campaign, feature, trait, bent, impulse, groove, platoon, organ stop, move (in chess), flight, migration," together with more than sixty other meanings ! The compiler of a Concise Dictionary cannot afford the space to give all the possible meanings and synonyms of every word, and must therefore make a choice of the most usual ones, sacrificing the others on the altar of conciseness. The user of the dictionary, for his part, must use it intelligently, bearing in mind the context in which the word is found and, if the particular meaning is not listed, see whether he can get it from the general meaning plus the context. In probably ninety-five cases out of a hundred he will find the dictionary will solve his problems.

The Concise Dictionary contains over 10,000 words in each language, selected because of their frequency value. It is reckoned that a working vocabulary of 2,000 most frequently used words in any language will see one through most of the circumstances of every-day life, so that we are justified in saying that the number of words in the Concise Dictionary provides a very handsome margin. Moreover, it contains a fair proportion of words that have emerged during the last five years, and can therefore claim to be up-to-date.

A list of the parts of the principal German strong and irregular verbs is given in Appendix A, and a list of commonly used German abbreviations in Appendix B. Finally, we have added a Concise German Grammar, covering both Accidence and Syntax, with a wealth of illustrative examples. This happy combination of Dictionary and Grammar in such a handy form is, we believe, a unique and valuable addition to the student's armoury.

PREFACE TO THE REVISED EDITION

THE revised edition of this dictionary combines an attempt to bring the work up to date, which, as the original preface indicates, becomes necessary every decade, with an improved layout, the main feature of which is the inclusion of the plural of each noun in the German–English section. Another alteration is the replacement of the abbreviations indicating gender, *m, f, n,* in the English–German section by the actual Definite Article, *der, die, das*. Although this innovation lies outside the tradition of dictionaries, it has been recommended by teachers and scholars of German, and should correspond to modern methods of teaching the language and its grammar. Where listed meanings gave rise to ambiguity in the original work, synonyms or explanations have been added for clarification. Finally, some uncommon words were omitted from both sections to make room for the alterations demanding extra space. We therefore hope that this present edition may now fulfil the needs of the student of German more adequately, and represent more accurately the vocabulary of modern German.

PREFACE TO THE REVISED EDITION

CONTENTS

ACKNOWLEDGMENTS

The Publishers gratefully acknowledge the special services in the preparation of the original dictionary of Major H. E. Husey, Mr. and Mrs. Maximilian Fourman, Mrs. C. M. Stevenson, Mr. Norman Scarlyn Wilson and Mr. P. G. Wilson; also of Mr. and Mrs. B. C. Price in preparing the revised edition.

The Publishers also express their appreciation to Messrs. Burgess and Bowes Ltd. for the use of certain of their copyright material.

A GERMAN-ENGLISH DICTIONARY

ABKÜRZUNGEN
ABBREVIATIONS

f = weiblich = feminine		*n* = sächlich = neuter	
m = männlich = masculine		*pl* = Mehrzahl = plural	
	fig = figuratively		

adj. noun = adjectival noun (see p. 275)

+ acc. ⎫
+ gen. ⎬ expression followed by accusative, genitive, or
+ dat. ⎭ dative case respectively

A

Aal *m*, (-e) eel
Aalbeere *f* (-n) black-currant
Aar *m* (-e) eagle
Aas *n* (Äser) carrion
ab off; - **und zu** now and then
abändern alter
Abänderung *f* (-en) alteration
abarbeiten overwork
Abart *f* (-en) variety
abätzen cauterize
Abbau *m* working (of a mine)
abbeissen bite off
abberufen recall
abbestellen annul
abbezahlen pay off
Abbild *n* (-er) image; portrait
abbinden bind off
abbitten apologize
abblasen blow off
abblättern strip off the leaves
abbrechen break off, pull down
abbrennen burn down
abbringen divert
abbröckeln crumble
Abbruch *m* (-̈e) breaking off, demolition
abbürsten brush off
abbüssen expiate
abdämmen dam up
abdanken abdicate; resign

abdecken uncover, clear the table
Abdruck *m* (-̈e) print, copy
abdrucken to print, copy
abdrücken press off, discharge, squeeze heartily
Abend *m* (-e) evening; **heute**-to-night; **gestern** - last night
Abendblatt *n* (-̈er) evening newspaper.
Abenddämmerung *f* twilight
Abendessen *n* supper
Abendland *n* occident
Abendmahl *n* Holy Communion
Abendröte *f* sunset sky
Abendzeit *f* eventide
Abenteuer *n* (-) adventure
Abenteurer *m* (-) adventurer
Abenteurerin *f* (-nen) adventuress
aber but
Aberglaube *m* (-n) superstition
abergläubisch superstitious
abermalig repeated
abermals again
abfahren depart, start (a journey)
Abfahrt *f* departure
Abfall *m* (-̈e) waste, refuse; slope, recession
abfallen slope, fall off; desert, break away
abfärbren stain; lose colour

abfassen seize; compose (write)
abfertigen dispatch; finish
abfinden indemnify; come to terms with a person
Abfindung f (-en) settlement
abfliessen flow off
Abfluss m (⁒e) outlet, gutter
abfordern demand from
abführen lead away; (medical) purge
Abführmittel n (-) purgative
Abgabe f (-n) fees, excise, tax
Abgang m (⁒e) departure
abgeben deliver
abgebrannt burnt down
abgebrochen abrupt; broken off
abgedroschen trite, hackneyed
abgehen depart, go off
abgelagert seasoned, matured (wine)
abgelaufen expired
abgelebt decrepit
abgelegen remote, distant
abgemacht agreed, all right
abgemessen measured, slow
abgeneigt disinclined
abgenutzt worn out
Abgeordnete m (adj. noun) deputy, member of Parliament
Abgeordnetenhaus n Parliament, chamber of deputies
Abgesandte m f (adj. noun) envoy, delegate
abgeschieden secluded, dead
Abgeschiedenheit f solitude
abgeschmackt tasteless, insipid, absurd
abgesehen von irrespective of
abgespannt tired, low spirited
abgestanden stale (beer)
abgestorben dead, paralyzed
abgestumpft blunt; indifferent
abgewinnen (+ dat.) win from
abgewöhnen wean from
abgiessen pour off, decant
Abgott m (⁒er) idol
Abgötterei f idolatry
abgöttisch idolatrous
abgrämen pine away
abgrenzen limit; define
Abgrund m (⁒e) abyss, precipice
Abguss m (⁒e) casting; sink
abhacken chop off

abhalten detain; prevent
abhanden mislaid, missing
Abhandlung f (-en) treatise, essay
Abhang m (⁒e) slope
abhängen von depend on
Abhängigkeit f dependence
abhauen cut off
abheben lift off
abhelfen remedy
Abhilfe f help, remedy
abholen fetch, call for
abkaufen buy
Abklatsch m (-e) cheap copy
Abkomme m (-n) descendant
Abkommen n agreement
abkühlen cool down
Abkunft f (⁒e) descent
abkürzen abridge, abbreviate
abladen unload
Ablass m (⁒e) (religious) indulgence
ablassen drain
Ablauf m expiration; gutter
ablaufen flow off, expire
ablecken lick off
ablegen lay aside, take off
ablehnen refuse, decline
Ablehnung f (-en) refusal
ableiten divert, derive
ablenken divert
ableugnen deny; disown
Ableugnung f (-en) denial
abliefern deliver
ablösen relieve
abmachen settle
Abmachung f (-en) agreement
abmagern grow thin
Abmarsch m (⁒e) marching off, departure
abmessen measure
abmühen (sich) exert oneself
Abnahme f (-n) decline, waning (moon)
abnehmen take off, amputate, decline
Abnehmer m (-) buyer
Abneigung f (-en) aversion
abnutzen wear out; use up
Abnutzung f wear and tear
Abonnent m (-en) subscriber
abonnieren auf (+ acc.) subscribe to

Abort *m* (-e) water-closet (W.C.)

abpacken unpack

abprallen rebound

abputzen cleanse; clean

abrahmen skim

abräumen clear away

abrechnen settle accounts; deduct

Abrechnungshaus *n* (ᴄer) clearing-house

Abrede *f* (-n) agreement; in - stellen deny

abreden (+ dat.) dissuade

abreiben rub off

Abreise *f* (-n) departure

abreisen leave, start

Abreisskalender *m* (-) tear-off calendar

abrichten train, break in (horse)

Abriss *m* (-e) sketch; summary

abrüsten disarm

abrutschen glide down

absagen decline; refuse

Absatz *m* (ᴄe) pause; heel (shoe); landing; sale; market; paragraph

abschaffen abolish

Abschaffung *f* (-en) abolition

abschätzen, Abschätzung *f* (-en) estimate

Abscheu *m* horror

abscheulich abominable

abschicken dispatch

Abschied *m* (-e) departure; - nehmen take leave; -sbesuch *m* (-e) farewell-visit

abschiessen shoot down, discharge

Abschlag (auf) *m* on account; -szahlung *f* (-en) instalment

abschlagen knock off; refuse

abschlägige Antwort *f* refusal

abschliessen lock; end; terminate; settle

abschnallen unbuckle

abschneiden cut off

Abschnitt *m* (-e) section; coupon

abschöpfen skim

abschrauben unscrew

abschrecken deter; scare away

abschreiben, Abschrift *f* copy

Abschuss *m* (ᴄe) discharge

abschüssig sloping

abschweifen deviate

Abschweifung *f* (-en) digression

abschwören abjure

abseits apart

absenden send, dispatch

Absender *m* (-) sender

absetzen depose; sell

Absetzung *f* (-en) deposition

Absicht *f* (-en) intention

absichtlich intentional

absolut absolute

absolvieren acquit, complete

absonderlich peculiar

absondern separate

abspenstig estranged

absperren shut; stop

Absperrhahn *m* (ᴄe) stop-cock

absprechend peremptory

abstammen descend

Abstammung *f* (-en) descent

Abstand *m* (ᴄe) distance; interval

abstatten make; render

abstauben dust

Abstecher *m* (-) trip; detour

abstehen von desist from

absteigen descend; dismount

abstellen redress; stop; turn off

abstempeln stamp

absterben die, fade away

Abstieg *m* (-e) descent

Abstimmung *f* (-en) vote; division

abstossen repel

abstreiten contest

abstumpfen blunt; dull

Absturz *m* (ᴄe) fall, precipice

Abt *m* (ᴄe) abbot; -ei *f* (-en) abbey

Abteil *n* (-e) compartment

Abteilung *f* (-en) division, department

abtragen wear out; take away

abtrennen separate

abtreten cede; retire

Abtritt *m* (-e) retreat; exit

abtrocknen dry; wipe

abtrünnig faithless, rebellious

abwägen weigh

abwarten wait for; wait and see

abwärts downward

abwaschen wash off

Abwaschung *f* (-en) ablution

Abwässer *pl.* waste water

abwechseln change; alternate
abwechselnd alternate(ly)
Abwechselung f (-en) change
Abweg m (-e) wrong way; side-path
abweichen deviate; differ
abweisen reject; refuse
abwenden avert
abwerfen throw off; post
abwesend absent
Abwesenheit f absence
abwickeln wind off; wind up (a business)
abwischen wipe off
abzahlen pay off
Abzahlung f (-en) instalment
Abzehrung f consumption
Abzeichen n (-) badge; sign
abziehen divert; deduct; retreat; take off
Abzug m (-e) retreat; deduction, discount; proof-sheet; -srohr n. (-e) sewer
abzweigen branch off
Abzweigung f (-en) branch-line
abzwingen extort
Achat m (-e) agate
Achse f (-n) axis; shaft; axle (-tree)
Achsel f (-n) shoulder; -grube f (-n) armpit
acht eight
acht geben pay attention
achtbar respectable
Achtel n (-) eighth part
achten, Achtung f esteem, respect, attention
achtungsvoll respectful
Achtziger m (-) octogenarian
Acker m (-) field; -bau m agriculture; **ackern** plough, till
addieren add; **Addition** f (-en) addition
Adel m nobility; **adlig** noble
Ader (-n) vein; artery; **zur - lassen** bleed; -lass m blood-letting
adieu good-bye
Adjutant m (-en) aide-de-camp
Adler m (-) eagle; -nase f (-n) aquiline nose
Admiral m (-e) admiral

Admiralität f Admiralty
adoptieren adopt
Adressbuch n (-er) directory
Adresse f (-n) address
adressieren address, direct; Adressat m (-en) addressee
Advent m advent
Advokat m (-en) barrister, counsel
Affe m (-n) monkey; **äffen** ape
affektiert affected
After m (-) backside
Agent m (-en) agent; **Agentur** f (-en) agency
Ägypten Egypt
Ägypter m (-) **ägyptisch** Egyptian
Ahn m (-en) ancestor
ähneln (+ dat.) resemble
ahnen anticipate; sense
ähnlich like
Ähnlichkeit f (-en) likeness
Ahnung f (-en) presentiment
Ahorn m (-e) maple
Ähre f (-n) ear (corn)
Akademie f (-n) academy
Akazie f (-n) acacia
akklimatisieren acclimatize
Akkord m (-e) agreement, contract; -arbeit f piece-work
Akt m (-e) act
Akte f (-n) document; -ntasche (-n) brief-case
Aktie f (-n) share; -ngesellschaft (-en) f joint-stock company
Aktionär m (-e) shareholder
aktiv active
Akzent m (-e) accent
Akzise f excise
Alarm m (-e) alert; - aus! all clear!
Alaun m (-e) alum
albern silly, absurd
Album n (pl. Alben) album
Alkohol m alcohol
Alkoven m (-) alcove
all all; **alles** everything
Allee f (-n) alley, avenue
allein alone; **alleinig** only
alleinstehend detached, single
allemal always
allenfalls perhaps

aller-dings certainly; indeed; **-hand** various; **-liebst** charming; **-seits** on all sides

Allerheiligen(tag) *m* All-Saints Day

Allerseelen(tag) *m* All-Souls Day

allezeit always

allgemein general

allmächtig almighty

allwissend omniscient

Almosen *n* alms

Alpdrücken *n* (-) nightmare

Alpen *f pl* Alps; **-klub** *m* Alpine Club; **-stock** *m* (⁀e) alpenstock

Alphabet *n* alphabet; **-isch** alphabetical

als as; than; when; but

also thus, therefore

alt old; ancient; antique; second-hand; **-backen** stale; **-erschwach** decrepit; **-modisch** old-fashioned

Altar *m* (⁀e) altar

Alter *n* (-) age; **-sheim** *n* old people's home

älter elderly

altern grown old

Altertum *n* (⁀er) antiquity

Aluminium *n* aluminium

Amboss *m* (-e) anvil

Ameise *f* (-n) ant; **-nhaufen** *m* ant-hill; **-nsäure** *f* formic acid

Amme *f* wet-nurse; **-nmärchen** nursery-tale

Amphitheater *n* (-) amphitheatre

Amputation *f* (-en) amputation

amputieren amputate

Amsel *f* (-n) blackbird

Amt *n* (⁀er) government office, municipal office; **Steuer-** income-tax office; **Zoll-** customs office

Amtstracht *f* (-en) official dress

amüsieren amuse

Ananas *f* (-se) pineapple

Anarchist *m* (-en) anarchist

Anatom *m* (-en) anatomist

Anbau *m* (-e) cultivation; annex

anbauen cultivate; annex

anbei enclosed

anbeten adore

anbetreffs (+ gen.) concerning

anbieten offer

Anblick *m* (-e) sight; **anblicken** look at

Anbruch *m* (⁀e) beginning; daybreak; **-** der Nacht nightfall

Anchovis *f* anchovy

Andacht *f* (-en) devotion; **andächtig** devout

Andenken *n* (-) remembrance

ander other; **-nfalls, anders** otherwise; **-seits** on the other hand; **-swo(hin)** elsewhere

anderthalb one and a half

ändern, Änderung *f* (-en) change

andeuten, Andeutung *f* (-en) hint

Andrang *m* crowd, throng; congestion

andrehen turn on

aneignen (**sich**) appropriate

anekeln disgust

Anerbieten *n* offer

anerkennen acknowledge

Anerkennung *f* (-en) acknowledgment

Anfall *m* (⁀e), **anfallen** attack

Anfang *m* (⁀e) beginning; **anfangen** begin; **Anfänger** (-) beginner; **anfangs** at first

anfassen take hold of, seize, touch

anfertigen manufacture

anfeuchten moisten

anfeuern inflame

anflehen implore

Anfrage *f* (-n) inquiry; **anfragen** inquire

anführen lead; quote, cite; deceive, dupe

Anführer *m* (-) leader

Anführung *f* (-en) leadership; **-szeichen** *n* inverted commas

Angabe *f* (-n) declaration

angeben declare; denounce

Angeber *m* (-) denouncer, informer

angeblich ostensible; alleged

angeboren innate

Angebot *n* (-e) offer; supply

angeheitert tipsy

angehen concern; begin

angehören belong

Angehörige (adj. noun) relative

Angel f (-n) hinge; fishing-hook; **-rute** f (-n) fishing-rod; **-schnur** f (¨e) line

angeln angle

Angelegenheit f (-en) matter

Angelsachse m (-n) Anglo-Saxon

angemessen appropriate, suitable

angenehm agreeable; pleasant

angesehen respectable

Angestellte (adj. noun) employee

Angler m (-) angler

angreifen attack; fatigue

angrenzend adjacent

Angriff m (-e) attack; **-skrieg** (-e) offensive war

Angst f (¨e) fear, anxiety

ängstigen frighten; **ängstlich** anxious, nervous

anhalten stop; last; propose

Anhang m (¨e) appendage, hangers on; **anhängen** hang; attach

Anhänger m (-) adherent

Anhängewagen m (-) trailer car

anhänglich attached; devoted

anhäufen accumulate

anheften fasten

Anhöhe f (-n) hill; height

anhören listen to

Animosität f animosity

Ankauf m (¨e), **ankaufen** purchase

Anker m (-), **ankern** anchor; armature; **vor -** at anchor

Anklage f (-n) accusation; **anklagen** accuse; **Ankläger** m (-) accuser

Anklang finden meet with approbation

ankleiden dress

anklopfen knock

ankommen arrive

ankündigen announce

Ankunft f (¨e) arrival

Anlage f (-n) design; investment; pleasure-ground; talent; plant

anlangen arrive; concern

Anlass m (¨e) occasion

anlassen start; temper (metal)

anlegen put on; invest; build; to apply

Anlehen n (-) loan

anlehnen lean against

Anleihe f (-n) loan

Anliegen n (-) request

anliegend adjacent; tight

anlocken allure

anmachen fasten; fix; light; dress

anmassend arrogant

anmelden announce

Anmerkung f (-en) note; comment

anmessen measure

Anmut f grace; **anmutig** graceful

annähen sew on

annähernd approximative

Annahme f (-n) acceptance; supposition; **annehmbar** acceptable

annehmen accept; receive; suppose

Annonce f (-n) advertisement

annoncieren advertise

anordnen arrange; order

Anordnung f (-en) direction; arrangement; order

anprobieren try, fit on

anraten (+ dat.) recommend

anrechnen charge

Anrecht n (-e) right, claim

anreden, Anrede f (-n) address

anrichten dress, do, serve (up) a meal

Anruf m (-e) (telephone) call

anrufen telephone

ansässig settled, resident

anschaffen procure

Anschauung f (-en) point of view; contemplation

Anschein m appearance

anschicken (sich) prepare

Anschlag m (¨e) plot; estimate; placard; bill; project

anschlagen affix; estimate

anschliessen join

anschliessend subsequently

Anschluss m (¨e) communication, connection, **-station** f (-en) junction

anschrauben screw on

anschreiben put to account

anschwellen swell

Anschwellung f (-en) swelling

ansehen look at
Ansehen *n* appearance; reputation; credit; esteem
ansehnlich considerable
Ansicht *f* (-en) view; opinion; zur - on approval
Ansichts-postkarte *f* (-n) pictorial post-card; **-sache** *f* (-n) matter of opinion
ansiedeln (sich) settle
Ansiedler *m* (-) settler
anspannen put to; rack; yoke to; harness
anspielen (auf) allude (to)
Anspielung *f* (-en) allusion
Ansprache *f* (-n) address, speech
Anspruch *m* (¨e) claim; pretension
anspruchsvoll (-los) (un-)pretentious
Anstalt *f* (-en) establishment
Anstand *m* (¨e) decency; **-sbesuch** *m* (-e) formal visit
anständig decent, respectable
anstechen broach; prick
anstecken infect; light
ansteckend contagious
Ansteckung *f* (-en) infection
anstellen place; appoint
Anstellung *f* (-en) appointment
anstossen push; shock; clink
anstossend adjacent
anstössig shocking; offensive
anstreichen paint; **Anstreicher** *m* (-) house-painter
anstrengen (sich) exert oneself
Anstrengung *f* (-en) exertion
Anstrich *m* (-e) paint
anstürmen assault; charge
Anteil *m* (-e) share; interest
Antenne *f* (-n) ariel
Antiquar *m* (-e) antiquary; second-hand bookseller
antiseptisch antiseptic
Antrag *m* (¨e) proposal; (Parl.) motion
antreiben incite
antreten enter upon, line up
Antrieb *m* (-e) impulse
Antwort *f* (-en), **antworten** answer
anvertrauen confide, entrust
Anwalt *m* (¨e) solicitor

Anwärter *m* (-) expectant, aspirant
anweisen assign; order
Anweisung *f* (-en) bill; cheque; instruction
anwenden apply; employ
anwerben enlist
anwesend present
Anwesenheit *f* presence
Anzahl *f* number
Anzeige *f* (-n) notice; advertisement; **anzeigen** advertise; notify
anziehen put on; dress; attract
anziehend attractive
Anziehung *f* (-en) attraction
Anzug *m* (¨e) suit; dress; costume
anzünden light
Apfel *m* (¨) apple; **-baum** *m* (¨e) apple tree; **-kuchen** *m* (-) apple tart; **-wein** *m* cider
Apfelsine *f* (-n) orange
Apostel *m* (-) apostle; **-geschichte** *f* Acts of the Apostles
Apotheke *f* (-n) chemist's shop
Apotheker *m* (-) chemist
Apparat *m* (-e) apparatus
appellieren appeal
Appetit *m* appetite
appetitlich appetizing
applaudieren applaud
Applaus *m* (-se) applause
Aprikose *f* (-n) apricot
April *m* April
Aquarium *n* (-rien) aquarium
Aquarell *n* (-e) water-colour
Äquator *m* equator
Arbeit *f* (-en), **arbeiten** work, labour; **-geber** *m* (-) employer; **-er** *m* (-) workman; **-nehmer** *m* (-) employee; **-sam** industrious; **-samt** *n*. (¨er) labour-exchange; **-seinstellung** *f* (-en) strike; **-slohn** *m* (¨e) wages; **-slos** out of work; **-slosenunterstützung** *f* dole; **-sministerium** *n* Ministry of Labour
Architekt(ur) *m* (-en) (*f*) architect(ure)
arg bad; wicked
Ärger *m* anger; **ärgerlich** angry; **ärgern** to vex; **sich -** get angry

Ärgernis n (-se) scandal
arglos harmless
Argwohn m suspicion
argwöhnisch suspicious
argwöhnen suspect
Arie f (-n) air; aria
Aristokratie f aristocracy
arm poor; **-selig** wretched
Arm m (-e) arm; **-band** n (¨er)
  bracelet; **-leuchter** m chandelier
Armee f (-n) army
Ärmel m (-) sleeve
Ärmelkanal m English Channel
Armen-haus n (¨er) almshouse;
  -pflege f relief; **-pfleger** m (-)
  relieving officer
Armut f poverty
Aroma(tisch) n aroma(tic)
arretieren, Arrest m (-e) arrest
Arsch m (¨e) arse
Arsenik n arsenic
Art f (-en) kind; sort; manner
Arterie f (-n) artery
artig nice; polite
Artikel m (-) article
Artillerie f (-n) artillery
Artillerist m (-en) gunner
Artischocke f (-n) artichoke
Arznei(mittel) f (n-) medicine
Arzt m (¨e) physician; doctor
ärztlich medical
As n (-se) ace
Asbest m asbestos
Asche f ashes pl; **-nkasten** ash-
  box; **-nbecher** m ash-tray
Aschenbrödel n Cinderella
Aschermittwoch m Ash-Wed-
  nesday
Asphalt m (-e) asphalt
Ast m (¨e) branch
ästhetisch æsthetic
Asthma n asthma; **-tisch**
  asthmatic
Astronom m (-en) astronomer
Astronomie f astronomy
Asyl n (-e) asylum
Atelier n (-s) studio
Atem m breath; **atemlos**
  breathless
Atemlosigkeit f breathlessness
athletisch athletic
Atlas m atlas; satin
atmen breathe

Atmosphäre f (-n) atmosphere
atmosphärisch atmospheric
Atom n (-e) atom; **-bombe** f
  (-n) atomic bomb; **-forschung**
  f (-en) nuclear research; **-kraft**
  f (¨e) atomic power
Attest n (-e) certificate
attestieren certify
ätzen corrode, etch
Ätzung f (-en) etching, cauteriz-
  ation
au! oh!
auch also; - **nicht** nor
Audienz f (-en) audience
auf on, upon; up
Aufbau m (-ten) building
aufbewahren keep; take care of
Aufbewahrungsort m (-e)
  cloakroom
aufbrechen break up; start out
aufbügeln iron; do up
aufdecken expose, reveal
aufdringlich importunate
Aufenthalt m (-e) stay; stop
auferlegen impose
Auferstehung f resurrection
auferwecken resuscitate
Auferweckung f (-en) resusci-
  tation
auffahren start up; ascend
auffallen be conspicuous
auffallend striking
Auffassung f conception, opinion
auffordern summon, order
aufführen perform
Aufführung f (-en) performance;
  behaviour
Aufgabe f (-n) task; lesson
aufgeben post; book; give up
Aufgebot n (-e) banns; levy
aufgebracht irritated
aufgehen rise; open
aufgesprungen chapped
Aufguss m (¨e) infusion
aufhalten stop, detain, stay
auf-hängen hang up; **-heben**
  lift up; **-hellen, -klären**
  enlighten, clear up; **-hören**
  cease; **-knöpfen** unbutton;
  -krempeln turn up; **-laden**
  load; **-lauern** waylay
Aufhebung f (-en) suspension
Auflage f (-n) edition, tax, rate

Auflauf *m* (⁻e) crowd; soufflé
auf-leben revive; **-legen** impose; **-lösen** dissolve, solve; **Auflösung** *f* (-en) (dis)solution; **- merken** listen, pay attention; **-merksam** attentive; **Aufmerksamkeit** *f* attention
Aufnahme *f* (-n) reception; survey; view, photograph
aufnehmen receive; survey; raise
auf-opfern sacrifice; **-passen** pay attention; **-räumen** put in order; **-recht** upright; **-regen, -reizen** excite; **Aufregung** *f* (-en) agitation; **-richten** raise, erect; **-richtig** sincere
Aufrichtigkeit *f* sincerity
Aufrührer *m* (-) rebel
Aufruhr *m* (-e) revolt, riot
Aufsatz *m* (⁻e) essay, composition
aufschieben postpone, delay
Aufschlag *m* (⁻e) increase, rise;
aufschlagen open; raise (price)
aufschliessen unlock, open
Aufschluss *m* (⁻e) information
aufschneiden cut up; brag
Aufschneider *m* (-) boaster
aufschrauben unscrew
aufschreiben note
Aufschrift *f* (-en) inscription; address; label
Aufschub *m* delay
Aufsehen *n* sensation
Aufseher *m* (-) overseer
aufsetzen put on; compose
Aufsicht *f* inspection, care, supervision
auf-spannen, -sperren open; **-stehen, -steigen** rise; **-stellen** erect; fit up; **Aufstieg** *m* (-e) ascent; **-stöbern, -treiben** find out; **-suchen** seek out; **-tauen** thaw
Aufstand *m* (⁻e) insurrection, riot
Auftrag *m* (⁻e) commission; order; **auftragen** charge, order
auftreten enter, appear
Auftrieb *m* (-e) buoyancy; impetus
Auftritt *m* (-e) scene
auf-wachen awake; **-wachsen** grow up; **-wärmen** warm up
Aufwand *m* (⁻e) expense; display

aufwarten wait upon
Aufwärter *m* (-) waiter
Aufwartung *f* attendance
aufwärts upwards
auf-weichen soak, soften; **-wischen** mop up; **-zählen** enumerate; **-ziehen** raise; hoist; wind up; breed; bring up
Aufwiegler *m* (-) mutineer
Aufzug *m* (⁻e) procession; elevator
Auge *n* (-n) eye; **aus den -n verlieren** lose sight of; **ins - fallen** strike; **Augapfel** *m* (⁻) eyeball
Augenarzt *m* (⁻e) oculist
Augen-blick *m* (-e) moment, instant; **-braue** *f* (-n) eyebrow; **-entzündung** *f* inflammation of the eye; **-glas** *n* (⁻er) eye-glass; **-licht** *n* eyesight; **-lid** *n* (-er) eye-lid; **-schirm** *m* (-e) eye-shade; **-stern** *m* (-e) pupil; **-wimper** *f* (-n) eye-lash; **-zeuge** *m* (-n) eye-witness
Auktion *f* (-en) auction
aus out of; over; **-arten** degenerate; **-bedingen** stipulate; **-bessern** repair; **-beuten** work; exploit; **-bilden** train; **-blasen** blow out; **-bleiben** stay away; **-blick** *m* (-e) outlook; **-brechen** break out; **-breiten** spread, extend; **Ausbruch** *m* (⁻e) outbreak; eruption; **-bürsten** brush; **Ausbeute** *f* (-n) gain
Ausbeutung *f* (-en) exploitation
Ausdauer *f* perseverance
ausdauern persevere
ausdehnen extend
Ausdehnung *f* (-en) extent; expansion
Ausdruck *m* (⁻e) expression; **ausdrücken** express; **ausdrücklich** express; **-svoll** expressive
auseinander asunder
aus-erlesen choice; **-erwählen** select; **-fahren** take a drive; **-fertigen** draw up
Ausfall *m* (⁻e) result; sally, loss
ausfallen turn out

Ausflucht *f* (̈e) subterfuge; excuse

Ausflug *m* (̈e) excursion, trip

Ausflügler *m* (–) tourist

ausfragen question

Ausfuhr *f* exportation

ausführen execute; export

ausführlich detailed, complete

Ausführung *f* (-en) execution

ausfüllen fill (up)

Ausgabe *f* (-n) delivery; edition; expense

Ausgang *m* (̈e) exit

ausgeben deliver, publish, spend

ausgehen go out

ausgelassen boisterous; **-genommen** except; **-gesucht** choice; **-gewachsen** full-grown; **-gezeichnet** excellent

ausgiessen pour out

ausgleiten slide, slip

ausgraben excavate

Ausgrabung *f* (-en) excavation

Ausguss *m* (̈e) sink; spout

aus-halten bear; **-händigen** deliver; **-harren** persevere; **-helfen** help; **-hungern** starve; **-kehren** sweep; **-kleiden** undress; **-klopfen** beat, dust; **-kommen** agree

Auskommen *n* livelihood; getting on with others

Auskunft *f* (̈e) information

aus-lachen laugh at; **-laden** unload

Auslage *f* (-n) expense; show, display

Ausland *n* foreign country; **Ausländer** *m* (–) foreigner; **ausländisch** foreign

auslassen omit

auslegen display; pay; explain; **ausleihen** lend

Auslese *f* (-n) selection

ausliefern deliver; **Auslieferung** *f* delivery; extradition

auslösen redeem

auslöschen put out; extinguish; erase

ausmachen make out; constitute; settle; matter

Aus-nahme *f* (-n) exception; **-nahmsweise** exceptionally;

-nehmen except; **-nehmend** exceeding

aus-nutzen profit by; **-packen** unpack; **-pfeifen** hiss; **-probieren** try; **-quetschen** squeeze out; **-radieren** erase; **-rangieren** reject; **-rechnen** calculate; **-reichen** suffice; **reissen** tear out, decamp; **-richten** accomplish; **-rotten** exterminate; **-rufen** exclaim, proclaim; **-ruhen** rest; **-rüsten** fit out, arm

Ausrede *f* (-n) subterfuge; excuse

Ausruf *m* (-e) exclamation; **-szeichen** *n* (–) exclamation mark

Aussage *f* (-n) statement, deposition

aussagen depose; report

Aussatz *m* (̈e) leprosy

Ausschank *m* (̈e) retailing beer; bar

aus-schelten scold; **-schiffen** disembark; **-schlafen** sleep enough

Ausschlag *m* (̈e) eruption, rash; turn; decision

ausschlagen kick; shoot; refuse

ausschliessen exclude; **-schliesslich** exclusive

Ausschuss *m* (̈e) refuse, damaged goods; committee

ausschweifend dissolute

Ausschweifung *f* (-en) debauch

aussehen look; **Aussehen** *n* appearance

aussen out; on the outside

ausser except, besides (+ dat.); **- sich** beside oneself; **-dem** besides, moreover; **-halb** outside (+ gen.); **-ordentlich** extraordinary

äussere exterior

äusserlich external

äussern utter

äusserst extreme

Äusserung *f* (-en) utterance

aussetzen expose; set; set out; promise; find fault with

Aussicht *f* (-en) prospect, view; **-wagen** *m* (–) observation-car

aus-spannen unharness, relax; **-sperren** lock out

Aussprache *f* (-n) pronunciation
aussprechen pronounce
Ausspruch *m* (-̈e) sentence
aus-spucken spit; **-spülen** rinse
Aus-stattung (-en), **-steuer** *f*
(-n) outfit, dowry; **ausstatten**
endow
aus-stehen bear; **-steigen** get
out; **-stellen** exhibit
Ausstellung *f* (-en) exhibition
aussterben become extinct
aus-stopfen stuff; **-stossen** expel; utter; **-strahlen** radiate;
-strecken stretch; **-streichen**
erase; **-strömen** escape; **-su-
chen** select; **-tauschen, Austausch** *m* (-e) exchange; **-teilen**
distribute
Auster(bank) *f* (-n) oyster(-bed)
austragen deliver
aus-trinken drink up; empty;
-trocknen dry; **-üben** exercise;
practise; **-verkaufen** sell out
Auswahl *f* (-en) choice; **auswählen** choose
Auswanderer *m* (-) emigrant;
auswandern emigrate; **Auswanderung** *f* (-en) emigration
auswärtig foreign; **Auswär-
tiges Amt** *n* Foreign Office
auswaschen wash out
auswechseln exchange
Ausweg *m* (-e) way out: expedient
ausweichen evade; make way
Ausweis *m* (-e) statement; identi-
fication
ausweisen expel; **Ausweisung**
f (-en) expulsion; **sich -** prove
one's identity
ausweiten widen, stretch
auswendig external; **-lernen**
learn by heart
auswerfen throw out; emit
auswischen wipe out, efface
Auswuchs *m* (-̈e) excrescence
Auswurf *m* (-̈e) expectoration;
refuse
Auszahlung *f* (-en) payment
Auszehrung *f* consumption
auszeichnen distinguish
Auszeichnung *f* (-en) distinction

ausziehen draw out; take off; undress; remove; extract
Ausziehtisch *m* (-e) extension-
table
auszischen hiss
Auszug *m* (-̈e) extract; removal
authentisch authentical
Auto *n* (-s) motor-car; **-bahn** *f*
(-en) motorway; **-bus** *m* (-se)
motor-coach; **-führer** *m* (-) driver;
-mat *m* (-en) automatic machine; **-vermietung** *f* car-hire
Autograph *n* (-e) autograph
Autor *m* (-en) author
Avis *m* (-e) advice; **avisieren**
advise
Axt *f* (-̈e) axe
Azur *m*, **azurn** azure

B

babbeln babble; prattle
Bach *m* (-̈e) brook; **-stelze** *f* (-n)
wagtail
Back *f* (-e) forecastle
Backbord *m* port, larboard
Backe *f* (-n) cheek
backen bake; fry
Bäcker *m* (-) baker
Backfisch *m* (-e) fish for frying;
flapper
Back-obst *n* dried fruit; **-ofen**
m (-) oven; **-werk** *n* pastry
Bad *n* (-̈er) bath; watering-place;
Bade-anstalt *f* (-en) bathing-
establishment; **-gast** *m* (-̈e)
visitor; **-hose** *f* bathing-
drawers; **-kur** *f* use of medicinal
waters; **-meister** *m* (-) baths-
attendant; **-ort** *m* (-e) watering-
place; **-reise** *f* (-n) visit to a
watering-place; **-wanne** *f* (-n)
bath(ing)-tub; **-zelle** *f* (-n)
bathing-cabin; **-zimmer** *n* (-)
bath-room
baden bathe; bath
Bagger *m* (-) dredger; **baggern**
dredge
Bahn *f* (-en) path, way; railway;
-hof *m* (-̈e) station; **-hofs-
vorsteher** *m* (-) station-master;
-restaurant *n* (-e) refreshment-

room; **-steig(karte)** m (-e) (f) platform (ticket); **-übergang** m (¨e) level crossing; **-wärter** m (-) signalman; line-keeper

bahnen clear, smooth

Bahre f (-n) stretcher; bier

Bai f (-en) bay

Bajonett n (-e) bayonet

Bakterie f (-n) microbe

bald soon; **baldig** early, speedy; **baldigst** as soon as possible

Baldrian m valerian

balgen fight, wrestle

Balken m (-) beam

Balkon m (-e) balcony

Ball m (¨e) ball; dance

Ballast m (-e) ballast

Ballen m (-) bale; ball

Ballett n (-e) ballet

Ballon m (-s) balloon

Balsam m (-e) balm; **-isch** balmy

Bambus m (-se) bamboo

Band m (¨e) volume; binding; n (¨er) band, tie; tape; ribbon; **-wurm** m (¨er) tape-worm

Bande f (-n) gang

Bandenkrieg m (-e) guerilla-warfare

bändigen tame; break in

Bandit m (-en) bandit

bange afraid; anxious

Bank f (¨e) bench; form; seat; pl. (-en) bank; **-ier** m (-s) banker; **-geschäft** n (¨e) banking house; **-konto** n (-ten) bank account; **-note** f (-n) bank-note; **-rott** m bankruptcy

Bann m ban; spell; excommunication; **Banner** n (-) banner

Bar f (-s) bar

bar devoid; **-fuss** barefooted

Bär m (-en) bear; **-enfell** n bearskin; **-enzwinger** m bear pit

Baracke f (-n) barrack

Barbar m (-en), **barbarisch** barbarian

bares Geld cash; **gegen bar** for cash

barhäuptig bareheaded

barmherzig merciful

Barometer m (-) barometer

Baron m (-e) baron

Barren m bar; ingot; parallel bars

Barsch m (-e) perch

barsch rude, rough

Bart m (¨e) beard

bärtig bearded

Barverkauf m (¨e) cash sale

Barzahlung f (-en) cash payment

Bass m (¨e) bass; **-ist** m bass-singer

Bataillon n (-e) battalion

Batist m (-e) cambric

Bau m (-ten) **-werk** n (-e) building; **-fällig** dilapidated; **-holz** n timber; **-kasten** m box of bricks; **-kunst** f architecture; **-meister** m (-) architect, builder; **-sparkasse** f (-n) building society; **-stil** m style of architecture; **-stelle** f (-n) building plot; **-unternehmer** m contractor

Bauch m (¨e) belly; **-fell** n peritoneum; **-redner** m ventriloquist; **-weh** n colic

bauen build; rely on

Bauer m (-n) peasant, farmer; pawn; knave; n (-) cage

Bauernfänger m (-) (card)-sharper

Baum m (¨e) tree; **-schule** f (-n) nursery; **-wolle** f cotton

baumeln dangle

bäumen rear; **sich bäumen** resist, put up one's back

beabsichtigen intend

beachten, Beachtung f (-en) notice

Beamte m (adj. noun) official, functionary, civil servant

beanspruchen claim

beantragen move; apply for

beantworten, Beantwortung f (-en) answer

bearbeiten work, treat; cultivate

beauftragen commission

Becher m (-) goblet, cup

Becken n (-) basin

bedächtig cautious

bedanken thank

Bedarf m want, demand

bedauerlich deplorable

bedauern, Bedauern n pity, regret

bedecken cover
bedenken consider; **sich -** hesitate; **bedenklich** dubious; critical; grave; **Bedenkzeit** *f* time for consideration
bedeuten mean, signify; **bedeutend** important; **Bedeutung** *f* (-en) significance, importance
bedienen serve, wait on; **sich -** help oneself; **Bediente** *m* (adj. noun) servant; **Bedienung** *f* attendance, service
bedingen stipulate
Bedingung *f* (-en) condition
bedrohen threaten
bedrücken oppress
Bedürfnis *n* (-se); **bedürfen** (+ gen.) need, want; **-anstalt** *f* lavatory
bedürftig indigent, poor, needy
Bedürftigkeit *f* need; destitution
beehren honour, favour
beeilen (sich) hurry up
beend(ig)en finish
beerdigen bury; **Beerdigung** *f* (-en) burial; funeral
Beere *f* (-n) berry
Beet *n* (-e) bed, border
befähigen enable
Befähigung *f* ability
befangen embarrassed
Befehl *m* (-e), **befehlen** (+ dat.) command, order
Befehlshaber *m* (-) commander
befestigen fasten; fortify; **Befestigung** *f* (-en) fortification
befinden find; **sich -** be; feel
befolgen follow, observe
befördern promote; forward
befragen interrogate
befreien deliver; **Befreiung** *f* (-en) deliverance
befremden surprise
befreunden befriend; **sich -** (mit) become friends with
befriedigen satisfy; **-d** satisfactory; **Befriedigung** *f* (-en) satisfaction
befürchten, Befürchtung *f* (-en) fear, misgiving
begabt gifted
Begabung *f* (-en) capacity; talent

begeben (sich) proceed, go
begegnen (+ dat.) meet
Begegnung *f* (-en) meeting
begehen commit
begehren desire; want
begeistern inspire
Begeisterung *f* enthusiasm
begierig desirous
begiessen water
beginnen begin; **Beginn** *m* beginning
beglaubigen attest; certify; legalize
Beglaubigungsschreiben *n* credentials
begleiten accompany
Begleitung *f* (-en) accompaniment
beglückwünschen congratulate
begnadigen, Begnadigung *f* (en) pardon
begnügen (sich) content oneself
begraben bury; **Begräbnis** *n* (-se) burial, funeral
begreifen comprehend; handle
begrenzen border, limit
Begriff *m* (-e) conception; idea
begründen found; prove
Begründung *f* (-en) foundation; motivation; reason(s)
begrüssen greet; salute
begünstigen favour
behaglich comfortable
Behaglichkeit *f* (-en) comfort
behalten keep; retain
Behälter *m* (-) container, reservoir
behandeln treat; use
Behandlung *f* treatment
beharren persevere; **beharrlich** constant, persevering
Beharrlichkeit *f* perseverance
behaupten affirm; assert
Behauptung *f* (-en) assertion
behelfen (sich) make shift
behend(e) nimble, quick
Behendigkeit *f* nimbleness
beherrschen rule; master
beherzigen take to heart
behilflich helpful
Behörde *f* authorities *pl*
behüten guard; **Gott behüte!** God forbid!

bei (+ dat.) at; near; with
beibringen produce; teach
Beichte *f* (-n) confession; **-stuhl** *m* confessional
beichten confess
beide both; **beides** either
beiderseitig mutual
Beifall *m* applause; assent
Beil *n* (-e) hatchet, axe
Beilage *f* supplement
beiläufig by the way; casual
beilegen enclose; settle
Beileid(sbezeigung) *n* (*f*) condolence; **-bezeigen** condole; **-sschreiben** *n* letter of condolence
beiliegend enclosed
Bein *n* (-e) leg; bone
beinahe almost, nearly
Beiname *m* (-n) surname, nickname
Beinbruch *m* fracture of the leg
beisammen together
Beischlaf *m* coitus
beiseite aside, apart
Beispiel *n* (-e) example; **zum -** for example
beissen bite
Beistand *m* (-̈e), **beistehen** (+ dat.) aid, help
beistimmen, Beistimmung *f* assent; agree(ment)
Beitrag *m* (-̈e) contribution
beitragen contribute
beitreten (+ dat.) accede; join
beiwohnen (+ dat.) attend; be present
beizeiten in time, early
bejahen affirm
bejammern bewail
bekämpfen combat, oppose
bekannt known; **-machen** publish; **Bekannte** *m f*, (adj. noun)
Bekanntschaft *f* acquaintance
bekehren convert
bekennen confess
Bekenntnis *n* (-se) confession, creed
beklagen deplore
bekleiden dress; fill
bekommen get, receive; obtain
beköstigen, Beköstigung *f* board

bekräftigen confirm
bekümmern grieve
beladen, belasten load
belagern besiege
Belagerung *f* (-en) siege
belästigen molest, trouble
Belästigung *f* (-en) molestation
belaufen amount to
beleben animate
belegt reserved; furred; **-es Brot** sandwich
belehren instruct
beleidigen offend; insult
Beleidigung *f* (-en) offence; insult
belesen well-read
beleuchten light
Beleuchtung *f* (-en) lighting, illumination
belieben please
beliebig any; whatever; at will
beliebt popular
Beliebtheit *f* popularity
bellen bark
Belohnung *f* (-en), **belohnen** reward
belustigen amuse
Belustigung *f* (-en) amusement
bemächtigen (sich) (+ gen.) seize (upon)
bemerkenswert remarkable
Bemerkung *f* (-en), **bemerken** remark
bemitleiden pity
bemittelt wealthy
Bemühung *f* (-en), **bemühen** trouble; endeavour
benachbart neighbouring
benachrichtigen inform
Benachrichtigung *f* information
benachteiligen injure; wrong
Benehmen *n*, **benehmen (sich)** conduct
beneiden envy; **-swert** enviable
benetzen wet, moisten
Bengel *m* (-) rude fellow
benutzen use
Benzin *n* petrol
beobachten observe
Beobachtung *f* (-en) observation
bequem convenient, comfortable
Bequemlichkeit *f* (-en) convenience, comfort

beraten counsel; consult
berauben rob; deprive
berauschen intoxicate
berechnen calculate
Berechnung f (-en) calculation
berechtigen authorize, entitle
bereden persuade; confer
Beredsamkeit f eloquence
beredt eloquent
Bereich m (-e) reach; sphere
bereichern enrich
bereisen travel over
bereit, -willig ready, willing
bereiten prepare
bereits already
bereuen repent
Berg m (-e) mountain; **- akademie** f School of Mines; **-bau**
m mining; **-mann** m (pl. **-leute**)
miner; **-steigen** n mountaineer-
ing; **-steiger** m mountaineer;
-sturz m landslip; **-werk** n
mine; **-auf (-ab)** up (down)-
hill
bergen salve, save
bergig mountainous
Bericht m (-e), **berichten** report;
-erstatter m reporter
berichtigen correct
Bernstein m amber
berüchtigt ill-famed
berücksichtigen consider
Beruf m (-e) profession, occupation, trade; **-sschule** f (-n)
continuation school; **-ssoldat**
m (-en) regular soldier
Berufung f (-en) call; appeal
beruhen rest, depend (on)
beruhigen, besänftigen calm
berühmt celebrated; famous
berühren touch; **Berührung** f
(-en) contact
Besatz m (¨e) trimming; border
Besatzung f (-en) garrison;
occupation
beschädigen, Beschädigung f
(-en) damage
beschäftigen occupy; employ
Beschäftigung f (-en) occupation
beschämt ashamed
Bescheid m (-e) answer; decision;
¨ ***wissen** (be in the) know

bescheiden modest; **Bescheidenheit** f modesty
bescheinigen attest, certify
Bescheinigung f (-en) certificate
beschenken, bescheren present
with; **Bescherung** f distribution
of presents
beschiessen bombard; shell
beschimpfen insult
beschlagen mount; shoe; **gut -**
conversant
beschleunigen accelerate; hasten
beschliessen decide; close
Beschluss m (¨e) resolution
beschmieren, beschmutzen
soil
Beschneidung f circumcision
beschönigen palliate
beschränken limit
beschreiben describe
Beschreibung f (-en) description
beschuldigen accuse (+ gen. of)
beschützen protect; **Beschützer**
m (-) protector
Beschwerde f (-n) complaint
beschweren (sich) complain
beschwerlich troublesome
beschwindeln cheat
beschwören conjure; confirm by
oath
besehen view; **beseitigen** remove
Besen m (-) broom
besessen possessed
besetzen occupy, garrison
besichtigen inspect; survey
besiegen conquer
besinnen reflect; remember
Besinnung f consciousness
Besitz m possession; **besitzen**
possess; **Besitzer** m (-) owner;
Besitzung f (-en) property
besoffen drunk
besohlen sole
Besoldung f (-en) pay; salary
besonder particular; **-s** especially
besorgen procure
besorgt anxious
Besorgung f (-en) care; management; purchase
besprechen review, discuss;
sich - confer

Besprechung *f* (**-en**) conference
bespritzen splash
bessern improve
Besserung *f* (**-en**) improvement;
  -sanstalt *f* (**-en**) reformatory
best best; **zum -en geben**
  treat; **zum -en haben** mock
beständig constant
bestärken, bestätigen confirm
bestatten bury
bestaubt covered with dust,
  dusty
bestechen bribe; corrupt
bestechlich corruptible
Bestechung *f* (**-en**) bribery
Besteck *n* (**-e**) case; set; knife
  and fork; cutlery
bestehen exist; pass; (**auf**)
  insist on; (**aus**) consist of
bestehlen rob
besteigen ascend; mount
Besteigung *f* (**-en**) ascent
bestellen order; deliver; summon
Bestellung *f* (**-en**) order; delivery
besteuern tax
Besteuerung *f* (**-en**) taxation
bestimmen determine; destine
bestimmt certain; positive
Bestimmung *f* (**-en**) destination;
  decision
bestrafen punish
Bestrafung *f* (**-en**) punishment
bestreben endeavour
Bestrebung *f* (**-en**) endeavour
bestreichen spread (a surface)
bestreiten contest; defray
bestürzt alarmed, perplexed
Bestürzung *f* (**-en**) consternation
Besuch *m* (**-e**) visit; **auf -** on a
  visit; **- machen** pay a visit;
  -stag *m* visiting day; **-szim-
  mer** *n* drawing-room; **-er** *m*
  visitor
besuchen go to see, call on; visit
betasten touch; handle
betäuben stun, deafen, narcotize
beteiligen share
beteiligen (sich) participate
beten pray; say grace
beteuern protest
betrachten consider, **Betrachtung** *f* (**-en**) reflection; meditation

beträchtlich considerable
Betrag *m* (**-̈e**) amount; **-en** *n*
  behaviour
betragen amount to; **sich - behave**
betrauern mourn
betreffen concern; to befall
betreffs, in betreff (+ gen.)
  with regard to
betreten tread upon, enter; embarrassed; perplexed
Betrieb *m* (**-e**) working; **-san-
  lage** *f* plant; **-sdirektor** *m*
  manager; **-skosten** *pl* working
  expenses
betrinken (sich) get drunk
betroffen perplexed; affected
betrüben afflict; grieve
Betrug *m*, **Betrüger** *m*, **betrügen**
  cheat
betrunken drunk; intoxicated
Bett *n* (**-en**) bed; **-decke** *f* (**-n**)
  blanket, counterpane, quilt;
  -lägerig bed-ridden; **-stelle** *f*
  bedstead; **-tuch** *n* (**-̈er**) sheet;
  -vorleger *m* bedside carpet;
  -zeug *n* bed-linen
betteln beg
Bettler *m* (**-**) beggar
beugen bend; **sich -** stoop; submit
Beule *f* (**-n**) bump, bruise, boil
beunruhigen, Beunruhigung *f*
  (**-en**) alarm, trouble
beurlauben give leave of absence
beurteilen judge
Beute *f* booty
Beutel *m* (**-**) bag, purse
bevölkern people
Bevölkerung *f* (**-en**) population
Bevollmächtigte *m* (adj. noun)
  plenipotentiary; proxy, deputy
bevor before; **-stehen** impend
bevorzugen to favour
bewachen guard, watch
bewaffnen arm
bewahren preserve
bewähren verify; **sich -** prove
  true
bewaldet wooded, woody
bewandert versed
bewässern water, irrigate
Bewässerung *f* (**-en**) irrigation

bewegen move; **Beweggrund** *m* (¨e) motive; **beweglich** movable; **Bewegung** *f* (-en) motion; emotion

Beweis *m* (-e) proof; **beweisen** prove

bewerben um (**sich**) apply for; woo; **Bewerber** *m* (-) candidate; suitor

bewerkstelligen effect, contrive

bewilligen allow; grant

bewillkommen welcome

bewirken effect; cause

bewirten entertain

bewohnen inhabit; reside in

Bewohner *m* (-) inhabitant

bewölkt clouded, cloudy

bewundern admire; **-swürdig** admirable

Bewunderung *f* admiration

bewusst conscious

Bewusstsein *n* consciousness

bezahlen, pay; **Bezahlung** *f* (-en) payment

bezaubern charm; enchant

bezeichnen mark; designate

bezeugen attest; certify

beziehen move into; receive; **sich - auf** refer to

Beziehung *f* (-en) connection

Bezirk *m* (-e) district

Bezug *m* (¨e) reference; covering; **in Bezug** with respect to

Bezugsbedingung *f* (-en) term of delivery

bezwecken intend

bezweifeln doubt

bezwingen overcome

Bibel *f* (-n) Bible

Biber *m* (-) beaver

Bibliothek *f* (-en) library; **-ar** *m* (-e) librarian

bieder honest, upright

biegen bend; **biegsam** flexible; **Biegung** *f* (-en) bend, turn

Biene *f* (-n) bee; **-nstock**, **-korb** *m* (¨e) bee-hive

Bier *n* beer; **-brauer** *m* (-) brewer; **-haus** *n* (¨er) beer-house

bieten bid

Bilanz *f* (-en) balance; result

Bild *n* (-er) painting; picture; **-erbuch** picture-book; **-funk** *m*

television; **-hauer** *m* sculptor; **- säule** *f* statue

bilden form; cultivate

bildhübsch extremely pretty

bildlich figurative

Bildung *f* (-en) formation; education

Billard *n* billiards *pl*

billig cheap

billigen approve

Billigung *f* approbation

Bimsstein *m* pumice

Binde *f* (-n) band; sling; tie; cravat; **-strich** *m* hyphen

binden bind; tie

Bindfaden *m* (¨) pack-thread; twine, string

binnen within; **Binnen** inland

Binse *f* (-n) bulrush

Biographie *f* (-n) biography

Birke *f* (-n) birch

Birne *f* (-n) pear; globe, bulb

bis till; as far as; **-her** hitherto; **-weilen** sometimes

Bischof *m* (¨e) bishop; **bischöf-lich** episcopal

Biss *m* (-e) bite; **Bissen** *m* morsel

bisschen, ein - little

Bistum *n* (¨er) diocese

Bitte *f* (-n) entreaty; request

bitte please; do not mention it; I beg your pardon; all right

bitten (**um**) ask (for)

bitter bitter

Bittschrift *f* (-en) petition

Blähung *f* (-en) puffing; wind

blamieren (**sich**) make a fool of oneself

blank bright

Blase *f* (-n) bubble; bladder; vesicle; blister; **-balg** *m* bellows *pl*

blasen blow

Blasinstrument *n* (-e) wind-instrument

Blasrohr *n* pea-shooter

blass pale; **Blässe** *f* paleness

Blatt *n* (¨er) leaf; newspaper; drawing; sheet of paper

Blatter *f*, **-n** *pl* smallpox

blättern turn over (leaves of a book)

blau, blauen blue; **Blaubuch** n blue-book; **-säure** f prussic acid; **-stift** m (-e) blue pencil

bläulich bluish

Blech n sheet-iron; tin-plate; **-instrument** n (-e) brass instrument; **-schmied** m tin-worker

Blei n lead; **-stift** m lead-pencil; **-weiss** n white-lead; **-arbeiter** m plumber

bleiben remain

bleich pale; faint

bleichen bleach

blenden blind

Blendlaterne f (-n) dark lantern

blicken, Blick m (-e) look, glance

blind blind; **-lings** blindly

Blind-darm m appendix; **-darm- entzündung** f appendicitis; **-schleiche** f blind-worm; **-ekub** f blindman's buff

Blindheit f blindness

blinzeln twinkle; wink

Blitz m (-e) lightning; **-strahl** m flash; **-ableiter** m lightning-conductor; **-licht** n flash-light

blitzen lighten, flash

Block m (⁻e) block

blockieren, Blockade f (-n) blockade

blödsinnig silly; **blöde** bashful

blöken bleat, low

blond fair

bloss naked; only; merely; **-stellen** expose

blühen bloom; flourish

Blume f (-n) flower; bouquet

Blumen-ausstellung f flower-show; **-kohl** m cauliflower; **-strauss** m nosegay; **-tisch** m flower-stand; **-reich** flowery

Blut n blood; **-andrang** m congestion; **-arm** anæmic; **-ge- schwür** n boil; **-probe** f blood-test; **-sturz** m hæmorrhage; **-kreislauf** m circulation of the blood; **-wurst** f black-pudding

Blüte f blossom

bluten bleed; **blutig** bloody

Bö f sudden squall

Bock m (⁻e) buck; frame, trestle; box; blunder; he-goat

Boden m (⁻) ground; bottom; floor; loft; **-satz** m sediment

Bogen m (-) arc; bow; curve; arch; sheet; **-brücke** f arched bridge; **-gang** m arcade; **-licht** n arc-light; **-schütze** m archer

Bohle f (-n) plank

Bohne f (-n) bean; **grüne (-n)** French beans

bohnern wax; polish

bohren bore; **Bohrer** m (-) drill; **Bohrmaschine** f boring-engine

Boje f (-n) buoy

Bollwerk n (-e) bulwark

Bolzen m (-) bolt

Bombe f (-n) bomb; **-nangriff** m raid

bombenfest bomb-proof

Bonbon m (-s) sweet(meat)

Boot n (-e) boat; **-fahren** n boating

Bord m board; **-ell** n brothel

Borg m credit; **borgen** borrow

Börse f (-n) purse; exchange

Börste f (-n) bristle; **borstig** bristly

bösartig malicious

Böschung f (-en) slope

böse bad; angry; **boshaft** malicious

Bösewicht m (-e) villain; wretch

böswillig malevolent

Bosheit f malice

Botanik f botany; **-er** botanist

botanisieren botanize

Bote m (-n) messenger

Botschaft f (-en) message; embassy; **-er** m (-) ambassador

Böttcher m (-) cooper

Bottich m (-e) vat

Bowle f (-n) cup; drink

boxen box; **Boxer** m (-) boxer

Boxkampf m (⁻e) boxing match

boykottieren boycott

brach fallow; waste

Brand m (⁻e) fire; gangrene; **-bombe** f incendiary bomb; **-mal** n stigma; **-stifter** m incendiary; **-wunde** f burn; **-zeichen** n brand, mark

brandmarken brand; stigmatize

Brandung f (-en) breakers, surf

Branntwein *m* (-e) spirits; brandy; -brennerei *f* distillery
Bratfisch *m* fried fish; -kartoffeln fried potatoes; -huhn *n* roast fowl; -pfanne *f* frying-pan; -wurst *f* sausage
braten roast; fry; grill; Braten *m* roast (meat)
Brauch *m* (¨e) custom
brauchbar handy, useful
brauchen want
Braue *f* (-n) eyebrow
brauen brew; Brauer *m* brewer
Brauerei *f* (-en) brewery
braun brown; bräunlich brownish
Bräune *f* quinsy, croup; brown
Brause *f* rose; -bad *n* shower-bath; -limonade *f* lemonade
brausen roar; effervesce
Braut *f*, Bräutigam *m* fiancé(e); bride, bridegroom; -führer *m* best man; -jungfer *f* (-n) bridesmaid; -paar *n* engaged couple
brav good; brave
bravo, Bravo *n* bravo
Brech-bohnen *f pl* French beans; -eisen *n* crow-bar; -mittel *n* emetic, vomitive
brechen break; sich - vomit
Brei *m* (-e) pap
breit broad; Breite *f* (-n) breadth
Breitseite *f* broadside
Bremse *f* (-n) brake; horse-fly
Bremser *m* (-) brakesman
Brenn-eisen *n* curling-iron; -essel *f* stinging-nettle; -glas *n* burning-glass; -punkt *m* focus; -stoff *m* fuel; -bar combustible
brennen burn; curl; sting
Brenner *m* (-) burner, distiller
Brennerei *f* (-en) distillery
Bresche *f* (-n) breach
Brett *n* (-er) board
Brezel *f* (-n) cracknel, pretzel
Brief *m* (-e) letter; -beschwerer *m* letterweight; -kasten *m* letter-box; -marke *f* postage-stamp; -papier *n* note-paper; -tasche *f* wallet; -taube *f* carrier-pigeon; -träger *m* postman;

-umschlag *m* envelope; -waage *f* letter-balance; -wechsel *m* correspondence
brieflich by letter
Brigade *f* brigade; Brigg *f* brig
brillant, Brillant *m* (-en) brilliant
Brille *f* (pair of) spectacles
Brillenschlange *f* (-n) cobra
bringen bring; take
Brise *f* (-n) breeze
Brocken *m* (-) crumb, bit
Brombeere *f* (-n) blackberry
Bronze *f* bronze
Brosche *f* (-n) brooch
broschieren stitch (books)
Broschüre *f* pamphlet
Brot *n* (-e) bread; loaf; -schnitte *f* slice of bread; geröstetes - toast; belegtes - sandwich
Brötchen *n* (-) roll
Bruch *m* (¨e) fracture, rupture; hernia; fraction; breach; quarry; -band *n* truss; -stein *m* quarry-stone; -stück *n* fragment
Brücke *f* bridge; -npfeiler *m* pier
Bruder *m* (¨) brother; brüderlich brotherly; -schaft *f* fraternity
Brühe *f* (-n) sauce; gravy, broth
brüllen roar
brummen growl; grumble
brünett dark
Brunnen *m* (-) well; fountain; -kur *f* mineral water cure; - trinken take the waters
Brust *f* (¨e) breast, chest; -bild *n* half-length portrait; -fellentzündung *f* pleurisy -umfang *m* chest measurement
Brüstung *f* (-en) parapet
brüsten (sich) boast (of)
Brut *f* (-en), brüten brood
brutto gross
Bube *m* (-n)boy; knave
Bubenstreich *m* (-e) prank
Buch *n* (¨er) book; quire; -binder *m* bookbinder; -drucker *m* printer; -druckerei *f* printing-works; -halter *m* book-keeper; -haltung *f* book-keeping; -händler *m* book-seller; -handlung *f* book(seller's) shop; -prüfer *m*

accountant; **-stabe** *m* letter; **grosser -** capital letter
Buche *f* (**-n**) beech
Buchecker *f* beech-nut
Bücher-brett *n* (**-er**) bookshelf; **-ei** *f* library; **-schrank** *m* (**-̈e**) book-case
Buchsbaum *m* box-tree
Büchse *f* (**-n**) tin; rifle; box
buchstabieren spell
buchstäblich literal
Bucht *f* (**-en**) bay
Buckel *m* (**-**) hump; hunchback
bücken (**sich**) stoop
Bucklige (adj. noun) hunchback (pers.)
Bückling *m* (**-e**) red herring
Bude *f* (**-n**) booth; room; hovel
Büfett *n* (**-s**) sideboard; bar
Büffel *m* (**-**) buffalo
Bug *m* (**-e**) bow; **-spriet** *n* bowsprit
Bügelbrett *n* (**-er**) ironing-board
Bügeleisen *n* (**-**) flat-iron
bügeln smooth, iron, press
Buhle *m* or *f* (**-n**) lover
Bühne *f* (**-n**) stage
Bukett *n* (**-e**) bouquet
Bulle *m* (**-n**) bull; **Bulle** *f* (**-n**) (papal) bull
Bulldogge *f* (**-n**) bull-dog
Bummel *m* (**-**) stroll
Bummelzug *m* (**-̈e**) slow train
Bummler *m* (**-**) loiterer, loafer
Bund *m* (**-̈e**) confederation; **-esbahn** *f* state railways; **-esgenosse** *m* ally; **-estag** federal diet; **-eswehr** *f* Federal armed forces
Bündel *n* bundle
Bündnis *n* (**-se**) alliance
bunt many (brightly) coloured
Bürde *f* (**-n**) burden
Burg *f* (**-en**) castle
Bürge *m* (**-n**), **Bürgschaft** *f*, **bürgen** bail
Bürger *m* (**-**) citizen; **-krieg** *m* civil war; **-meister** *m* mayor; **pflicht** *f* civic duty; **-recht** *n* freedom, citizenship; **-steig** *m* pavement; **-stand** *m* middle class
bürgerlich civil; common, middle class

Büro *n* (**-s**) office
Bursche *m* (**-n**) lad; youth; fellow
Bürste *f* (**-n**), **bürsten** brush
Busch *m* (**-̈e**) bush; **Büschel** *m* (**-**) tuft
Busen *m* (**-**) bosom, breast
Busse *f* (**-n**) penance; fine
büssen expiate; **Büsser** *m* (**-**) penitent
Büste *f* (**-n**) bust; **Bütte** *f* (**-n**) tub
Butter *f* butter; **-brot** *n* sandwich; (slice of) bread and butter; **-dose** *f* b.-dish; **-fass** *n* churn; **-milch** *f* butter-milk; **-schnitte** *f* bread and butter
buttern churn
Butzen *m* (**-**) clod; clot

C (see K, Z and SCH)

Café *n* (**-s**) café; coffee-house
Cellist *m* (**-en**) violoncellist
Cello *n* (**-s**) violoncello
Chamäleon *n* (**-s**) chameleon
Champagner *m* champagne
Champignon *m* (**-s**) mushroom
Chaos *n* chaos; **chaotisch** chaotic
Charakter *m* (**-e**) character; **-zug** *m* trait
Chauffeur *m* (**-e**) chauffeur
Chaussee *f* (**-n**) high-road
Chef *m* (**-s**) chief; principal; boss
Chemie *f* chemistry; **Chemiker** *m* chemist; **chemisch** chemical
Chemikalien *f pl* chemicals
Chicoree *m* chicory
China *n* China
Chinese *m* (**-n**) Chinese
Chirurg *m* (**-en**) surgeon; **-ie** *f* surgery
Chlor *n* chlorine
Chloroform *n* chloroform
Cholera *f* cholera
Chor *m* (**-̈e**) chorus; choir; **-al** *m* hymn; **-hemd** *n* surplice; **-verein** *m* choral society
Christ *m* (**-en**) Christian; **-enheit** *f* Christendom; **-entum** *n*

Christianity; **-lich** Christian;
-us Christ
Chronik f (-en) chronicle
chronologisch chronological
Courtage (-n) brokerage

D

da then; there; as; when
dabei besides; present
Dach n ("er) roof; **-decker** m
tiler; slater; **-kammer** f garret;
-rinne f gutter; **-ziegel** m tile
Dachs m (-e) badger; **-hund** m
dachshund
dagegen against; on the contrary
daheim at home
daher thence; therefore
dahinter behind there
Dahlie f (-n) dahlia
damals then; at that time
Damast m damask
Dame f (-n) lady; **-spiel** n
draughts
Damen-abteil n ladies' compartment; **-klub** m ladies' club
damit in order that; so that
Damm m ("e) dike; embankment;
causeway
dämmern dawn
Dämmerung f twilight, dawn
Dampf m ("e) steam; smoke;
-bad n vapour-bath; **-boot** n,
-heizung f steam-heating;
-kessel m boiler; **-maschine** f
steam-engine; **-schiff** n steamboat; **-turbine** f steam-turbine;
-walze f steam-roller
dampfen steam; smoke
dämpfen damp; stew
Dampfer m (-) steamer; **-fahrt**
f steamer-trip
Dank m thanks pl; **schönen -**
many thanks
dankbar grateful
Dankbarkeit f gratitude
danken steam (+ dat.)
dann, darauf then, thereupon
darlegen disclose; explain
Darlehen n (-) loan; **-skasse**
f loan society
Darm m gut; **Därme** pl bowels

darstellen represent, depict
Darstellung f (-en) represen-
tation
Dasein n existence
datieren, Datum n date
Dattel f (-n) date; **-palme** f
date-palm
Daube f stave
Dauer f duration; **dauerhaft**
durable; **dauern** last
Dauerwellen f pl permanent
waves
Daumen m (-) thumb
Daune f (-n) down
davon hence
davontragen carry off
davor before it
dawider against it
dazwischentreten intervene
Debatte f (-n), **debattieren**
debate
Debit m sale; market
Deck n (-e) deck
Deckblatt n ("er) wrapper
Decke f (-n) cover; ceiling
Deckel m (-) cover; lid
decken cover; **Tisch -** lay the
table
defekt defective
Defizit n deficit
Degen m (-) sword
dehnbar ductile, elastic, flexible
dehnen extend, stretch
Deich m (-e) dike
Deichsel f (-n) pole
Dekan m (-e) dean
deklamieren recite
deklinieren decline
Dekoration f (-en) decoration;
scenery
Dekret n (-e) **dekretieren** decree
delikat delicate, nice
Delikatesse f (-n) delicacy
Delphin m dolphin
demnach accordingly
Demokratie f democracy
demokrat(isch) democrat(ic)
Demut f humility
demütig, demütigen humble
denkbar conceivable; imaginable

denken think; imagine
Denkmal *n* (-e) monument
Denkmünze *f* (-n) medal
denkwürdig memorable
denn for, then; -och nevertheless
Depesche *f* (-n) telegram
Depot *n*, deponieren deposit
derart such
derb solid, rude
dergleichen such, the like
deshalb therefore
desinfizieren disinfect
Dessert *n* dessert
destillieren distil
desto the more; je mehr, desto besser the more, the better
Detail(list) *n* (*m*) retail(er)
Detektiv *m* (-e) detective
deuten interpret; deutlich distinct; Deutlichkeit *f* distinctness
Devise *f* (-n) device, motto; foreign currency
Dezember *m* December
Dezimalbruch *m* (¨e) decimal fraction
Diakon *m* (-e) deacon
Dialekt *m* (-e) dialect
Dialog *m* (-e) dialogue
Diamant *m* (-en) diamond
Diät *f* diet, regimen
dicht dense; -bei close by
Dichter *m* (-) poet; dichterisch poetical; Dichtung *f* (-en) poetry; fiction
dick thick, big; stout
Dickicht *n* (-e) thicket
Dieb *m* (-e) thief; -stahl *m* (¨e) theft
Diele *f* (-n) board, plank; hall; lounge
dienen serve (+ dat.); Diener *m* (-) servant
Dienst *m* (-e) service; -alter *n* seniority; -bote *m*, -mädchen *n* maid(-servant); -mann *m* porter, commissionaire
Dienstag *m* Tuesday
diesmal this time
diesseits (+ gen.) on this side
Dietrich *m* picklock
Diktat *n* (-e) dictation; diktieren dictate

Dilettant *m* (-en) amateur; dilettante
Diner *n* dinner; dinieren dine
Ding *n* (-e) thing
dingen hire
Diphtheritis *f* diphtheria
Diplom *n* (-e) diploma; charter
Diplomat *m* (-en) diplomat
direkt direct; Direktor *m* (-en) director, manager
Dirigent *m* (-en) conductor, leader
Dirne *f* (-n) wench; prostitute
diskontieren, Diskont *m* discount
Dissident *m* (-en) dissenter
Distanz *f* (-en) distance
Distel *f* (-n) thistle
Disziplin *f* discipline
Dividende *f* (-n) dividend; dividieren divide
Division *f* division
doch yet, however; surely
Docht *m* (-e) wick
Dock *n* (-s) dock, -arbeiter *m* docker
Dogge *f* (-n) bulldog
Dohle *f* (-n) jackdaw
Doktor *m* (-en) doctor
Dokument *n* (-e) document
Dolch *m* (-e) dagger; -stich *m* (-e) stab
Dolmetscher *m* (-) interpreter
Dom *m* (-e) cathedral
Domäne *f* (-n) domain, demesne
Domino *m* or *n* (-s) domino
Donau *f* Danube
Donner *m* thunder; -schlag *m* thunder-clap; -stag Thursday
donnern thunder
Doppel-ehe *f* bigamy; -gleis *n* double track; -punkt *m* colon; -sinnig ambiguous
doppelt double; -wirkend double acting
Dorf *n* (¨er) village
Dorn *m* (-en) thorn; -röschen *n* Sleeping Beauty
dornig thorny
dorren dry
dort(hin) there; -her thence
Dose *f* (-n) tin
Dosis *f* dose

Dozent m (**-en**) teacher at university

Drache m (**-n**) dragon; kite

Dragoner m (**-**) dragoon

Draht m (**ِّe**) wire; **-bürste** f wire-brush; **-los** wireless; **-seil** n wire-cable; **-stift** m wire-tack

drahten telegraph, wire

Drama n (**-men**) drama; **-tisch** dramatic

drängen press; crowd; force

draussen outside; out of doors

drechseln turn; shape (on a lathe); **Drechsler** m turner

Dreck m dirt; **dreckig** dirty

Dreh-bank f turning-lathe; **-brücke** f turn-bridge; **-gestell** n bogie; **-kreuz** n turnstile; **-orgel** f barrel-organ; **-punkt** m pivot; **-scheibe** f turntable; **-stuhl** m swivel-chair

drehen, Drehung f (**-en**) turn

drei three; **-mal** thrice; **-blätterig** three-leaved

Drei-eck n triangle; **-eckig** triangular; **-fach, -fältig** threefold; **-faltigkeit** f Trinity; **-fuss** m tripod; **-königsfest** n Twelfth Night; **-master** m three-master

dreist bold

dreschen thresh; **Drescher** m thresher

Dreschmaschine f (**-n**) threshing machine

dressieren train; break in

drillen drill

dringend urgent

drinnen within

Drittel n (**-**) third

Droge f (**-n**) drug; **-rie, -nhandlung** f drug store; **-nhändler** m druggist

Drohbrief m (**-e**) threatening letter

drohen threaten; **Drohung** f threat

drollig droll; facetious

Dromedar n (**-e**) dromedary

Droschke f (**-n**) cab; **-nstand** m cab-stand: **-kutscher** m cab-man

Drossel f (**-n**) thrush

drüben on other side

Druck m pressure; print(ing); **-fehler** m erratum; **-fehlerverzeichnis** n errata; **-sache** printed matter

drucken print

drücken press, oppress; **sich -** sneak away

Drucker m (**-**) printer; **-presse** f printing-press; **-schwärze** f printer's ink; **-ei** f printing-office, press

Drücker m (**-**) latch; trigger

Drüse f (**-n**) gland

du thou, you

ducken (sich) stoop, duck

Dudelsack m bag-pipe

Duell n (**-e**) duel

duellieren (sich) fight a duel

Duett n (**-e**) duet, duo

Duft m (**ِّe**) fragrance; perfume

duftend fragrant

dulden tolerate, suffer

duldsam tolerant

Duldung f toleration

dumm stupid

Dummheit f (**-en**), stupidity; prank

Dummkopf m (**ِّe**) blockhead

dumpf hollow; dull; **-ig** musty

Düne f (**-n**) dune

Dünger m, **düngen** dung, manure

dunkel dark

Dünkel(haft) m conceit(ed)

Dunkel-kammer f dark room (phot.); **-heit** f darkness

dunkeln darken

dünn thin

Dunst m (**ِّe**) vapour

dunstig vaporous; damp

Dur n major

durch through; **-aus** thoroughly; **-aus nicht** not at all; **-bohren, -löchern** pierce, perforate; **-bringen** dissipate; **-dringen,** penetrate; **-einander** (in) confusion; **-kommen** pass; **-fahrt** f, **-reise, -marsch, -lass, -weg** passage; **-fall** m diarrhœa; failure; **-fallen** fail; **-fuhr** f, **-gang** m corridor; **-gangsverkehr** m transit; **-gangszug** m corridor-train; **-gehender**

Wagen *m* through-carriage; **-gebraten** well done; **-lochen** punch; **-messer** *m* diameter; **-schnitt** *m* average; **-schnittlich** on an average; **-sehen** examine; **-sichtig** transparent; **-streichen** cross out; **-suchen** search through; **-trieben** artful; **-weg** throughout; **-weichen** steep, soak; **-wirken** interweave; **-ziehen** pass through;

Durchzug *m* passage, draught

dürfen be allowed; may

dürftig indigent; poor

dürr dry, arid

Dürre *f* aridity

Durst *m*, **dürsten** thirst

durstig thirsty

düster gloomy, dark

Dutzend *n* (-e or –) dozen

duzen address with **du**

Dynamit *m* (-e) dynamite

Dynamo *m* (-s) dynamo

Dynastie *f* (-n) dynasty

D-Zug *m* (ˑe) corridor-train

E

Ebbe *f* (-n) ebb (tide)

eben flat, level; just; **-falls** likewise

Ebene *f* (-n) plain

Ebenholz *n* ebony

Eber *m* (–) boar

Eberesche *f* (-n) mountain-ash

ebnen level, smooth

Echo *n* (-s) echo

echt genuine; real; true

Ecke *f* (-n) corner

Eckplatz *m* (ˑe) corner-seat

eckig angular; awkward

edel noble

Edel-mann *m* nobleman; **-mut** *m* generosity; **-mütig** generous; **-stein** *m* precious stone

Edikt *n* (-e) edict

Efeu *m* ivy

Effekt *m* (-e) effect; **-en** personal effects

eggen, Egge *f* (-n) harrow

Egoist(isch) *m* (-en) egoist(ic)

Ehe *f* (-n) matrimony; **-brecher** *m* adulterer; **-bruch** *m* adultery; **-frau** *f* wife; **-mann** *m* husband; **-paar** *n* married couple; **-ring** *m* wedding-ring; **-scheidung** *f* divorce; **-stand** *m* matrimony

ehe before; **-dem** formerly

ehelich conjugal

ehemalig former

ehemals formerly

eher sooner; rather

ehrbar honourable

Ehre *f* (-n), **ehren** honour

Ehren-amt *n* honorary post; **-mann** *m* man of honour; **-mitglied** *n* honorary member; **-pforte** *f* triumphal arch; **-sache** *f*, **-handel** *m* affair of honour; **-voll** honourable; **-wort** *n* word of honour; **-zeichen** *n* decoration

ehrerbietig respectful

ehrlich honest

Ehrlichkeit *f* honesty

Ehr-geiz *m* ambition; **-geizig** ambitious **-würdig** venerable

Ei *n* (-er) egg; **-dotter** *m*, **-gelb** *n* yolk; **-weiss** *n* white of an egg; albumen

Eiche *f* (-n), **eichen** oak

Eichel *f* (-n) acorn; (cards) club

Eichmass *n*, gauge

eichen gauge

Eichhörnchen *n* (–) squirrel

Eid *m* (-e) oath; **-bruch** *m* perjury; **-brüchig** perjured; **-genosse** *m* confederate

Eidechse *f* (-n) lizard

Eiderdaunen *pl* eiderdown

eidlich sworn, on oath

Eier-becher *m* egg-cup; **-kuchen** *m* omelet; **-likör** *m* egg-liqueur; **-schale** *f* egg-shell

Eifer *m* zeal; **-sucht** *f* jealousy; **-süchtig** jealous

eifrig zealous; keen

eigen proper; own; **-tümlich** peculiar; **Eigen-liebe** *f* self-love; **-lob** *n* self-praise; **-name** *m* proper name; **-mächtig** arbitrary; **-nutz** *m* selfishness; **-nützig** selfish; **-sinn** *m* obstinacy; **-sinnig** obstinate; **-schaft** *f* (-en) quality; **-tum** *n* (ˑer) property; **-tümer** *m* owner; **-tümlich(keit)** *f* peculiar(ity); **eigentlich** proper, exact, actually; **eigens** expressly

eignen (sich) suit, be suitable

Eil-bote *m* courier; **-gut** *n* express goods; **-marsch** *m* forced march; **-(post)wagen** *m* mailcoach; **-zug** *m* express train

Eile *f* haste; **eilen** hasten, make haste; **eilends** in haste; **eilig** speedy, urgent, pressing

Eimer *m* (-) bucket

ein one; **-ander** one another; **-armig** one-armed; **-äugig** oneeyed

einatmen breathe in

Einbahnstrasse *f* (-n) one-way street

einbalsamieren embalm

Einband *m* ("-e) binding

einbiegen turn in

einbilden (sich) imagine; be conceited

Einbildung(skraft) *f* imagination

einbinden bind

einbrechen break in; **Einbrecher** *m* burglar; **Einbruch** *m* breaking in; burglary; **- der Nacht** nightfall

einbringen yield

einbürgern naturalize

Einbusse *f* (-n) loss, forfeit

einbüssen lose, forfeit

Eindecker *m* (-) monoplane

eindrängen (sich) intrude

eindringen penetrate

eindringlich impressive

Eindruck *m* ("-e) impression

Einer *m* (-) unit

einerlei (of) the same (kind)

ein-fach, -fältig simple; plain

Ein-fachheit *f* simplicity

einfahren enter; run in (car)

Einfahrt *f* (-en) entrance; gateway

Einfall *m* ("-e) idea; invasion

einfallen fall in; invade; collapse

Einfalt *f* simplicity

einfältig simple, silly

einfassen border

einfinden (sich) appear; acclimatize

einflössen inspire

Einfluss *m* ("-e) influence; **-reich** influential

einförmig uniform; **-keit** *f* uniformity

einfriedigen fence

Einfuhr *f* (-en) import

einführen introduce; import

Eingang *m* ("-e) entrance

eingeben give; suggest

eingebildet imaginary, conceited, vain

eingeboren native

eingedenk mindful

eingefallen dilapidated; sunken

eingehen enter; cease; agree to

eingelegt inlaid

Eingemachtes *n* preserves *pl*

eingestehen avow, confess

Eingeweide *n* bowels, intestines

eingezogen retired; called up

eingiessen pour in

eingreifen intervene; encroach

Einhalt *m*, **einhalten** stop

einhändigen hand over; deliver

einheimisch native

Einheit *f* (-en) unity; unit; **-lich** uniform

einholen overtake

Einhorn *n* unicorn

einig agreed; in harmony

einige several, some

einigen unite; agree

Einigkeit *f* concord

Einkauf *m* ("-e) purchase; **-en** do shopping; **-spreis** *m* prime cost

einkehren put up at an inn

einklammern put in brackets

Einkommen(steuer) *n* (*f*) income (-tax)

einladen invite

Einladung *f* (-en) invitation

Einlage *f* enclosure; deposit

Einlass *m* admission

einlassen admit

einlaufen enter; shrink

Einleitung *f* (-en) introduction

einleuchtend evident

einliegend enclosed

einmachen preserve, pickle

einmal (all at) once

Einmaleins *n* multiplicationtable

einmischen (sich) interfere

einmütig unanimous

Einnahme f (-n) capture; receipt; takings

einnehmen take; receive; **-d** captivating

Einnehmer m (-) collector

ein-packen pack; **-pökeln** pickle; **-prägen** impress; **-quartieren** quarter, billet; **-rahmen** frame; **-räumen** admit; **-reiben** rub (in); **-rechnen** include; **-reibung** f embrocation; **-reihig** single-breasted; **-renken** set; **-richten** arrange, furnish; **-rücken** insert; **-salzen** salt

eins one; **einsam** lonely

Einsatz m (⁀e) stake; shirt-front

einsaugen absorb

einschärfen enjoin; impress

Einschätzung f assessment

ein-schieben insert; **-schiffen** embark; **-schlafen** fall asleep; **-schlagen** break in; wrap, pack up; strike; take; **-schliessen** lock up, include; **-schliesslich** inclusive; **-schmeicheln** insinuate; **-schmieren** grease; **-schränken** limit; **-schreibebrief** m registered letter; **-schreiben** book, enter, register; **-schreiten** interfere; **-schüchtern** intimidate; **-sehen** understand; **-seifen** soap, lather; **-seitig** partial; **-senden** send, transmit; **-setzen** institute, stake, appoint, install

Einschlag m (⁀e) impact; weft

Einschnitt m (-e) incision; cutting

Einsicht f insight; intelligence

Einsiedler m (-) hermit

Einspänner m one-horse carriage

einsperren lock up

einspritzen inject

Einspritzung f (-en) injection

Einspruch m (⁀e) objection

einst once, one day; **-weilen** meanwhile

ein-stecken pocket; **-stehen für** answer for; **-steigen** get in; **-stellen** stop; strike; focus; **-stimmig** in unison; **-stürzen** collapse; **-tauchen** immerse;

-tauschen exchange; **-teilen** divide; **-teilung** f division; **-tönig** monotonous

Eintracht f concord

Eintrag m (⁀e) entry; damage

Eintragung f entry, entering

ein-tragen enter; yield; **-träglich** profitable; **-treffen** arrive; **-treiben** collect; **-treten** enter

Eintritt m (-e) entrance; admission; beginning

einüben practise

einverleiben incorporate; annex

einverstanden! agreed!

Einwanderer m (-) immigrant; **einwandern** immigrate; **Einwanderung** f immigration

ein- weichen steep, soak; **-weihen** inaugurate; **-wenden** object; **-wickeln** wrap up; **-willigen, Einwilligung** f consent

Einwohner m (-) inhabitant

Einwurf m (⁀e) objection; (letter-box) slot

Einzahl f singular

einzahlen pay

Einzahlung f (-en) payment

einzäunen fence

Einzelheit f (-en) detail

einzeln single; separate

einziehen draw in; move into; call up

einzig only

Einzug m (⁀e) entry

Eis n ice; **-bahn** f skating rink; **-bär** m polar bear; **-berg** m iceberg; **-brecher** m icebreaker; **-keller** m ice-house; **-maschine** f ice-machine; **-meer** n Arctic, Antarctic Ocean; **-schrank** m ice-box; **-zapfen** m icicle

Eisen n iron; **-bahn** f railway; **-bahnwagen** m railway-carriage; **-blech** n sheet-iron; **-draht** m iron-wire; **-giesserei** f iron-foundry; **-händler** m ironmonger; **-hammer** m forge; **-hüttenwerk** n ironworks; **-ware** f hardware

eisern iron; **eisig** icy

eitel vain

Eitelkeit f vanity

Eiter *m* pus; **eitern** fester
Ekel *m*, **ekeln** disgust
ekelhaft disgusting
elastisch elastic
Elastizität *f* elasticity
Elefant *m* (-en) elephant
elegant elegant
Eleganz *f* elegance
Elegie *f* (-n) elegy
Elektriker *m* (-) electrician
elektrisch electric(al)
elektrisieren electrify
Elektrisiermaschine *f* electrical machine
Elektrizität *f* electricity; **-swerk** *n* electricity works *pl*
Elektromagnet *m* (-e) electromagnet
Element(ar) *n* (-e) element(ary)
Elend *n* misery; **elend** miserable
Elentier *n* (-e) elk
elf eleven; **Elf** *m* (-en) elf, fairy
Elfenbein *n* ivory
Elle *f* (-n) ell; **Ellbogen** *m* (-) elbow
Elster *f* (-n) magpie
Eltern *pl* parents
Email *n*, **emaillieren** enamel
emanzipieren emancipate
Empfang *m* (¨e) reception; **empfangen** receive; **Empfänger** *m* receiver; **empfänglich** susceptible; **Empfängnis** *f* conception; **Empfangs** **-dame** *f* receptionist; **-schein** *m* receipt; **-tag** *m* at home (day); **-zimmer** *n* reception-room
empfehlen recommend; **-swert** recommendable; **Empfehlungsbrief** *m* letter of recommendation
empfinden feel; **empfindlich** sensible; sensitive; irritable
empfindsam sentimental
empor upwards; **-kommen** rise
empören, Empörung *f* revolt; **(sich) -** get angry
Emporkömmling *m* upstart
emsig assiduous, active
Ende, *n* (-n), **enden** or **endigen** end
End-station *f* terminus; **-zweck** *m* final aim; **-ziel** *n* destination; **-gültig** final

endlich final; at last
endlos endless
Endung *f* (-en) ending; termination
Energie *f* energy
eng narrow; tight
Engel *m* (-) angel
England *n* England; **Engländer** *m* (-) Englishman; **-in** (-nen) Englishwoman
englisch English; **-es Pflaster** court-plaster
Engpass *m* (¨e) defile
Enkel *m* (-) grandson; **-in** *f* (-nen) granddaughter
entarten degenerate
entbehren want; do without
Entbehrung *f* (-en) want, privation
entbinden dispense; deliver
Entbindung *f* (-en) delivery; accouchement
entblössen bare, deprive
entdecken discover
Entdeckung *f* (-en) discovery
Ente *f* (-n) duck; hoax, canard; **-nbraten** *m* roast duck
entehren dishonour
enteignen expropriate
Enteignung *f* (-en) expropriation
enterben disinherit
entfahren, entfallen slip
entfalten display; unfold
entfernen remove; **entfernt** distant
Entfernung *f* (-en) distance
entfliehen flee, escape
entführen abduct
entgegen towards; against; **-gehen** go to meet; **-gesetzt** opposite; **-kommen** come to meet; **-stellen** oppose
entgegnen reply
entgehen escape; fail
entgleisen get off the rails
Entgleisung *f* (-en) derailment
enthalten contain; abstain
enthaupten behead
enthüllen reveal
entkleiden undress
entkommen, -laufen escape
entkorken uncork

entladen, Entladung *f* (-en) unload

entlang along

entlassen, dismiss; discharge

entlasten unburden; relieve

Entlastung *f* (-en) easing; relief

entledigen deliver, get rid of

entlegen remote; distant

entlehnen borrow

entleihen to borrow

entmannen castrate

entmutigen discourage

enträtseln decipher; solve

entreissen snatch from

entrüsten exasperate

Entrüstung *f* indignation

entsagen resign; abandon

entschädigen indemnify

Entschädigung *f* (-en) indemnity

entscheiden decide; entscheidend decisive; Entscheidung *f* decision

entschliessen (sich) resolve; entschlossen resolute; Entschluss *m* (-̈e) resolution

entschuldigen, Entschuldigung *f* (-en) excuse

Entsetzen *n* horror

entsetzlich horrible

entsinnen (sich) remember

entsprechen answer; correspond

ent-stehen arise; -stellen disfigure; -täuschen disappoint; -völkern depopulate; -waffnen disarm; -wässern drain; -weichen escape; -weihen profane; -wickeln develop

entweder . . . oder either . . . or

entwerfen design, plan

Entwertung *f* (-en) depreciation

entwickeln develop

Entwickelung *f* (-en) development

entwöhnen wean; disaccustom

Entwurf *m* (-̈e) sketch; design

entziehen withdraw

entziffern decipher

entzücken charm

Entzückung *f* (-en) rapture

entzündbar inflammable

entzünden inflame

Entzündung *f* (-en) inflammation

entzwei in two; broken; -en disunite, separate

Epidemie *f* (-n), epidemisch epidemic

Epoche *f* (-n) epoch

Epos *n* (Epen) epic poem

Equipage *f* carriage

erbarmen (sich), Erbarmen *n* pity

erbärmlich pitiful, miserable

erbauen build; edify

Erbe *m* (-n) heir; *n* inheritance; erben inherit; Erbin *f* heiress; Erbfolge *f* succession

erbieten (sich) offer

erbittern embitter, exasperate

erblassen, erbleichen grow pale

erblich hereditary

erblicken perceive

erbrechen break open; sich - vomit

Erbschaft *f* (-en) inheritance

Erbschaftssteuer *f* succession duty; death duty

Erbse *f* (-n) pea

Erbsünde *f* original sin

Erd-achse *f* axis of the earth; -arbeiter *m* navvy; -beben *n* earthquake; -leitung (Electricity) *f* earth connection; -beere *f* strawberry; -geschoss *n* ground-floor; -kugel *f* terrestrial globe; -kunde *f* geography; -rutsch *m* land-slip; -teil *m* continent

Erde *f* earth; ground

erdenken imagine, invent

erdenklich imaginable

erdichten feign; invent

erdrosseln strangle

erdrücken crush

erdulden suffer

ereignen happen

Ereignis *n* (-se) event

erfahren learn; experience

Erfahrung *f* (-en) experience

erfinden invent; Erfinder *m* inventor; Erfindung *f* (-en) invention

erfinderisch inventive

Erfolg *m* (-e) success

erfolgreich successful

erfordern require

erforderlich necessary
erforschen investigate; explore
Erforscher *m* (-) explorer
Erforschung *f* (-en) exploration
erfreuen, ergötzen delight
erfreulich pleasing
erfrieren freeze to death
erfrischen refresh
ergänzen complete
ergeben devote; surrender, submit to; result; **ergebenst** respectfully
Ergebnis *n* (-se) result
ergreifen seize; touch
erhaben sublime
erhalten receive; obtain; preserve; maintain
erhängen hang
erheben raise; levy
erheblich considerable
erheitern cheer
erhitzen heat
Erhöhung *f* (-en) elevation; increase
erholen (sich) recover
Erholung *f* (-en) recovery; recreation
erinnern remind; **sich -** remember
Erinnerung *f* (-en) remembrance
erkalten, erkälten cool; **sich -** catch cold
erkennen recognize
erkenntlich grateful
Erkerfenster *n* (-) bay-window
erklären declare; explain
Erklärung *f* (-en) declaration; explanation
erkranken fall ill
erkühnen (sich) dare
erkundigen (sich) inquire
Erkundigung *f* (-en) inquiry
erlangen obtain
erlauben allow, permit
Erlaubnis *f* permission
erläutern explain
Erläuterung *f* (-en) explanation
Erle *f* (-n) alder
erleben live to see; experience
Erlebnis *n* (-se) experience
erledigt settled
erleichtern facilitate; relieve

erleiden suffer
erleuchten illuminate
erlogen false
Erlöser *m* (-) redeemer, saviour
erlöschen go out
ermächtigen empower, authorize
ermahnen admonish, exhort
ermangeln fail, lack
ermässigen reduce
ermorden, Ermordung *f* murder
ermüden, Ermüdung *f* fatigue
ermutigen encourage
ernähren nourish
ernennen appoint
Ernennung *f* (-en) appointment
erneuern renew
Ernst *m* earnest; **ernsthaft** serious
Ernte *f* (-n) harvest
ernten gather, reap
Eroberer *m* (-) conqueror
erobern conquer
Eroberung *f* (-en) conquest
eröffnen open
erörtern discuss
erpressen extort
Erpressung *f* (-en) exaction; blackmail
erproben try; test
erquicken refresh
erraten guess
erregen excite; cause
Erregung *f* excitement
erreichen reach; attain
errichten erect, establish
erröten blush
Ersatz *m* compensation; substitute; **-wahl** *f* by-election
erschaffen create
Erschaffung *f* (-en) creation
erscheinen appear
Erscheinung *f* (-en) appearance; apparition; vision
erschiessen shoot dead
erschlagen slay
erschöpfen exhaust
Erschöpfung *f* (-en) exhaustion
erschrecken frighten
erschüttern shake
erschweren aggravate
ersehen see
ersetzen replace; compensate
ersichtlich visible

ersinnen contrive
ersinnlich imaginable
ersparen save
Ersparnis *f* (-se) savings *pl*
erst first; only; not until
erstarken to grow strong
erstatten compensate, restore
Erstaufführung *f* (-en) first night
Erstaunen *n* astonish(ment)
erstaunlich astonishing
erstens firstly
ersticken (to be) suffocate(d)
erstrecken (sich) extend
ersuchen request
ertappen catch
Ertrag *m* (⸚e) produce
ertragen endure
erträglich endurable
ertränken drown
ertrinken be drowned
erwachen awake
erwachsen adult; grown up
erwägen consider
Erwägung *f* (-en) consideration
erwähnen, Erwähnung *f* mention
erwarten expect
Erwartung *f* (-en) expectation
erweichen soften
erweisen do, render
erweitern enlarge
erwerben acquire
erwidern, Erwiderung *f* reply, reciprocate
erwischen catch
erwünscht desired
erwürgen strangle
Erz *n* (-e) ore
erzählen tell; relate
Erzählung *f* (-en) tale; story
Erzbischof *m* (⸚e) archbishop
erzeugen, Erzeugnis *n* (-se) produce
Erzherzog *m* (⸚e) archduke
erziehen bring up; educate
Erzieherin *f* (-nen) governess
Erziehung *f* education; -sanstalt *f* educational establishment
erzielen attain, reach
Esche *f* (-n) ash
Esel *m* (-) ass; -sbrücke *f* crib; -sohr *n* dog's ear (in book)
Espe *f* (-n) asp

essbar eatable
Esse *f* (-n) chimney; forge
essen eat; zu mittag - dine; zu Abend - sup
Essenszeit *f* (-en) mealtime
Essig *m* vinegar; -gurke *f* gherkin; -säure *f* acetic acid
Esslöffel *m* (-) table-spoon
Etage *f* (-n) storey; floor; -nwohnung *f* flat
etliche some; a few
Etui *n* (-s) case
etwa perhaps; roughly
etwas something; some
euch you
euer your
Eule *f* (-n) owl
Europa *n* Europe; europäisch, Europäer *m* (-) European
evangelisch evangelic
Evangelium *n* (-lien) gospel
ewig eternal
Ewigkeit *f* eternity
Examen *n* (-) examination
Exemplar *n* (-e) copy
exemplarisch exemplary
exerzieren, Exerzitium *n* exercise; drill
Existenz *f* (-en) existence
existieren exist
exotisch exotic
expedieren forward
Experiment *n* (-e) experiment
explodieren explode
Explosion *f* (-en) explosion
Export *m* (-e), exportieren export
Expressgut *n* express goods
Expresszug *m* (⸚e) express train
extra extra; E-blatt *n* special edition; -zug *m* special train
Extrakt *m* (-e) extract
Extrem *n* (-e) extreme
Exzellenz (-en) excellency

F

Fabel *f* (-n) fable; -dichter *m* writer of fables; -haft fabulous
Fabrik *f* (-en) factory; -arbeiter *m* factory worker; -stadt *f* manufacturing town; -zeichen *n* trade-mark

Fabrikant *m* (-en) manufacturer

Fabrikat *n* (-e), **fabrizieren** manufacture

Fach *n* (¨er) compartment; drawer; profession; subject; branch; **-mann** *m* professional, expert

fächeln, Fächer *m* (-) fan

Fackel *f* (-n) torch; **-beleuchtung** *f* torchlight; **-träger** *m* torch-bearer; **-zug** *m* torchlight procession

fade stale; insipid

Faden *m* (¨) thread; fathom; filament; **-nudeln** *f pl* vermicelli

fadenscheinig threadbare

Fagott *n* (-e) bassoon

fähig capable

Fähigkeit *f* (-en) capability

fahl fallow, pale

Fahne *f* (-n) flag; **-nträger** *m* standard-bearer

Fähnrich *m* (-e) ensign

Fahr-geld *n*, **-preis** *m* fare; **-karte** *f* ticket; **-kartenschalter** *m* booking-office; **-plan** *m* time-table; **-planmässig** regular; **-rad** *n* cycle; **-schein** *m* ticket; **-schule** *f* driving-school; **-stuhl** *m* lift; **-weg** *m*, **-damm** *m* roadway; **-zeug** *n* vehicle; vessel

Fähre *f* (-n) ferry

fahren drive; ride

Fahrer *m* (-) driver

fahrlässig careless

Fährmann *m* (¨er) ferryman

Fahrt *f* (-en) drive; journey

Fährte *f* (-n) track, trail

faktisch real

Faktur *f* (-en) invoice

Falke *m* (-n) falcon

Fall *m* (¨e) fall; reverse; case; **-beil** *n* guillotine; **-brücke** *f* drawbridge; **-sucht** *f* epilepsy; **-schirm** *m* parachute; **-tür** *f* trap-door

Falle *f* (-n) trap; snare

fallen fall; sink; **fällen** fell; **fällig** due

falls in case (that)

falsch false; wrong; **fälschen** forge; adulterate; **Fälschung** *f* forgery, falsification

Falschmünzer *m* (-) coiner

Falte *f* (-n) fold, plait, crease

falten fold, plait, crease

Falz *m* (-e), **falzen** groove, fold

Familie *f* (-n) family

famos famous; capital

Fang *m* (¨e), **fangen** catch

Farbe *f* (-n) colour; **färben** colour; dye; **Färber** *m* dyer; **farbig** coloured

Farb-film *m* colour-film; **-stift** *m* coloured pencil; **-ton** *m* tint

Farn *m* (-e) fern

Fasan *m* (-en) pheasant

Fasching *m* (-e) carnival

Faser *f* (-n) fibre; **faserig** fibrous

Fass *n* (¨er) cask, barrel; **-binder** *m* cooper

fassen seize; take; set; learn; contain; hold; **sich -** compose

Fassung *f* (-en) mounting; self-control; version; **-skraft** *f* power of comprehension

fast almost; nearly

fasten fast; **Fastenzeit** *f* Shrovetide, Lent; **Fastnacht** *f* Shrove Tuesday; **Fasttag** *m* fasting-day

faul rotten, putrid; idle; **faulen** rot; **Faulenzer** *m* idler

Faulheit *f* laziness

Faultier *n* (-e) sloth

Faust *f* (¨e) fist

Februar *m* February

fechten fence

Fechtmeister *m* fencing-master

Feder *f* (-n) feather; pen; spring; **-ball** *m* shuttle-cock; **-halter** *m* pen-holder; **-messer** *n* penknife

Fee *f* (-n) fairy

Fegefeuer *n* purgatory

fegen sweep

Fehl *m* error, **-er**, **-griff** *m* fault, mistake; **-geburt** *f* miscarriage; **-schlagen** fail; **-treten** slip; **-tritt** *m* false step

fehl amiss

Fehlbetrag *m* (¨e) deficit

fehlen be wanting, be absent

fehlerhaft faulty

Feier (-n) celebration; **-tag** *m*

holiday; **feierlich** solemn, ceremonious; **feiern** celebrate

feige cowardly

Feige f (-n) fig

Feigheit f cowardice

Feigling m (-e) coward

Feile f (-n), **feilen** file

feilschen bargain

fein fine; elegant

Feind m (-e) enemy; **-lich, -selig** hostile; **-schaft** f enmity

Feinschmecker m (-) gourmet

Feld n (-er) field; **-bett** n campbed; **-herr** m general; **-huhn** n partridge; **-messer** m surveyor; **-stuhl** m camp-stool; **-webel** m sergeant-major; **-zug** m campaign

Fell n (-e) skin; hide

Fels(en) m rock

felsig rocky

Fenchel m fennel

Fenster n (-) window; skylight; **-laden** m shutter; **-riegel** m window-bolt; **-scheibe** f pane

Ferien pl holidays; vacation

Ferkel n (-) young pig

fern far; distant; **Ferne** f distance; **Fernglas** n telescope; **-leitung** f long-distance line; **-sehen** n television; **-sehapparat** m television-set; **-sprechamt** n telephone-office; **-sprecher** m telephone; **-sprechzelle** f call-box

ferner further; moreover

Ferse f (-n) heel

fertig ready-made, ready

Fertigkeit f facility

Fessel f (-n), **fesseln** fetter, chain

fest firm; solid; fast; **-machen** fasten; **-nehmen** arrest

feststellen ascertain, state

Fest, -essen n, **-tag** m feast, festival

Festland n continent

Festung f (-en) fortress; **-swerk** n fortification

fett, Fett n fat; **-fleck** m spot of grease; **-leibig** corpulent; **fettig** greasy

Fetzen m (-) rag, tatter

feucht moist; damp

Feuchtigkeit f moisture

Feuer n (-) **feuern** fire; **-bestattung** f cremation; **-fest** fireproof; **-haken** m poker ; **-melder** m fire-alarm; **-spritze** f fire-engine; **-sbrunst** f fire; **-stein** m flint; **-versicherung** f fire-insurance; **-wehr** f firemen; **-werk** n fireworks

Feuerzeug n lighter

feurig fiery

Fibel f (-n) spelling-book

Fichte f (-n) pine, spruce-fir

fidel merry

Fieber n fever; **-haft** feverish

Fiedel(bogen) f (m) fiddle (-stick)

fiedern feather; fledge

Figur f (-en) figure

Filet n (-s) loin, fillet

Filiale f (-n) branch office

Film m (-e) film

Filter m (-), **filtrieren** filter

Filz m (-e) felt; **-hut** m felt-hat

Finanzminister m (-) minister of finance; (Engl.) Chancellor of the Exchequer

finden find; **Finder** m finder

findig clever

Finger m (-) finger

Fingerabdruck m (-̈e) fingerprint

Fingerhut m (-̈e) thimble

Fink m (-en) finch

finster dark

Finsternis f (-se) darkness

Firma f (pl **Firmen**) firm

firmen confirm (R.C. church)

Firnis m (-se), **firnissen** varnish

First m (-e) ridge

Fisch m (-e), **fischen** fish; **-bein** n whale-bone; **-fang** m fishing; **-tran** m fish-oil; **Fischer** m fisherman, **-ei** f fishery

Fiskus m exchequer

Fixstern m fixed star

flach flat

Fläche f (-n) plain; **-ninhalt** m area

Flachrennen n flat race

Flachs m (-e) flax

flackern flare; flicker

Flagge f (-n) flag

Flak *f* anti-aircraft-gun
Flamme *f* (-n) **flammen** flame
Flanell *m* (-e) flannel
Flanke *f* (-n) **flankieren** flank
Flasche *f* (-n) bottle; **-nbier** *n* bottled beer; **-nzug** *m* tackle
flatterhaft fickle
flattern flutter; float
flau dull; faint; insipid
Flaum(feder) *m* (*f*) down (feather)
Flechte *f* (-n) tress; lichen; ringworm
flechten plait
Fleck(en) *m* spot; **fleckig** spotted
Fledermaus *f* (¨e) bat
Flegel *m* (-) flail; churl
flehen implore
Fleisch *n* flesh; meat; pulp; **-brühe** *f* beef-tea; **-er** *m* butcher; **-extrakt** *m* extract of meat; **-fressend** carnivorous; **-ig** fleshy
Fleiss *m* diligence; **-ig** diligent
flicken mend
Flickschneider *m* botcher
Flickschuster *m* cobbler
Flieder *m* (-) elder; lilac
Fliege *f* (-n) fly
fliegen fly; **-fänger** *m* fly-catcher; **fliehen** flee
Flieger *m* airman
fliessen flow
flink quick; agile; nimble
Flinte *f* (-n) gun, musket
Flitterwochen *f pl* honeymoon
Flocke *f* (-n) flake
Floh *m* (¨e) flea
Flor *m* (-e) crape
florieren flourish, thrive
Floss *n* (¨e) raft; **Flosse** *f* (-n) fin
Flöte *f* (-n) flute
flott afloat; free, quick
Flotte *f* fleet; navy
Flöz *n* (-e) seam; layer
fluchen, Fluch *m* (¨e) curse
Flucht *f* (-en) flight; **flüchten** flee
Flüchtling *m* (-e) refugee
flüchtig fugitive; hasty
Flug *m* (¨e) flight; **-abwehr** *f* A.A. (army); **-karte** *f* air-ticket;

-platz *m* aerodrome; **-sand** *m* quicksand; **-schrift** *f* pamphlet; **-zeug** *n* aeroplane; **-zeughalle** *f* hangar; **-zeugmutterschiff** *n* aircraft-carrier
Flügel *m* wing; blade; grand-piano; **-tür** *f* folding-door
Flur *f* (-en) field; *m* (-e) floor; hall
Fluss *m* (¨e) river; flux; **-pferd** *n* hippopotamus
flüssig, Flüssigkeit *f* liquid
Flut *f* (-en) flood; high tide
Fockmast *m* fore-mast
Fohlen *n* (-) foal
Föhre *f* (-n) fir, pine
Folge *f* (-n) consequence; **folgen** (+ dat.) follow; succeed
folgern conclude
folglich consequently
folgsam obedient
Folie *f* (-n) foil
foltern, Folter *f* (-n) torture
Fonds *m* funds
foppen, Fopperei *f* hoax
fördern further; raise
fordern ask; demand
Forderung *f* (-en) claim
Forelle *f* (-n) trout
Form, *f* (-en), **Formular** *n* (-e), **form(ier)en** form; **Format** *n* (-e) size; **Formel** *f* (-n) formula; **formell** formal; **Förmlich(keit)** *f* formal(ity)
forschen, Forschung *f* (-en) search
Forst *m* (-e) forest
Förster *m* (-) forester; ranger
fort forward; away; **-dauern, -fahren, -setzen** continue; **-schritt** *m* (-e) progress; **-setzung** *f* continuation; **-während** continual
forthin in the future
Fracht *f* (-en) freight; **-brief** *m* bill of lading
Frack *m* (¨e) dress-coat; **-anzug** dress-suit; **-hemd** *n* dress-shirt
Frage *f* (-n) question; **-zeichen** *n* question-mark
fragen ask
fraglich doubtful
frankieren stamp, prepay

franko (carriage) paid
Frankreich France
Franse *f* (**-n**) fringe
Franzose *m* (**-n**) Frenchman
französisch French
Frau *f* (**-en**) woman, lady, wife;
 -enabteil *n* ladies' compartment
frauenhaft womanly
Frauenschneider *m* ladies' tailor
Fräulein *n* (**–**) young lady, Miss
frech insolent
Frechheit *f* insolence
Fregatte *f* (**-n**) frigate
frei free; vacant, frank; paid;
 disengaged; **im Freien** in the
 open air; **-geben** give a holiday;
 release; **-gebig** generous; **-geist**
 m freethinker; **-gepäck** *n* allowed
 luggage; **-hafen** *m* free port;
 -halten treat; **-handel** *m* free
 trade; **-lassen** release, set free;
 -marke *f* stamp; **-maurer** *m*
 freemason; **-mütig(keit)** *f* frank-
 (ness); **-sinnig** liberal; **-spre-
 chen** acquit; **-stehend** detached;
 -tag *m* Friday; **-treppe** *f* door-
 steps; **-willig** voluntary
freien woo, court
Freier *m* (**–**) wooer, suitor
Freiheit *f* liberty
freilich certainly; indeed
fremd strange; foreign; **Fremder**
 (adj. noun) stranger, foreigner;
 Fremde *f* foreign lands; **Fremd-
 sprache** foreign language; **-wort**
 n foreign word
Fremden-buch *n* visitors' book;
 -führer *m* guide; **-zimmer** *n*
 spare room
Freskogemälde *n* fresco painting
fressen eat; devour
Freude *f* (**-n**) joy; **-nfeuer** *n*
 bonfire
freuen (**sich**) rejoice
Freund *m* (**-e**) friend; **-lich** kind;
 friendly; **-lichkeit** *f* friendliness;
 -schaft *f* friendship
Friede *m* peace; **friedlich, -lieb-
 end** peaceable; **Friedensrich-
 ter** *m* justice of the peace
Friedhof *m* (**-̈e**) cemetery
frieren freeze
Fries *m* (**-e**) frieze

frisch fresh, new, new-laid, clean,
 cool
Friseur *m* (**-e**) hair-dresser
frisieren dress the hair
Frist *f* (**-en**) term; delay
Frisur *f* (**-en**) hair-style
froh, fröhlich glad; joyful
frohlocken exult
fromm pious
Frömmelei *f* bigotry
Frömmigkeit *f* piety
Fronleichnamsfest *n* Corpus
 Christi
Front *f* (**-en**) front, face
Frosch *m* (**-̈e**) frog
Frost *m* frost; **-beule** *f* chilblain
frösteln shiver; **frostig** frosty
frottieren rub
Frucht *f* (**-̈e**) fruit; **-barkeit** *f* fer-
 tility; **-bar** fertile; **-los** fruit-
 less
früh early; **Frühjahr** *n* spring;
 morgen - to-morrow morning;
 -er former(ly); **-estens** at the
 earliest; **-reif** precocious
Frühe *f* early morning
Frühling *m* spring
Frühstück *n*, **-en** breakfast
Fuchs *m* (**-̈e**) fox
Fuder *n* (**–**), **Fuhre** *f* (**-n**) cart-
 load
Fuge *f* (**-n**) joint; fugue
fühlbar appreciable; **fühlen** feel
führen conduct; lead; guide;
Führer *m* conductor, leader,
 guide; manager; **-schein** *m*
 driving-licence; **Führung** *f* conduct
Fuhr-mann *m* carter; **-lohn** *m*
 carriage; **-werk** *n* conveyance
füllen fill, stuff; **Fülle** *f* fullness,
 plenty
Füllen *n* foal
Füllfeder *f* (**-n**) fountain-pen
Fund *n* (**-e**) thing found, discovery
Fundament *n* (**-e**) foundation
funkeln sparkle
funkelneu brand-new
Funke *m* (**-n**) spark; **funken**
 broadcast
Funkentelegraphie *f* radio telegraphy; **Funkspruch** *m* wire-
 less-message

Furche f (-n), **furchen** furrow
Furcht f, **sich fürchten vor** fear
furchtbar fearful, terrible
furchtlos fearless; **-sam** timid
Fürsorge f care, welfare
Fürsprache f intercession
Fürst m (-en) prince; **-in** f princess
Fürstentum n (¨er) principality
Furt f (-en) ford
Furz m (¨e), **furzen** fart
Fuss m (¨e) foot; **zu -** on foot; **-bad** n foot-bath; **-ball** m football; **-bank** f foot-stool; **-boden** m floor; **-gänger** walker; **-pfad** m footpath; **-soldat** m foot-soldier; **-tour** f walking-tour; **-tritt** m kick
Futter n food; lining; **-beutel** m nose-bag
Futteral n (-e) case
füttern feed; line
Fütterung f feeding, lining

G

Gabe f (-n) gift, talent
Gabel f (-n) fork; **-frühstück** n lunch; **gabeln** fork, divide
gackern cackle
gaffen gape
gähnen yawn
Gala f pomp, gala
galant gallant, polite
Galanterie f (-n) gallantry; **-waren** f fancy goods
Galeere f (-n) galley
Galerie f (-n) gallery
Galgen m (-) gallows
Galle f (-n) bile
Gallert n (-e) jelly
Galopp m, **galoppieren** gallop
Galosche f (-n) galosh
galvanisieren galvanize
Gamasche f (-n) gaiter
Gang m (¨e) walk; errand; working; course; corridor; round
gangbar practicable
Gans f (¨e) goose
Gänse-blümchen n daisy; **-braten** m roast goose; **-marsch** m Indian file; **-klein** n giblets

Gänserich m gander
ganz all; whole; quite
gar done; **- nicht** not at all
Garantie f (-n), **garantieren** guarantee
Garbe f (-n) sheaf
Garde f guard; **Gardist** m guardsman
Garderobe f wardrobe, cloakroom; **-nständer** m hall-stand
Gardine f (-n) curtain
gären ferment
Garn n (-e) yarn, thread
garnieren garnish; trim
Garnison f (-en) garrison
Garnitur f (-en) set
garstig nasty, ugly
Garten m (¨) garden
Gärtner m (-) gardener
Gärung f fermentation
Gas n (-e) gas; **-anstalt** f gasworks; **-behälter** m gasometer; **-beleuchtung** f gas-lighting; **-brenner** m gas-burner; **-glühlicht** n incandescent light; **-uhr** f gas-meter; **-ofen** m gas-furnace; **-rohr** n gas-pipe
Gasse f (-n) lane
Gassenjunge m (-n) street boy
Gast m (¨e) guest; **-freundlich** hospitable; **-geber** m host; **-haus** n inn; **-hof** m hotel; **-wirt** m hotel-keeper; **-zimmer** n general room, spare room
Gatte m (-n) husband; **Gattin** f wife
Gattung f (-en) species; kind
gaukeln juggle, play tricks
Gaukler m (-) juggler
Gaul m (¨e) horse
Gaumen m (-) palate
Gauner m (-) sharper
Gaze f (-n) gauze
Gebäck n pastry
Gebärde f (-n) air, mien
gebärden behave
gebären bring forth, bear
Gebärmutter f womb
Gebäude n (-) building
Gebeine n pl bones
geben give; **es gibt** there is (are)
Gebet n (-e) prayer

Gebiet *n* (**-e**) territory
Gebieter *m* (**-**) master, lord
gebieten order
gebieterisch imperious
gebildet well-educated
Gebirge *n* (**-**) mountains; mountain range
gebirgig mountainous
Gebiss *n* (**-e**) (set of) teeth *pl*
geboren born
geborgen saved, sheltered
Gebot *n* (**-e**) command(ment)
Gebrauch *m* (**ö**e), **gebrauchen** use
gebräuchlich usual, customary
Gebrechen *n* (**-**) infirmity
Gebühr *f* (**-en**) duty; **gebührend** due
Geburt *f* (**-en**) birth; **-shelfer** *m* accoucheur; **-stag** *m* birthday; **gebürtig** native
Gebüsch *n* bush
Gedächtnis *n* (**-se**) memory; **-tag** *m* anniversary
gedämpft subdued
Gedanke *m* (**-n**) thought; **-nlos- (igkeit)** *f* thoughtless(ness); **-nstrich** *m* dash
Gedärme *n pl* intestines
Gedeck *n* (**-e**) cover
gedeihen thrive
gedenken (**+** gen.) remember
Gedenkstein *m* (**-e**) commemorative stone
Gedicht *n* (**-e**) poem
gediegen solid; pure; sound
Gedränge *n* crowd; scrummage
gedrängt crowded; concise
Geduld *f* patience; **-ig** patient
gedulden (**sich**) have patience
geeignet fit, suitable
Gefahr *f* (**-en**) danger
gefährden endanger
gefährlich dangerous
Gefährte *m* (**-n**) companion
Gefallen *m* pleasure; favour
gefallen (**+** dat.) please
gefällig pleasing; kind
gefälligst please
Gefälligkeit *f* (**-en**) favour
Gefangene *m* (adj. noun) prisoner
Gefängnis *n* (**-se**) prison
Gefäss *n* (**-e**) vessel

gefasst calm; prepared
Gefecht *n* (**-e**) fight
gefleckt spotted
Geflügel *n* poultry
Geflüster *n* whisper
Gefolge *n* suite, attendance
gefrässig voracious
Gefrässigkeit *f* voracity
Gefreite (adj. noun) lance-corporal
gefrieren freeze
Gefrierpunkt *m* freezing-point
Gefrorenes *n* ice
gefügig pliant
Gefühl *n* (**-e**) feeling
gefühlvoll (**-los**) (un)feeling
gegen (**+** acc.) towards, against
Gegen- counter; **-befehl** *m* counter-order; **-besuch** *m* return visit; **-gewicht** *n* counterpoise; **-gift** *n*, **-mittel** *n* antidote; **-seitig** mutual; **-stand** *m* object; **-stück** *n* counterpart; **-teil** *n* contrary; **-über** (**+** dat.) opposite; **-wart** *f* presence; **-wärtig** present; **-wehr** *f* defence; **-zeichnen** countersign
Gegend *f* (**-en**) country; neighbourhood; region
Gegner *m* (**-**) adversary; opponent
Gehalt *n* (**ö**er) salary; stipend
gehässig hateful
Gehäuse *n* (**-**) case
Gehege *n* (**-**) enclosure
Geheimnis *n* (**-se**), **geheim** secret
geheimnisvoll mysterious
gehen go; walk
geheuer (**nicht -** eerie)
Geheul *n* howling
Gehilfe *m* (**-n**) assistant
Gehirn *n* (**-e**) brain
Gehölz *n* wood, copse
Gehör *n* hearing
gehorchen (**+** dat.) obey
gehören (**+** dat.) belong; **sich gehören** to be proper
gehörig proper, due
gehorsam obedient
Gehorsam *m* obedience
Gehrock *m* frock-coat
Geier *m* (**-**) vulture

Geige *f* (-n) violin; **-r** *m* violinist

geil lascivious

Geiss *f* (-en) she-goat

Geissblatt *n* honeysuckle

Geissel *f* (-n) scourge

Geist *m* (-er) spirit; **-esgegenwart** *f* presence of mind; **-eskrank** insane; **geistig** spiritual; intellectual; **geistlich** ecclesiastical; **Geistliche** *m* (adj. noun) clergyman; **Geistlichkeit** *f* clergy

Geiz *m* avarice; **-hals** *m* miser

geizig avaricious

Gelächter *n* laughter

Geländer *n* railing; parapet

gelangen get; arrive

gelassen composed

geläufig fluent

gelaunt disposed; humoured

gelb(lich) yellow(ish)

Gelbsucht *f* jaundice

Geld *n* (-er) money; **bares -** cash; **kleines -** change; **-beutel** *m* purse; **-postamt** *n* money-order office; **-schrank** *m* safe; **-strafe** *f* fine; **-sendung** *f* remittance; **-tasche** *f* leather purse

gelegen situated; convenient

Gelegenheit *f* (-en) opportunity

gelegentlich occasional

gelehrig docile; **gelehrt** learned

Geleise *n* track

Geleit *n* (-e) **geleiten** escort

Geleitzug *m* convoy

Gelenk *n* (-e) joint; hinge

gelenkig supple

Geliebte *m* (adj. noun) lover; *f* sweetheart

gelind mild, gentle

gelingen succeed

gellend shrill

geloben, Gelöbnis *n* (-se) vow

gelten be worth; **- für** pass for

Gelübde *n* vow

gemach, gemächlich gentle; slowly

Gemahl *m* (-e) consort

Gemälde *n* (-) painting; picture

gemäss (+ dat.) according to

gemässigt temperate

gemein common; mean

Gemeinde *f* (-n) community; congregation; parish; **-steuer** *f* local rate

Gemeinheit *f* meanness

gemeinsam, -schaftlich common; jointly

Gemeinwesen *n* commonwealth

Gemenge *n*, **Gemisch** *n* mixture

Gemme *f* (-n) gem

Gemse *f* (-n) chamois

Gemüse *n* vegetables; **-händler** *m* greengrocer

gemustert figured

Gemüt *n* (-er) mind; heart

gemütlich comfortable

genau exact; **Genauigkeit** *f* accuracy

genehmigen approve; sanction

Genehmigung *f* (-en) approval

geneigt inclined; disposed

General *m* (-e) general; **-postmeister** *m* postmaster-general

genesen recover

Genesung *f* recovery

Genf Geneva

Genick *n* (-e) nape, back of the neck

Genie *n* (-s), **Genius** *m* genius

genieren trouble

geniessen eat and drink; enjoy

Genosse *m* (-n) companion, comrade

Genossenschaft *f* syndicate; co-operative society

Genua Genoa

genug enough; **genügen** suffice; **-d** sufficient; **genügsam** frugal; **Genugtuung** *f* satisfaction

Genuss *m* (-e) enjoyment; pleasure

Geograph *m* geographer

Geographie *f* geography

Gepäck *n* luggage; **-annahme** *f*, **-ausgabe** *f* luggage-office; cloakroom; **-netz** *n* rack; **-schein** *m* receipt; **-träger** *m* porter; **-wagen** *m* luggage-van; **-zettel** *m* label

Geplänkel *n* skirmish

Gepolter *n* loud noise, din

Gepräge *n* impression

gerade straight; even, just, exactly; **-aus** straight ahead

Gerät *n* (-e) tool, implement

geraten get into; come to

Geratewohl *n,* **aufs -** at random

geräumig spacious

Geräusch *n* (-e) noise; **-voll** noisy

gerben tan; **Gerber(ei)** *m* (*f*) tanner(y)

gerecht just; **Gerechtigkeit** *f* justice

Gericht *n* (-e) dish; court of justice

Gericht(shof) *n* (*m*) court of justice; **jüngste-** last judgment; **-svollzieher** *m* bailiff

gering little; **-fügig** insignificant

gerinnen curdle; clot

Gerippe *n* (-) skeleton

gern willingly, gladly

Geröll *n* rubble

Gerste *f* barley

Gerte *f* (-n) switch, rod

Geruch *m* (-e) smell

Gerücht *n* (-e) rumour

geruhen deign

Gerüst *n* (-e) scaffold(ing)

gesamt, Gesamtheit *f* total

Gesandte *m* (adj. noun) ambassador

Gesandtschaft *f* embassy

Gesang *m* (-e) song; singing

Geschäft *n* (-e) business; shop; **-lich** commercial; **-santeil** *m* share in business; **-sfreund** *m* business-friend; **-sführer** *m* manager; **-sreisender** *m* (adj. noun) commercial traveller; **-sstunden** *pl* business-hours; **-sträger** *m* chargé d'affaires; **-sviertel** *n* shopping-centre

geschehen happen

gescheit clever

Geschenk *n* (-e) present

Geschichte *f* (-n) history; story; affair

geschichtlich historical

Geschichtsschreiber *m* historian

Geschick *n* (-e) fate; **-lichkeit** *f* skill

geschickt skilled, clever

Geschirr *n* dishes, crockery; harness

Geschlecht *n* (-er) sex; gender

geschlechtlich sexual

Geschmack *m* (-e) taste; **-los** tasteless; **-voll** tasteful

Geschöpf *n* (-e) creature

Geschrei *n* cries *pl*; shrieking

Geschütz *n* (-e) cannon; gun

Geschwader *n* (-) squadron

Geschwätz *n* idle talk

geschwätzig talkative

geschwind quick, swift

Geschwindigkeit *f* speed

Geschwister *pl* brothers and sisters

Geschworene (adj. noun) juryman; **-ngericht** *n* court of assizes

Geschwulst *f* (-e) swelling; tumour

Geschwür *n* (-e) abscess

Geselle *m* (-n) journeyman; fellow

gesellig sociable

Geselligkeit *f* sociability

Gesellschaft *f* (-en) society; party; **-lich** social; **-sanzug** *m* evening-dress; **-sspiel** *n* round-game; **-er** *m* partner

Gesetz *n* (-e) law; Act of Parliament; **-buch** *n* code of law; **-gebend** legislative; **-geber** *m* legislator; **-mässig, -lich** legal, lawful; **-vorschlag** *m* bill; **-widrig** illegal

gesetzt steady; grave

Gesicht *n* (-er) face; sight; **-sfarbe** *f* complexion; **-skreis** *m* horizon

Gesims *n* (-e) cornice

Gesinde *n* (-) servants

Gesindel *n* mob

gesinnt, gesonnen disposed

Gesinnung *f* (-en) disposition; sentiment

Gespann *n* (-e) team

gespannt tense, taut; **- sein** wonder

Gespenst *n* (-er) ghost

Gespräch *n* (-e) conversation

gesprächig talkative

Gestalt *f* (-en), **gestalten** form; shape

geständig sein confess

Geständnis *n* (-se) confession

Gestank *m* stench

gestatten allow
gestehen confess, admit
Gestell *n* (-e) frame; stand
gestern yesterday; **- abend** last night
gestirnt starry
Gesträuch *n*, **Gestrüpp** *n* shrubs
gestreift striped
Gesuch *n* (-e) petition
gesund healthy; sound; wholesome
Gesundheit *f* health, **-slehre** *f* hygiene
Getöse *n* noise, din
Getränk *n* (-e) drink, beverage
Getreide *n* corn, grain; **-börse** *f* corn-exchange
geübt experienced
Gewächshaus *n* (¨er) hothouse
gewachsen sein be equal (or match) to
gewahr aware
gewähren grant
gewährleisten warrant, guarantee
Gewalt *f* (-en) power; force
gewaltig powerful
Gewand *n* (¨er) garment
gewandt active; clever
Gewebe *n* (-) web; tissue
Gewehr *n* (-e) gun, rifle
Geweih *n* (-e) antlers *pl*
Gewerbe *n* (-) trade; profession; **gewerbmässig** professional
Gewerbfleiss *m* industry
Gewerkschaft *f* (-en) trade union
Gewicht *n* (-e) weight
Gewinn *m* (-e) profit, success
gewinnen win; gain
gewiss certain; sure
Gewissen *n* conscience; **-sbiss** *m* remorse
gewissenhaft conscientious
gewissenlos unscrupulous
Gewissheit *f* certainty
Gewitter *n* (-) thunderstorm
gewöhnen accustom; **Gewohnheit** *f* (-en) custom; **gewöhnlich** usual
Gewölbe *n* (-) vault
Gewürz *n* (-e) spice; **-händler** *m* grocer; **-nelke** *f* clove

gezahnt toothed
geziert affected
Gicht *f* gout; **-isch** gouty
Giebel *m* (-) gable
Gier *f* greed; **-ig** greedy
Giessbach *m* (¨e) torrent
giessen pour; cast, found
Giesser *m* founder; **-ei** *f* foundry
Giesskanne *f* (-n) watering-can
Gift *n* (-e) poison; **-ig** poisonous
Giftgas *n* (-e) poison gas
Ginster *m* broom
Gipfel *m* (-) summit; top
Gips *m* plaster of Paris
Gipsabguss *m* (¨e) plaster-cast
Giro *n* (-s) endorsement
Girokonto *n* (-ten) drawing-account
Gitarre *f* (-n) guitar
Gitter *n* (-) grate; lattice; iron bars
Glacehandschuh *m* (-e) kid-glove
Glanz *m* splendour; **-leder** *m* patent-leather
glänzen shine; **-d** brilliant
Glas *n* (¨er) glass; **-hütte** *f* glassworks *pl*; **Glaser** *m* glazier
Glasur *f* (-en), **glasieren** glaze
glätten, **glatt** smooth
Glatze *f* (-n) bald head
glauben believe; **Glauben** *m* faith, belief; **-sbekenntnis** *n* creed; **-ssatz** *m* dogma; **glaubhaft**, **-lich** credible; **gläubig** believing
Gläubiger *m* creditor
gleich equal; like; immediately; **-berechtigt** possessing equal rights; **-falls** likewise; **-gewicht** *n* equilibrium; **-gültig** indifferent; **-gültigkeit** *f* indifference; **-heit** *f* equality; **-kommen** equal; **-mut** *m* equanimity; **-viel** no matter; **-zeitig** simultaneous
gleichen resemble
Gleichnis *n* (-se) parable, simile
gleichsam as it were
Gleichschaltung *f* equalization
Gleichung *f* equation
Gleis *n* (-e) track
Gleitbahn *f*, **gleiten** slide
Gletscher *m* (-) glacier

Glied *n* (-er) limb; rank; member
glimmen glimmer
Glocke *f* (-n) bell; globe
glorreich glorious
Glück *n* fortune; happiness;
-**wünschen** congratulate;
-**wunsch** *m* congratulation;
glücken succeed; **glücklich**
happy; -**erwise** fortunately
Glüh-hitze *f* red-heat; -**licht**
incandescent light; -**strumpf** *m*
mantle; -**wein** *m* mulled wine;
-**wurm** *m* glow-worm; **glühen**
glow; **glühend** red-hot; ardent
Gnade *f* mercy; **gnädig** gracious
Gold *n* gold; -**grube** *f* gold-mine;
-**münze** *f*, -**stück** *n* gold coin;
-**schnitt** *m* gilt edge; **golden**
gold; **goldig** golden
Golf *m* (-e) gulf
Golf *n* golf; -**platz** *m* golf links
Gondel *f* (-n) gondola
gönnen not grudge, wish, grant
Gönner *m* (-) patron
Gosse *f* gutter; drain
gotisch Gothic
Gott *m* (-̈er) God; -**esdienst** *m*
divine service; -**eslästerung** *f*
blasphemy; **Göttin** *f* goddess;
göttlich divine
gottlos impious
Götze(nbild) *m* (*n*) idol; -**ndie-
ner** *m* idolater
Grab *n* (-̈er) grave; tomb;
-**schrift** *f* epitaph; -**stein** *m*
tombstone
Graben *m* (-̈) ditch; **graben** dig
Grad *m* (-e) degree, grade
Graf *m* (-en) count, earl; -**schaft**
f county
Gram *m* grief; **sich grämen**
grieve
Grammatik *f* grammar
Grammophon *n* (-e) gramophone
Granate *f* (-n) grenade; shell
Granit *m* (-e) granite
Graphit *m* (-e) plumbago
Gras *n* (-̈er) grass; **grasen** graze
grässlich horrible
Gräte *f* (-n) fish-bone
gratis gratis
Gratulation *f* (-en) congratula-
tion

gratulieren (+ dat.) congratulate
grau grey; -**enhaft** dreadful
Graupen *f pl* hulled barley
Graupeln *pl*, **graupeln** sleet
grausam cruel; **Grausamkeit**
f cruelty
grausig awful
gravieren engrave
graziös graceful; **Grazie** *f* (-n)
grace
greifen grasp, seize
Greis *m* (-e) old man
Greisenalter *n* old age
grell glaring; shrill
Grenze *f* (-n) boundary
grenzen border; -**los** boundless
greulich atrocious
Grieche *m* (-n), **griechisch**
Greek; -**nland** *n* Greece
Griff *m* (-e) grasp, handle
Griffel *m* slate-pencil
Grille *f* (-n) cricket; whim
Grimasse *f* (-n) grimace
grimmig grim
grinsen grin
Grippe *f* influenza
grob coarse; **Grobheit** *f* coarseness
Grobschmied *m* blacksmith
Groll *m* ill-will
Gros *n* (-se) gross
gross large; big; great; tall;
-**enteils** mostly; -**artig** grand;
-**britannien** *n* Great Britain;
-**eltern** *pl* grand-parents; -**enkel**
m great-grandson; -**handel** *m*
wholesale trade; -**händler** *m*
merchant; -**herzog** *m* grand
duke; -**jährig** of age; -**mut**
f generosity; -**mütig** generous;
-**mutter** *f* grandmother;
-**sprecher** *m* boaster; -**tun**
boast; -**vater** *m* grandfather
Grösse *f* (-n) tallness; size;
greatness
grösstenteils for the most part
Grotte *f* (-n) grotto
Grübchen *n* dimple
Grube *f* (-n) pit; mine
grübeln meditate; brood
Gruft *f* (-̈e) vault
grün green; **grünlich** greenish

Grün-donnerstag m Maundy Thursday; **-span** m verdigris
Grund m (⁼e) ground, bottom; reason; **im -e** after all; **-besitzer** m landed proprietor; **-fläche** f, **-lage** f base; **-satz** m principle; **-stein** m foundation-stone; **-steuer** f rate(s)
gründen found; **gründlich** thorough; **Gründung** f foundation
grunzen grunt
Gruppe f (-n), **gruppieren** group
Gruss m (⁼e) greeting; compliment
grüssen greet, salute
gucken peep
Gulden m (-) florin; guilder
gültig valid; **Gültigkeit** f validity
Gummi n (-s) india-rubber; **- arabikum** gum arabic; **gummieren** gum
Gunst f favour; **günstig** favourable; **Günstling** m favourite
Gurgel f (-n) throat
gurgeln gargle
Gurke f (-n) cucumber
Gurt m (-e) girth; **Gürtel** m (-) belt
Guss m (⁼e) cast(ing); **-eisen** n cast iron
gut good; well; **-artig** good-natured; **-heissen** approve; **- machen** repair; **-mütig** kind-hearted; **-willig** voluntary
Gut n (⁼er) estate; **-achten**, **-dünken** n opinion; **-haben** n credit; **-sbesitzer** m landowner
Güte f goodness
Güter pl goods; **-bahnhof** m goods station; **-wagen** m goods van; **-zug** m goods train ,
gütig kind; **gütlich** amicable
Gymnasium n (-sien) grammar-school
Gymnastik f gymnastics

H

Haag m The Hague
Haar n (-e) hair; **-bürste** f hair-brush; **-färbemittel** n hair-dye; **-schneiden** n hair-cutting; **-schneider** m hair-dresser

haarig hairy; **haarlos** bald
haben have
habgierig avaricious
Habicht m (-e) hawk
hacken, Hacke f (-n) hoe; chop
Hacken m (-) heel
Hackfleisch n minced meat
Häcksel n chaff
Hafen m (⁼) harbour; port; **-damm** m pier
Hafer m oats; **-schleim** m gruel
Haft f custody
haftbar liable; responsible
haften be liable; **-an** stick to
Haftpflicht f liability
Hagel m, **hageln** hail; **-korn** n hailstone
Hagedorn m hawthorn
hager lean, haggard
Hagestolz m bachelor
Hahn m (⁼e) cock; tap; **-rei** m cuckold
Haifisch m (-e) shark
Hain m (-e) grove
häkeln crochet
Haken m (-), **haken** hook
halb half; **-bruder** m half-brother; **-insel** f peninsula; **-kugel** f hemisphere; **-messer** m radius; **-mond** m crescent; **-wegs** halfway
halbieren halve
Hälfte f (-n) half
Halfter f (-n) halter
Halle f (-n) hall; **hallen** sound, resound
Halm m (-e) blade; stalk
Hals m (-e) neck; **-band** n necklace; **-binde** f (neck)tie; **-entzündung** f inflammation of the throat; **-kragen** m collar
Halt m (-e), **halt!** halt; stop; hold!
haltbar durable
halten hold; keep; think; stop
Haltestelle f (-n) (bus, tram) stop
Haltung f (-en) attitude
Halunke m (-n) rascal
Hammel m **-fleisch** n mutton; **-braten** m roast-m.; **-keule** f leg of mutton
Hammer m (⁼) hammer
Hand f (⁼e) hand; **-arbeit**

handwork, needlework; -buch
n manual; -fläche f palm; -geld
n earnest-money; -gelenk n
wrist; -gepäck n small luggage;
-haben handle, manage; -koffer
m suit-case; portmanteau; -lich
handy; -schrift f manuscript;
-schuh m glove; -schuhmacher
m glover; -tuch n towel; -voll f
handful; -werk n trade; -wer-
ker m artisan; -werkszeug n
tools

Händedruck m handshake
Handel m commerce
handeln act; trade, deal; bargain
Handels-flotte f merchant navy;
-mann m trader; -minister
m (in Engl.) president of the
Board of Trade; -schiff n
merchantman; -schule f commercial school; -stadt f commercial town

Handlanger m (-) handy man
Händler m (-) tradesman
Handlung f (-en) action; shop;
-sgehilfe m clerk; -sreisender
m (adj. noun) commercial traveller

Hanf m hemp
Hänge-brücke f suspension-
bridge; -matte f hammock
hängen, hangen hang
Hanswurst m clown, buffoon
Harfe f (-n) harp
Harke f (-n), harken rake
harmlos harmless
Harmonika f concertina
harmonisch harmonious
Harn m urine; -blase f bladder;
-röhre f urethra
harren to wait for
hart hard; -herzig hard-hearted;
-hörig hard of hearing; -leibig
constipated; -näckig obstinate;
-näckigkeit f obstinacy
Härte f hardness; -n pl rigours
Harz n (-e) resin; harzig resinous
haschen catch, snatch
Hase m (-n) hare
Haselnuss f (-e) hazel-nut
Haspel f (-n), haspeln reel
Hass m hatred; hassen hate
hässlich ugly

Hässlichkeit f ugliness
Hast f hurry
hastig hasty, rash
Haube f (-n) cap; tuft
Hauch m (-e) breath
hauchen breathe
hauen cut, hew, strike
häufen, Haufen m (-) heap
häufig frequent
Haupt n (-er) head; chief
Haupt-buch n ledger; -mann
m captain; -postamt n general
post-office; -quartier n headquarters; -schlüssel m master
key; -stadt f capital; -wort n
noun

Häuptling m (-e) chief; leader
hauptsächlich mainly, chiefly
Haus n (-er) house; zu Hause at
home; nach Hause home; -boot
n house-boat; -besitzer m landlord; -flur m hall; -hälter(in) m
(f) housekeeper; -halt m house-
hold; -lehrer m tutor; -meister
m caretaker; -putz m spring-
cleaning; -schlüssel m front-
door key; -tier n domestic
animal; -tür f front door; -wirt
m l andlord; -zins m house rent

hausieren peddle
Hausierer m pedlar
häuslich domestic
Haut f (-e), häuten skin
Häutchen n (-) membrane
Hautfarbe f complexion
Hebamme f (-n) midwife
Hebel m (-) lever
heben lift; raise
Heber m (-) siphon
hebräisch, Hebräer Hebrew
Hecht m (-e) pike
Heck n (-e) stern
Hecke f (-n) hedge
Heer n (-e) army
Hefe f (-n) yeast
Heft n (-e) handle; copy-book;
-pflaster n sticking-plaster;
-zwecke f drawing-pin
heften fasten; stitch
heftig vehement
hegen foster
Heide m (-n), heidnisch heathen
Heide f (-n) heath; moor

Heidekraut *n* heather
Heidelbeere *f* (**-n**) bilberry
heil sound; **Heil** *n* welfare; salvation
Heiland *m* (**-e**) Saviour
heilbar curable
heilen cure; heal
heilig holy; **-sprechen** canonize; **Heilige** *m* and *f* (adj. noun) saint; **Heiligtum** *n* sanctuary; **heiligen** hallow
Heilmittel *n* (**-**) remedy
heilsam salutary
Heilsarmee *f* Salvation Army
Heim *n* (**-e**), **heim** home; **-kehr** *f*, **-kehren**, **-kommen** return; **-suchen** visit, inflict, infest; **-weh** *n* homesickness; **-weh haben** be homesick
Heimat *f* (**-en**) native country
Heimchen *n* (**-**) cricket
heimlich secret
Heirat *f* (**-en**) marriage; **-santrag** *m* proposal of marriage; **Bruch des -sversprechens** breach of promise; **-urkunde** *f* marriage-certificate; **-stifter** *m* match-maker
heiraten marry
heiser hoarse; **Heiserkeit** *f* hoarseness
heiss hot
heissen be called; **das heisst** (**d.h.**) that is to say
heiter serene; cheerful
heizen heat; **Heizung** *f* heating
Held *m* (**-en**) hero; **-enmut** *m* heroism; **-entat** *f* exploit
heldenmütig heroic
helfen (**+** dat.) help
hell bright; clear; light
Helm *m* (**-e**) helmet
Hemd *n* (**-en**) shirt; chemise
hemmen stop, check
Hemmschuh *m* (**-e**) skid-pan, brake
Hemmung *f* (**-en**) escapement, inhibition
Hengst *m* (**-e**) stallion
Henkel *m* (**-**) handle
Henker *m* hangman; executioner
Henne *f* (**-n**) hen
her hither, here; **lange -** long ago

herab down; **-bringen** bring down; **-lassend** condescending; **-setzen** reduce, belittle
heran near, along; **herauf** upwards
heraus out; **-fordern** provoke; **-geben** edit, publish; give change; **Herausgeber** *m* editor, publisher; **-rufen** call before the curtain; call a person out
herb tart; harsh; dry
herbei hither; near
Herberge *f* (**-n**) inn, shelter
Herbst *m* autumn; **-lich** autumnal
Herd *m* (**-e**) hearth; cooker
Herde *f* (**-n**) herd; flock
herein in; come in!
hergebracht customary
Hering *m* (**-e**) herring
Herkommen *n* custom
Herkunft *f* (**¨e**) origin
Hermelin *n* ermine
hernach afterwards
Herold *m* (**-e**) herald
Herr *m* gentleman; master; the Lord
Herrenzimmer *n* study
herrisch imperious
herrlich excellent; splendid
Herrschaft *f* (**-en**) dominion, rule; master and mistress
herrschen rule, reign; **Herrscher** *m* (**-**) sovereign
hersagen recite
herstellen make; restore
herüber, over here, across
herum (a)round; about
herunter down there (here)
hervor forth; **-bringen** bring forth, produce; **-gehen** result; **-ragend** prominent; **(sich) -tun** distinguish; **-treten** stand out
Herz *n* (**-en**) heart; **-klopfen** *n*, **-schlag** *m* palpitation; heart attack; **herzlich** hearty; **Herzlichkeit** *f* cordiality
herzhaft bold; **herzig** dear
herzlos heartless
Herzog *m* (**¨e**) duke; **-in** *f* duchess; **-lich** ducal; **-tum** *n* duchy
hetzen hunt; rush about
Hetzjagd *f* hunt
Heu *n* hay; **-boden** *m* hay-loft;

-schober m haystack; **-schrecke** f grasshopper
Heuchelei f hypocrisy; **Heuchler** m hypocrite
heucheln feign
heulen howl
heute to-day; **-abend** to-night; **heutzutage** nowadays; **heutig** of this day; present; modern
Hexe f (-n) witch; **-rei** f witchcraft
Hexenschuss m lumbago
Hieb m (-e) blow; cut
hienieden here below
hier, hierher here
hiesig of this place, local
Hilfe f (-n) help; aid
Hilfs-mittel n (-) remedy; **-quelle** f resource
Himbeere f (-n) raspberry
Himmel m (-) sky; heaven; **-bett** n four-poster; **himmelblau** sky-blue; **Himmelsgewölbe** n firmament; **-fahrt(stag)** Ascension (day); **-reich** n kingdom of heaven; **-skörper** m celestial body; **-schreiend** disgraceful
himmlisch celestial, heavenly
hin here; **-ab** down; **-an, -auf** up; **-aus** out; **-durch** through; **-ein** in; **-fällig** frail; **-fort** henceforth; **-gegen** on the contrary; **-reichend** sufficient; **-richten** execute; **-sichtlich** with regard to; **-über** over; **- und her** to and fro; **-unter** down; **-weg** away; **-weisen** refer to
hindern hinder; prevent
Hindernis n (-se) obstacle; **-rennen** n steeplechase
hinken limp; be lame
hinten, hinter behind
Hinter-bein n hind-leg; **-grund** m background; **-halt** m ambush; **-haus** n back building; **-list(ig)** f cunning; **-treppe** f backstairs; **-zimmer** n back-room; **Hintere** m back(-side); **hinterst** hindmost
hintergehen deceive
hinzufügen add; subjoin
Hirn n (-e) brain; **-schale** f skull

Hirsch m (-e) stag, hart
Hirt m (-en) shepherd
hissen hoist
historisch historical
Hitze f, **hitzen** heat
hitzig hot; ardent
Hitz-schlag m sunstroke; **-blatter** f pimple
Hobel m (-), **hobeln** plane
Hoboe f (-n) oboe
hoch high; **-achtung(svoll)** f respect(ful); **-bahn** f elevated railway; **-druck** m high pressure; **-ebene** f tableland; **-genuss** m treat; **-mut** m pride; **-mütig** haughty; **-ofen** m blast-furnace; **-sprung** m high jump; **-verrat** m high treason
höchstens at most
Hochzeit f wedding; **-sreise** f honeymoon
Hocker m (-) stool
Höcker m (-) hump
Hode f (-n) testicle
Hof m (¨e) court; hall; **-lieferant** m purveyor to the court; **-mann** m courtier; **-narr** m jester
Hoffart f vainglory
hoffen, Hoffnung f (-en) hope
hoffnungslos hopeless
höflich polite; **H-keit** f politeness
Höhe f (-n) height; **-punkt** m climax
Hoheit f (-en) Highness
hohl hollow
Höhle f (-n) cave; **Höhlung** f (-en) cavity
Hohlspiegel m (-) concave mirror
Hohn m scorn; **höhnisch** scornful
hohnlächeln, höhnen sneer
hold gracious
holen fetch; **- lassen** send for
Holländer m (-) Dutchman
Hölle f hell; **-nstein** m lunar caustic
höllisch infernal
holperig rough; jolting
Holunder m (-) elder, lilac
Holz n (¨er) wood; **-kohle** f charcoal; **-schnitt** m wood-cut; **hölzern** wooden; **holzig** woody

Honig *m* honey
Honigkuchen *m* gingerbread
Honorar *n* (-e) fee
Hopfen *m*, hopfen hop(s)
hörbar audible
horchen listen
Horde *f* (-n) horde, troupe; tribe
hören hear; - auf listen to; von Hörensagen by hearsay; Hörapparat *m* deaf-aid; -spiel *n* radio-drama; -weite *f* earshot
Horizont *m* horizon
Horn *n* (ⁿer) horn; hörnern horny
Hornisse *f* (-n) hornet
Hort *m* (-e) hoard, treasure
Hose *f* trousers; -nbandorden *m* Order of the Garter; -nträger *m pl* braces
Hospital *n* hospital
Hotel *n* (-s) hotel
hübsch pretty
Huf *m* (-e) hoof; -eisen *n* horseshoe; -schmied *m* farrier
Hüfte *f* (-n) hip
Hügel *m* (-) hill; -ig hilly
Huhn *n* (ⁿer) fowl; hen; junges - chicken
Hühner-auge *n* corn; -hund *m* pointer
Huld *f* homage
Hülle *f* (-n) envelope, cover
Hülse *f* (-n) husk
Hummel *f* (-n) humble-bee
Hummer *m* (-) lobster
Humor *m* humour
Hund *m* (-e) dog; Hündin *f* bitch
Hundstage *m pl* dog-days
hundert hundred; -fältig hundredfold;-jährig centennial;-ste hundredth; -weise by hundreds
hundertgradig centigrade
Hüne *m* (-n) giant
Hunger *m* hunger
hungrig hungry
Hungersnot *f* famine
hüpfen skip, hop
Hürdenrennen *n* (-) hurdle race
Hure *f* (-n) whore
hurtig quick, brisk
Husar *m* (-en) hussar
husten, Husten *m* (-) cough

Hut *m* (ⁿe) hat; -schachtel *f* hat-box
Hut *f* guard, care
hüten watch, take care
Hüter *m* (-) guardian
Hütte *f* (-n) hut, cottage; -nwerk *n* smelting-works
Hyäne *f* (-n) hyena
Hymne *f* (-n) hymn
Hypochonder *m* (-) hypochondriac
hypnotisieren hypnotize
Hypothek *f* (-en) mortgage
Hypothese *f* (-n) hypothesis
hysterisch hysteric

I

i-ah! heehaw; i-ahen bray
Ich *n* I, self (ego); ich I, myself
Ideal *n* (-e) ideal; Idee *f* (-n) idea
ideenreich full of ideas
identisch identical
Identität *f* identity
Idiom *n* (-e) idiom
Idiot *m* (-en) idiot
Idyll(isch) *n* (-e) idyll(ic)
Igel *m* (-) hedgehog
ignorieren ignore
ihm (to) him
ihn him
ihr her, its, their; Ihr your
illuminieren illuminate
Illusion *f* (-en) illusion
illustrieren illustrate
Iltis *m* (-se) polecat
Imbiss *m* (-e) cold repast, snack
Imbiss-stube *f* (-n) snack-bar
Imker *m* (-) bee-keeper
immer always; auf- for ever; -dar, -fort forever; -grün evergreen; -während unceasing; immer noch still
impfen vaccinate; inoculate
Impfung *f* (-en) vaccination
Import *m* (-e), -importieren import
imposant imposing
imstande sein be able
in in, into, at
Inanspruchnahme *f* use
Inbegriff *m* (-e), summary; sum total; epitome; essence

Inbrunst *f* fervour
inbrünstig fervent
indem while, as
Inder *m* (-) Indian
indessen meanwhile, however
Indianer *m* (-) Red Indian
Indien the Indies, India
indirekt indirect
indiskret indiscreet
Individuum *n* (-uen) individual
Industrie *f* industry
Infanter-ie *f* infantry; **-ist** foot-soldier
Inflation *f* inflation
infolge (+ gen.) in consequence of
informieren inform
Ingenieur *m* (-e) engineer
Ingwer *m* ginger
Inhaber *m* (-) possessor
Inhalt *m* (-e) contents; volume
Inhaltsverzeichnis *n* table of contents
Inland *n* inland; home(land)
Inländer *m*, **inländisch** native
innehaben hold, possess
innehalten stop
innen, innerhalb (+ gen.) within
inner, Innere *n* interior; **Minister des Innern** Secretary of State for Home Affairs
innerlich internal
innewerden (+ gen.) become aware of
innig hearty; intimate
Innung *f* (-en) guild
Insasse *m* (-n) inmate
Inschrift *f* (-en) inscription
Insektenpulver *n* insect powder
Insel *f* (-n) island; **-bewohner** *m* islander
Inserat *n* (-e) advertisement
inserieren advertise
insgeheim secretly
insofern as far as
instand-halten maintain; **-setzen** restore
inständig instant
Instanz *f* (-en) instance, resort
Instinkt *m* (-e) instinct; **instinktiv** instinctive
Institut *n* (-e) institution
Instrument *n* (-e) instrument

Inszenierung *f* (-en) production
interessant interesting; **interessieren, Interesse** *n* (-n) interest
Internat *n* (-e) boarding-school
Interne *m* (adj. noun) boarder
Interpunktion *f* punctuation
intim intimate
invalid, Invalide *m* (adj. noun) invalid
Inventar *n* (-e) inventory
Inventur *f* stock-taking
inwendig internal
inwiefern how; to what extent
inzwischen in the meantime
irden earthen
irdisch earthly
irgend any, some
irgendwo anywhere
Ironie *f* irony
Irre *m* (adj. noun) insane, madman; **-nanstalt** *f*, **-nhaus** *n* lunatic asylum
irre astray; wrong; **-gehen** lose one's way; **- machen** mislead
irren err; **Irrenarzt** *m* mental specialist; **sich -** be mistaken
irrig, irrtümlich erroneous
Irrlehre *f* heresy
Irrlicht *n* will-o'-the-wisp
Irrtum *m* (-̈er) error; **irrtümlich** erroneous
Islam *m* Islamism
Island *n* Iceland
isolieren isolate; insulate
Israelit *m* (-en) Israelite

J

ja yes; **- doch** yes, yes; **-wohl** yes indeed
Jacht *f* (-en) yacht
Jacke *f* (-n) jacket
Jackett *n* (-e) coat
Jagd *f* (-en) chase; hunt(ing); **-tasche** *f* game-bag; **-wagen** *m* dog-cart
jagen chase; shoot
Jäger *m* (-) hunter; sportsman; (military) rifleman; fighter aircraft
jäh precipitous
Jahr *n* (-e) year; **-buch** *n* year-

book; **-hundert** *n* century;
-estag *m* anniversary; **-eszeit**
f season; **-market** *m* fair
jährlich annual
jähzornig irascible
Jalousie *f* (-n) Venetian blind
Jammer *m* distress
jämmerlich pitiful
jammern lament
Januar *m* January
jäten weed
jauchzen shout, exult
Jazz *m* jazz; **-kapelle** *f* jazz-band
je, jemals ever; **- mehr desto
besser** the more the better;
jedenfalls at all events; **jeder**
every, each; **-mann** everybody
jedoch however
jemals ever
jemand somebody
jener that; the former
jenseit(s) (+ gen.) beyond
jenseitig opposite
Jenseits *n* the other world
Jesuit *m* (-en) Jesuit; **-isch** Jesuitical
jetzt now; **jetzig** present
Joch *n* (-e) yoke; col
Jockei *m* (-s) jockey
jodeln yodel
Johannis *n* Midsummer; **-beere**
f currant; **-wurm** *m* glow-worm
Joppe *f* (-n) jacket
jubeln jubilate
Jubiläum *n* (-äen) jubilee
Juchten *n* Russian leather
jucken itch
Jude *m* (-n) Jew
jüdisch Jewish
Jugend *f* youth; **-lich** youthful;
-herberge *f* youth hostel
jung young; **Jungfrau** *f* maid,
virgin; **-gesell** *m* bachelor;
Junge *m* boy; **Jungfernrede** *f*
maiden speech; **Jungfernschaft**
f virginity; **Jüngling** *m* young
man; **Junggesellenwohnung** *f*
bachelor's chambers; **jüngstes
Gericht** last judgment; **jüngster
Tag** doomsday
jüngst lately; last
Junker *m* (-) aristocrat, squire

Jurist *m* (-en) lawyer; **Jury** *f*
jury
just just now
Justiz *f* justice; **-minister** Lord
Chancellor; minister of justice
Juwel *n* (-en) jewel
Juwelier *m* (-e) jeweller; **-arbeit**
f jewelry; **-laden** *m* jeweller's
shop
Jux *m* (-e) joke

K

Kabale *f* (-n) plot; intrigue
Kabel *n* (-), **kabeln**, cable
Kabeljau *m* (-s) codfish
Kabine *f* (-n) cabin
Kabinett *n* (-e) cabinet, closet
Kachel *f* (-en) Dutch tile
Kadett *m* (-en) cadet
Käfer *m* (-) beetle
Kaffee *m* (-s) coffee; **-geschirr** *n*
(**-tasse**, **-kanne**) *f* coffee-service
(-cup, -pot)
Käfig *m* (-e) cage
kahl(köpfig) bald(headed)
Kahn *m* (-̈e) boat, punt
Kai *m* (-s) quay, wharf
Kaiser *m* (-) emperor; **-in** *f* empress; **kaiserlich** imperial;
-reich, **-tum** *n* empire
Kajüte *f* (-n) cabin
Kakao *m* cocoa
Kaktus *m* (-teen) cactus
Kalb *n* (-̈er) calf; **-fleisch** *n* veal;
-sbraten *m* roast veal
Kalender *m* (-) calendar; almanac
Kaliber *n* (-) calibre
Kalk(stein) *m* (-e) lime(-stone)
kalt cold; **-blütig** cool, calm;
-herzig cold-hearted; **-sinnig**
cold, indifferent
Kälte *f* cold
Kambüse *f* (-n) ship's galley
Kamel *n* (-e) camel
Kamelie *f* camelia
Kamerad *m* (-en) comrade
Kamille *f* (-n) camomile
Kamin *m* (-e) chimney, fireside;
-sims *m* mantelpiece
Kamm *m* (-̈e), **kämmen** comb

Kammer(jungfer) *f* chamber-(maid); **-diener** *m* valet
Kammgarn *n* worsted
Kampf *m* (¨e), **kämpfen** fight; **- ums Dasein** struggle for existence
Kampfer *m* camphor
Kämpfer *m* fighter
Kanal *m* (¨e) canal
Kanapee *n* (-s) sofa, settee
Kanarienvogel *m* (¨) canary bird
Kandidat *m* (-en) candidate
Kaninchen *n* (-) rabbit
Känguruh *n* (-s) kangaroo
Kanne *f* (-n) can; tankard; jug
Kanone *f* (-n) cannon; **-nboot** *n* gun-boat; **Kanonier** *m* gunner
Kante *f* (-n) edge
kantig angular
Kantine *f* (-n) canteen
Kanzel *f* (-n) pulpit
Kanzler *m* (-) chancellor
Kap *n* (-s) cape
Kapaun *m* (¨e) capon
Kapelle *f* (-n) chapel; band
Kapital *n* capital; **-ist** *m* (-en) capitalist
Kapitän *m* (-e) captain
Kapitel *n* (-) chapter
kapitulieren capitulate
Kaplan *m* (¨e) chaplain
Kappe *f* (-n) cap
Kapsel *f* (-n) case; box
kaputt broken, ruined
Kapuze *f* (-n) hood
Karabiner *m* (-) carbine
Karaffe *f* (-n) decanter
Karat *n* (-e) carat
Karawane *f* (-n) caravan
Karbolsäure *f* carbolic acid
Karbunkel *m* (-) carbuncle
Kardinal *m* (¨e) cardinal
Karfreitag *m* Good Friday
karg, kärglich sparing, poor
kariert checked
Karikatur *f* (-en), **karikieren** caricature
Karl *m* Charles
karmesin crimson
Karneval *m* (-e) carnival
Karpfen *m* (-) carp
Karren *m* (-) cart

Karriere *f* career; gallop
Karte *f* (-n) card; map
Kartoffel *f* (-n) potato; **-brei** *m* mashed potatoes
Karussell *n* (-s) merry-go-round
Karwoche *f* Passion week
Kaschmir *m* cashmere
Käse *m* cheese
Kaserne *f* (-n) barracks *pl*
Kasse *f* (-n) cash; booking-office
Kassierer *m* (-) cashier
Kastanie *f* (-n) chestnut
Kasten *m* (¨) box
Katalog *m* (-e) catalogue
Katarrh *m* catarrh
Katechismus *m* catechism
Kater *m* (-) male cat
Käthe Kate
Katheder *m* (-) lecturing desk
Kathedrale *f* cathedral
Katholik *m*, **katholisch** Catholic
Kattun *m* calico
Katze *f* (-n) cat
Kätzchen *n* (-) kitten
Kauderwelsch *n* gibberish
kauen chew
Kauf *m* (¨e) purchase; **-mann** *m* tradesman; merchant; **-haus** *n* department store, bazaar; **-fahrteischiff** *n* merchantman; **kaufen** buy; **Käufer** *m* buyer; **käuflich** for sale, venal
kaum scarcely, hardly
Kautschuk *m* india-rubber
Kavaller-ie *f* cavalry; **-ist** *m* horseman
Kaviar *m* caviar
keck bold, daring
Kegel *m* (-) cone; ninepin; **-bahn** *f* bowling-green; skittle-ground
Kehle *f* (-n) throat; **Kehlkopf** *m* larynx
kehren sweep; **Kehrbesen** *m* (-) broom
Kehricht *m* sweepings
Keil *m* (-e) wedge
Keim *m* (-e) germ; seed
keimen germinate
kein no; **-eswegs** by no means
Keks *m* (-e) biscuit
Kelch *m* (-e) cup; chalice
Kelle *f* (-n) trowel, ladle

Keller *m* (–) cellar; **-geschoss** *n* basement

Kellner(in) *m* (*f*) wait(e)r(ess)

Kelter *f* (-n), keltern press

kennen know; Kenner *m* connoisseur; Kenntnis *f* (-se) knowledge

Kennzeichen *n* (–) mark

kentern capsize

Kerbe *f* (-n) notch, indent

Kerker(meister) *m* jail(er)

Kerl *m* (-e) fellow

Kern *m* (-e) kernel; stone; grain

kernig, kernhaft pithy

Kerze *f* (-n) candle

Kessel *m* (–) kettle; boiler

Kette *f* (-n) chain; **-nbrücke** suspension-bridge

Ketzer *m* (–) heretic; **-ei** *f* heresy

keuchen pant

Keuchhusten *m* whooping cough

Keule *f* (-n) club; leg (meat)

keusch chaste; **-heit** *f* chastity

kichern titter

Kiefer *m* (–) jaw; *f* (-n) fir, pine

Kiel *m* (-e) keel; quill

Kies *m* (-e) gravel

Kiesel *m* (–) pebble

Kind *n* (-er) child; **-heit** *f* childhood; **-isch** childish; **-lich** filial, childlike; Kinder-frau *f*, **-mädchen** *n* nurse; **-lähmung** *f* poliomyelitis; **-stube** *f* nursery

Kinn *n* (-e) chin; **-backen** *m* jaw

Kippkarren *m* tip-cart

Kirche *f* (-n) church; **-nlied** *n* hymn; **-nstuhl** *m* pew; Kirchhof *m* churchyard; **-spiel** *n* parish; **-turm** *m* steeple; kirchlich ecclesiastical

Kirmes *f* kermess, fair

Kirsche *f* (-n) cherry

Kissen *n* (–) cushion; pillow

Kiste *f* (-n) chest, box

Kitt *m* (-e), kitten cement; putty

Kittel *m* (–) tunic, coat

kitzelig ticklish

kitzeln tickle

Kladde *f* (-n) rough draft; exercise book; day-book

kläffen yelp

Klage *f* (-n) complaint; action;

Kläger *m* plaintiff; klagen, sich be- complain

Klammer *f* (-n) cramp; bracket; holdfast; peg; fastener

Klang *m* (⁻e) sound

Klappe *f* (-n) damper; flap; key; valve; Klapphut *m* crush-hat; Klappstuhl *m* folding-chair

klappern rattle

Klapper(schlange) *f* rattle-(snake)

Klaps *m* (-e) clap, slap

klar, (sich) klären clear

Klarheit *f* clearness

Klarinette *f* (-n) clarinet

Klasse *f* (-n) class; form

klassisch classical

klatschen clap; applaud; gossip

klatschhaft gossiping

Klaue *f* (-n) claw

Klaviatur *f* (-en) key-board

Klavier *n* (-e) piano

kleben stick

klebrig sticky

Klecks *m* (-e), klecksen blot

Klee *m* clover

Kleid *n* (-er), -ung *f*, kleiden dress

Kleider *pl* clothes; **-bürste** *f* clothes-brush; **-schrank** *m* wardrobe

Kleie *f* (-n) bran

klein little; small; **-es Geld** change

Klein-händler *m* retailer; **-bahn** *f* branch-line; **-kinderbewahranstalt** *f* infant-asylum; **-städter** *m* provincial; Kleinigkeit *f* trifle; kleinlich mean, paltry

Kleister *m*, kleistern paste

klemmen pinch; squeeze

Klemmer *m* (–) pince-nez

Klempner *m* (–) plumber

Klepper *m* (–) hack

Klette *f* (-n) bur

klettern, klimmen climb

Klima *n* (-te) climate; **-tisch** climatic

Klinge *f* (-n) blade

Klingel *f* (-n) bell; **-zug** *m* bell-rope; klingeln ring the bell

klingen sound

Klinik *f* (-en) hospital

Klinke *f* (-n) latch
Klippe *f* (-n) cliff
klirren clatter; clash
Kloake *f* (-n) sewer
klopfen knock; Klopfer *m* knocker
Klöppel *m* (-) clapper (bell)
Klosett *n* (-e) water-closet
Kloss *m* (:e) dumpling
Kloster *n* (:) convent; monastery
Klotz *m* (:e) block; log
Klub *m* (-s) club
klug prudent, clever; Klugheit *f* prudence; cleverness
Klumpen *m* (-) lump
Klumpfuss *m* club-foot
knabbern nibble
Knabe *m* (-n) boy
knacken crack
Knall *m* (-e) report; detonation
knallen detonate
knapp scanty; scarce; close
Knarre *f* (-n), knarren rattle
Knäuel *m* (-) ball; coil
Knauser *m* (-) niggard
knauserig, knickrig niggardly
knebeln, Knebel *m* (-) gag
Knecht *m* (-) servant
kneifen pinch
Kneifer *m* (-) pince-nez
Kneifzange *f* nippers, pincers
Kneipe *f* (-n) tavern, public-house
kneipen tipple; pinch
kneten knead
knicken crack
Knicks *m* (-e) curtsy
Knie *n* (-) knee; -scheibe *f* knee-cap
knien kneel
Kniff *m* (-e) pinch, crease, trick
knipsen take a photograph
knirschen gnash
knistern crackle
Knoblauch *m* garlic
Knöchel *m* (-) knuckle; ankle
Knochen *m* (-) bone
knochig bony
Knollen *m* (-) bulb
Knopf *m* (:e), knöpfen button; stud; -haken *m* button-hook; -loch *n* button-hole; -stiefel *m* button-boot
Knöpfer *m* button-hook

Knorpel *m* (-) gristle, cartilage
Knospe *f* (-n), knospen bud
Knoten *m* (-) knot; -punkt *m* junction
knüpfen tie; bind
Knüppel *m* (-), Knüttel *m* (-) cudgel; truncheon
knurren growl
Koch *m* (:e), Köchin *f* cook -buch *n* cookery-book; -löffel *m* ladle
kochen cook; boil
ködern, Köder, *m* (-) bait
Koffer *m* (-) trunk; -träger *m* porter
Kohl *m* (-köpfe) cabbage
Kohle *f* (-n) charcoal; coal
kohlen char
Kohlen-bergwerk *n*, -grube *f* coal-mine; -kasten *m* scuttle; -säure *f* carbonic acid; -stoff *m* carbon; -wasserstoff *m* carburetted hydrogen
Koje *f* (-n) berth
Kokette *f* coquette
kokett coquettish; -ieren flirt
Kokosnuss *f* (:e) coco-nut
Koks *m* (-e) coke
Kolben *m* (-) butt
Kolik *f* colic
Kolonie *f* (-n) colony; Kolonist *m* colonist; kolonisieren colonize
Kolonne *f* (-n), Kolumne *f* (-n) column
Koloss *m* (-e) colossus
kolossal huge, immense; terrific
kombinieren combine
Komet *m* (-en) comet
komisch comic; funny; queer
Komitee *n* (-s) committee
Kommandant *m* (-en) commander; kommandieren command
kommen come; - lassen send for
Kommis *m* (-) clerk
Kommode *f* (-n) chest of drawers
Komödie *f* (-n) comedy
Kompanie *f* (-n) company
Kompagnon *m* (-s) partner
Kompass *m* (-e) compass
komponieren compose
Komponist *m* (-en) composer
Kompott *n* (-e) stewed fruit

Konditor *m* (-en) confectioner; -ei *f* confectioner's shop
Kondolenzkarte *f* card of condolence
Konfekt *n* (-e) sweets
Konfektion *f* (-en) ready-made clothes
konfiszieren confiscate
Kongress *m* (-e) congress
König *m* (-e) king; -in *f* queen; -lich royal; -reich *n* kingdom; -tum *n* royal dignity
konjugieren conjugate
konkav concave; **konvex** convex
Konkurrenz *f* (-en) competition
Konkurs *m* insolvency
können can; know
konservativ conservative
Konserve *f* (-n), **konservieren** preserve
Konsul(at) *m* (*n*) consul(ate)
Konsument *m* (-en) consumer
Konsumverein *m* (-e) co-operative society
Kontinent *m* continent
Konto *n* (-ten) bank account
Kontor *n* (-e) office; counting house
Kontrakt *m* (-e) contract
Kontrolle *f*, **kontrollieren** control
Konversationslexikon *n* encyclopædia
Konzert *n* (-e) concert
Konzession *f* (-en) licence
Kopf *m* (¨e) head; -kissen *n* pillow; -rechnen *n* mental arithmetic; -weh *n* headache
köpfen behead; head (ball)
Kopierpresse *f* copying-press
Koppe *f* (-n) hill-top; summit
koppeln couple
Koralle *f* (-n) coral
Korb *m* (¨e) basket
Korinthe *f* currant
Kork(zieher) *m* cork(screw)
Korn *n* (¨er) grain; corn
Kornblume *f* (-n) corn-flower
Körper *m* (-), -schaft *f* body
körperlich bodily
Korpsgeist *m* esprit de corps
Korrektur *f* (-en) correction; -bogen *m* proof-sheet

Korrespondenz *f* correspondence
korrespondieren correspond
Korridor *m* (-e) corridor; passage
korrigieren correct
Korsar *m* (-en) corsair
Korsett *n* (-e) corset
Kost *f*, -geld *n* board; -gänger *m* boarder; -haus *n* boarding-house
kost-bar precious; -spielig expensive
kosten cost; taste; **Kosten** *pl* costs, expense
köstlich delicious
Kostüm *n* (-e) costume
Kot *m* dirt; excrement; **kotig** dirty
Krabbe *f* (-n) crab, shrimp
krabbeln crawl
krachen crack
krächzen croak
Kraft *f* (¨e) strength, force, power; -anlage *f* power-plant; -omnibus *m* motor-bus; -wagen *m* motor-car; -werk *n* power-station
kraft (+ gen.) by virtue of
kräftig strong; vigorous
kräftigen strengthen
Kragen *m* collar
Krähe *f* (-n), **krähen** crow
Kralle *f* (-n) claw
Krämer *m* (-) shopkeeper
Krampf *m* (¨e) cramp; convulsion
krampfhaft convulsive
Kran *m* (-e), **Kranich** *m* (-e) crane
krank ill
Kranke *m* (adj. noun) patient
kränkeln be sickly
kränken grieve; vex
Kranken-haus *n* (¨er) hospital; -kraftwagen *m* motor-ambulance; -pflege *f* nursing; -wärter(in) *m* (*f*) sick-nurse
krankhaft morbid
Krankheit *f* (-en) disease; illness
kränklich sickly
Kranz *m* (¨e) wreath
kränzen crown
Krater *m* (-) crater

Kratz-bürste f, **-eisen** n scraper
Krätze f itch, scabies
kratzen scrape, scratch
kraus crisp; frizzled; curly
Krause f (-n) ruff
kräuseln frizzle
Kraut n (¨er) herb; cabbage
Krawatte f (-n) cravat, neck-tie
Krebs m (-e) crayfish; cancer
Kredenztisch m (-e) sideboard
Kredit m (-e), **kreditieren** credit
Kreditbrief m (-e) letter of credit
Kreide f (-n) chalk
Kreis m (-e) circle; **-förmig** circular; **-lauf** m circulation; **-säge** f circular saw
kreischen shriek
Kreisel m (-) spinning top
kreissen labour (with child)
Krempe f (-n) brim
Krepp(flor) m crape
Kresse f (-n) cress
Kreuz n (-e), **kreuzen** cross; **-band** n wrapper; **unter -band verschicken** send by book-post; **-fahrer** m crusader; **-gang** m cloisters; **-verhör** n cross-examination; **-zug** m crusade
kreuzigen crucify
Kreuzigung f (-en) crucifixion
Kreuzung f (-en) crossing; **-spunkt** m junction
kriechen creep; sneak
Krieg m (-e) war; **-er** m warrior; **-erisch** warlike; **-führend** belligerent
Kriegs-flotte f navy; **-gefangene** m prisoner-of-war; **-gericht** n court-martial; **-list** f stratagem; **-schiff** n man-of-war; **-zug** m military expedition
Krim f Crimea
Kriminal, -polizei f criminal investigation police; **-roman** m detective novel
Krippe f (-n) crib, nursery
Kristall m (-e) crystal
Kritik f (-en) critique
Kritiker m (-) critic
kritisch critical
kritisieren criticize; review
kritzeln scribble
Krokodil n (-e) crocodile

Krone f (-n), **krönen** crown
Krönung f (-en) coronation
Kronleuchter m (-) lustre, chandelier
Kronprinz m (-en), **-prinzessin** f (-en) Crown Prince, Princess
Kropf m goitre
Kröte f (-n) toad
Krücke f (-n) crutch
Krug m (¨e) pitcher; jug
Krume f (-n) crumb
krumm crooked
krümmen bend
Krümmung f (-en) curve
Krüppel m (-) cripple
Kruste f (-n) crust
Kruzifix n (-e) crucifix
Krypta f (-ten) crypt
Kübel m (-) tub
kubik cubic
Küche f (-n) kitchen; **-nschrank** m dresser; **-ngerät** n utensils (pl.)
Kuchen m (-) cake; **-bäcker** m pastry-cook
Küchlein n (-) chicken
Kuckuck m (-e) cuckoo
Küfer m (-) cooper
Kugel f (-n) ball; bullet; sphere; globe; **-stossen** n putting the shot; **kugelsicher** bullet-proof
Kuh f (¨e) cow; **-pocken** pl cowpox
kühl, kühlen cool
Kühle f coolness
kühn bold
Kühnheit f boldness
Kulisse f (-n) side-scene, wing
Kultur f (-en) culture; civilization
Kultus m (-te) worship
Kummer m grief
kümmern (sich) grieve for; afflict; care for
kummervoll sorrowful
Kummet n (-e) collar (horse)
kundbar notorious
Kunde m (-n) customer
Kunde f (-n) news; science
Kundgebung f (-en) statement
kündigen give notice
Kündigung f (-en) notice; warning

Kundschaft f (-en) custom; customers
künftig future
Kunst f (-̈e) art; **-ausdruck** m technical term; **-ausstellung** f art exhibition; **-griff** m, trick; **-kenner** m connoisseur; **-sammlung** f collection of works of art; **-stück** n trick; **-seide** f artificial silk, rayon; **-werk** n work of art; **Künstler** m artist; **künstlerisch** artistical; **künstlich** artificial
Kupfer n copper; **-stich** m copper-engraving
Kuppel f (-n) cupola; dome
Kuppelung f (-en) coupling
Kuppler(in) m (f) procurer
Kur f (-en), **kurieren** cure; **-fürst** m elector; **-liste** f list of visitors; **-ort** m watering-place; spa
Kürass(ier) m cuirass(ier)
Kurbel f (-n) crank
Kürbis m (-se) pumpkin
Kurier m (-e) courier
Kuriosität f curiosity
Kurs m (-e) exchange; course
Kursbuch n time-table
Kürschner m (-) furrier
Kursivschrift f italics
Kursus m (-se) course
Kurve f (-n) curve
kurz short; **-um** in short; **-sichtig** short-sighted; **-wellig** amusing; **Kurzschluss** m short circuit
Kürze f brevity; **kürzen** shorten; **kürzlich** recently
Kuss m (-̈e), **küssen** kiss
Küste f (-n) coast, beach
Küster m (-) sexton
Kutsche f (-n) coach
Kutscher m (-) coachman
Kutte f (-n) cowl
Kutteln pl tripe
Kuvert n (-e) cover, envelope
Kux m (-e) share, claim

L

Labe f refreshment, comfort
laben refresh
Laberdan m salt cod

Laboratorium n (-rien) laboratory
lächeln, Lächeln n smile
lachen, Lachen n laugh
lächerlich ridiculous
Lachs m (-e) salmon
Lack m (-e), **lackieren** varnish; **-stiefel** m patent-leather shoe
Lade f (-n) chest; box
laden load; charge
Laden m (-̈) shop, store; shutter; **-tisch** m counter
Ladung f (-en) load; cargo; charge
Lafette f (-n) gun-carriage
Laffe m (-n) fop
Lage f (-n) situation; layer
Lager n (-) bed; camp; bearing; store(house); **-bier** n lager
lagern rest; store; encamp
lahm lame
lähmen paralyse
Lähmung f (-en) paralysis
Lahn m (-e) tinsel
Laib m (-e) loaf
Laich m, **laichen** spawn
Laie m (-n) layman, amateur
Laken n (-) sheet
Lakritze f (-n) liquorice
Lamm n (-̈er) lamb
Lampe f (-n) lamp
Land n (-̈er) land; country; **-enge** f isthmus; **-gut** n estate; **-karte** f map; **-mann** m countryman; **-messer** m surveyor; **-schaft** f landscape; **-sitz** m country-seat; **-smann** m fellow-countryman; **-strasse** f highway; **-streicher** m tramp; **-wirt** m farmer; **-wirtschaft** f agriculture
Ländereien pl landed property
Landauer m (-) landau
landen land
ländlich rural
Landungsbrücke f (-n) pier
lang, lange long
Länge f (-n) length; longitude; **-ngrad** m degree of longitude; **-nmass** n long measure
langen suffice; hand, pass on
Langeweile f tediousness; **langweilig** tedious; **langweilen** bore

länglich oblong
Langmut f patience
längs (+ gen.) along
langsam slow
längst long ago
Lanze f (-n) lance
Lanzette f (-n) lancet
Lappen m (-) rag
läppisch foolish, silly
Lärche f (-n) larch
Lärm m noise
lärmen make a noise
lärmend noisy
Larve f (-n) larva; mask
lassen (zu-) let; allow; suffer; make, cause
lässig inactive, sluggish
Last f (-en) load; burden; **-wagen** m waggon; lorry
lasten to weigh on
Laster n (-) vice
lasterhaft vicious
lästern, Lästerung f (-en) slander
lästig troublesome
Latein n, **lateinisch** Latin
Laterne f (-n) lantern; **-nanzünder** m lamplighter; **-npfahl** m lamp-post
latschig shuffling
Latte f (-n) lath
Lattich m (-e) lettuce
Latz m (-e) bib (pinafore)
lau, lauwarm lukewarm
Laub n foliage; leaves pl; **-wald** m deciduous wood
Laube f (-n) arbour, summer-house
Lauch m (-e) leek; garlic
lauern lurk, lie in ambush
Lauf m (-e) course; run; race; barrel; **-bahn** f career; **-bursche** m errand boy; **laufen** run
Läufer m runner
Laune f (-n) humour; whim
launisch capricious
Laus f (-e), **lausen** louse
Lausbube m young scamp; blackguard
lauschen listen
laut loud; **Laut** m (-e) sound
Laute f (-n) lute
läuten ring, peal

lauter clear; pure
Lautlehre f phonetics, phonology
Lautsprecher m (-) loudspeaker
Lautstärke f volume
Lava f lava
Lavendel m lavender
Lawine f (-n) avalanche
laxieren purge
Lazarett n (-e) military hospital
Lebehoch n cheer
leben live; **- Sie wohl!** goodbye
Leben n (-) life
lebendig living, lively
Lebens-art f manners pl; **-beschreibung** f life; biography; in **-grösse** full-length; **-gefahr** f danger of life; **-länglich** for life; **-mittel** n pl victuals; **-versicherung** f life-insurance
Leber f (-n) liver; **-tran** m cod-liver oil
Leberwurst f (-e) liver-sausage
lebhaft vivid; lively
Lebkuchen m gingerbread
leblos lifeless
Leck n (-e), **lecken** leak
leck leaky
lecken lick
lecker, Leckerbissen m (-) dainty
Leder n (-) leather, skin
ledern of leather; dull
Lederwaren f pl leather goods
ledig free, single
leer, leeren empty
Legat n (-e) legacy
legen lay; **sich -** lie down
Legende f (-n) legend
Legierung f, **legieren** alloy
Legitimationspapier n (-e) identity papers
Lehm m (-e) loam, clay
Lehne f (-n) support; back (chair), arm-rest; **lehnen** lean; **Lehnstuhl** m (-e) easy-chair
Lehr-anstalt f (-en) educational establishment; **-buch** n textbook; **-jahre** pl apprenticeship; **-saal** m lecture-room
Lehre f (-n) lesson; doctrine; apprenticeship
lehren teach; **Lehrer(in)** m (f)

teacher; **-seminar** *n* teachers' training-college
Lehrling *m* (-e) apprentice
lehrreich instructive
Lehrsatz *m* ("e) theorem
Leib *m* (-er) body; **-binde** *f* sash; **-chen** *n* corset; **-gericht** *n* favourite dish; **-schmerzen** *pl* colic; **-rente** *f* annuity; **-wäsche** *f* body linen
Leibes-pflege *f* hygiene; **-übungen** *pl* physical training
Leiche *f* (-n), **Leichnam** *m* (-e) dead body; corpse
Leichen-bestatter *m* undertaker; **leichenblass** as pale as death; **-(schau)haus** *n* mortuary; **-stein** *m* tombstone; **-verbrennung** *f* cremation; **-verbrennungsofen** *m* crematorium; **-wagen** *m* hearse
leicht easy; light; **-gläubig** credulous; **-sinnig** frivolous
Leichtathletik *f* athletics
Leichtigkeit *f* facility
Leid *n* grief; **es tut mir leid** I am sorry; **Leiden** *n* (-) suffering, complaint; **-schaft** *f* passion; **leidenschaftlich** passionate
leiden suffer
leider unfortunately
leidlich tolerable
Leierkasten *m* (") barrel-organ
Leih-bibliothek *f* circulation library; **-haus** *n* pawnshop
leihen lend, borrow
Leim *m* (-e), **leimen** glue
Leine *f* (-n) line; string
Leinöl *n* linseed-oil
Leinwand *f*, **leinen** linen
leise low; soft
Leiste *f* (-n) border; ledge
leisten perform; render; take
Leisten *m* (-) last, shoe-tree
Leistung *f* (-en) performance
Leitartikel *m* (-) leader
leiten lead; conduct; manage; **Leiter** *m* leader, conductor, manager; **Leitung** *f* management, control, transmission; **-s-draht** *m* conducting-wire; **-s-rohr** *n* conduit
Leiter *f* (-n) ladder

Leitmotiv *n* theme (music)
Lektion *f* (-en) lesson
Lektüre *f* (-n) reading
Lende *f* (-n) loin
lenkbar dirigible
lenken direct; guide; steer
Leopard *m* (-en) leopard
Lerche *f* (-n) lark
lernen learn; **kennen -** become acquainted with
Lesart *f* (-en) version; **Lesung** *f* (-en) reading
lesen read; **lesbar** readable; **Lesezimmer** *n* (-) reading-room
Leser *m* (-) reader
letzt last
leuchten light, shine
Leuchter *m* (-) candlestick
Leucht-gas *n* gas (light); **-käfer** *m* glow-worm; **-turm** *m* lighthouse
leugnen deny
Leute *pl* people
Leutnant *m* (-e) lieutenant
leutselig affable
Leutseligkeit *f* affability
Levante *f* Levant
Levkoje *f* (-n) stock, gillyflower
Lexikon *n* (-ka) dictionary
Licht *n* (-er) light; **-mess** *f* Candlemas; **-spiel** *n* cinema
lichten weigh (anchor)
Lid *n* (-er) eye-lid
lieb dear; **es ist mir -** I am glad
Liebe *f*, **lieben** love; **liebenswürdig** amiable; **lieber** rather; **lieber mögen** like better
Liebes-brief *m* love-letter; **-erklärung** *f* declaration of love, proposal; **-paar** *n* loving couple; **Liebhaber** *m* lover, amateur; **liebkosen** caress; **lieblich** lovely; **Liebchen** *n* sweetheart; **Liebling** *m* darling, favourite
Lied *n* (-er) song
liederlich dissolute; slovenly
Lieferant *m* (-en) purveyor; **liefern** supply; **Lieferung** *f* delivery
liegen lie; be situated; **- lassen** leave behind
Likör *m* (-e) liqueur
lila lilac

Lilie f (-n) lily
Limonade f (-n) lemonade
Limone f (-n) lemon
Linde f (-n) lime-tree
lindern mitigate
Lineal n (-e) ruler
Linie f (-n) line; -nschiff n battleship
linieren rule
link left; Linke f left; linkisch awkward, clumsy; links left (hand, side); -händig left-handed
Linse f (-n) lentil; lens
Lippe f (-n) lip
lispeln lisp; whisper
List f (-en), listig cunning
Liste f (-n) list
Litanei f (-en) litany
literarisch literary
Literatur f (-en) literature
Lithograph m (-en) lithographer
Lithographie f (-n) lithography
Livree f (-n) livery
Lob n, loben praise
lobenswert praiseworthy
Loch n (-̈er) hole
lochen punch
Locke f (-n) curl
locken allure; curl
locker loose; lockern loosen
lockig curled
Lockmittel n (-), -speise f bait
Löffel m (-) spoon; -voll spoonful
Loge f (-n) box (theatre)
Logik f logic
Logis n (-) lodging
logisch logical
Lohgerber m (-) tanner
Lohn m (-̈e) reward; wages
lohnen reward, recompense
löhnen, Löhnung f pay (wages)
Lohnsteuer f (-n) income-tax
Lokal n (-e) locality; premises
Lokomotive f (-n) locomotive; -führer m engine-driver
Lorbeer m (-en) laurel
Los n (-e) lot; ticket; fate, destiny
los, lose loose; was ist -? what's

the matter?; -binden unbind; -gehen go off, rush; -spannen unyoke; -sprechen absolve
löschen extinguish; quench
Löschblatt n, -papier n blotting-paper
Lösegeld n ransom
losen draw lots
lösen untie; solve
Lösung f (-en) solution
loten sound; löten solder
Lothringen n Lorraine
lotrecht perpendicular
Lötrohr n (-e) blowpipe
Lotse m (-n) pilot
Lotterie f (-n) lottery
Löwe m (-n) lion
Luchs m (-̈e) lynx
Lücke f (-n) gap
lückenhaft defective
Ludwig Lewis
Luft f (-̈e), lüften air; -angriff m air-raid; -aufklärung f air-reconnaissance; -ballon m balloon; -blase f bubble; l-dicht air-tight; -druck m atmospheric pressure; -pumpe f air-pump; -schiffahrt f aeronautics; -schlösser n pl castles in the air; -schutz(raum) m A.R.P. (air-raid-shelter); -spähdienst m Observer Corps; -spiegelung f mirage; -streitkräfte n pl air-forces; -verkehrslinie f air-line; -veränderung f, -wechsel m change of air; -zug m draught
Lüge f (-n), lügen lie
Lügner m (-) liar
Luke f (-n) hatch
Lümmel m (-) lout, boor
Lump m (-e) rascal
Lumpen m (-) rag
lumpig shabby
Lunge f (-n) lungs pl; -nentzündung f inflammation of the lungs; -nschwindsucht f pulmonary consumption
Lunte f slow match; Lunte riechen smell a rat
Lupe f (-n) magnifying glass
Lust f (-̈e) desire; pleasure; - haben feel inclined; -spiel n

comedy; **lustwandeln** take a walk
lustig merry; **Lustigkeit** f mirth
lutherisch Lutheran
lutschen suck
Luxus m luxury; **-zug** m saloon-train
lynchen lynch
Lyra f (-ren) lyre
Lyrik f lyric poetry
lyrisch lyric

M

Maat m (-e) mate
machbar practicable
machen make; do
Machenschaft f (-en) intrigue
Macht f (¨e) power
mächtig powerful
Mädchen n (-) girl; maid; **- für alles** maid of all work; **höhere -schule** f girls' college
Made f (-n) maggot
Magd f (¨e) maid-servant
Magen m (¨) stomach; **-schmerzen** stomach-ache; **beschwerden** pl indigestion
mager meagre; lean
Magerkeit f leanness
Magnet m (-e) magnet; **-nadel** f magnetic needle; **-ismus** m magnetism; **-isieren** magnetize
Mahagoni n mahogany
mähen mow; **Mäher** m mower; **Mähmaschine** f mowing-machine
Mahl(zeit) n (f) meal(time)
mahlen grind
Mähne f (-n) mane
mahnen remind; warn
Mahnung f (-en) warning
Mai m May; **-glöckchen** n lily-of-the-valley; **-käfer** m May-bug
Mailand n Milan
Mais m maize; (Indian) corn
Maische f (-n), **maischen** mash
Majestätsbeleidigung f lese-majesty
Major m (-e) major
Makel m (-) stain, blemish
mäkeln find fault

Makler m (-) broker
Makrele f (-n) mackerel
Makrone f (-n) macaroon
Makulatur f (-en) waste-paper
mal time; **Mal** n (-e) time; mark, mole
malen paint; **Maler** m painter, **-ei** f painting; **-isch** picturesque
Malve f (-n) mallow
Malz n, **mälzen** malt
man one; people
manch many
manchmal sometimes
Mandel f (-n) almond
Mange(l) f (-n), **mange(l)n** mangle
Mangel m (¨) want; defect; **mangeln** lack
mangelhaft deficient
Manie f (-n) mania
Manier f (-en) manner
Mann m (¨er) man; husband; **mannhaft** manly; **männlich** male, masculine; **Männlichkeit** f, **Mannesalter** n manhood
Männchen n (-) male
Männerchor m (¨e) male voice choir
mannigfaltig various
Mannschaft f (-en) team; crew
Mannszucht f discipline
Manöver n (-) manœuvre
Mansarde(nstube) f (-n) garret
Manschette f (-n) cuff; **-nknopf** m cuff-link
Mantel m (¨) cloak; overcoat
Manufakturwaren f pl manufactured goods
Manuskript n (-e) manuscript
Mappe f (-n) portfolio; brief-case
Märchen n (-) fairy-tale
Maria Mary
Marine f navy
Marineflieger m (-) naval airman
marinieren cure, pickle
Marionette f (-n) puppet
Mark n marrow
Mark f mark (coin); boundary
Marke f (-n) mark, counter; postage-stamp; brand, quality
markten haggle

Markt(platz) *m* (¨e) market (-place)
Marktschreier *m* (–) quack
Marmelade *f* (-n) marmalade; jam
Marmor *m*, **-ieren** marble
Marsch *m* (¨e), **marschieren** march
Marschallstab *m* marshal's baton
Marter *f* (-n), **martern** torture
Märtyrer *m* (–) martyr; **-tum** *n* martyrdom
März *m* March
Marzipan *m* (-e) marchpane
Masche *f* (-n) mesh
Maschine *f* (-n) machine, engine
Maschinenbau *m* construction of machines; engineering
Maschinerie *f* machinery
Maser *f* (-n) mark; spot
Masern *pl* measles
Maske *f* (-n), **maskieren** mask; **-nball** *m* fancy-dress ball
Mass *n* (-e), **-liebchen** *n* daisy; **-nahme** *f* measure; **-regel** *f* measure; **-stab** *m* scale
Masse *f* (-n) mass
massenhaft numerous
massieren massage
mässig, mässigen moderate
Mässigkeitsverein *m* temperance society; **-ler** *m* abstainer
massiv massive
Mast *m* (-e) mast
mästen fatten
Material *n* (-ien) material
Materialwaren *pl* groceries
Mathematik *f* mathematics
Mathematiker *m* (–) mathematician
Matratze *f* (-n) mattress
Matrose *m* (-n) sailor
matt faint, weak
Matte *f* (-n) mat; meadow
Mattigkeit *f* languor
Mauer *f* (-n) wall; **-werk** *n* masonry
Maul *n* (¨er) mouth (animal's); **-affe** *m* gaper, loafer; **-beerbaum** *m* mulberry tree; **-esel** *m*, **-tier** *n* mule; **-korb** *m* muzzle; **-wurf(shügel)** *m* mole(-hill)

Maurer *m* (–) mason
Maus *f* (¨e) mouse; **-efalle** *f* mouse-trap
mausern, Mauser *f* moult
Maximum *n* (-a) maximum
Mechanik *f* mechanics; **-er** *m* mechanic; **mechanisch** mechanical
meckern bleat; grouse
Medaille *f* (-n) medal
Medizin *f* (-en) medicine
Meer *n* (-e) sea, ocean; **-busen** *m* gulf; **-enge** *f* strait; **-esspiegel** *m* level of the sea; **-rettich** *m* horse-radish; **-schaum(pfeife)** *m* (*f*) meerschaum; **-schweinchen** *n* guinea-pig
Mehl *n* flour, meal; **-ig** mealy
mehr more; **-mals** several times; **mehrere** several; **Mehrheit** *f*, **-zahl** *f* majority; **mehrfach** repeated(ly)
meiden avoid
Meierei *f* (-en) dairy-farm
Meile *f* (-n) mile
Meineid *m* (-e) perjury; **meineidig** perjured
meinen think; **Meinung** *f* (-en) opinion; **meiner - nach** in my opinion
Meise *f* (-n) titmouse
Meissel *m* (–), **meisseln** chisel
meist most; **-ens** mostly
Meistbietende *m* (adj. noun) highest bidder
Meister *m* (–) master; champion; **-haft** masterly; **-schaft** *f* championship; **-werk** *n* masterpiece
Melancholie *f*, **melancholisch** melancholy
melden announce; report
melken milk
Melodie *f* (-n) melody
melodisch melodious
Melone *f* (-n) melon
Meltau *m* mildew
Menagerie *f* (-n) menagerie
Menge *f* (-n) quantity; crowd
mengen mingle; mix
Mensch *m* (-n) human being, man
Menschenfeind *m* misanthrope; **-fresser** *m* cannibal; **-gesch-**

lecht *n* mankind; **gesunder Menschenverstand** *m* common sense

Menschheit *f* mankind

Menschlich(keit) *f* human(ity)

Menuett *n* (-e) minuet

Meridian *m* (-e) meridian

merken perceive; **merkbar** noticeable; **merklich** perceptible; **merkwürdig** remarkable; **-würdigkeit** *f* curiosity

Messbuch *n* (¨er) missal

Messe *f* (-n) mass; fair

messen measure

Messer *n* (-) knife; **-schmied** *m* cutler

Messing *n* brass

Messkunde *f* surveying

Metall *n* (-e) metal; **metallisch** metallic

Meteor *n* (-e) meteor; **-stein** *m* aerolite

Methode *f* (-n) method

Metzelei *f* (-en) slaughter

Metzger *m* (-) butcher

Meute *f* (-n) pack of hounds

Meuterei *f* (-en), **meutern** mutiny

miauen mew

Michaelis *n* Michaelmas

Mieder *n* (-) corset, bodice

Miene *f* (-n) look, mien

Miete *f* (-n), **mieten** hire; rent; **-r** *m* tenant, lodger; **Mietvertrag** *m* lease; **Mietswohnung** *f* flat, lodgings

Mieze *f* (-en) puss

Mikroskop *n* (-e) microscope

Milbe *f* (-n) mite

Milch *f* milk; **-brötchen** *n* roll; **-strasse** *f* milky way; **-topf** *m* milk-jug

mild mild; **-tätig** charitable

Milde *f* mildness, mercy

mildern mitigate

Militär *n*, **militärisch** military

Miliz *f* (-en) militia

Million(är) *f* (*m*) million(aire)

Milz(krankheit) *f* spleen

minder less; **-jährig** minor; **Minderheit** *f*, **-jährigkeit** *f*; **-zahl** *f* minority

mindern, sich diminish

mindest least; **-ens** at least

Mine *f* (-n) mine

Mineral *n* (-ien) mineral; **-wasser** *n* mineral water

Miniatur *f* (-en) miniature

Minister *m* (-) minister; Secretary of State; **-präsident** *m* Prime Minister; **- des Innern** Secretary of State for Home Affairs; **Ministerium** *n* (-rien) ministry

Minute *f* minute

Mischehe *f* (-n) mixed marriage

mischen mix; (cards) shuffle

Mischling *m* (-e) mongrel

Mischung *f* (-en) mixture

miss-achten, Miss-achtung *f* disregard; **-billigen** disapprove; **-brauch** *m*, **-brauchen** abuse; **-deuten** misinterpret; **-erfolg** *m* failure; **-fallen** displease; **-geburt** *f* miscarriage; **-gestaltet** deformed; **-gönnen** envy; **-griff** *m* mistake; **-günstig** envious; **-handeln** ill-treat; **-heirat** *f* mésalliance; **-kredit** *m* discredit; **-lingen** fail; **-ton** *m* discord; **-trauen** distrust; **-trauisch** suspicious; **-verhältnis** *n* disproportion; **-verständnis** *n* misunderstanding; **-vergnügt** displeased; **-wachs** *m* failure of crops

Mission(ar) *f* (*m*) mission(ary)

misslich doubtful; awkward

Mist *m* dung; **-gabel** *f* pitchfork

Mistel *f* (-n) mistletoe

mit with; **Mitarbeiter** *m* fellow-labourer, collaborator; **Mitbewerber** *m* competitor; **-einander** together; **Mitgefühl** *n* sympathy; **-hilfe** *f* aid; **-gift** *f* dowry; **-glied** *n* member; **-leid** *n* pity; **-leidig** compassionate; **-mensch** *m* fellow man; **-schuldige** (adj. noun) accomplice; **-schüler** *m* schoolfellow; **-spieler** *m* fellow-player, partner

Mittag *m* midday, noon; **-essen** *n* luncheon; **-schläfchen** *n* nap, siesta

Mitte *f* middle

mitteilen communicate

Mitteilung *f* (**-en**) communication

Mittel *n* (**-**) means, remedy; **-alter** *n* middle ages; **-alterlich** mediæval; **-finger** *m* middle finger; **-mässig** mediocre; **-mässigkeit** *f* mediocrity; **-meer** *n* Mediterranean; **-punkt** *m* centre; **-stand** *m* middle class; **-stürmer** *m* centre-forward

mittelbar indirect

mittels (+ gen.) by means of

mitten in in the midst of

Mitternacht *f* midnight

mittlere middle, mean; **in mittleren Jahren** middle-aged

mittlerweile in the meantime

Mittwoch *m* Wednesday

Mitwelt *f* present generation

Mitwirkung *f* co-operation

Möbel, Mobiliar *n*, **Möblierung** *f* furniture

Möbelwagen *m* (**-**) furniture-van

Mobilmachung *f* (**-en**) mobilization

möblieren furnish

Mode *f* (**-n**) fashion; **-händler(in)** *m* (*f*) milliner; **modisch** fashionable

Modell *n* (**-e**), **modellieren** model

Moder *m* mould; **modern** moulder

modern modern

mogeln cheat

mögen like; may

möglich possible; **-st (viel)** as (much) as possible

Möglichkeit *f* (**-en**) possibility

Mohammedaner *m* (**-**) Mohammedan

Mohn *m* (**-e**) poppy

Mohr *m* (**-en**) Moor

Möhre *f* (**-n**) carrot

Molch *m* (**-e**) salamander

Molken *f pl* whey

Molkerei (**en**) *f* dairy

Moll *n* minor key (music)

Moment *m* (**-e**) moment; **-aufnahme** *f* instantaneous photography; snapshot

Monarch *m* (**-en**) monarch; **-isch** monarchical; **Monarchie** *f* monarchy

Monat *m* (**-e**) month; **monatlich** monthly; **Monatsschrift** monthly journal

Mönch *m* (**-e**) monk

Mond *m* (**-e**) moon; **-finsternis** *f* eclipse of the moon; **-jahr** *n* lunar year; **-schein** *m* moonlight; **-wechsel** *m* change of the moon

Monolog *m* (**-e**) monologue

Monopol *n* (**-e**) monopoly

monoton monotonous

Montag *m* Monday

Moor *n* (**-e**) moor

Moos *n* (**-e**) moss

Mops *m* (**-̈e**) pug

Moral *f*, **moralisch** moral

Morast *m* (**-̈e**) morass

Mord *m* (**-e**) **morden** murder; **Mörder** *m* murderer; **-isch** murderous

morgen to-morrow; **-früh** to-morrow morning

Morgen *m* (**-**) morning; **morgens** in the m.; **-anzug** *m* morning-dress; **-dämmerung** *f* dawn; **-land** *n* East; **-röte** *f* aurora; **-stern** *m* morning star

Morphium *n* morphia; morphine

morsch rotten

Mörser *m* (**-**) mortar

Mosaik *f* (**-en**) mosaic

mosaisch Mosaic

Moschee *f* (**-n**) mosque

Moschus(tier) *m* (*n*) musk (**-deer**)

Mosel(wein) *f* (*m*) Moselle

Moskitonetz *n* (**-e**) mosquito-net

Most *m* must; grape-juice

Motor *m* (**-en**) motor; **-rad** *n* (**-̈er**) motor-bicycle

Motte *f* (**-n**) moth

Motto *n* (**-s**) motto

moussieren effervesce

Möwe *f* (**-n**) gull

Mücke *f* (**-n**) gnat

Mucker *m* (**-**) hypocrite

müde weary; tired

Müdigkeit *f* weariness; fatigue

Muff *m* (**-̈e**) muff; **muffig** musty

Mühe *f* (**-n**) pains; **sich - geben, sich mühen** take pains

mühsam painful

Mühle *f* (-n) mill
Mulatte *m* (-n) mulatto
Mulde *f* (-n) trough
Müll *m* dust, rubbish
Müller *m* (-) miller
multiplizieren multiply
Mumie *f* (-n) mummy
Mund *m* ("er), Mündung *f*
mouth; halte den - hold your
tongue; -voll mouthful; -vorrat
m provisions; münden flow,
fall into; mündlich oral
Mündel *n* (-) ward, minor
mündig of age
Munition *f* (-en) ammunition
munter merry; lively
Münze *f* (-n), münzen coin;
mint; change; medal
Münzfuss *m* monetary standard
mürbe tender; friable
Murmel *m* (-n) marble
murmeln murmur
Murmeltier *n* (-e) marmot
murren grumble
mürrisch sulky
Mus *n* (-e) jam
Muschel *f* (-n) shell, mussel
Muse *f* (-n) Muse
Museum *n* (-een), museum
Musik *f*, -alien *pl* music
musikalisch musical
Musikant, Musiker *m* musician
musizieren have music
Muskatnuss *f* ("e) nutmeg
Muskel *m* (-n) muscle
muskulös muscular
Musse *f* leisure
Musselin *m* (-e) muslin
müssen be obliged; must
müssig idle; -gang *m* idleness;
-gänger *m* idler
Muster *n* (-) model; sample; design; example; standard
musterhaft exemplary
mustern muster; review
Mut *m* courage; mutig courageous; mutlos discouraged;
-massen suppose; -masslich
probable; -massung *f* conjecture; -wille *m* wantonness;
-willig wanton, mischievous
Mutter *f* (") mother; nut (of
screw); -korn *n* ergot; -milch

f mother's milk; -schaft *f*
maternity; -sprache *f* native
tongue; -witz *m* common sense
Mütze *f* (-n) cap
Mystik *f* mysticism
Mythe *f* (-n) myth
Mythologie *f* mythology

N

na! now, then!
Nabe *f* (-n) nave, hub
Nabel *m* (") navel
nach, nachdem after, to
Nachachtung *f* observance
nachäffen ape
nachahmen imitate; copy
Nachahmung *f* (-en) imitation
nacharten take after
Nachbar *m* (-n) neighbour;
-schaft *f* neighbourhood
nachdenken meditate
Nachdenken *n* (-) meditation
nachdenklich thoughtful
Nachdruck *m* ("e) energy;
pirated edition; reprint
nachdrücklich energetical; forcible
nacheinander one after another
Nachen *m* (-) boat; bark
Nachfolge *f* succession; -r *m*
successor
nachfolgen follow, succeed
nachforschen inquire, search
Nachfrage *f* demand
nachgeben yield
nachgehen follow; lose; be
slow
Nachgeschmack *m* after-taste
nachher afterwards
nachholen make up for
Nachhut *f* rearguard
Nachkomme *m* (-n) descendant
Nachlass-steuer *f* (-n) death-
duty
nachlassen diminish; abate:
cease
nachlässig careless
nachmachen imitate
Nachmittag *m* (-e) afternoon;
-svorstellung *f* matinée; afternoon performance

Nachnahme *f* reimbursement; cash on delivery
Nachrede *f* slander; epilogue
Nachricht *f* (-en) news
nachschlagen consult, look up
Nachschlagebuch *n* ("er) book of reference
Nachschlüssel *m* (–) pick-lock
Nachschrift *f* postscript
nachsehen examine
Nachsicht *f* indulgence
nachsichtig indulgent
Nachspiel *n* (-e) epilogue; sequel
nachsprechen repeat
nächst next; nearest
nächstens shortly
nachstehen be inferior
nachstellen put back; waylay
Nächste *m* (adj. noun) fellow-creature
Nächstenliebe *f* charity
Nacht *f* ("e) night; **-asyl** *n* casual ward; **-essen** *n* supper; **-geschirr** *n* chamber-pot; **-hemd** *n* night-shirt; **-lager** *n* night's lodging; **-stuhl** *m* commode; **wächter** *m* watchman; **-wandler** *m* somnambulist
nachts at night
Nachteil *m* (-e) disadvantage
nachteilig disadvantageous
Nachtigall *f* (-en) nightingale
Nachtisch *m* dessert
nächtlich nightly
Nachtrab *m* rear
Nachtrag *m* ("e) supplement
Nachwahl *f* (-en) by-election
Nachweisbureau *n* inquiry-office
nachweisen show, prove
Nachwelt *f* posterity
nachzahlen pay the difference
nachzählen count over again
Nachzügler *m* (–) straggler
Nacken *m* (–) neck, nape
nackt naked
Nadel *f* (-n) needle
Nagel *m* ("), **nageln** nail
nagen gnaw
nah, nahe bei near, nigh
Nähe *f* (-n) proximity; neighbourhood
nähen sew; stitch

Näheres *n* particulars, details
Näherin *f* (-nen) seamstress
nähern approach
Nähmaschine *f* (-n) sewing-machine
nähren nourish, suckle
nahrhaft nutritious
Nahrung *f* food
Nahrungsmittel *n pl* victuals
Naht *f* ("e) seam
naiv ingenuous, naïve
Name *m* (-n) name; **dem -n nach** by name
namentlich especially
nämlich namely
Namenstag *m* name-day
Namensvetter *m* (–) namesake
Napf *m* ("e) bowl
Narbe *f* (-n) scar
narkotisch narcotic
Narr *m* (-en) fool; **zum -en haben** make a fool of
närrisch foolish
Narzisse *f* (-n) daffodil
naschen eat titbits
Näscherei *f*, **naschhaft** eating dainties on the sly
Nase *f* (-n) nose; **-nloch** *n* nostril; **-nschleim** *m* mucus; **naseweis** saucy
näseln speak through the nose
Nashorn *n* ("er) rhinoceros
nass wet
Nässe *f* humidity
nasskalt damp and cold
Nation *f* (-en) nation
Nationalflagge *f* (-n) national flag
Natron *n* soda; **doppelt kohlensaures -** bicarbonate of soda
Natter *f* (-n) adder
Natur *f* (-en) nature; **-erscheinung** *f* phenomenon; **-forscher** *m* naturalist; **-lehre** *f* natural philosophy; **-schutz** *m* national trust; **-wissenschaften** *f pl* natural science
Naturaliensammlung *f* natural history collection
naturalisieren naturalize
natürlich natural; of course
nautisch nautical
Neapel Naples

Nebel *m* (-) fog
nebelig foggy
neben by the side of, beside; **-an** close by, next door; **-bei** by the way
Neben-arbeit *f* extra work; **-buhler** *m* rival; **-einnahmen** *f pl* perquisites; **-fluss** *m* tributary river; **-gleis** *n* side-track; **-mensch** *m* fellow-creature; **-produkt** *n* by-product; **-sache** *f* trifle; **-sächlich** subordinate; **-strasse** *f* by-street; **-zimmer** *n* adjoining room
nebst in addition to
Necessaire *n* (-s) dressing-case
necken tease
Neffe *m* (-n) nephew
negativ, Negativ *n* (-e) negative (photo)
Neger *m* (-) negro
nehmen take; capture
Neid *m* envy
neidisch envious
neigen incline
Neigung *f* (-en) inclination
nein no
Nelke *f* (-n) carnation, clove
nennen name; call
nennenswert worth mentioning
Nenner *m* (-) denominator
Nennwert *m* (-e) nominal value
Nerv *m* (-en) nerve
Nervenschwäche *f*, **Nervosität** *f* nervousness
nervig, nervös nervy
Nessel *f* (-n) nettle
Nest *n* (-er) nest
nett neat; nice
netto net
Nettopreis *m* (-e) net price
Netz *n* (-e) net; rack
Netzhaut *f* retina
netzen wet, moisten
neu new; **von -em** anew
neuere modern
neuerdings lately
Neuerer *m* innovator
Neuerung *f* (-en) innovation
Neu-fundland *n* Newfoundland; **-geboren** new-born; **-gier** *f* curiosity; **-gierig** curious; **-heit** *f* novelty; **-igkeit** *f* news; **-lich**

late(ly); **-ling** *m* novice; **-jahrsgeschenk** *n* New Year's gift; **-modisch** new fashioned; **-mond** *m* new moon; **-schottland** Nova Scotia; **-seeland** New Zealand; **-zeit** *f* modern times
neun nine
neutral neutral
Neutrum *n* neuter
nicht not; **-raucher** *m* non-smoker
Nichte *f* (-n) niece
nichtig null, void
nichts nothing; **-destoweniger** nevertheless; **-würdig** vile
Nickel *n* (-) nickel
nicken nod
nie never; **nieder** down
niedere low; inferior
Nieder-druckmaschine *f* low-pressure engine; **-gang** *m* decline; **-geschlagen** dejected; **-knien** kneel down; **-kommen** be confined; **-kunft** *f* confinement; **-lage** *f* defeat; warehouse; **-lande** *n pl* Netherlands; **-lassen** establish; **-lassung** *f* establishment; **sich -legen** lie down; **-reissen** pull down; **-schlag** *m* deposit; **-trächtig** mean; **-ung** *f* lowland
niedlich neat; pretty
niedrig low
niemals never
niemand nobody
Niere *f* (-n) kidney; **-nbraten** *m* roast loin
niesen sneeze
Niessbrauch *m* usufruct
Niet *n* (-en), **nieten** rivet
Niete *f* (-n) blank (in lottery, etc.)
Nihilist *m* (-en) nihilist
Nil *m* Nile
Nilpferd *n* (-e) hippopotamus
nimmermehr never more
nippen sip; **Nippsachen** *pl* knick-knacks
nirgends nowhere
Nische *f* (-n) niche
nisten nest
Niveau *n*, **nivellieren** level

Nizza Nice
noch still; yet
nochmals again
nominell nominal
Nonne f (**-n**) nun
Nord(en) m north; **-licht** n aurora borealis; **-see** f North Sea; **-west** north-west; **nordisch, nördlich** northern
nörgeln grumble, nag
normal normal
Norwegen Norway
Not f (¨e) necessity; distress; want; **-ausgang** m emergency-door; **-bremse** f communication cord; **-brücke** f temporary bridge; **-dürftig** scanty; **-fall** m case of need; **-landung** f forced landing; **-leidend** needy; **-signal** n signal of distress; **-wehr** f self-defence; **-wendig** necessary; **-wendigkeit** f necessity; **-zucht** f rape; **-züchtigen** ravish
Notar m (**-e**) notary
Note f (**-n**), **notieren** note
Notenpapier n music-paper
nötig necessary; **- haben** want
nötigen force; compel
Notizbuch n (¨er) note-book
notorisch notorious
Novelle f (**-n**) short story
November m November
Nu m instant, trice; **im Nu** in a flash
nüchtern sober
Nudeln f pl macaroni
Null f (**-en**) zero
numerieren, Nummer f (**-n**) number
nun now; **von - an** henceforth
nur only
Nuss f (¨e) nut; **-baum** m walnut tree; **-kern** m kernel; **-knacker** m nut-cracker; **-schale** f nut-shell
Nüster f (**-n**) nostril
Nute f (**-n**) groove
nutz useful
Nutzen m use, profit
Nutzholz n timber
nützlich useful
nutzlos useless

Nützlichkeit f utility
Nutzniessung f usufruct
Nutzung f (**-en**) yield, produce
Nymphe f (**-n**) nymph

O

Oase f (**-n**) oasis
ob whether, if; **als - as if**
Obacht f heed, care
Obdach n shelter; lodging
Obelisk m (**-en**) obelisk
oben above; upstairs; **-drein** into the bargain
obenan in the first place
obenauf upon; above
ober upper, superior; **-arm** m upper-arm; **-bau** m superstructure; **-befehl** m chief command; **-fläche** f surface; **-flächlich** superficial; **-halb** above; **-hand** f upper hand; **-haupt** n head, chief; **-haus** n House of Lords; **-hemd** n dress-shirt; **-herrschaft** f supremacy; **-kellner** m head waiter; **-kiefer** (**-lippe** f) m upper jaw (lip); **-licht** n sky-light; **-schenkel** m thigh; **-stübchen** n attic; **-welt** f upper world
oberst uppermost; highest
Oberst m (**-en**) colonel; chief
obgleich though, although
Obhut f guard, care
obig above-mentioned
Objekt n (**-e**) object
Oblate f (**-n**) wafer
obliegend incumbent
obligatorisch compulsory
Obrigkeit f (**-en**) authorities
obschon though
Observatorium n (**-rien**) observatory
Obst n fruit; **-garten** m orchard; **-händler(in)** m (f) fruiterer; **-torte** f fruit-cake; **-wein** m cider
Ochse m (**-n**) ox; **-enfleisch** n beef; **-enschwanz** m ox-tail
Ode f (**-n**) ode; **öde** deserted
oder or

Ofen *m* (⁻) stove; oven; furnace; kiln; **-röhre** *f* flue; **-schirm** *m* fire-screen

offen open; frank; **-bar** evident; **-baren** manifest; **Offenbarung** *f* revelation; **Offenheit** *f* frankness

Offensive *f* (-n), **offensiv** offensive

öffentlich public

Öffentlichkeit *f* publicity

offerieren, Offerte *f* (-n) offer

offiziell official

Offizier *m* (-e) officer

öffnen open

Öffnung *f* (-en) opening

oft, oftmals often

Oheim, Ohm *m* (-e) uncle

ohne without

ohnehin besides

Ohnmacht *f* (-en) swoon; unconsciousness

ohnmächtig, -werden faint

Ohr *n* (-en) ear; **-feige** *f* box on the ear; **-läppchen** *n* lobe of the ear; **-ring** *m* ear-ring; **-enschmalz** *n* ear-wax; **-enschmerz** *m* ear-ache

Oktav *n,* **-band** *m* octavo

Oktave *f* (-n) octave

Oktober *m* October

Okzident *m* occident

Öl *n* (-e), **ölen** oil; **ölig** oily; **-baum** *m* olive-tree; **-berg** *m* Mount of Olives; **-bild** *n* oil-painting; **-druckbild** *n* chromo-lithography

Oleander *m* (-) oleander

Olive *f* (-n) olive

Ölung (letzte) *f* oiling; extreme unction

Omnibus *m* (-se) omnibus, bus

Onkel *m* (-) uncle

Opal *m* (-e) opal

Oper *f* (-n) opera; opera-house; **-ngucker** *m* opera-glass; **-ntext** *m* libretto

operieren operate

Opfer *n* (-), **opfern** sacrifice; **-tier** victim; **-gabe, -ung** *f* offering; **-kasten, -stock** *m* poor-box

Opium *n* opium

opponieren oppose

Opposition *f* (-en) opposition

Optik *f* optics

Optiker *m* (-) optician

optische Täuschung *f* (-en) optical illusion

Orakel(spruch) *n* (*m*) oracle

Orange *f* (-n) orange

Oratorium *n* (-rien) oratorio

Orchester *n* (-) orchestra

Orchidee *f* (-n) orchid

Orden *m* (-) order; decoration

ordentlich orderly

ordinieren ordain

ordnen arrange

Ordnung *f* (-en) order; **-smässig** orderly; **-swidrig** irregular

Ordonnanz *f* (-en) orderly; order

Organ *n* (-e) organ

organisch organic

organisieren organize

Organist *m* (-en) organist

Orgel *f* (-n) organ (music); **-spieler** *m* (-) organist; **-zug** *m* (⁻e) organ stop

Orient *m* Orient; East

orientieren find out one's bearings

originell, Original *n* (-e) original

Orkan *m* (-e) hurricane

Ornat *m* (-e) official robes

Ort *m* (⁻er) place; **örtlich** local

Orthographie *f* orthography

orthographisch orthographical

Ortsverkehr *m* local traffic

Ortszeit *f* local time

Öse *f* (-n) eye, loop

Ost, Osten *m* east; **-indien** *n* India, the East Indies; **-see** *f* Baltic; **-wärts** eastward; **-wind** *m* east wind

Ostern *pl* Easter

Österreich *n* Austria

Österreicher *m* Austrian

Otter *m* (-) otter

Otter *f* (-n) viper

Ouvertüre *f* (-n) overture

oval oval

Oxyd(o-ieren) *n* (-e) oxyd(iz)e

Ozean *m* (-e) ocean

Ozon *n* ozone

P

Paar *n* (-e), **paaren** pair; couple; -weise in pairs; **Paarungszeit** *f* pairing-time
Pacht(**kontrakt**) *f* (*m*) lease; -gut *n* farm; -zins *m*, **pachten** rent
Pächter *m* (-) farmer, tenant
Pack *n* rabble
Pack *m* (-e) packet, bale; -esel *m* drudge; -knecht *m* packer; -leinwand *f* packcloth; -pferd *n* pack-horse; -träger *m* porter; -wagen *m* luggage van
packen grasp, decamp; pack
Pädagog *m* (-en) pedagogue
Paddelboot *n* (-e) canoe
paffen whiff, puff
Paket *n* (-e) parcel; -annahmestelle *f* parcel-office; -boot *n* packet-boat
Palast *m* (¨e) palace
Palme *f* (-n) palm; **Palmsonntag** *m* Palm-Sunday; -zweig *m* palm-branch
Pampelmuse *f* (-n) grapefruit
Panier *n* (-e) banner
panisch panic
Panne *f* (-n) break-down
Panther *m* (-) panther
Pantoffel *m* (-n) slipper
Pantomime *f* (-n) pantomime
Panzer *m* (-) armour; armour-plated tank; -abteilung *f* tank-battalion; -hemd *n* mail-shirt; -platte *f* armour-plate; -schiff *n* iron-clad; -tier *n* armadillo
Papa *m* (-s) papa
Papagei *m* (-en) parrot
Papier *n* (-e) paper; -fabrik *f* paper mill; -handlung *f* stationery-shop; -korb *m* waste-paper basket
Pappe *f* (-n) pasteboard; paste
Pappel *f* (-n) poplar
Papst *m* (¨e) pope
Papsttum *n* papacy
Papstwürde *f* papacy
päpstlich papal
Paradeplatz *m* (¨e) parade-ground
Paradies *n* (-e) paradise

parallel parallel
Parasit *m* (-en) parasite
Parfüm *n* (-e), **parfümieren** perfume
pari (at) par
parieren parry
Pariser *m* Parisian
Park *m* (-e) park
Parkett *n* (-e) inlaid floor; stalls
Parlament *n* (-e) parliament
parlamentarisch parliamentary
Partei *f* (-en) party; -gänger *m* partisan; -lichkeit *f* partiality
parteilich partial
parteilos impartial
Parterre *n* (-s) ground-floor; pit
Partie *f* (-n) party; game; excursion; match
Partitur *f* (-en) score
Parzelle *f* (-n) lot; allotment
Pass *m* (¨e) pass; passport
Passagier *m* (-e) passenger
Passatwind *m* trade-wind
passen fit; suit
passieren pass; happen
Passierschein *m* (-e) pass
Passion *f* (-en) passion
Passkontrolle *f* passport examination
Pastete *f* (-n) pie
Pastille *f* (-n) lozenge
Pastor *m* (-en) clergyman
Pate *m*, *f* (-n) godfather; godmother
Patent *n* (-e), **patentieren** patent
Patient *m* (-en) patient
Patriot(**ismus**) *m* (-en) patriot(ism)
patriotisch patriotic
Patrone *f* (-n) cartridge
Patrouille *f* (-n) patrol
Patsch *m* (-e) smack; slab
Patsche *f* (-n) puddle, scrape
Pauke *f* (-n) kettledrum
Pause *f* (-n), **pausieren** pause
Pauspapier *n* tracing-paper
Pavian *m* (-e) baboon
Pech *n* (-e) pitch; ill luck
Pedant *m* (-en), **p-isch** pedant(ic)
Pegel *m* (-) water-gauge
Pein *f*, **peinigen** torment
peinlich painful
Peitsche *f* (-n), **peitschen** whip

Pellkartoffeln *f pl* potatoes in their jackets
Pelz *m* (-e) fur
Pendel *n* (-) pendulum
Pension *f* (-en) pension, board; -at *n* boarding-school; **Pensionär** *m* pensioner; boarder
pensionieren pension
Pensum *n* (-en) task; course
Pergament *n* (-e) parchment
Periode *f* (-n) period
Perle *f* (-n) pearl; bead; **Perlhuhn** *n* guinea-fowl; **Perlmutter** *f* mother-of-pearl
perlen sparkle
Persien *n* Persia; **Perser** *m* Persian
Person *f* (-en) person; **-al** *n* staff; **-enwagen** *m* passenger-carriage (-train); **-enaufzug** *m* lift; **persönlich** personal
Personenzug *m* (-̈e) slow train
Perspektive *f* (-n) perspective
Perücke *f* (-n) wig
Pest *f* (-en) plague
Petersilie *f* parsley
Petroleum *n* petroleum
Petschaft *n* (-e) seal
Pfad *m* (-e) path
Pfahl *m* (-̈e) pile; post
Pfalz *f* Palatinate
Pfand *n* (-̈er) pawn; **-haus** *n* pawn-shop; **-leiher** *m* pawnbroker; **Pfänderspiel** *n* game of forfeits
Pfänden seize (as a pledge)
Pfändung *f* (-en) seizure
Pfanne *f* (-n) pan; **Pfannkuchen** *m* pancake
Pfarrei *f* (-en) parish; **Pfarrhaus** *n* parsonage; **Pfarrer** *m* clergyman, parson
Pfau *m* (-en) peacock
Pfeffer *m*, **pfeffern** pepper; **-büchse** *f* pepper-box; **-gurke** *f* gherkin; **-kuchen** *m* gingerbread; **-minz plätzchen** *n* peppermint drop
Pfeife *f* (-en), **pfeifen** whistle; pipe
Pfeil *m* (-e) arrow
Pfeiler *m* (-) pillar
Pferch *m* (-e), **pferchen** fold

Pferd *n* (-e) horse
Pferde-bahn *f* tramway, horse tram; **-knecht** *m* groom; **-kraft** *f* horse-power; **-rennen** *n* horse race; **-stärke** *f* horse-power
Pfiff *m* (-e) whistle (sound)
pfiffig cunning, sly
Pfingsten *pl* Whitsuntide
Pfirsich *m* (-e) peach
Pflanze *f* (-n), **pflanzen** plant; **-nreich** *n* vegetable kingdom; **-r** planter
Pflanzung *f* (-en) plantation
Pflaster *n* (-) pavement; plaster; **englisches** court-plaster
pflastern pave
Pflaume *f* (-n) plum
Pflaumenmus *n* plum jam
Pflege *f* nursing
Pflegekind *n* (-er) foster-child
pflegen take care of; nurse; be accustomed to
Pfleger(in) *m* (*f*) nurse
Pflicht *f* (-en) duty
Pflock *m* (-̈e), **pflocken** peg
pflücken gather; pluck
Pflug *m* (-̈e), **pflügen** plough
Pforte *f* (-n) gate
Pförtner *m* (-) porter
Pfosten *m* (-) post
Pfote *f* (-n) paw
Pfropfen *m* (-) stopper; cork; **-zieher** *m* cork-screw
pfropfen cork; graft
Pfründe *f* (-n) benefice
pfui ! fie ! for shame !
Pfund *n* (-e) pound
pfuschen bungle; cheat
Pfuscher *m* (-) bungler
Pfütze *f* (-n) puddle
Phantasie *f* (-n) fancy
phantasieren wander; rave
Philologe *m* (-n) philologist
Philologie *f* philology
Philosoph *m* (-en) philosopher
Philosophie *f* (-n) philosophy
Phiole *f* (-n) phial
phlegmatisch phlegmatic
Phonetik *f* phonetics
phonetisch phonetic
Phonograph *m* (-en) phonograph
Phosphor *m* (-e) phosphorus

Photograph *m* (-en) photographer; -ie *f*, -ieren photograph
Phrase *f* (-n) phrase
Physik *f* natural philosophy
Pickel *m* (-) pimple
picken peck
Picknick *n* picnic
piepen chirp
Pik *n* (cards) spade
Pilger *m* (-) pilgrim
Pilgerfahrt *f* (-en) pilgrimage
Pille *f* (-n) pill
Pilz *m* (-e) mushroom, fungus
Pinguin *m* (-e) penguin
Pinne *f* (-n) peg, tack
Pinsel *m* (-), pinseln brush
Pionier *m* (-e) pioneer
pissen urinate, piss
Pistole *f* (-n) pistol
Plage *f* (-n) plague, torment
plagen torment; sich - drudge
Plaid *n* (-s) plaid; rug
Plakat *n* (-e) placard; poster
Plan *m* (¨e), planen plan
Planet *m* (-en) planet
Planke *f* (-n) plank
planmässig scheduled
plappern babble
plastisch plastic
Platane *f* (-n) plane-tree
Platin *n* platinum
plätschern splash
platt flat; plain
Platte *f* (-n) plate; slab
plätten iron
Plätteisen *n* (-) flat-iron
Plätterin *f* (-nen) ironer
Platz *m* (¨e) place; square; seat
platzen burst
Platzregen *m* downpour
Plauderei *f*, plaudern talk, chat
plombieren stop teeth
plötzlich sudden
plump clumsy
Plunder *m* lumber, rubbish
plündern plunder
Plüsch *m* plush
Pneumatik *f* pneumatics
Pöbel *m* mob
pöbelhaft vulgar
pochen knock; boast

Pocken *f pl* small-pox; -narbe *f* pock-mark
Poesie *f* (-n) poetry; poem
poetisch poetic
Pokal *m* (-e) goblet; cup; trophy
Pökelfleisch *n* salt meat
Pökel *m* brine; -n pickle
Pol *m* (-e) pole
Pole *m* (-n) Pole
Polen *n* Poland
Police *f* (-n) policy
polieren, Politur *f* (-en) polish
Politik *f* politics
Politiker *m* (-) politician
politisch politic(al)
politisieren talk politics
Polizei *f* police
Polizist *m* (-en) policeman
Polster *n* bolster; cushion; -möbel *pl* upholstery
polstern stuff
Pomade *f* (-n) pomade, pomatum
Pomp *m* pomp
pomphaft pompous
Ponton *m* (-s) pontoon
Pony *m* and *n* (-s) pony
Popularität *f* popularity
Pore *f* (-n) pore; porös porous
Portal *n* (-e) porch
Portier *m* (-s) porter
Porto *n* postage
Porträt *n* (-e) portrait
Portwein *m* port
Porzellan *n* china
Posaune *f* (-n) trombone
positiv, Positiv *n* positive
Posse *f* (-n) burlesque; farce
possenhaft burlesque, farcical
possierlich droll
Post *f* (-en) post; -amt *n* post-office; -anweisung *f* money-order; -fachnummer *f* box-number; -karte *f* postcard; -karte mit Antwort double postcard; -lagernd to be called for; -paket *n* postal parcel; -scheck *m* postal order; -verein *m* postal union; -zug *m* mail-train
Postament *n* (-e) pedestal
Posten *m* (-), postieren post
Pottasche *f* potash
Pracht *f* splendour

prachtvoll, prächtig splendid
prägen coin
prahlen boast
Prahler m (-) boaster
praktisch practical
Prämie f (-n) premium; prize
Pranger m (-) pillory
Pranke f (-n) paw; claw; clutch
Präsentierteller m (-) tray
Präsident m (-en) chairman; president
prassen lead a gay life
Praxis f practice
präzis, precise, exact
Präzedenzfall m (-e) precedent
predigen preach
Prediger m (-) preacher
Predigt f (-en) sermon
Preis m (-e) price; prize; **-bewerbung** f competition; **-liste** f price list
preisen praise
Preisselbeere f (-n) whortleberry
prellen cheat
Premierminister m prime minister, premier
Presse f (-n), **pressen** press; **-freiheit** f liberty of the press; **Presskohle** f (-n) briquette
Preussen n Prussia; **Preusse** m, **preussisch** Prussian
priemen chew tobacco
Priester m (-) priest
Prima f highest; sixth form
prima prime, first-class
Primel f (-n) primrose
Prinz m (-en) prince
Prinzessin f (-nen) princess
Prinzip n (-ien) principle
Prinzipal m (-e) master, head
Prise f (-n) pinch of snuff; capture
privat private
Probe f (-n) trial; sample; rehearsal; **probieren** try
Problem n (-e) problem; **p-atisch** problematic
Produzent m (-en) producer
produzieren, Produkt n produce
Professor m (-en) professor
Profil n (-e) profile
Programm n (-e) programme

Prokurist m (-en) chief clerk
Proletarier m (-) proletarian
Promenade f (-n) promenade
Propaganda f propaganda
Propeller m (-) propeller
Prophet m (-en) prophet
prophetisch prophetic
prophezeien prophesy
Prophezeiung f (-en) prophecy
Prosa f prose
Prosaiker m (-) prose-writer
prosaisch prosaical
prosit! to your health!
Prospekt m (-e) prospectus
Protest m (-e), **protestieren** protest
Protestant (p-isch) Protestant
Protokoll n (-e) minutes pl; protocol
Proviant m (-e) provisions
Provinz f (-en) province
provisorisch provisional
Prozent n per cent.
Prozess m (-e) process; lawsuit
Prozession f (-en) procession
prüfen examine
Prüfstein m touchstone
Prüfung f (-en) examination
prügeln cudgel, beat
Prunk m pomp
Psalm m (-e) psalm; **-ist** psalmist
Publikum n public
Pudding m (-s) pudding
Pudel m (-) poodle
Puder m powder; **-beutel** m powder-bag
Puffer m (-) buffer
Puls m (-e) pulse
Pulsader f (-n) artery
Pult n (-e) desk
Pulver n (-), **pulvern** powder; gunpowder; **-verschwörung** f gunpowder plot
Pumpe f (-n), **pumpen** pump; give or take on tick
Punkt m (-e) point; **pünktlich** punctual; **Pünktlichkeit** f punctuality
Punsch m (-e) punch
Puppe f (-n) doll, puppet; chrysalis

Purpur *m*, **purpurn** purple
purzeln tumble
pusten puff, blow; huff
Pute *f* (-n) turkey-hen
Puter *m* (-) turkey-cock
Putsch *m* (-e) revolt; unsuccessful rising
Putz *m* finery
Putzmacherin *f* (-nin) milliner
putzen clean, polish; wipe; adorn
putzig droll, funny
Pyramide *f* (-n) pyramid

Q

quabblig flabby
Quacksalber *m* (-) quack
Quadrat *n* (-e) square; **-fuss** *m* sq. foot; **-wurzel** *f* sq. root
Qual *f* (-en), **quälen** torment
Qualität *f* (-en) quality
Qualle *f* (-n) jelly fish
Qualm *m* smoke
Quantität *f* (-en), **Quantum** *n* (-s) quantity
Quark *m* curd, milk-cheese
Quartal *n* (-e) quarter of a year
Quartband *m* (-̈e) quarto volume
Quartett *n* (-e) quartet
Quartier *n* (-e) quarter(s)
Quarz *m* quartz
Quast *m* (-e) tassel, tuft
Quatsch *m* foolishness, twaddle, bosh
Quecke *f* (-n) couch-grass
Quecksilber *n* mercury
Quelle *f* (-n), **quellen** spring
Quendel *m* (-) wild thyme
quer cross, slanting
quetschen, Quetschung *f* (-en) bruise
quieken squeak
quirlen twirl
quitt quit; even
Quitte *f* (-n) quince
quittieren, Quittung *f* (-en) receipt
Quote *f* (-n) quota
quotieren quote (prices)

R

Rabatt *m* (-e) discount
Rabbiner *m* (-) rabbi
Rabe *m* (-n) raven; **-nmutter** *f* unnatural mother
Rache *f* revenge; **rächen** avenge
Rachen *m* (-) throat; jaws
Rad *n* (-̈er) wheel; cycle; **-dampfer** *m* paddle-steamer; **-eln** cycle; **-fahrbahn** *f* cycle-track; **-fahren** cycle; **-fahrer** *m* cyclist; **-kranz** *m* rim; **-reifen** *m* tyre; **-rennen** *n* bicycle-race
Radar *n* radar; **-anlage** *f* radar unit
radebrechen break on the wheel; speak a language imperfectly
Rädelsführer *m* (-) ringleader
radieren erase, etch
Radiergummi *m* (-s) eraser
Radierung *f* (-en) etching
Radieschen *n* (-) radish
Radio *n* radio, **-apparat** *m* wireless set
raffen snatch, sweep
raffiniert refined; artful
ragen project
Rahm *m* cream
Rahmen *m* (-) **rahmen** frame
Rakete *f* (-n) rocket
Ramme *f* (-n) pile-driver
rammeln ram, press, rut
Rampe *f* (-n) slope; platform
Ramsch (im) in the lump
Ramsch *m* (-e) job goods
Rand *m* (-̈er) edge; margin
Rang *m* (-̈e) rank
rangieren shunt
rank slender
Ranke *f* (-n) tendril
Ränke *pl* intrigues
Ranzen *m* (-) wallet; bag
ranzig rancid
Rappe *m* (-n) black horse
Rarität *f* (-en) curiosity
rar rare
rasch quick; brisk
rasen rage
Rasen *m* (-) turf; lawn
Rasenplatz *m* (-̈e) lawn
rasieren shave
Rasiermesser *n* (-) razor

Rasse *f* (-n) race; breed; **-nabsonderung** *f* racial segregation
rasseln rattle
rasten, Rast *f* rest
Rat *m* advice, counsel; council; **Ratgeber** *m* councillor; **-haus** *n* town hall; **-los** helpless; **-sam** advisable; **-schlag** *m* advice
Rate *f* (-n) instalment
raten (+ dat.) advise; guess
ratifizieren ratify
Rätsel *n* (-) riddle
rätselhaft enigmatic
Ratte *f* (-n) rat
Rattengift *n* ratsbane
Raub *m* (-e) robbery; prey; **-tier** *n* beast of prey; **rauben** rob; **Räuber** *m* robber; **räuberisch, raubgierig** rapacious
Rauch *m*, **rauchen, räuchern** smoke; **-abteil** *n* smoking-compartment; **-fleisch** *n* smoked meat; **-los** smokeless; **-er** *m* smoker; **-ig** smoky; **-werk** *n* furs
räudig mangy; scabby
rauh rough; raw
Raum *m* (ˈ-e) space, room, hold
räumen clear, leave
Rauminhalt *m* volume
Räumlichkeit *f* locality
Raupe *f* (-n) caterpillar
Rausch *m* (ˈ-e) intoxication
rauschen rustle; roar
räuspern (sich) clear one's throat
realisieren realise
Reb-huhn *n* partridge; **-stock** *m*, **Rebe** *f* (-n) vine
Rebell *m* (-en) **rebellieren** rebel
Rechen *m* (-) rake
Rechenschaft *f*, **ablegen** render an account; **zur - ziehen** call to account
rechnen calculate; count
Rechnung *f* (-en) account; invoice
Recht *n* (-e) **recht** right; **- haben** be right; **-eck** *n* rectangle; **-schreibung** *f* orthography; **-eckig, -winklig** rectangular; **-fertigen** justify; **-mässig** leg-

al; **-schaffen** honest; **rechts on** (to) the right; **-sanwalt** *m* solicitor, barrister; **-sgelehrter** *m* lawyer; **-spflege** *f* administration of justice; **-sstreit** *m* lawsuit; **-swidrig** illegal
Rechte *f* right hand
recken stretch
Redakteur *m* (-e) editor
Rede *f* (-n) speech; **reden** speak; **Redensart** *f* expression; **Redner** *m* orator; **redselig** talkative
redlich honest
Redlichkeit *f* honesty
Reede *f* (-n) roadstead (harbour)
Reeder *m* (-) shipowner
Reform(ation) *f* reform(ation)
Regal *n* (-e) book-shelf
Regatta *f* (-en) regatta
rege lively
Regel *f* (-n) rule; **-mässig, -mässigkeit** *f* regular(ity)
regeln regulate
Regen *m* rain; **-bogen** *m* rainbow; **-guss** *m* shower; **-mantel** *m* waterproof; **-schirm** *m* umbrella; **-wetter** *n* rainy weather; **-wurm** *m* earth-worm
Regent *m* (-en) regent
Regentschaft *f* regency
regieren govern; reign
Regierung *f* (-en) government; reign
Regiment *n* (-e) regiment
Register *n* (-) register; record
registrieren register
regulieren regulate
regnen rain
regnerisch rainy
Reh *n* (-e) roe; **-bock** roebuck
Rehbraten *m* roast-venison
reiben rub
Reibung *f* (-en) friction
reich, -haltig rich
Reich *n* (-e) empire; kingdom
reichen reach; hand; suffice
reichlich copious
Reichtum *m* (ˈ-er) riches; wealth
reif ripe; **reifen** ripen
Reif *m* hoarfrost; circle
Reife *f* maturity
Reifen *m* (-) hoop, tyre
Reihe *f* (-n) row; rank

Reihenfolge f succession
Reiher m (-) heron
Reim m (-e), **reimen** rhyme
rein pure; clean; **Reinheit** f purity; **reinigen** clean; **reinlich** cleanly
Reinlichkeit f cleanliness
Reis m (uo pl.) rice; n (-er) twig
Reise f (-n) journey; voyage; **-anzug** m travelling suit; **-handbuch** n traveller's guide; **-decke** f rug; **-gepäck** n luggage; **-koffer** m trunk; **-korb** m dress-basket; **-necessaire** n dressing-case; **-pass** m pass-port; **-scheck** m traveller's cheque; **-tasche** f portmanteau; **-zeit** f tourist season
reisen travel
Reisende m (adj. noun) traveller
Reisig n brushwood, faggots
Reisige m soldier, warrior
Reissbrett n (-er) drawing-board
reissen tear
reissend rapid; rapacious
Reisszeug n mathematical instrument case
reiten ride; **Reiter** m horseman; **Reiterstandbild** n equestrian statue
Reiterei f cavalry
Reitpeitsche f (-n) riding-whip
reizen, Reiz m (-e) charm; irritate
reizend charming
Reizmittel n (-) stimulant
rekeln (sich) loll
Reklame f (-n) advertisement
reklamieren protest; claim
rekognoszieren reconnoitre
Rekrut m (-en), **rekrutieren** recruit
Rektor m (-en) rector, principal, headmaster
Relief n (-s) relief
Religion f (-en) religion
religiös religious
Reling f (-en) rail
Reliquie f (-n) relic
Remise f (-n) coach-house
Remonte f (-n) new horse, re-mount
rempeln jostle
Rendant m (-en) accountant

Renegat m (-en) renegade
Rennbahn f (-en) racecourse
Rennen n (-) race
rennen run, race
Renner m (-) racer
Rennpferd n (-e) racehorse
Renntier n (-e) reindeer
renommieren boast; brag
Rente f (-n) pension, income
rentieren pay
Reparatur f (-en), **reparieren** repair
Repetieruhr f (-en) repeater
Reporter m (-) reporter
Repressalie f (-n) reprisal
Reptil n (-e) reptile
Republik f (-en) republic
Reserve f (-n) reserve
reservieren reserve
Residenz f (-en) residence
Respekt(voll) m (-e) respect(ful)
Rest m (-e) rest, remainder
Restaurant n (-s) restaurant
Resultat n (-e) result
retten save
Rettich m (-e) radish
Rettung f (-en) rescue
Rettungsboot n (-e) lifeboat
Reue f repentance
Reuegeld n (-er) forfeit
Revolution f (-en) revolution
Revolver m (-) revolver
Revue f (-n) review
rezensieren, Rezension f (-en) review
Rezept n (-e) prescription, recipe
Rhabarber m rhubarb
Rhein m Rhine
Rheinwein m hock
Rheumatismus m rheumatism
richten direct, pass sentence, judge
Richter m (-) judge
richtig right; correct
Richtschnur f ("e) line; rule
Richtung f (-en) direction
riechen smell
Riechfläschchen n (-) smelling bottle
Ried n (-e) reed, bog
Riegel m (-) bolt, bar
Riemen m (-) strap
Ries n (-e) ream

Riese *m* (-n) giant; **-nschlange** *f* boa

rieseln flow; drizzle

riesig gigantic

Riff *n* (-e) reef

Rind *n* (-er) heifer; **-fleisch** *n* beef; **-vieh** *n* cattle; **-erbraten** *m* roast beef

Rinde *f* (-n) bark

Ring(finger) *m* (-e) ring(-finger)

ringen wrestle; wring

Ringkampf *m* (-̈e) wrestling match

rings, -um (a) round

Rinne *f* (-n) channel; gutter

rinnen flow; leak

Rinnstein *m* (-e) gutter

Rippe *f* (-n), rib; **-nfellentzündung** *f* pleurisy

Risiko *n* (-s), **riskieren** risk

Riss *m* (-e) rent, split, schism

Ritt *m* (-e) ride; **-er** *m* knight

ritterlich chivalrous

rittlings astride

Rittmeister *m* (—) captain (cavalry)

Ritze *f* (-n) fissure; **ritzen** scratch

Rivalität *f* (-en) rivalry

Rizinusöl *n* castor-oil

Robbe *f* (-n) seal

Robe *f* (-n) gown

Rock *m* skirt; coat; gown

Roggen *m* rye

roh raw; rude

Roheisen *n* pig-iron

Roheit *f* rudeness

Rohr *n* (-e), **Röhre** *f* (-n) tube; pipe; **-stock** *m* cane; **-stuhl** *m* cane-bottomed chair; **-zucker** *m* cane-sugar

Rolle *f* (-n) roll(er); pulley; mangle; part (play)

rollen roll; mangle

Roller *m* (—) scooter

Rollschuh *m* (-e) roller-skate

Rollwagen *m* (—) dray, truck

Roman *m* (-e) novel

romantisch romantic

Römer (—), **römisch** Roman

rosa rose-coloured

Rose *f* (-n) rose; **-nkohl** *m* Brussel sprouts; **-nkranz** *m* rosary, beads; **-nstock** *m* rosebush

Rosette *f* (-n) rosette

Rosine *f* (-n) raisin

Rosmarin *m* (-e) rosemary

Ross *n* (-e) horse

Rost *m*, **rosten** rust

Rost *m* (-e) grate; grill

rösten roast, grill, fry

rostig rusty

Rot *n*, **rot** red; **-glühend** red-hot; **-haarig** red-haired; **-kehlchen** *n* robin; **-kohl** *m* red cabbage; **Röte** *f* redness; **röten** redden; **rötlich** reddish

Rotte *f* (-n) gang; file

Rübe *f* (-n) (weisse) turnip; - (rote) beetroot; **-nzucker** *m* beet-sugar

Rubin *m* (-e) ruby

ruchbar notorious

ruchlos villainous

Ruck *m* (-e) jerk, sudden push

Rückberufung *f* recall; **-blick** *m* retrospect; **-datieren** antedate; **-erinnerung** *f* reminiscence; **-fahrt** *f* return-journey; **-fahrkarte** *f* return-ticket; **-fall** *m* relapse, reversion; **-gabe** *f* restitution; **-gang** *m* return, decline; **-gängig** retrograde; **-grat** *n* spine, backbone; **-halt** *m* support; **-kauf** *m* repurchase; **-kehr** *f*, **-kunft** *f* return; **r-lings** backward(s); **-ruf** *m* recall; **-schreiben** *n* reply; **-schritt** *m* step back, reaction; **-seite** *f* reverse; **-sicht** *f* regard, consideration; **-sichtslos** ruthless, uncouth; **-sitz** *m* back-seat; **-sprache** *f* conference, consultation; **-ständig** still due; **-stoss** *m* recoil; **-tritt** *m* retirement, resignation; **-versichern** reinsure; **-wärts** backward(s); **-wirkung** *f* reaction; **-zug** *m* retreat

rücken move, draw

Rücken *m* (—) back; **-mark** *n* spinal cord

Ruder *n* (—) oar; **-er** *m* rower; **rudern** row; **-sport** *m* boating, rowing; **-wettfahrt** *f* boat-race

Ruf *m* (-e), **rufen** call, cry; **guter-** good reputation

Rüge f (-n), **rügen** reprimand
Ruhe f (-n), **ruhen** rest, repose
Ruhebett n (-en) couch; **-gehalt** n pension; **-stand** m retirement
ruhig quiet; silent
Ruhm m glory
rühmen praise, boast
rühmlich glorious
Ruhr f (-en) dysentery
Rührei n scrambled eggs
rühren stir; touch
rührig active; nimble
Rührung f (-en) emotion
Ruin m (-e), **ruinieren** ruin; **die Ruine** f (-n) ruin (building)
rülpsen belch
Rum m rum
Rumpelkammer f lumber-room
Rumpf m (-̈e) trunk; hull
rümpfen (**Nase**) turn up
rund round
Runde f (-n) round; circle
runden (grow) round; rounding off
Rundfunk m broadcasting
Rundreise (**fahrkarte**) f (-n) circular tour (ticket)
Rundschreiben n (-) circular (letter)
Rundung f (-en) roundness
rundweg roundly, plainly
Runkelrübe f (-n) mangel-wurzel
Runzel f (-n), **runzeln** wrinkle; **runzelig** wrinkled
rupfen pluck, fleece
ruppig shabby, paltry
Russ m soot; **russig** sooty
Russe m (-n) Russian
Rüssel m (-) trunk; snout
Russland n Russia
rüsten arm
rüstig alert
Rüstung f (-n) armour, armament
Rute f (-n) rod
rutschen glide, slide, skid
rütteln shake; winnow

S

Saal m (**Säle**) hall; room
Saat f (-en) seed(s), young crops; **-korn** n seed-corn; **-krähe** f rook

Säbel m (-), **säbeln** sabre
Sache f (-n) thing; affair
sachlich real, objective
sächlich neuter
sacht soft; gentle
sachverständig expert
Sack m (-̈e), **sacken** sack; bag; **-gasse** f blind alley; **-leinwand** f sack-cloth
säen sow
Saffian m morocco
Saft m (-̈e) juice; **saftig** juicy
Sage f (-n) legend
Säge f (-n) **sägen** saw; **-späne** pl sawdust; **-mühle** f sawmill
sagen say; tell; **- lassen** send word
Sago m sago
Sahne f cream
Saite f (-n) string (violin, etc.)
Sakristei f (-en) vestry
Salat m (-e) salad; **-schüssel** f salad-bowl
Salbe f (-n) ointment
Salbei f sage
salben anoint
Saldo m (-di), **saldieren** balance
Salm m (-e) salmon
Salon m (-s) drawing-room; **-dampfer** m saloon-steamer; **-fähig** presentable
Saltpeter m saltpetre
Salut m (-e) salute
Salve f (-n) volley
Salz n (-e), **salzen**, **salzig** salt; **-fass** n salt-cellar; **-säure** f hydrochloric acid
Samen m seed
sammeln collect
Sammler m (-) collector
Sammlung f (-en) collection
Samstag m Saturday
Samt m velvet
sämtlich all; complete
Sand m (-e) sand; **-bank** f sand-bank; **-uhr** f hour-glass
Sandale f (-n) sandal
sandig sandy
sanft, **-mütig** gentle
Sang m (-̈e) song
Sänger m (-) singer
Sanitäter m (-) medical orderly
Sankt Saint

Saphir *m* (-e) sapphire
Sardelle *f* (-n) anchovy
Sardine *f* (-n) sardine
Sarg *m* (⸚e) coffin
sarkastisch sarcastic
Satan *m* Satan
Satellit *m* (-en) satellite
satiniert glazed
Satire *f* (-n) satire
satirisch satirical
satt satisfied
Sattel *m* (⸚), **satteln** saddle
sättigen satisfy; saturate
Sattler *m* (-) saddler
Satz *m* (⸚e) sentence; leap; sediment; composition
Satzung *f* (-en) statute
Sau *f* (⸚e) sow
sauber, säubern clean
Saubohne *f* (-n) broad bean
Sauce *f* (-n) sauce; gravy
sauer sour
Sauerampfer *m* (-) sorrel
säuerlich sourish
Sauerstoff *m* oxygen
saufen drink (animals); drink to excess
Säufer *m* (-) habitual drunkard
Säugamme *f* (-n) wet-nurse
saugen, säugen suck; suckle
Säugetier *n* (-e) mammal
Säule *f* (-n) column; **-ngang** *m* colonnade; **-nhalle** *f* portico
Saum *m* (⸚e) seam, hem
saumselig, säumig tardy, negligent
säumen hem; delay
Säure *f* (-n) acid
sausen whiz, buzz
Schabe *f* (-n) cockroach
schaben scrape
Schab-eisen *n* (-), **-messer** *n* (-) scraper
Schabernack *m* (-e) practical joke, trick
schäbig shabby
Schablone *f* (-n) pattern
Schach *n* chess; **-brett** *n* chessboard
schachern haggle
Schacht *m* (⸚e) shaft
Schachtel *f* (-n) box
Schädel *m* (-) skull

Schaden *m*, **schaden, schädigen** damage, harm; **-ersatz** *m* indemnity; **-froh** malicious
schadhaft damaged
schädlich injurious
Schaf *n* (-e) sheep; ewe; **-skopf** *m* blockhead
Schäfer *m* (-) shepherd; **-hund** *m* sheepdog
schaffen do, make
Schaffner *m* (-) guard; conductor
Schafott *n* (-e) scaffold
Schaft *m* (⸚e) shaft, legging
Schakal *m* (-e) jackal
Schäker *m* (-) jester
schäkern jest
schal stale; flat; insipid
Schale *f* (-n) shell; peel; scale; husk; cup, bowl, dish
schälen shell, peel
Schalk *m* (⸚e) wag; rogue
Schall *m* (-e), **-platte** *f* record; **schallen** sound
Schalter *m* (-) booking-office; **-beamte** *m* (adj. noun) booking-clerk
Schaltjahr *n* (-e) leap year
Schaluppe *f* (-n) sloop
Scham *f* shame; privy parts; **s-haft** bashful; **-los** impudent; **-rot** blushing
schämen (sich) be ashamed
Schande *f* (-n) shame; disgrace
schänden dishonour, rape
Schandfleck *m* blemish
schändlich disgraceful; infamous
Schar *f* (-en) troop, crowd
scharen (sich) assemble
scharf sharp; **Scharfblick** *m* penetration; **scharfsinnig** sagacious; **Schärfe** *f* sharpness, (Schneide) edge
schärfen sharpen
Scharlach *m* scarlet
Scharmützel *n* (-) skirmish
Scharnier *n* (-e) hinge
Schärpe *f* (-n) scarf, sash
scharren scrape
Scharte *f* (-n) notch; gap
Schatten *m* (-) shadow; shade; **-riss** *m* silhouette; **-seite** *f* drawback
schattieren shade

schattig shady

Schatulle f (-n) cash-box

Schatz m (¨e) treasure

schätzen esteem; **ab-** estimate

Schätzung f (-en) estimate

Schau f (-en) show; exhibition; **-fenster** n shop-front; **-platz** m scene; **-spiel** n spectacle, play; **-spieler** m actor; **-spielhaus** n theatre

Schauder m (-), **schaudern** shudder

schauderhaft horrible

schauen see; look

Schauer m (-) awe; fit; shower

schauern shudder, shiver

Schaufel f (-n), **schaufeln** shovel

Schaufelrad n (¨er) paddle-wheel

Schaukel f (-n) swing; see-saw; **-stuhl** m rocking-chair

schaukeln swing; rock

Schaum m, **schäumen** foam; froth; **-gummi** m sponge-rubber; **-wein** m champagne

Scheck m (-s) cheque

scheckig spotted

Scheffel m (-) bushel

Scheibe f (-n) disk: pane; slice; target

Scheide f (-n) sheath; **-münze** f change; **-wand** f partition-wall; **-wasser** n aqua-fortis

scheiden separate; divorce; **Scheidung** f (en) separation, divorce

Schein m (-e) light; appearance; certificate; note; **-bar** apparent; **-heilig** hypocritical; **-werfer** m reflector, searchlight

scheinen appear; shine

Scheit n (-er) log

Scheitel m (-) crown; parting; **scheiteln** part

Scheiterhaufen m (-) funeral pile; pyre, stake

scheitern founder; fail

Schelle f (-n) bell

schellen ring the bell

Schellfisch m (-e) haddock

Schelm m (-e) rogue

schelmisch roguish

Schelte f (-n) scolding

schelten scold

Schemel m (-) footstool

Schenke f (-n) public-house

Schenkel m (-) thigh

schenken give; present

Schenktisch m (-e) bar

Schenkung f (-en) donation

Schenkwirt m (-e) publican

Scherbe f (-n) fragment, piece

Schere f (-n) scissors pl;

Scherenschleifer m (-) grinder

scheren shear

Schererei f (-en) vexation

Scherz m (-e), **scherzen** jest, joke

scherzhaft droll, funny

scheu, scheuen shy; fear

Scheuerfrau f (-en) charwoman

scheuern scour

Scheune f (-n) barn

Scheusal n (-e) monster

scheusslich hideous

Schicht f (-en) layer; shift

schicken send; become

schicklich fit, becoming

Schicksal n (-e) fate

Schiebedach n (¨er) sliding roof

Schiebefenster n (-) sash-window

schieben push

Schieber m (-) slide; slide-valve; profiteer

Schieds-gericht n court of arbitration; **-richter** m umpire

schief oblique; inclined

Schiefer m (-) slate

schielen squint

Schienbein n shin

Schiene f (-n) rail

Schienenstrang m track

schier sheer, pure

Schierling m (-e) hemlock

Schiess-baumwolle f gun-cotton; **-pulver** n gun-powder; **-scharte** f embrasure; **-stand** m shooting stand

schiessen shoot

Schiff n (-e) ship, vessel, nave; **-bau** m shipbuilding; **-bruch** m ship-wreck; **-brüchig** shipwrecked; **-brücke** f pontoonbridge; **-bar** navigable; **-en** navigate; **-er** m sailor; **-fahrt** f navigation; **-sladung** f cargo; **-smannschaft** f crew; **-sma-**

schine *f* marine engine; **-sraum** *m* hold; tonnage; **-sschraube** *f* propeller

Schild *m* (-e) shield; *n* (-er) sign-board; **-krötensuppe** *f* turtle-soup; **-patt** *n* tortoise-shell; **-wache** *f* sentinel

schildern describe

Schilderung *f* (-en) description

Schilf *n*, **-rohr** *n* (-e) reed

schillern glitter; change colour

Schimmel *m* (-) white horse, mould

Schimmer *m* (-), **schimmern** glitter

Schimpf *m* (-e) insult, disgrace

schimpfen revile; call names

schimpflich disgraceful

Schindeldach *n* shingle-roof

schinden flay; grind down

Schinder *m* (-) knacker; **-ei** *f* drudgery

Schinken *m* (-) ham; **-brötchen** *n* ham-sandwich

Schirm *m* (-e) screen; umbrella; **-ständer** *m* umbrella-stand

schlabbern lap, babble

Schlacht *f* (-en) battle; **-feld** *n* battlefield; **-haus** *n* slaughter-house

schlachten kill, slaughter

Schlächter *m* (-) butcher

Schlacke *f* (-n) slag, dross

Schlaf *m*, **schlafen** sleep; **-los** sleepless; **-anzug** *m* pyjamas; **-mittel** *n* soporific; **-rock** *m* dressing-gown; **-saal** *m* dormitory; **-sofa** *n* sofa-bed; **-wagen** *m* sleeping-car; **-zimmer** *n* bed-room; **Schläfen** *n* nap; **schläfrig** sleepy

Schläfe *f* (-n) temple

schlaff slack, loose

Schlag *m* (⸚e) blow; shock; beat; apoplexy; **-anfall** *m* apoplectic fit; **-baum** *m* turnpike; **-uhr** *f* chiming clock

schlagen beat; strike

schlagend striking

Schlägerei *f* (-en) fight; row

schlagfertig ready-witted

Schlagwort *n* (⸚er) catch-word

Schlamm *m* mud

schlammig muddy

Schlange *f* (-n) serpent

schlängeln (sich) meander

schlank slender

schlapp slack

schlau sly

Schlauch *m* (⸚e) leather hose, tube

Schlauheit *f* slyness

schlecht bad

schlechtweg simply

Schlegel *m* (-) mallet, drum-stick

Schlehe *f* (-n) sloe

schleichen creep, crawl, slink

Schleier *m* (-) veil

Schleife *f* (-n) bow

schleifen grind; drag

Schleifer *m* (-) grinder

Schleifstein *m* (-e) grindstone

Schleim *m* mucus, slime

schleimig mucous, slimy

schleissen wear out

schlendern loiter, stroll

Schlendrian *m* routine

schlenkern dangle

Schleppe *f* (-n) train

schleppen drag; tow

Schlepper *m* (-), **-schiff** *n* (-e) tug

Schleppnetz *n* (-e) drag-net

Schleuder *f* (-n), **schleudern** sling

schleunig quick, speedy

Schleuse *f* (-n) lock, drain

Schlich *m* (-e) trick

schlicht plain, simple, smooth

schlichten settle

schliessen close; shut; conclude

schliesslich final

Schliff *m* polish

schlimm bad

Schlinge *f* (-n) sling; snare

Schlingel *m* (-) rascal

schlingern roll

Schlingpflanze *f* (-n) creeper

Schlips *m* (-e) tie, bow

Schlitten *m* (-) sledge

schlittern slide

Schlittschuh *m* (-e), **-laufen** skate; **-läufer** *m* skater

Schlitz *m* (-e) slit

Schloss *n* (⸚er) castle; lock

Schlosse f (-n) hailstone
Schlosser m (-) locksmith
Schlot m (¨e) chimney
Schlucht f (-en) gorge; ravine
schluchzen sob
Schluck m (¨e) draught, gulp
Schlucker m (-) poor fellow
schlucken swallow
Schlummer m, **schlummern** slumber
Schlund m (¨e) gullet, gorge
schlüpfen glide, slip
schlüpfrig slippery; obscene
Schlupfwinkel m (-) hiding-place
schlürfen sip
Schluss m (¨e) close, end; conclusion; - **der Debatte** closure; -**stein** m keystone
Schlüssel m (-) key; -**bein** n collar-bone; -**loch** n keyhole
Schmach f ignominy
schmachten languish
schmächtig slender
schmackhaft savoury
schmähen abuse, revile
schmählich ignominious
Schmähschrift f libel
schmal narrow
schmälern curtail
Schmalz n dripping, lard
Schmarotzer m (-) parasite
Schmarre f (-n) scar
Schmaus m (¨e), **schmausen** feast
schmecken taste
Schmeichelei f (-en) flattery
schmeicheln flatter
Schmeichler m (-) flatterer
schmeissen cast, throw, strike
Schmelz m (-e) enamel
schmelzen melt; smelt
Schmerz m (-en), **schmerzen** pain; -**haft**, -**lich** painful
Schmetterling m (-e) butterfly
Schmied m (-e) smith
schmieden forge
Schmiede f (-n) smithy; forge; -**eisen** n wrought iron
schmiegsam pliant
schmieren grease; scribble
schmierig greasy; dirty
Schminke f, **schminken** paint, rouge

Schmirgel m emery
schmollen pout, sulk
schmoren stew; **Schmorbraten** m braised meat
Schmuck m (-e) ornament; jewel(s); -**kästchen** n casket
schmücken adorn
schmuggeln smuggle
Schmuggler m (-) smuggler
Schmuggelware f (-n) contraband goods
schmunzeln smile
Schmutz m dirt
schmutzig dirty
Schnabel m (¨) bill, beak
Schnake (-n) crane-fly
Schnalle f (-n), **schnallen** buckle
Schnappschloss n spring-lock
schnappen snap
Schnaps m (¨e) strong liquor, brandy
schnarchen snore
schnattern cackle, chatter
schnauben (sich) blow one's nose
schnaufen snort
Schnauze f (-n) snout
Schnecke f (-n) snail; -**nlinie** f spiral line
Schnee m snow; -**flocke** f snowflake; -**gestöber** n snow-storm; -**glöckchen** n snowdrop; -**schuh** m ski; -**verwehung** f snow-drift
Schneide f (-n) edge
schneiden cut
Schneider m (-) tailor
Schneiderin f (-nen) dressmaker
schneidig smart
schneien snow
schnell quick, fast
Schnelldampfer m (-) fast steamer
Schnelligkeit f (-en) speed
Schnellzug m (¨e) express (train)
Schnepfe f (-n) snipe
schneuzen (sich) blow one's nose
schnippisch pert, snappish
Schnitt m (-e), -**wunde** f cut
Schnitte f (-n) slice, sandwich
Schnitter m (-) reaper
Schnittwaren pl retail goods (drapery)

Schnitzel *n* (-) cutlet; (**Wiener**) - *n* veal-cutlet; *pl* clippings, shavings

schnitzen carve

Schnitzer *m* (-) wood-carver; pointed knife; blunder

Schnitzerei *f* (-en) carved work

schnöde base; scornful

Schnörkel *m* (-) flourish

schnüffeln snuffle

Schnupfen *m* (-) cold in the head

schnupfen take snuff

Schnupftabak(sdose) *m* (*f*) snuff(-box)

Schnuppe *f* (-n) snuff

Schnur ("e) string; cord

schnüren lace

Schnürnadel *f* (-n) bodkin

Schnurrbart *m* ("e) moustache

schnurren purr

schnurrig droll

Schnürstiefel *m* (-) laced-boot

Schober *m* (-) stack

Schokolade *f* chocolate

Scholle *f* (-n) clod; plaice

schon already

schön beautiful; fine

schonen spare; save

Schönheit *f* (-en) beauty

Schopf *m* ("e) tuft

schöpfen draw (water)

Schöpfer *m* (-) creator

Schöpfung *f* (-en) creation

Schöpf-eimer *m* pail; **-kelle** *f* scoop; **-löffel** *m* ladle

Schorf *m* dandruff

Schornstein *m* (-e) chimney; **-feger** *m* chimney-sweep

Schoss *m* ("e) lap; skirt

Schote *f* (-n) pod, husk

Schoten *pl* green peas

Schott *n* (-e) bulkhead

Schotte *f* (-n) Scotsman

schottisch Scottish

Schottland *n* Scotland

schraffieren hatch (of a map)

schräg oblique; inclined

Schramme *f* (-n) scratch, scar

Schrank *m* ("e) cupboard

Schranke *f* (-n) barrier; list, bound

Schraube *f* (-n), **schrauben** screw; **-ndampfer** *m* screw-steamer; **-nzieher** *m* screwdriver

Schrecken *m* (-) fright

schrecken frighten

schrecklich terrible

Schrei *m* (-e), **schreien** cry

schreiben write; **Schreiber** *m* (-) writer, secretary, clerk

Schreib-feder *f* pen; **-maschine** *f* typewriter; **-pult** *n* writing-desk; **-stube** *f* office; **-unterlage** *f* blotting-pad; **-waren** *pl* stationery; **-zeug** *n* ink-stand; writing material

Schreiner *m* (-) joiner

schreiten step; proceed

Schrift *f* (-en) writing, script, publication; **-führer** *m* secretary; **-steller** *m* author; **-setzer** *m* compositor; **-wechsel** *m* correspondence

schriftlich in writing

Schritt *m* (-e) step; **-macher** *m* pacemaker

schroff steep; rough

schröpfen cup (draw blood)

Schrot *n* (-e) small shot; bruised corn, coarse meal

Schrotthändler *m* scrap-dealer

Schrulle *f* (-n) whim, fad

schrumpfen shrink

Schrunde *f* (-n) crevice

Schublade *f* (-n) drawer

Schubkarren *m* (-) wheelbarrow

schüchtern timid

Schuft *m* (-e) scoundrel

Schuh *m* (-e) shoe; **-anzieher** *m* shoe-horn; **-macher** *m* bootmaker; **-putzer** *m* shoeblack; **-wichse** *f* shoe-polish

Schuld *f* (-en) debt; guilt; **-schein** *m* promissory note, I O U; **schulden**, **schuldig sein** owe; **schuldig** guilty; **-ner** *m* debtor; **-igkeit** *f* duty

Schule *f* (-n) school; **Schul-amt** *n* education authority; **-buch** *n* school-book; **-direktor** *m* headmaster; **-jahr** *n* scholastic year; **-bank** *f* form; **-lehrer** *m* schoolmaster, teacher; **-zimmer** *n* school-room

Schüler *m* (-) scholar; pupil

Schulter f (-n) shoulder; **-blatt** n shoulder-blade

Schuppe f (-n) scale; dandruff

Schuppen m (-) shed

Schüreisen n (-) poker

schüren stir

Schurke m (-n) rascal

Schürze f (-n) apron

Schuss m (¨e) shot; **-waffe** f fire-arm; **-weite** range (bullet gun)

Schüssel f (-n) dish

Schuster m (-) shoemaker

Schutt m rubbish

schütteln shake

schütten pour

Schutz m protection; shelter; **-engel** m guardian angel; **-heilige** m patron saint; **-herrschaft** f protectorate; **-mann** m police-man; **-marke** f trade-mark; **-mittel** n preservative; **-zoll** m protective duty

Schütze m (-n) rifleman

schützen protect

Schwabe f (-n) cockroach

schwach weak

Schwäche f weakness

schwächen weaken

schwächlich weakly

Schwadron f (-en) squadron

schwadronieren swagger

Schwager m (-) brother-in-law; coachman

Schwägerin f (-nen) sister-in-law

Schwalbe f (-n) swallow

Schwamm m (¨e) sponge; mush-room; tinder

Schwan m (¨e) swan

schwanger pregnant

Schwangerschaft f pregnancy

Schwank m (¨e) farce

schwanken stagger; fluctuate

Schwanz m (¨e) tail

schwänzen play truant

Schwäre f (-n) abscess, ulcer, boil

schwären ulcerate

Schwarm m craze, swarm

schwärmen swarm, enthuse

schwärmerisch enthusiastic

Schwarte f (-n) rinh

schwarz black

schwärzen blacken

schwatzen chat, gossip

Schwätzer m (-) gossip

Schwebe f suspense

schweben float; soar

schwebend floating

Schwede(n) m (n) Swede(n)

Schwefel m sulphur; **-säure** f sulphuric acid

Schweif m (-e) tail

Schweigen n silence

schweigen be silent

schweigend silent

schweigsam taciturn

Schwein n (-e) pig

Schweine-braten m roast pork; **-fleisch** n pork

Schweinerei f (-en) obscenity, nastiness

Schweiss m perspiration

Schweiz f Switzerland

Schweizer m (-) Swiss

Schweizerkäse m gruyère

schwelgen feast, revel

Schwelle f (-n) threshold, sleeper

schwellen swell

Schwengel m (-) lever, handle

schwenken swing; rinse

Schwenkung f turning about; change of mind

schwer heavy; difficult; **-fällig** clumsy; **-hörig** hard of hearing; **-mut** f, **-mütig** melancholy; **-punkt** m centre of gravity

Schwere f weight

schwerlich hardly; scarcely

Schwert n (-er) sword

Schwester f (-n) sister

Schwiegervater m father-in-law; **-mutter** f mother-in-law

schwielig callous, horny

schwierig difficult

Schwierigkeit f (-en) difficulty

Schwimm-anstalt f, **-bad** n swimming-bath; **-blase** f bladder; **-gürtel** m life-belt; **-haut** f web; **-hose** f bathing-drawers

schwimmen swim

Schwindel m giddiness; swindle

schwindelig giddy

schwindeln swindle

Schwindler m (-) swindler

schwinden disappear; diminish
Schwindsucht *f* consumption
schwindsüchtig consumptive
schwingen swing
Schwingung *f* (-en) vibration
schwitzen sweat; perspire
schwören swear
schwül sultry; Schwüle *f* sultriness
schwulstig bombastic
Schwungrad *n* ("er) fly-wheel
schwunghaft flourishing
schwungvoll enthusiastic
Schwur *m* ("e) oath
Schwurgericht *n* (-e) jury
sechs six
See *m* (-n) lake; *f* (-n) sea; -bad *n* (-eort) (*m*) seaside resort; -fischerei *f* sea-fishery; -gras *n*, -tang *m* sea-weed; -handel *m* maritime trade; -hund *m* seal; -krank(heit) *f* sea-sick(ness); -krieg *m* naval war; -mannsheim *n* sailor's home; -meile *f* nautical mile; -räuber *m* pirate; -soldat *m* marine; -tüchtig seaworthy; -zunge *f* sole
Seele *f* (-n) soul
Seelenruhe *f* tranquillity of mind
Segel *n* (-), segeln sail; -flugzeug *n* glider; -schiff *n* sailing ship; -sport *n* yachting; -tuch *n* canvas
Segen *m* (-) blessing
segensreich blessed
segnen bless
sehen see; look at
sehenswert worth seeing
Sehenswürdigkeit *f* (-en) curiosity; sight
Sehne *f* (-n) sinew; string
sehnen (sich) long
sehnig sinewy
sehnlich ardent
Sehnsucht *f*, sehnsüchtig longing
sehr very
seicht shallow
Seide *f* (-n), seiden silk
Seidenraupe *f* (-n) silk-worm
Seife *f* soap; -nblase *f* bubble
seihen filter
Seihe *f* (-n) strainer

Seil *n* (-e) rope; -bahn *f* cable-railway
Seiler *m* (-) ropemaker
Seilerbahn *f* (-en) rope-walk
Seiltänzer *m* (-) rope dancer
seit, seitdem since
Seite *f* (-n) side; page
Seiten-ansicht *f* side-view; -blick *m* leer; -schiff *n* aisle; -stechen *n* stitch; -strasse *f* by-street; -stück *n* counterpart
seitens on the part of
seitlich lateral
Sekretär *m* (-e) secretary
Sekt *m* champagne
Sekte *f* (-n) sect
Sekunde *f* (-n) second
selbst self; even
selbständig independent
Selbständigkeit *f* independence
Selbst-beherrschung *f* self-control; -gespräch *n* soliloquy; -achtung *f* self-esteem; -hilfe *f* self-help; -kostenpreis *m* cost price; -mord, -mörder *m* suicide; -süchtig selfish; -tätig automatic; -verleugnung *f* self-denial; -verständlich evident, of course; -verwaltung *f* self-government; -wirkend self-acting
selig blessed
seligsprechen beatify
Sellerie *m* celery
selten rare, seldom
Seltenheit *f* (-en) rarity
Selterwasser *n*, seltzer water
seltsam strange
Seminar *n* (-e) training college
Semmel *f* (-n) roll
Senat *m* (-e) senate
Senator *m* (-en) senator
senden send
Sendung *f* (-en) consignment
Senf *m* mustard
sengen singe
senken lower; sich - sink
Senkgrube *f* (-n) cesspool
senkrecht vertical
Sense *f* (-n) scythe
September *m* September
Serie *f* (-n) series
servieren serve

Serviette _f_ (-n) napkin
Sessel _m_ (-) seat
setzen set; put; appoint; settle
Setzer _m_ (-) compositor
Seuche _f_ (-n) epidemic
seufzen, Seufzer _m_ (-) sigh
sezieren dissect
Sibirien _n_ Siberia
Sichel _f_ (-n) sickle; crescent
sicher safe; certain
Sicherheit _f_ security; -sventil _n_ safety-valve
sichern secure
Sicht (auf) (in) _f_ at (in) sight
sichtbar, sichtlich visible
Sieb _n_ (-e) sieve
sieben, sichten sift
sieben seven
siebenfach sevenfold
siech sickly
siedeln settle
sieden boil
Siedler _m_ (-) settler
Sieg _m_ (-e) victory
Siegel _n_ (-), **siegeln** seal; **-lack** _m_ sealing-wax; **-ring** _m_ signet-ring
siegen conquer
Sieger _m_ (-) conqueror, victor
siegreich victorious
Signal _n_ (-e), **signalisieren** signal
Silbe _f_ (-n) syllable
Silber _n_ silver
Silbergeschirr _n_ plate
Silvester(abend) _m_ New Year's Eve
singen sing
Singvogel _m_ (¨) singing-bird
sinken sink
Sinn _m_ (-e) sense; mind; **-bild** _n_ emblem; **-gedicht** _n_ epigram; **-lich** sensual; **-reich** ingenious; **-spruch** _m_ motto
sinnen meditate
sinnig appropriate
sintern trickle
Sintflut _f_ flood, deluge
Sirup _m_ syrup
Sitte _f_ (-n) custom
sittenlos dissolute; immoral
Sitten-losigkeit _f_ immorality; **-verderbnis** _f_ corruption of morals
sittlich moral

Sittlichkeit _f_ morality
sittsam modest
Sitz _m_ (-e) seat
Sitzbad _n_ (¨er) hipbath
sitzen sit; fit; **- bleiben** get on the shelf; remain in same form (school); **- lassen** abandon
Sitzung _f_ (-en) sitting; **-speriode** _f_ session
Skala _f_ (-len) scale
Skandal _m_ (-e) scandal
Skelett _n_ (-e) skeleton
Skizze _f_ (-n), **skizzieren**, sketch
Skizzenbuch _n_ (¨er) sketch-book
Sklave _m_ (-n) slave; **-nhandel** _m_ slave trade; **Sklaverei** _f_ slavery
Skorbut _m_ scurvy
Skorpion _m_ (-e) scorpion
Smaragd _m_ (-e) emerald
Smoking _m_ (-s) dinner-jacket
so so; thus; **- gross wie** as great as; **-bald als** as soon as; **-eben** just now; **-fort, -gleich** immediately; **-gar** even; **-mit** therefore
Socke _f_ (-n) sock
Sockel _m_ (-) basement; base (monument)
Sodawasser _n_ soda-water
Sodbrennen _n_ heartburn
Sofa _n_ (-s) sofa
Sohle _f_ (-n), **sohlen** sole
Sohn _m_ (¨e) son
solch such
Sold _m_ pay
Soldat _m_ (-en) soldier
Söldner _m_ (-) mercenary
Sole _f_ brine
solid solid
Soll _n_ debit
sollen be obliged; shall; be said
Sommer _m_ (-) summer
Sommersprosse _f_ (-n) freckle
Sonate _f_ (-n) sonata
sonderbar strange
Sonderling _m_ (-e) odd fellow
Sonderzug _m_ (¨e) special train
sondieren sound
Sonett _n_ (-e) sonnet
Sonnabend _m_ Saturday
Sonne _f_ (-n) sun
Sonnen-aufgang _m_ sunrise; **-blume** sunflower; **-dach** _n_,

-segel *n* awning; -finsternis *f* eclipse of the sun; -flecken *m pl* sun-spot; -schein *m* sunshine; -schirm *m* sun-shade; parasol; -stich *m* sunstroke; -uhr *f* sundial; -untergang *m* sunset

sonnig sunny

Sonntag *m* Sunday

sonst else; otherwise; - noch etwas? anything else; -ig other; -wo elsewhere

Sopran *m* (-e) soprano

Sorge *f* (-n), Sorgfalt *f* care; -tragen, sorgen take care; sorgfältig, -sam careful; sorglos careless; sorgenlos free from care; -voll anxious

Sorte *f* (-n), sortieren sort

Souffleur *m* (-e) prompter

Souterrain *n* (-s) basement

Souverän *m* (-e) sovereign

Sozialdemokrat *m* (-en) social democrat

Sozietät *f* society

Spalierobst *n* wall-fruit

Spalte *f* (-n) crevice; column

spalten split

Spaltung *f* (-en) division

Span *m* (⁀e) chip; *pl* shavings

Spanferkel *n* (-) sucking pig

Spange *f* (-n) clasp

Spanien *n* Spain

Spanier *m* (-) Spaniard

spanisch Spanish

Spann *m* (-e) instep

spannen stretch; excite

Spannkraft *f* elasticity

Spannung *f* (-en) tension; suspense

Spar-büchse *f* money-box; -kasse *f* savings-bank; -kassenbuch *n* savings-bank book; sparen save; spärlich scanty; sparsam economical; Sparsamkeit *f* economy

Spargel *m* asparagus

Sparren *m* (-) rafter

Spass *m* (⁀e), spassen joke; -macher *m* jester

spasshaft funny

spät late; -estens at the latest

Spaten *m* (-) spade

Spatz *m* (-en) sparrow

spazieren take a walk

Spazier-fahrt *f* drive; -gang *m*, -ritt *m* ride; -stock *m* walking-stick; -weg *m* walk

Specht *m* (-e) woodpecker

Speck *m* bacon

spedieren forward

Spediteur *m* (-e) forwarding agent

Speditionsgeschäft *n* (-e) forwarding business

Speer *m* (-e) spear

Speiche *f* (-n) spoke

Speichel *m* saliva

Speicher *m* (-) granary; warehouse

speien spit

Speise *f* (-n) food; dish; -haus *n* eating-house; -kammer *f* pantry; -karte *f* bill of fare; -röhre *f* gullet; -saal *m* dining-room; -schrank *m* meat-safe; -wagen *m* dining-car

speisen entertain; eat

Spektakel *m* (-) noise, show

Spende *f* (-n) gift

Spender *m* (-) donor

Sperling *m* (-e) sparrow

sperren bar; lock up

Sperrsitz *m* (-e) stall

Spesen *pl* expenses

speziell special

Sphäre *f* (-n) sphere

spicken lard

Spiegel *m* (-) (looking-)glass; -ei *n* poached egg; -glas *n* plate glass

spiegeln reflect

Spiel *n* (-e) play; game; -bank *f*, -haus *n*, -hölle *f* gambling-house; -dose *f*, -uhr *f* musical box; -marke *f* counter; -platz *m* playground; -sache *f* toy

spielen play; gamble; perform

Spieler *m* (-) player, gambler

Spielerei *f* (-en) fun; play

Spiess *m* (-e) spear; spit

Spinat *m* spinach

Spindel *f* (-n) spindle

Spinne *f* (-n) spider

spinnen spin; purr

Spinnengewebe *n* cobweb

Spinnerei *f* (-en) spinning-mill

Spinnmaschine *f* (-n) spinning-machine
Spinnrad *n* (¨er) spinning-wheel
Spion *m* (-e), **spionieren** spy
Spiralfeder *f* (-n) spiral spring
Spirituosen *pl* spirits
Spiritus *m* alcohol
Spital *n* (¨er) hospital
spitz, spitzig pointed
Spitz-bogen *m* pointed arch; -**bube** *m* rogue; -**findig** subtle; -**name** *m* nickname
Spitze *f* (-n) point; top; lace
spitzen point; prick
Sporn *m* (-ren), **spornen** spur
Sport *m* (-arten) sport
Spott *m* derision
spottbillig very cheap
spotten mock, scoff
Spottgedicht *n* (-e) satire
spöttisch mocking
Sprache *f* (-n) language
Sprach-forscher *m* (-) linguist; -**lehrer** *m* teacher of languages; -**los** speechless; -**rohr** *n* speaking-trumpet
sprechen speak
Sprecher *m* (-) speaker
Sprechstunde *f* (-n) hour of consultation
Sprechzimmer *n* (-) consulting-room
sprengen burst, blast; break; sprinkle, water
Sprengwagen *m* water-cart; -**bombe** *f* high explosive bomb
sprenkeln spot, speckle
Spreu *f* chaff
Sprichwort *n* (¨er) proverb
sprichwörtlich proverbial
Springbrunnen *m* (-) fountain
springen jump; burst; crack
Springer *m* (-) knight
Spritze *f* (-n) syringe, injection, fire engine
spröde brittle; prudish
Spross *m* (-en) shoot, sprout, sprig; scion; offspring
Sprosse *f* (-n) rung, step
sprossen sprout
Sprössling *m* (-e) offspring
Sprotte *f* (-n) sprat
Spruch *m* (¨e) sentence; saying

sprudeln bubble
sprühen sparkle; drizzle
Sprung *m* (¨e) jump, leap; crack; -**feder** *f* spring
spucken spit; expectorate
Spule *f* (-n) bobbin; coil
spülen rinse; wash up
spunden, Spund *m* bung
Spur *f* (-en) trace; -**weite** *f* gauge
spüren track; feel
sputen (**sich**) make haste
Staat *m* (-en) state
staatlich public
Staats-angehörigkeit *f* nationality; -**anwalt** *m* public prosecutor; -**bürger** *m* citizen; -**kirche** *f* Established Church; -**mann** *m* statesman; -**wirtschaft** *f* political economy; -**wohl** *n* public welfare
Stab *m* (¨e) staff
Stabeisen *n* bar-iron
Stachel *m* (-) **stacheln** sting; -**beere** *f* gooseberry; -**beerwein** *m* gooseberry wine; -**draht** *m* barbed wire; -**schwein** *n* porcupine
Stadt *f* (¨e) town; city; -**bahn** *f* metropolitan railway; -**leute** *pl* townsfolk; -**rat** *m* town council(lor); -**verwaltung** *f* local administration
städtisch municipal
Städter *m* (-) townsman
Staffel *f* (-n) step; degree; echelon
Staffelei *f* (-en) easel
Stahl *m*, **stählen, stählern** steel; -**feder** *f* steel pen; -**quelle** *f* chalybeate spring; -**stich** *m* steel-engraving
Stall *m* (¨e) stable; sty; -**knecht** *m* groom, hostler
Stamm *m* (¨e) stem, trunk; tribe, race; -**baum** *m* pedigree; -**buch** *n* album; -**gast** *m* regular customer; -**tafel** *f* genealogical table
stammeln stammer
stämmig sturdy
stampfen ram, trample
Stand *m* (¨e) stand; condition; rank; profession; **imstande**

able; **-bild** *n* statue; **-esamt** *n* registrar's office; **-punkt** *m* point of view; **-recht** *n* martial law; **-rede** *f* harangue
Ständchen *n* (–) serenade
Ständer *m* (–) stand
standhaft constant
Standhaftigkeit *f* constancy
ständig permanent
Standuhr *f* (-en) grandfather clock
Stange *f* (-n) pole; rod; stick
Stanniol *n* (-e) tinfoil
Stapel *m* (–) support, stocks
Stapelplatz *m* (-̈e) warehouse
Star *m* (-e) starling; cataract
stark strong; **Stärke** *f* strength, starch; **stärken** strengthen, starch
Starkstrom *m* (electricity) high-tension current
starr rigid; fixed; **-köpfig** stubborn
starren stare
Station *f* (-en) station
Statist *m* (-en) super; extra
statistisch statistical
Statt *f* place; **(an)statt** instead of
stattfinden take place
statthaft admissible
stattlich stately
Statue *f* (-n) statue
Statut *n* (-en) regulation
Staub *m* dust; **-mantel** *m* dust coat; **-regen** *m* drizzling rain; **-tuch** *n* duster
staubig dusty
Staude(ngewächs) *f* (*n*) shrub
stauen stow; dam
staunen be astonished
Staunen *n* astonishment
stechen sting; prick; engrave
Stechpalme *f* holly
stecken stick; **- bleiben** stop, break down
Steckenpferd *n* (-e) hobby(-horse)
Stecknadel *f* (-n) pin
Steg *m* (-e) path; foot-bridge
Stegreif *m* (-e) stirrup; **aus dem Stegreif** extempore
Stehbierhalle *f* (-n) bar
stehen stand; suit
stehen bleiben stop

Stehkragen *m* (–) stand-up collar
stehlen steal, rob
steif stiff; rigid
Steigbügel *m* (–) stirrup
steigen ascend; mount
steigern raise; increase
Steigkraft *f* force of ascent
Steigung *f* (-en) ascent, gradient
steil steep
Stein *m* (-e) stone; **-bruch** *m* quarry; **-butt** *m* turbot; **-druck** *m* lithography; **-gut** *n* pottery-ware; **-kohle(ngrube)** *f* coal-(-mine); **-ig** stony; **-salz** *n* rock salt
steinigen stone
Steiss *m* (-e) rump
Stelldichein *n* rendezvous
Stelle *f* (-n) place; situation; passage; office; **auf der** - on the spot
stellen put, place; set; feign
Stellschraube *f* (-n) adjusting-screw
Stellung *f* (-en) position
Stellvertreter *m* (–) substitute
Stelze *f* (-n) stilt
Stempel *m* (–) **stempeln** stamp; **-papier** *n* stamped paper
Stengel *m* (–) stalk
Stenograph *m* (-en) stenographer
Stenographie *f* stenography, shorthand
Steppdecke *f* (-n) **steppen** quilt
Steppe *f* (-n) steppe
Sterbehemd *n* (-en) shroud
sterben die
sterblich mortal
Sterblichkeit *f* mortality
stereotypieren stereotype
Stern *m* (-e) star; **-chen** *n* asterisk; **-bild** *n* constellation; **-schnuppe** *f* shooting star; **-warte** *f* observatory
stetig steady, stable
stets always
Steuer *n* (–) helm; steering-wheel; *f* (-n) tax; **-einnehmer** *m* collector (of taxes); **-frei** tax-free; **-mann** *m* helmsman, mate; **-pflichtig** taxable; **-wesen** *n* taxation; **-zahler** *m* taxpayer
steuern steer

Steuerung f (-en) gear; steering
Stich m (-e) thrust; prick; sting;
  stitch; engraving; **-wahl** f
  second ballot; **-wort** n catch-
  word
Stichel m (-) chisel
sticheln stitch; taunt
stichhaltig valid
sticken embroider
Stickerei f (-en) embroidery
Stickstoff m nitrogen
Stief- step-; **-vater** step-father;
  -mutter step-mother
Stiefel m (-) boot; **-knecht** m
  boot-jack; **-putzer** m shoeblack;
  -wichse f blacking
Stiege f (-n) staircase
Stieglitz m (-e) goldfinch
Stiel m (-e) handle, stick
Stier(kampf) m (-e) bull (-fight)
stier fixed; **stieren** stare
Stift m (-e) pin; pencil
Stift(-ung) n (f) foundation
stiften found
Stifter m (-) founder
Stil m (-e) style
still still; silent; **-schweigen** n
  silence
stillen appease; quench; stop
Stimme f (-n) voice; vote; **ent-
  scheidende** - casting vote
stimmen agree; tune; vote
Stimmeneinheit f unanimity
Stimmenmehrheit f majority (of
  votes)
Stimmgabel f (-n) tuning-fork
Stimmung f (-en) humour, disposition, atmosphere
Stimmzettel m (-) voting paper
stinken stink
Stinktier n (-e) skunk
Stipendium n (-ien) scholarship
Stirn f (-en) forehead
stochern stir; pick
Stock m (-e) stick; **-werk** n story,
  floor; **-fisch** m (dried) cod
stocken stop; stagnate
Stoff m (-e) matter; stuff
stöhnen groan
stolpern stumble
stolz proud; **Stolz** m pride
stopfen fill; darn
Stoppel f (-n) stubble

stoppen stop
Stöpsel m (-) stopper
stöpseln cork
Stör m (-e) sturgeon
Storch m (-e) stork
stören disturb; trouble
störrisch stubborn
Störung f (-en) disturbance;
  trouble; **-sangriff** m nuisance-
  raid
Stoss m (-e) shock; blow; pile
stossen push; knock
stottern stutter
stracks straightway
Straf-anstalt f house of correction; **-arbeit** f imposition;
  -gefangene m convict; **strafbar** punishable, guilty; **-ge-
  setz** n penal law; **-porto** n
  surcharge
Strafe f (-n) punishment, fine
strafen punish; fine
straff tight
Sträfling m (-e) convict
Strahl m (-en) ray; jet
strahlen beam; radiate
stramm tight; strong
Strand m (-e) beach
stranden run aground
Strang m (-e) rope; track
Strapaze f (-n) fatigue
Strasse f (-n) street
Strassen-bahn f tramway;
  -bahnwagen m tram-car;
  -damm m road; **-junge** m
  street-arab; **-kehrer** m scavenger; **-räuber** m highwayman;
  -übergang m crossing
sträuben (sich) resist; bristle
Strauch m (-e) shrub
straucheln stumble
Strauss m (-e) bouquet, nosegay;
  fight, combat; (pl -e) ostrich
Strebe f (-n) stay, **-bogen** m
  arch-buttress; **-pfeiler** m buttress
streben strive
strebsam assiduous; ambitious
Strecke f (-n) distance; line
strecken stretch
Streich m (-e) stroke; **-holz** n
  match; **-instrument** n stringed
  instrument; **-riemen** m strop
streicheln caress, fondle

streichen paint; efface; strike
Streif(en) *m* (-) streak; strip
streifen stripe, graze
Streik *m* (-s), streiken strike;
-brecher *m* blackleg
Streit *m* (-igkeiten), streiten
quarrel, fight
streitig disputed
streitsüchtig quarrelsome
streng severe
Strenge *f* severity
Streu *f* litter
streuen strew
Strich *m* (-e) stroke, line, passage
Strick *m* (-e) rope; -leiter *f* rope
ladder; -maschine *f* knitting
machine
stricken knit
Streime *f* (-n) stripe; weal
Stroh *n*, -halm *m* straw; -dach
n thatched roof; -hut *m* straw-
hat; -witwe(r) *f* (*m*) grass-
widow(er)
Strolch *m* (-e) tramp, loafer
Strom *m* (-̈e) river; current;
-schnelle *f* rapid; strömen
stream; Strömung *f* current;
in Strömen in torrents
Strophe *f* (-n) stanza
strotzen abound in
Strudel *m* (-) whirlpool
Strumpf *m* (-̈e) stocking; mantle;
-band *n* garter; -waren *f pl*
hosiery
struppig bristly; rough
Stube *f* (-n) room; -nmädchen *n*
chambermaid
Stuck *m* stucco
Stück *n* (-e) piece
Student *m* (-en) student
Studie *f* (-n), studieren, Studierzimmer *n*, Studium *n* study
Stufe *f* (-n) step; degree
stufenweise gradual(ly)
Stuhl *m* (-̈e) chair; -gang *m*
stool (bowels)
stumm dumb
Stummel *m* (-) stump; end
Stümper *m* (-) bungler
stumpf blunt; obtuse
Stumpf *m* (-̈e) stump; -nase *f*
snub-nose; -sinn *m* idiocy;
-sinnig stupid

Stunde *f* (-n) hour; lesson;
-nplan *m* timetable
stündlich hourly
Sturm *m* (-̈e), stürmen storm;
assault; -flut *f* spring-tide;
-glocke *f* tocsin; -wind *m* gale
stürmisch stormy; rough
Sturz *m* (-̈e) fall; stürzen fall;
rush; overthrow; -bach *m* torrent; -flug *m* nose-dive; -kar-
en *m* tilt-cart; -see *f* breaker
Stute *f* (-n) mare
Stütze *f* (-n), stützen prop; support
stutzen clip; trim
Stutzer *m* (-) fop; swell
stutzig machen, - werden stop
short, startle
Subskribent *m* (-en) subscriber
subskribieren subscribe
subtrahieren subtract
Suche *f* (-n) search
suchen seek; look for; try
Sucht *f* mania, passion
Süd *m*, -en *m* south; -früchte *f pl*
tropical fruits; -see *f* South Sea;
-west *m* south-west; -wind *m*
south wind
südlich southern
süffig tasty (drink)
Sühne *f* atonement
sühnen expiate
Sultan *m* (-e) sultan
Sülze *f* brawn
Summe *f* (-n) sum
summen hum, buzz
summieren sum up
Sumpf *m* (-̈e) marsh
sumpfig marshy
Sund *m* (-e) strait(s), Sound
Sünde *f* (-n), sündigen sin; -nfall
m fall of man
Sünder *m* (-) sinner
Sündflut *f* flood
sündig sinful
Suppe *f* (-n) soup; -nlöffel *m*
soup-spoon; -nschüssel *f* tureen;
-nteller *m* soup-plate
süss sweet
süssen sweeten
Süssholz *n* liquorice
Süssigkeit *f* (-en) sweetness
Süsswasser *n* fresh-water

Sympathie *f* sympathy
System *n* (-e), **(s-atisch)** system(atical)
Synagoge *f* (-n) synagogue
Synthese *f* (-n) synthesis
Szene *f* (-n) scene

T

Tabak *m* (-e) tobacco; snuff
Tabak-sbeutel *m* tobacco pouch; **-sdose** *f* snuff-box; **-händler** *m* tobacconist; **-spfeife** *f* tobaccopipe; **-pflanze** *f* tobacco-plant
Tabelle *f* (-n) table; index
Tablett *n* (-e) tray
Tablette *f* (-n) tablet
Tadel *m*, **tadeln** blame
tadellos faultless
tadelnswert blameable
Tadler *m* (-) fault-finder
Tafel *f* (-n) plate; table; slate
Täfelwerk *n* wainscot
Taffet *m* (-e) taffeta
Tag *m* (-e) day; **heute über** 8 (14) **Tage** this day week (fortnight); **bei Tagesanbruch** at daybreak; **bei Tage(slicht)** by daylight
Tageblatt *n* (¨er) daily paper
Tage-buch *n* diary; **-dieb** *m* idler; **-lohn** *m* daily wages; **-löhner** *m* day labourer; **-reise** *f* a day's journey; **szeit** *f* daytime; **-werk** *n* day's work
tagen dawn; **täglich** daily
Taille *f* (-n) waist
Takelage *f* rigging
Takt *m* (-e) measure: tact; **- halten** keep time
Taktik *f* tactics
Tal *n* (¨er) valley
Talar *m* (-e) gown
Talent (-e) **(t-voll)** *n* talent(ed)
Talg *m* tallow; suet
Talk *m* (-e) talc
tändeln trifle; flirt
Tang *m* (-e) seaweed
Tanne(nbaum) *f* (-n) (*m*) fir, spruce
Tante *f* (-n) aunt
Tanz *m* (¨e), **tanzen** dance; **-saal**
m ball-room; **-stunde** *f* dancing lesson
Tapete *f* (-n) tapestry; wallpaper
tapezieren paper
Tapezierer *m* (-) paper-hanger
tapfer brave
Tapferkeit *f* bravery
täppisch awkward
Tarif *m* (-e) tariff
Tasche *f* (-n) pocket; bag
Taschen-buch *n* notebook; **-dieb** *m* pickpocket; **-tuch** *n* pocket-handkerchief; **-uhr** *f* watch
Tasse *f* (-n) cup
Taste *f* (-n) key
tasten grope; touch
Tat *f* (-en) act; action; **in der -** indeed; **-kraft** *f* energy; **-sache** *f* fact
Täter *m* (-) perpetrator
tätig active
Tätigkeit *f* activity
tätlich violent
Tätlichkeit *f* violence
tätowieren tattoo
Tatze *f* (-n) paw
Tau *n* (-e) cable, rope; *m* dew
taub deaf; **-stumm** deaf and dumb; **Taubheit** *f* deafness
Taube *f* (-n) pigeon; **-nschlag** *m* dove-cote
Tauchboot *n* (-e) submersible boat
tauchen dive; **Taucher** *m* diver; **-glocke** *f* diving-bell
tauen thaw
Taufe *f* (-n) baptism; **taufen** baptize; **Taufbecken** *n* baptismal font; **Taufname** *m* Christian name
taugen be good, be worth
Taugenichts *m* good-for-nothing fellow
tauglich fit; useful
taumeln reel
Tausch *m* (-e) **tauschen** exchange
täuschen deceive
Täuschung *f* (-en) delusion; illusion
Taxe *f* (-n) tax; tariff
Taxus *m* (-) yew

Techniker *m* (-) technician, engineer

technisch technical

Tee *m* tea; **-brett** *n* tea-tray; **-büchse** *f* tea-canister; **-kanne** *f*, **-topf** *m* tea-pot; **-löffel** *m* tea-spoon; **-maschine** *f* tea-urn

Teer *m*, **teeren** tar

Teich *m* (-e) pond; **Teig** *m* dough

Teil *m* (-e) part; *n* share; **-bar** divisible; **-barkeit** *f* divisibility; **-chen** *n* particle; **-en** share; **-haben** participate; **-haber** *m* partner; **-nahme** *f* participation; sympathy; **-nehmen** participate, sympathize; **-nehmend** sympathetic; **-zahlung** *f* instalment

teilen divide; share

teils partly

Teilung *f* (-en) division

Teint *m* (-s) complexion

Telegramm *n* (-e) telegram

Telegraph *m* (-en), **-ieren** telegraph

Telegraphen-amt *n* telegraph-office; **-leitung** *f* telegraph line; **telegraphisch** telegraphic

Telegraphie *f* telegraphy

Telephon *n*, **-ieren** telephone

Telephonzelle *f* (-n) call-box

Teleskop *n* (-e) telescope

Teller *m* (-) plate

Tempel *m* (-) temple

Temperament *n* (-e) temper

Temperänzler *m* (-) abstainer

Temperatur *f* (-en) temperature

Tempo *n* (-s) time

Tendenz *f* (-en) tendency

Tender *m* (-) tender

Tenne *f* (-n) barn-floor; threshing-floor

Tennis *n* (lawn-)tennis; **-spielplatz** *m* tennis court

Tenor *m* tenor

Teppich *m* (-e) carpet

Termin *m* (-e) term

Terpentin *m* turpentine

Terrain *n* (-s) ground

Terrasse *f* (-n) terrace

Terrine *f* (-n) tureen

Territorium *n* (-ien) territory

Terzett *n* (-e) trio

Testament *n* (-e) testament; will

teuer dear

Teufel *m* (-) devil

teuflisch diabolical

Text *m* (-e) text; **-buch** *n* libretto

Theater *n* (-) theatre; **-stück** *n* play; **-zettel** *m* play-bill

Thema *n* (-en) theme; subject

Themse *f* Thames

Theolog *m* (-en) theologian

Theologie *f* theology

theoretisch theoretical

Theorie *f* (-n) theory

Thermometer *n* (-) thermometer

Thron *m* (-e) throne

Thunfisch *m* (-e) tunny

Thymian *m* thyme

ticken tick

tief deep; **-sinnig** thoughtful; melancholy

Tiefe *f* (-n) depth

Tiefgang *m* draught

Tiegel *m* (-) saucepan; crucible

Tier *n* (-e) animal; **-arzt** *m* veterinary surgeon; **-reich** *n* animal kingdom

tierisch animal; bestial

Tiger *m* (-) tiger

tilgen cancel, destroy

Tingeltangel *m* music-hall

Tinte *f* (-n) ink

Tinten-fass *n* ink-stand; **-fleck** *m* ink-blot; **-wischer** *m* penwiper

Tisch *m* (-e) table

Tischdecke *f* (-n) table-cover

Tischgebet *n* (-) grace

Tischler *m* (-) joiner, carpenter

Titel *m* (-) title

Titelbild *n* (-er) frontispiece

Toast *m* (-e) toast; **- ausbringen** propose

toben rave

Tobsucht *f* raving madness

Tochter *f* (-) daughter

Tod *m* (-esfälle) death; **-feind** *m* mortal enemy; **-esfall** *m* death; **-eskampf** *m* agony; **-esstrafe** *f* capital punishment; **tödlich** mortal, fatal

toll mad

tollen romp, rave

Tollheit *f* madness
tollkühn foolhardy
Tollkühnheit *f* temerity
Tollwut *f* hydrophobia
Tölpel *m* (-) awkward fellow
Tomate *f* (-n) tomato
Ton *m* (ˑe) **tönen** sound
Ton *m* clay
Tonart *f* (-en) tone; key
Tonleiter *f* (-n) scale
Tongeschirr *n* pottery
Tonne *f* (-n) cask; ton; **-nge-halt** *m* tonnage
Topf *m* (ˑe) pot
Töpfer *m* (-) potter
Töpferei *f* pottery
Tor *n* (-e) gate
Tor *m* (-en) fool; **Torheit** *f* (-en) folly; **töricht** foolish
Torf *m* peat
Tornister *m* (-) knapsack
Torpedoboot(zerstörer) *n* (*m*) torpedo-boat(-destroyer)
Torte *f* (-n) tart; flan
Torweg *m* (-e) gateway
tosen roar, rage
tot dead; **töten** kill
Toten-bahre *f* bier; **-bett** *n* death-bed; **-gräber** *m* grave-digger; **-schein** *m* certificate of death
Totschlag *m* manslaughter
Tourist *m* (-en) tourist
Trab *m*, **traben** trot
Tracht *f* (-en) costume; load
trächtig pregnant
trachten strive
Trag-bahre *f* stretcher; **-rie-men** *m* strap; **-sessel** *m* sedan-chair; **-weite** *f* range
tragbar portable
träge idle
Trägheit *f* idleness
tragen carry; wear; be pregnant
Träger *m* (-) bearer; girder
tragisch tragic
Tragödie *f* (-n) tragedy
trainieren train
traktieren treat
trampeln trample
Tran *m* train-oil, fish-oil
tranchieren carve
Tranchiermesser *n* carving-knife

Träne *f* (-n) tear
Trank *m* (ˑe) drink, beverage
tränken give to drink, water
Transport *m* (-e) **-ieren** transport
Trapez *n* (-e) trapeze
Traube *f* (-n) grape; bunch of grapes
trauen trust; marry
Trauer *f* mourning; **-marsch** *m* funeral march; **-spiel** *n* tragedy; **-weide** *f* weeping willow
trauern mourn
Traufe *f* (-n) gutter
traulich comfortable
Traum *m* (ˑe), **träumen** dream
Träumer *m* (-) dreamer
Traurig(keit) *f* sad(ness)
Trauring *m* (-e) wedding-ring
Trauung *f* (-en) wedding, marriage
Treber *pl* husks; dregs
Treff *n* (-e) club (cards)
treffen hit; meet
treffend striking
Treffer *m* (-) prize; good shot
trefflich excellent
Treib-eis *n* drift-ice; **-haus** *n* hot-house; **-jagd** *f* battue; **-rie-men** *m* driving-belt
treiben drive; do; carry on; float
trennen separate, divide
Trennung *f* (-en) separation
Treppe *f* (-n) stairs *pl*; staircase
Treppen-absatz *m* landing; **-geländer** *n* rail; **-haus** *n* staircase
Tresse *f* (-n) lace, galloon, stripe
treten tread; step; **fehl-** slip; **nähr-** approach
Tretmühle *f* (-n) tread-mill
treu faithful
Treue *f* fidelity
treulos faithless
Tribüne *f* (-n) tribune
Tribut *m* (-e) tribute
Trichter *m* (-) funnel
Trieb *m* (-e) impulse; shoot; **-kraft** *f* motive power; **-rad** *n* driving wheel; **-sand** *m* drift-sand
triefen drip
triftig urgent, valid

Trikot n hosiery, tricot
Triller m, **trillern** trill
trinkbar drinkable
trinken drink
Trinker m (-) drunkard
Trink-geld n gratuity, tip; **-geld geben** tip; **-spruch** m toast
trippeln trip
Tripper m gonorrhœa
Tritt m (-e) step; kick; footboard
Triumphbogen m triumphal arch
Triumph m (-e) (t-ieren) triumph
trocken, trocknen dry
Trockenheit f dryness; drought
Troddel (-n) f tassel
trödeln dawdle
Trödler m (-) dawdler, second-hand dealer
Trog m (¨e) trough
Trommel f (-n), **trommeln** drum; **-fell** n tympanum; **-er** m drummer
Trompete f (-n), **trompeten** trumpet
Trompeter m (-) trumpeter
Tropen pl tropics
tröpfeln drip; trickle
Tropfen m (-) drop
Tropfstein m stalactite
tropisch tropical
Tross m (-e) baggage
Trost m comfort
trostlos desolate
trösten console
Trottel m (-) idiot
trotz in spite of; **-dem** notwithstanding; **Trotz** m defiance
trotzen defy
trotzig defiant
trüb dull, troubled
trüben trouble; **sich -** grow dull
trübsinnig melancholy
Trüffel f (-n) truffle
trügen deceive
trügerisch delusive
Truhe f (-n) trunk, chest
Trümmer pl ruins
Trumpf m (¨e), **trumpfen** trump
Trunk m (¨e) drink; **-enbold** m drunkard; **-e(heit** f) drunken(ness)

Truppe f (-n) troop
Truthahn m turkey
Tuberkulose f tuberculosis
Tuch n (¨er) cloth; shawl
Tuchhändler m (-) draper
tüchtig able
Tücke f malice
tückisch malicious
Tugend f (-en) virtue; **-haft** virtuous
Tüll m (-e) tulle, net
Tulpe f (-n) tulip
Tümpel m (-) pool
Tumult(uarisch) m tumult(uary)
tun do; **es tut nichts** it does not matter; **-lich** feasible
Tünche f, **tünchen** whitewash
Tunke f (-n) sauce
Tunnel m (-s) tunnel
Tüpfel m (-) dot; **tupfen** dab, spot
Turban m (-e) turban
Turbine f (-n) turbine; **-ndampfer** m turbine-steamer
Tür f (-en) door; **-angel** f hinge; **-flügel** m leaf; **-klinke** f latch; **-klopfer** m knocker
Türke m (-n) Turk
Türkei f Turkey
Türkis m turquoise
Turm m (¨e) tower; steeple
turnen practise gymnastics
Turnhalle f (-n) gymnasium
Turnier n (-e) tournament
Turteltaube f (-n) turtle-dove
Tusch m (-e) flourish
Tusche f (-n) Indian ink
Tüte f (-n) paper bag
tuten toot; tootle
Typ m (-e) type; **-isch** typical
Type f, type (printing)
Typhus m typhoid fever
Tyrann m (-en) tyrant
tyrannisch tyrannical
tyrannisieren tyrannize

U

Übel n, **übel** evil; **-keit** f nausea; **ü-nehmen** take amiss; **-nehmerisch** touchy; **-stand** m evil, abuse, inconvenience; **-wollen** n ill-will; **ü-wollend** malevolent

Übelkeit *f* sickness
üben exercise; practise
über over; above; **-all** everywhere; **-arbeiten** overwork; over-exert
überbelichten over-expose
überbieten outbid; surpass
Überblick *m*, **ü-en** survey
Über-bleibsel *n* remains; **-bringer** *m* bearer; **überdies** besides; **-druss** *m* disgust
über-drüssig disgusted
übereilt over-hasty
übereinkommen, ü-einstimmen agree; **-einkunft** *f* agreement
überessen over-eat
über-fahren run over, cross; **-fahrt** *f* passage; **-fall(en)** *m* surprise, attack; **-fliessen** flow over; **-fluss** *m* abundance; **-flüssig** superfluous; **-fordern, -forderung** *f* overcharge; **-führen** convict; **-füllt** overcrowded
Übergabe *f* delivery, surrender
Übergang *m* crossing, transition
über-geben deliver; **sich -** be sick, vomit; **-gehen** pass over
Übergewicht *n* overweight
über-häufen overload; **-haupt** on the whole; at all; **-hitzen** overheat; **-holen** overtake; **-hören** overhear; **-irdisch** celestial; **-laden** overload; **-lassen** leave; **-kochen** boil over; **-leben** outlive; **-legen** consider
Überlegen(heit *f*) superior(ity)
Überlegung *f* (-en) reflection
Überlieferung *f* tradition
überlisten outwit; dupe
Übermacht *f* superiority
Übermass *n* excess
übermenschlich superhuman
übermorgen the day after tomorrow
Übermut *m* insolence
übermütig haughty; insolent
übernachten pass the night
übernatürlich supernatural
über-nehmen accept; take over; **-raschen, Überraschung** *f* surprise; **-reden** persuade; **Über-**

redung *f* persuasion; **-reichen** deliver; **-reizen** over-excite
Überrest *m* rest; remains
Überrock *m* overcoat
übergeschnappt crazy
überschlagen turn over, estimate
überschreiben superscribe
überschreiten cross
Überschrift *f* (-en) title; headline
Überschuh *m* (-e) galosh
Überschuss *m* surplus
überschwemmen inundate
Überschwemmung *f* (-en) inundation
über-seeisch oversea; **-sehen** overlook; **-senden** forward; **-setzen** translate; **Übersetzung** *f* translation
Übersicht *f* view, survey
übersichtlich succinct, lucid
übersiedeln remove
überspannt eccentric
übersteigen surpass; **-stimmen** outvote; **-stürzen** precipitate; **-teuern** overcharge; **-tragbar** transferable; **-tragen** transfer, transmit; **-treffen** surpass; **-treiben** exaggerate; **Übertreibung** *f* exaggeration; **-treten** transgress
Übertritt *m* (-e) conversion
über-vorteilen over-reach; **-wachen** superintend; **-wältigen, -winden** overcome; **-wintern** winter; **-zählig** supernumerary; **-zeugen** convince; **Überzeugung** *f* conviction; **-ziehen** cover
Überzieher *m* (-) overcoat
Überzug *m* cover
üblich usual; customary
übrig left; **die Ü-en** the rest; **-ens** as for the rest; **-bleiben** remain
Übung *f* (-en) exercise; practice
Ufer *n* (-) shore; bank
Uhr *f* (-en) clock; watch; **wieviel - ist es?** what is the time? **-werk** *n* clockwork; **-macher** *m* watchmaker
Uhu *m* horned owl
Ulk *m* fun; **-ig** funny
Ulme *f* (-n) elm

um (rund-) (a)round; over
um-ändern alter; **-arbeiten** recast; **-bringen** kill; **-drehen** turn round
Umdrehung f (-en) rotation
umfallen upset; fall down
Umfang m (¨e) extent; circumference, compass
umfassen embrace
umfassend extensive
Umgang m intercourse
umgänglich sociable
Umgangssprache colloquial language
umgeben surround
Umgebung, Umgegend f environs
umgehen mit keep company with
umgehend by return of post
umgekehrt opposite; contrary; vice-versa
Umhängetasche f satchel
umhauen cut down
umher around, about
Umkehr f, **umkehren** return
umkleiden (sich) change clothes
Umkreis m circuit
umlaufen circulate
umliegend surrounding
umpflanzen transplant
umrennen overrun
Umriss m (-e) outline
umrühren stir up
umschalten commute; reverse
Umschau f, - **halten,** looking round
umschiffen circumnavigate
Umschlag m (¨e) change; envelope; poultice
umschlagen change, shift; turn over
Umschrift f circular inscription; transcription
umsehen (sich) look about
umsetzen sell
Umsicht f circumspection
umsonst gratis; in vain
Umstand m (¨e) circumstance **-skleid** n maternity dress
umständlich circumstantial
umsteigen change
Umtausch (u-en) m exchange
Umwälzung f (-en) revolution

Umweg m (-e) detour
unwenden turn over
unwerfen overthrow; upset
umziehen remove; **sich -** change clothes
Umzug m (¨e) removal
unabhängig independent
Unabhängigkeit f independence
unabsichtlich unintentional
unähnlich unlike
unangenehm disagreeable
unanständig indecent
unappetitlich disgusting
unartig naughty
unaufhörlich incessant
unauflöslich insoluble
unaufmerksam inattentive
unauslöschlich indelible
unaussprechlich ineffable
unausstehlich intolerable
unbarmherzig pitiless
unbedeutend insignificant
unbedingt absolute
unbefangen ingenuous
unbegreiflich inconceivable
unbegründet unfounded
unbehaglich uneasy
unbeholfen awkward
unbekannt unknown
unbequem inconvenient
unbescheiden immodest
unbeschreiblich indescribable
unbesiegbar invincible
unbesonnen thoughtless
unbeständig inconstant
unbestellbar undeliverable
unbestimmt uncertain
unbestreitbar incontestable
unbeweglich immovable; real
unbewohnt uninhabited
unbewölkt cloudless
unbezahlbar invaluable
unbillig unfair
unbrauchbar useless
Undank m ingratitude
undankbar ungrateful
undenkbar inconceivable
undenklich immemorial
undeutlich indistinct
uneben uneven
unecht false; mock
unehelich illegitimate
unehrlich dishonest

uneinig disagreeing
uneinnehmbar impregnable
unempfindlich insensible
unendlich infinite
unentbehrlich indispensable
unentgeltlich gratuitous; gratis
unentschlossen irresolute
unerbittlich inexorable
unerfahren inexperienced
unerhört unheard of
unermesslich immense
unermüdlich indefatigable
unersättlich insatiable
unerschöpflich inexhaustible
Unerschrocken(heit f) intrepid-(ity)
unersetzlich irreparable
unerträglich intolerable
unerwartet unexpected
unfähig incapable
Unfähigkeit f incapacity
Unfall m (⁻e) accident
unfehlbar infallible
Unfehlbarkeit f infallibility
unfrankiert not prepaid
unfreiwillig involuntary
unfruchtgar sterile; barren
Unfug m nuisance; mischief
ungangbar impassable
Ungar m, ungarisch Hungarian
Ungarn n Hungary
ungebildet uneducated
ungebräuchlich unusual
ungebraucht unused
ungebrochen unbroken
Ungeduld f impatience
ungeduldig impatient
ungeeignet unfit
ungefähr about
ungeheuer enormous
Ungeheuer n (–) monster
ungehörig unbecoming
ungehorsam disobedient
Ungehorsam n disobedience
ungemütlich uncomfortable
ungenau inexact
ungenügend insufficient
ungerade uneven
ungerecht unjust
Ungerechtigkeit f injustice
ungern unwillingly
ungeschickt awkward
ungesetzlich illegal

ungestüm impetuous
ungesund unwholesome
ungewiss uncertain
ungewöhnlich unusual
ungewohnt unaccustomed
Ungeziefer n vermin
ungezogen ill-bred; naughty
ungläubig infidel
unglaublich incredible
ungleich unequal
Unglück n (-sfälle) misfortune
unglücklich unfortunate
Unglücksfall m (⁻e) accident
Ungnade f disgrace
ungültig invalid
ungünstig unfavourable
unheilbar incurable
unheimlich dismal
unhöflich impolite
unhörbar inaudible
Uniform f (-en) uniform
Universität f (-en) university
Unkenntnis f ignorance
unklug imprudent
Unklugheit f imprudence
Unkosten pl expenses
Unkraut n weeds pl
unlängst lately
unleserlich illegible
unleugbar undeniable
unmenschlich inhuman
unmerklich imperceptible
unmittelbar direct
unmöglich impossible
Unmöglichkeit f impossibility
unmoralisch immoral
unmündig minor
unnatürlich unnatural
unnötig unnecessary
unordentlich disorderly
unparteiisch impartial
unpassend unsuitable
unpässlich indisposed
unpraktisch unpractical
unpünktlich unpunctual
Unrecht n wrong
unredlich dishonest
unregelmässig irregular
Unregelmässigkeit f irregularity
Unruhe f (-n) restlessness; riot
unruhig restless
uns us
unschädlich harmless

unschätzbar inestimable
unschicklich unbecoming
Unschlitt n tallow
Unschuld f innocence
unschuldig innocent
unser our
unsicher uncertain
Unsicherheit f insecurity
unsichtbar invisible
Unsinn m nonsense
unsinnig absurd
unsittlich immoral
unsterblich immortal
Unsterblichkeit f immortality
unstreitig incontestable
untauglich unfit
unten below; downstairs
unter under; among
untere lower; inferior
Unter-arm m forearm; -bleiben
not take place; -brechen interrupt; -brechung f interruption, break; -bringen lodge;
-dessen in the meantime;
-drücken suppress; -gang m
fall, ruin, sinking; -geben subject; -gebene m inferior, subject; -gehen perish, sink, set;
-grundbahn f undergroundrailway; -halb below; -halt m
maintenance; -halten entertain,
amuse; sich - converse; -haltung f conversation; -handeln
negotiate; -handlung f negotiation; -haus n House of Commons; -hose f drawers pl, pants;
-irdisch underground, subterranean; -jacke f vest; -kiefer m
lower jaw; -kleid n under-garment; -kunft f accommodation;
-lassen omit; -leib m abdomen;
-liegen succumb; -lippe f lower
lip; -nehmen n enterprise;
-nehmend enterprising; -nehmer m contractor; -nehmung
f enterprise; -redung f conversation; -richt m instruction;
-richten instruct; -rock m
petticoat; -sagen forbid; -satz
m stand; -scheiden distinguish; -schenkel m shank;
-schied m difference; -schlagen
embezzle; -schreiben sign;

-schrift f signature; -seeboot
n submarine; -setzt thick-set;
-streichen underline; -stützen
support; -stützung f relief;
-suchen examine; -suchung f
examination, inquiry; -tan m
subject; -tänig humble; -tasse
f saucer; -tauchen dive; -treten take shelter; -wegs on the
way; -werfen subdue; (sich)-
submit; -zeichnen sign
Untiefe f shoal
untreu faithless
untröstlich disconsolate
Untugend f (-en) vice
unüberlegt inconsiderate
unüberwindlich invincible
unumschränkt absolute
unumstösslich irrefutable
unveränderlich invariable
unverantwortlich irresponsible
unverbesserlich incorrigible
unverdaulich indigestible
unverdient undeserved
unverdorben uncorrupted
unverdrossen indefatigable
unvereinbar incompatible
unverfroren impudent
unvergleichlich incomparable
unverheiratet unmarried
unverhofft unexpected
unvermeidlich inevitable
unvermutet unexpected
unvernünftig unreasonable
unverschämt impudent
Unverschämtheit f insolence
unversehens unawares
unverständig imprudent
unverständlich unintelligible
unverwüstlich indestructible
unverzeihlich unpardonable
unvollkommen imperfect
unvordenklich immemorial
unvorsichtig incautious
unwahr untrue; false
Unwahrheit f falsehood
unwahrscheinlich improbable
unwegsam impracticable
unweit not far
unwiderruflich irrevocable
Unwille m displeasure
unwillig angry
unwillkürlich involuntary

unwissend ignorant
Unwissenheit *f* ignorance
unwohl sick
Unwohlsein *n* indisposition
unwürdig unworthy
unzählig innumerable
unzart indelicate
Unzeit *f* wrong season; **zur -** at the wrong time; **-ig** untimely
unzertrennlich inseparable
Unzucht *f* debauchery
unzufrieden discontented
Unzufriedenheit *f* discontent
unzugänglich inaccessible
unzuverlässig unreliable
unzweifelhaft undoubted
üppig luxurious
Ur-enkel *m* great-grandson; **-grossvater** *m* great-grandfather; **-heber** *m* author; **-kunde** *f* document; **-laub** *m* leave; **-sache** *f* cause; **keine Ursache!** don't mention it; **-sprung** *m* origin; **-sprünglich** original; **-tell** *n* judgment; **-teilen** judge; **-wald** *m* primeval forest; **-welt** *f* primitive world
Urin *m*, urine; **urinieren** make water
Urne *f* (**-n**) urn
urteilen judge
Utensilien *pl* utensils
uzen tease, mock

V

Vagabund *m* (**-en**) vagabond
vakant vacant
Vakanz *f* (**-en**) vacancy; vacation
Vakuumbremse *f* (**-n**) vacuum-brake
Vampir *m* (**-e**) vampire
Vanille *f* vanilla
Vasall *m* (**-en**) vassal
Vase *f* (**-n**) vase
Vater *m* (**ˉ**) father; **-land** *n* native country; **-landsliebe** *f* patriotism; **-schaft** *f* paternity; **- unser** *n* Lord's Prayer
väterlich paternal
Vegetarier *m* vegetarian
Veilchen *n* (**-**) violet

Venedig Venice
Ventil *n* (**-e**) valve
ventilieren ventilate
verabreden agree
Verabredung *f* (**-en**) agreement; appointment
verabscheuen detest
verabschieden discharge; **sich -** take leave
verachten despise
verächtlich contemptible
Verachtung *f* contempt
verallgemeinern generalize
veraltet obsolete
veränderlich variable
verändern change; alter
veranlassen cause
Veranlassung *f* (**-en**) occasion
verantworten account for
verantwortlich responsible
Verantwortlichkeit *f* responsibility
Verantwortung *f* (**-en**) responsibility
verargen blame
verarmen become poor
verbannen banish
verbergen conceal; hide
verbessern (**sich**), improve
verbeugen (**sich**), **Verbeugung** *f* bow
verbieten forbid; **verbotener Eingang** no admission
verbinden join; connect; dress; oblige
verbindlich obliging
Verbindung *f* (**-en**) connection; **Eisenbahn-** junction
verbissen soured
verbittern embitter
verblenden blind
verblüffen dumbfound
verblühen fade
verbluten (**sich**) bleed to death
verborgen, lend; secret
Verbot *n* (**-e**) prohibition
Verbrauch *m* consumption
verbrauchen consume
Verbrechen *n* (**-**) crime
Verbrecher *m* (**-**) **verbrecherisch** criminal
verbreiten spread
verbrennen burn

Verbrennung f combustion
verbringen spend
verbrüdern (sich) fraternize
verbünden, Verbündete m (-n) ally
verbürgen warrant
Verdacht m suspicion
verdächtig suspicious
verdammen damn
Verdammnis f damnation
verdampfen evaporate
verdanken owe; be indebted for
verdauen digest
verdaulich digestible
Verdauung f digestion
Verdeck n (-e) deck, covering
verdenken take amiss, blame
verderben spoil; corrupt
Verderben n ruin
verdienen merit; earn
Verdienst m (-e) earnings; n merit
verdienstlich meritorious
verdolmetschen interpret
verdoppeln double
verdorren dry up, wither
verdreht crazy
verdriessen vex
verdriesslich peevish
Verdruss m annoyance
verduften vanish
verdunkeln obscure
verdünnen rarefy; dilute
verdunsten evaporate
verdursten die of thirst
verdutzt puzzled; taken aback
verehelichen marry
verehren revere; adore
Verehrer m (-) admirer
Verein m (-e) society; club
vereinbaren agree
vereinfachen simplify
vereinigen unite
vereinzeln isolate
vereiteln frustrate
verekeln disgust
vererben leave, bequeath
verewigen perpetuate
verfahren proceed
Verfahren n (-) proceeding, process
verfallen decay; be due
verfälschen adulterate

verfassen compose
Verfasser m (-) author
Verfassung f (-en) constitution; -smässig constitutional
verfaulen rot
verfehlen miss
verfeinern refine; polish
verfertigen make; manufacture
verfliessen elapse
verflogen flown away
verfluchen curse
verfolgen pursue; persecute; prosecute
Verfolgung f (-en) pursuit; persecution, prosecution
verfrachten freight, ship
verfrüht premature
verfügen über dispose of
Verfügung f disposal
verführen seduce
verführerisch seductive
vergangen, Vergangenheit past
vergänglich transient
vergeben, Vergebung f pardon
vergebens in vain
vergeblich fruitless
vergehen pass
Vergehen n (-) offence
vergelten repay
vergessen forget
Vergessenheit f oblivion
vergesslich forgetful
vergeuden lavish
vergewissern ascertain
vergiessen shed
vergiften poison
Vergiftung f poisoning
Vergissmeinnicht n (-e) forget me-not
Vergleich m (-e) comparison
vergleichen compare
vergnügen amuse
Vergnügen n (-) pleasure
vergnügt pleased
Vergnügungsreise f (-n) pleasure-trip
vergolden gild
Vergoldung f gilding
vergöttern deify, idolize, worship
vergraben bury
vergriffen out of print
vergrössern enlarge; **sich - increase**

Vergrösserungsglas n ('-er)
magnifying-glass
vergüten indemnify
verhaften, Verhaftung f (-en)
arrest
verhalten retain; sich - behave;
sich ruhig - keep quiet
Verhältnis n (-se) proportion;
relation(ship), connection
verhältnismässig proportional
verhandeln negotiate
Verhängnis n fate, doom
verhängnisvoll fatal
verhasst hated; odious
verhehlen, verheimlichen conceal
verheiraten marry
verheissen promise
verherrlichen glorify
verhexen bewitch
verhindern prevent
Verhör n (-e) trial; examination
verhören examine
verhungern die of hunger
verirren (sich) lose one's way
Verkauf m ('-e) sale
verkaufen sell
Verkäufer m (-) salesman
verkäuflich saleable; venal
Verkehr m intercourse; traffic;
-sstörung f interruption of
traffic; -zeichen n traffic-sign
verkehren visit; pervert
verkehrt wrong
verkennen mistake; misjudge
verklagen accuse
verkleiden, Verkleidung f (-en)
disguise
verkleinern diminish
verkohlen char
verkommen depraved
verkörpern embody
verkrüppelt crippled
verkünd(ig)en announce
verkürzen shorten
verladen load, ship
Verlag m publication; in - nehmen publish; -sbuchhändler m
publisher; -srecht n copyright
verlangen, Verlangen n demand
verlängern extend
Verlängerung f (-en) prolongation; extension

Verlass m reliance
verlassen leave; relinquish; forsake; sich - auf rely on
Verlauf m course
verlaufen subside; expire
verleben pass
verlegen misplace; remove; publish; postpone
verlegen embarrassed
Verlegenheit f embarrassment;
in - bringen embarrass
Verleger m (-) publisher
verleiden disgust
verleihen lend; grant
verleiten seduce
verlernen forget
verletzen hurt
verleugnen deny
verleumden calumniate
Verleumdung f calumny
verlieben (sich) fall in love
verlieren lose
verlobt engaged
Verlobung f (-en) engagement
Verlobungsring m (-e) engagement ring
verlockend tempting
verloren gehen be lost
Verlust m (-e) loss
vermachen leave; bequeath
Vermächtnis n (-se) legacy
vermählen marry
vermehren, Vermehrung f increase
vermeiden avoid
vermeintlich supposed
vermessen survey
vermieten let
vermindern diminish
vermischen mix
vermissen miss
vermitteln mediate
vermittels by means of
Vermittelung f (-en) mediation
vermöge by virtue of
Vermögen n be able; prevail
Vermögen n fortune
vermögend wealthy
vermuten suppose
vermutlich probable
Vermutung f (-en) conjecture
vernachlässigen neglect
vernarben cicatrize; scar

vernarrt in infatuated with
vernehmen perceive; hear
Vernehmung *f* examination
verneigen bow; curtsy
verneinen deny
Verneinung *f* negation
vernichten annihilate
vernickeln nickel
Vernunft *f* reason
vernünftig reasonable
veröffentlichen publish
Veröffentlichung *f* publication
verordnen order; prescribe
verpachten farm out, lease
verpacken pack up
verpassen miss
verpfänden pawn; pledge
verpflegen nurse
Verpflegung *f* nursing; board, provisioning
verpflichten oblige
Verrat *m* treason
verraten betray
Verräter *m* (-) traitor
verrechnen (sich) miscalculate
verreisen go on a journey
verrenken, Verrenkung *f* sprain
verriegeln bolt
verringern diminish
verrosten rust
verrückt insane; crazy
Verrücktheit *f* madness
verrufen ill-famed
Vers *m* (-e) verse
Versmass *n* (-e) metre
versagen refuse
versagt engaged
versalzen salt
versammeln assemble
Versammlung *f* (-en) meeting
Versand *m* transport, export
Versatz *m* (-̈e) pawning
Versatzschein *m* (-e) pawn ticket
versäumen omit; miss
verschaffen procure
verschämt bashful
verschanzen entrench
Verschanzung *f* entrenchment
verschenken give away
verscherzen forfeit
verschicken forward, send
verschieben put off, delay
verschieden different

Verschiedenheit *f* diversity
verschiessen fade
verschiffen ship
verschimmelt mouldy
verschlafen oversleep
verschlafen sleepy
Verschlag *m* (-̈e) partition; box
verschlagen cunning
verschlechtern deteriorate
verschleiern veil
verschleissen retail; wear out
verschlendern squander, waste
verschliessen lock up
verschlimmern make worse;
  sich - grow worse
verschlingen devour
verschlucken swallow
Verschluss (unter) under lock
  and key
verschmähen disdain
verschmelzen blend
verschmitzt artful; sly
verschmutzen soil; get dirty
verschneiden prune, clip, castrate
verschnupft sein have a cold;
  be offended
verschollen missing; lost
verschonen spare
verschönern embellish
Verschönerung *f* (-en) embellishment
verschreiben prescribe
verschreien decry
verschroben queer
verschuldet in debt
verschütten spill
verschweigen keep secret
verschwenden waste; squander
Verschwender(isch) *m* (-)
  prodigal
Verschwendung *f* dissipation
verschwiegen discreet
Verschwiegenheit *f* discretion
verschwinden disappear
verschwören conspire
Verschwörung *f* (-en) conspiracy
versehen furnish; sich - make a
  mistake
Versehen *n* (-) mistake
versenden forward, send away
versengen singe
versenken sink

Versenkung f (-en) sinking, submersion; trap-door

versetzen transplant; transfer; pawn; give; reply

versichern assure; insure

Versicherung f (-en) assurance; insurance; **-sgesellschaft** f insurance company

versiegeln seal

versilbern silver; plate; **elektrisch -** electro-plate

versinken sink down

versöhnen reconcile

Versöhnung f reconciliation

versorgen supply

verspäten retard; **sich -** be late

versperren bar; block up

verspielen lost (at play)

verspotten mock; deride

versprechen, Versprechen n (-) promise

Verstand m understanding; **gesunder -** common sense

verständigen inform; **sich -** come to an understanding

verständig reasonable

verständlich intelligible; **sich - machen** make oneself understood

verstärken strengthen

verstauchen sprain

Versteck n (-e) hiding-place

Versteck spielen play at hide-and-seek

verstecken hide

verstehen understand; **versteht sich!** of course!

versteigern sell by auction

versteinern petrify

Versteinerung f petrifaction

verstellen disguise; **sich -** dissemble

Verstellung f dissimulation

verstimmt out of tune; out of humour

verstockt hardened

verstohlenerweise on the sly

verstopft choked, constipated; **Verstopfung** f constipation

verstorben deceased

verstört bewildered

Verstoss m (¨e) offence; fault

verstossen offend; repudiate

verstümmeln mutilate

Versuch m (-e) trial, attempt

versuchen try; taste; tempt

Versuchung f (-en) temptation

versündigen (sich) sin

versüssen sweeten

vertagen adjourn

vertauschen (ex)change

verteidigen defend

Verteidigung f defence

verteilen distribute

Verteilung f (-en) distribution

verteuern raise the price of

verteufelt devilish

vertilgen exterminate

Vertrag m (¨e) treaty

vertragen bear, endure; **sich -** agree

verträglich conciliatory

vertrauen confide

Vertrauen n confidence

vertraulich confidential

Vertraulichkeit f familiarity

vertraut intimate; familiar

vertreiben drive away

vertreten represent; **Vertreter** m (-) representative

Vertrieb m (-e) sale

vertrinken spend in drink

vertrocknen dry up

vertuschen hush up

verübeln take amiss

verunehren dishonour

veruneinigen disunite

verunglücken meet with an accident

verunreinigen soil

verunstalten disfigure

veruntreuen embezzle

verursachen cause

verurteilen condemn

Verurteilung f condemnation

vervielfältigen multiply

vervollkommnen improve

vervollständigen complete

verwachsen deformed

verwahren keep guard

verwahrlost neglected

verwaist orphaned; bereft of parents

verwalten administer; manage

Verwaltung f administration

verwandeln transform

verwandt related (to)
Verwandte *mf* (**-n**) relative
Verwandtschaft *f* relationship
verwarnen reprimand
verwechseln confound
Verwechselung *f* (**-en**) mistake
verwegen daring, rash
verwehren hinder
verweichlicht effeminate
verweigern refuse
verweilen stay
Verweis *m* (**-e**) reprimand
verweisen auf refer to
verwelken fade, wither
verweltlichen secularize
verwenden employ; **sich -** intercede
verwerfen reject
verwerflich objectionable
verwerten turn to account
verwesen putrefy
Verwesung *f* putrefaction
verwickeln entangle
verwinden get over
verwirken forfeit
verwirklichen realize
Verwirklichung *f* (**-en**) realiza-
tion
verwirrt perplexed; confused
Verwirrung *f* (**-en**) confusion
verwischen efface
verwitwet widowed
verwöhnen spoil
verwundbar vulnerable
verwunden wound
verwundern astonish; **sich -**
wonder
Verwunderung *f* astonishment
verwünschen, **-ung** *f* curse
verwüsten devastate
verzagen despond
verzählen (**sich**) miscalculate
verzehren consume
verzeichnen note down, register
Verzeichnis *n* (**-se**) list
verzeihen pardon
verzeihlich pardonable
Verzeihung *f* pardon
verzerren distort
verzetteln squander, scatter
Verzicht *m* resignation
verzichten resign ; renounce
verziehen spoil; remove, move

verzieren decorate
Verzierung *f* (**-en**) decoration
verzinken zinc
verzinnen tin
verzinsen pay interest on
verzögern, **Verzögerung** *f*, **Ver-
zug** *m* delay
verzollen pay duty; **nichts zu -**
nothing to declare
verzweifeln, **Verzweiflung** *f*
despair
verzweifelt desperate
verzweigen (**sich**) branch off
verzwickt intricate
Vetter *m* (**-**) cousin
Vieh *n* beast; cattle; **-zucht** *f*
cattle-breeding
viehisch beastly
viel much; **-erlei** of many kinds;
-fach manifold; **-frass** *m* glutton; **-mals** many times; **-mehr**
rather; **-sagend** significant;
-versprechend very promising
vielleicht perhaps
vier four; **-fach** fourfold
Vier-eck(ig) *n* square; **-füsser**
m quadruped; **-schrötig** square
built; **-spänner** *m* four-in-hand
Viertel *n* (**-**) quarter; **-stunde** *f*
quarter of an hour
Viktualien *pl* victuals
Villa *f* (**-en**) villa; country house
violett violet
Violine *f* (**-n**) violin
Violoncell *n* (**-os**) violoncello
Visier *n* (**-e**) visor, sight
Visitenkarte *f* (**-n**) visiting card
visitieren search
Vivat *n* (**-s**) cheer
Vizekönig *m* viceroy
Vlissingen Flushing
Vogel *m* (**-**) bird; **-bauer** *n* bird-
cage; **-flinte** *f* fowling-piece;
-händler *m* bird fancier; **-haus**
n aviary; **-perspektive, -schau**
f bird's-eye view; **-scheuche**
f scarecrow; **-steller** *m* fow-
ler
Vogesen *pl* Vosges
Vokal *m* (**-e**) vowel
Volk *n* (**-er**) people; nation
Völkerbund *m* league of nations
Völkerrecht *n* law of nations

Völkerschaft f (-en) tribe
volkreich populous
Volks-lied n popular song; **-schule** f primary school; **-tümlich** popular; **-versammlung** f public meeting; **-vertreter** m deputy, representative; **-wirtschaft** f political economy; **-zählung** f census
voll full; **-bringen, -strecken** execute; **-jährig** of age; **-kommen(heit)** perfect(ion); **-macht** f power; **-mond** m full moon; **-ständig, -zählig** complete; **-ziehende Gewalt** executive power
vollenden, V-ung f finish; **vollends** entirely; **völlig** entire
Volumen n (-ina) volume
vor, -an, -aus before; **- allem** above all
Vorabend m eve
vorangehen precede; take the lead
Vorarbeiter m (-) foreman
voraus in advance
Voraus-sagung f prediction; **-sagen** predict; **-sehen** foresee; **-setzen** suppose; **-setzung** f supposition; **-sicht** f foresight; **-sichtlich** probable
Vorbedacht m premeditation
Vorbedeutung f (-en) omen
Vorbehalt m, **sich vorbehalten** reserve
vorbei past; **-gehen** pass
vorbereiten prepare
Vorbereitung f (-en) preparation
Vorbild n (-er) model
Vorbildung f schooling, preliminary training
vorder front; fore
Vorder-ansicht f front view; **-arm** m forearm; **-grund** m foreground; **-lader** m muzzle-loader; **-sitz** m front seat; **-zahn** m front tooth; **-zimmer** n front room
vorderst foremost
vordringen advance
voreilig rash
voreingenommen prepossessed

Voreingenommenheit f prepossession
vorenthalten withhold
Vorfahr m (-en) ancestor
Vor-fall, -gang m (-̈e) event
vorfallen happen; occur
Vorfrage f previous question
Vorgänger m (-) predecessor
Vorgarten m front garden
vorgeben pretend
Vorgebirge n cape
vorgeblich pretended
vorgefasst preconceived
vorgehen advance; be too fast; happen
vorgeschichtlich prehistoric
Vorgeschmack m foretaste
vorgesehen! look out!
Vorgesetzte m (adj. noun) superior
vorgestern the day before yesterday
vorgreifen anticipate
vorhaben, V-haben n plan
Vorhalle f (-n) porch; hall
vorhanden sein exist
Vorhang m (-̈e) curtain
Vorhängeschloss n (-̈er) padlock
Vorhemdknopf m (-̈e) stud
vorher previously
vorhergehen precede
vorherig previous
vorherrschen predominate
vorhin just now
Vorhut f van
vorig former; last
vorkommen happen, occur
Vorkommnis n (-se) occurrence
vorladen summon
Vorläufer m (-) forerunner
vorläufig for the present
vorlaut forward, pert
vorlegen propose, serve
Vorlegeschloss n (-̈er) padlock
vorlesen read
Vorlesung f (-en) lecture
vorletzt last but one
vorlieb nehmen be content
Vorliebe f predilection
vorliegend in question
vormals formerly

Vormittag *m* (-e) morning
Vormund *m* guardian
vorn, -heraus in front
Vorname *m* (-n) Christian name
vornehm of rank; distinguished
vornehmen (**sich**) intend
vornüber head foremost
Vorort *m* (-e) suburb
Vorposten *m* (-) outpost
Vorrang *m* precedence
Vorrat *m* (˝e) stock
vorrätig in stock
Vorrecht *n* (-e) privilege
Vorrede *f* preface
Vorrichtung *f* apparatus
vorrücken advance
Vorsatz *m* (˝e) intention
vorsätzlich intentionally
Vorschein *m* appearance; **zum -kommen** appear
vorschiessen advance
Vorschlag *m* (˝e) proposition
vorschlagen propose
vorschneiden carve
vorschreiben prescribe
Vorschrift *f* (-en) prescription
vorschuhen refoot
Vorschuss *m* (˝e) advance; **-verein** *m* loan society
vorschützen pretend
vorsehen (**sich**) take care
Vorsehung *f* Providence
vorsetzen set before
Vorsicht, Vorsorge *f* precaution
vorsichtig cautious
Vorsitz *m* chair; **- führen** preside
Vorsitzende *m* (adj. noun) chairman
Vorspann *m* relay
Vorspiegelung *f* (-en) pretence
Vorspiel *n* (-e) prelude
vorsprechen call on
Vorsprung *m* start; advantage
Vorstadt *f* (-n) suburb
Vorstecknadel *f* (-n) tie-pin
vorstehen project
Vorsteher *m* (-) director
Vorstehhund *m* (-e) pointer
vorstellen introduce; advance; perform; **sich -** imagine
Vorstellung *f* (-en) introduction; performance; idea; remonstrance
vorstrecken advance

Vorteil *m* (-e) advantage
vorteilhaft advantageous
Vortrab *m* vanguard
Vortrag *m* (˝e) lecture
vortragen recite
vortrefflich excellent
vortreten step forward
Vortritt *m* precedence
vorüber beyond; over
Vorurteil *n* (-e) prejudice
Vorwand *m* (˝e) pretext
vorwärts forward
vorwegnehmen anticipate
vorwerfen, Vorwurf *m* (˝e) reproach
vorwiegen preponderate
Vorwissen *n* foreknowledge, prescience
vorwitzig inquisitive
Vorwort *n* preface
vorzeigen show; exhibit
Vorzeit *f* olden times
vorzeitig premature
vorziehen prefer
Vorzimmer *n* (-) antechamber
Vorzug *m* (˝e) preference
vorzüglich excellent
vorzugsweise especially
votieren, Votum *n* (-a) vote
Vulkan *m* (-e) volcano
vulkanisch volcanic
vulkanisieren vulcanize

W

Waage *f* (-n) balance
Wabe *f* (-n) honeycomb
wach awake, astir
Wache *f* guard
wachen wake, be awake
wachhabend on duty
Wacholder *m* (-) juniper; **-branntwein** *m* gin
Wachs *n* (-e) wax; **-figur** *f* wax figure; **-leinwand** *f* oil-cloth; **-kerzchen, -licht** *n* waxlight; **-tuch** *n* oil-cloth
wachsam vigilant
wachsen grow
Wachstum *n* growth
Wacht *f* (-en) watch

Wachtel *f* (-n) quail
Wachtelhund *m* (-e) spaniel
Wächter *m* (-) watchman
wackeln shake, totter
wacklig shaky
wacker brave, gallant
Wade *f* (-n) calf (leg)
Waffe *f* (-n) arm; **-nschmied** *m* armourer; **-stillstand** *m* armistice
Wagschale *f* scale
wagen venture; risk
Wagen *m* (-) carriage, car; **-wechsel** *m* change of carriage; **-abteil** *n* compartment; **-schuppen** *m* coach-house
wägen weigh
Wahl *f* (-en) election; choice; **-recht** *n* franchise; **-spruch** *m* motto, device; **-verwandtschaft** *f* elective affinity; **-urne** *f* ballot-box; **-zettel** *m* ballot paper
wahlberechtigt, **-fähig** entitled to (a) vote; **-frei** optional
wählbar eligible
wählen elect; choose
Wähler *m* (-) elector
wählerisch fastidious
Wahnsinn *m* madness
wahnsinnig insane, mad
wahr true; **-haft(ig)**, **-lich** truly, in truth; **-nehmen** perceive; **-sagen** prophesy; **-sager(in)** *m* (*f*) fortune-teller; **-scheinlichkeit** *f* probability; **-spruch** *m* verdict
währen last
während during; while
Wahrheit *f* truth
wahrheitsliebend truthful
Währung *f* (-en) standard, currency
Waise *f* (-n) orphan; **-nhaus** *n* orphanage
Wald *m* (¨er) wood, forest
Waldhorn *n* (¨er) bugle
waldig woody
Walfisch *m* (-e) whale
Walfischfahrer *m* whaler
walken full
Wall *m* (¨e) rampart; **Wallfahrer** *m* pilgrim; **Wallfahrt** *f* pilgrimage

Walnuss(baum) *f* (¨e) (*m*) walnut(tree)
Walze *f* (-n) cylinder, roller
walzen, wälzen roll
Walzer *m* (-) walzen waltz
Walzwerk *n* (-e) rolling-mill
Wand *f* (¨er) wall; partition; **spanische-** folding screen; **-kalender** *m* sheet-almanac; **-karte** *f* map; **-schrank** *m* closet; **-tafel** *f* blackboard; **-teppich** *m* tapestry
Wandel *m* change; conduct
wandeln walk, wander
Wanderer *m* (-) wanderer
wandern wander
Wanderung *f* (-en) tour
Wange *f* (-n) cheek
wanken totter, stagger
wann when
Wanne *f* (-n) tub, bath
Wanst *m* (¨e) paunch, belly
Wanze *f* (-n) bug
Wappen *n* (-) coat of arms
Waren *f pl* merchandise, goods; **-haus** *n* department store; **-lager** *n* warehouse; **-probe** *f* sample; **-zeichen** *n* trade-mark
warm, wärmen warm
Wärme *f* warmth, heat; **-grad** *m* degree of heat; **-strahl** *m* thermal ray
Wärmflasche *f* (-n) hot-water bottle
Warmwasserheizung *f* hot-water heating
warnen warn
warten (auf) wait for
Wärter *m* (-) keeper
Wärterin *f* (-nen) nurse
Wartesaal *m* (-säle), **-zimmer** *n* (-) waiting-room
warum why
Warze *f* (-n) wart; nipple
was which, what; **- auch**, **- immer** whatever
Wasch-becken *n* wash-hand-basin; **-frau** *f* washerwoman; **-haus** *n*, **-küche** *f* wash-house; **-korb** *m* linen-basket; **-tisch** *m* wash-stand; **-weib** *n* gossip
Wäsche *f* washing; linen; **-geschäft** *n* ready-made linen ware-

house; **-schrank** *m* linen-cup-board
waschen wash
Wäscherin *f* (-nen) laundress
Wasser *n*, **wässern** water; **-behälter** *m* tank; **-dampf** *m* steam; **-dicht** waterproof; **-fall** *m* waterfall; **-farbenmalerei** *f* painting in water-colours; **-flasche** *f* carafe; **-glas** *n* tumbler; **-heilanstalt** *f* hydro; **-heizung** *f* hot-water heating; **-kraft** *f* water-power; **-leitung** *f* aqueduct, water-supply; **-messer** *m* water meter; **-partie** *f* boating excursion; **-pflanze** *f* aquatic plant; **-rad** *n* water-wheel; **-rübe** *f* turnip; **-scheide** *f* water-shed; **-scheu** *f* hydrophobia; **-sperre** *f* weir; **-spiegel**, **-stand** *m* level of the water; **-sport** *m* aquatics; **-stiefel** *m* waterproof boot; **-stoff** *m* hydrogen; **-sucht** *f* dropsy; **-wage** *f* water-level; **-werk** *n* waterworks; **-zeichen** *n* water-mark
wässerig watery
watscheln waddle
Watte *f* wadding; **wattieren** wad
weben weave; **Weber** *m* weaver; **Weberei** *f* weaving; **Webstuhl** *m* loom
Wechsel *m* change; bill of exchange; **-geschäft** *n* exchange-office; **-strom** *m* alternating current
wechseln change, vary
wechselweise alternately
Wechsler *m* (-) money-changer
wecken wake
Wecker *m* (-) alarm-clock
wedeln fan, wag
Weg *m* (-e) way; path
weg away; **-gehen** go away; **-fahren** drive away; **-fallen** drop off; **-lassen** omit; **-legen** lay aside; **-räumen** clear away; **-werfend** disdainful; **-ziehen** move
wegen on account of
Wegerich *m* (-e) plantain
Wegweiser *m* (-) signpost

weh sore; woe; **-klagen** lament; **-mütig** melancholy; **- tun** ache
wehen blow
Wehen *f pl* labour pains
Wehr *n* (-e) weir; *f* (-en) defence
wehren defend
wehrlos defenceless
Wehrmacht *f* (ˀe) armed forces
Wehrstand *m* military profession
Weib *n*, **-chen** *n* woman; wife; female; **-erfeind** *m* womanhater; **weibisch** effeminate; **weiblich** female, feminine
weich, **-lich** soft; tender
Weichbild *n* outskirts
Weiche *f* (-n) switch points; groin; **-nsteller** *m* pointsman
Weichselholz *n* cherrywood
Weide *f* (-n) willow: pasture
weiden graze; **-korb** *m* wicker-basket
Weidmann *m* (ˀer) hunter
weigern (**sich**) refuse
Weigerung *f* (-en) refusal
Weihbischof *m* (ˀe) suffragan
Weihe *f* ordination
weihen consecrate; ordain
Weiher *m* (-) pond
Weihnacht-en *f pl* Christmas; **-sabend** *m* C. Eve; **-sbaum** *m* C.-tree; **-sgeschenk** *n* C.-box
Weihrauch *m* incense; **-fass** *n* censer
Weihwasser *n* holy water
weil because
weiland formerly; late
Weile *f* while
weilen stay, tarry
Weiler *m* (-) hamlet
Wein *m* (-e) wine; **-beere** *f* grape; **-berg** *m* vineyard; **-brand** brandy; **-essig** *m* French vinegar; **-flasche** *f* wine bottle **-geist** *m* spirits of wine; **-karte** *f* wine list; **-kühler** *m* wine-cooler; **-lese** *f* vintage; **-rebe** *f*, **-stock** *m* vine; **-traube** *f* bunch of grapes
weinen cry, weep
weise wise
Weise *m* (adj. noun) sage; *f* manner
weisen show; teach

Weisheit f wisdom
weismachen make believe
weiss white
weisslich whitish
Weiss-blech n tin-plate; **-brot** n white bread; **-fisch** m whiting; **-kohl** m white cabbage; **-ware** f linen
weissen whitewash
Weisung f (-en) direction
weit far; large; **bei-em** by far; **- und breit** far and near; **-läufig**, **-schweifig** vast; **-sichtig** far-sighted
Weite f width
weiten widen, stretch
weiter further on; **und so -** and so on; **ohne - es** without ceremony; **- gehen** go on
Weizen m wheat
welk withered
welken wither
Wellblech n corrugated-iron plate
Welle f (-n) wave; shaft; **-nbrecher** m breakwater; **-nförmig** undulatory
welsch foreign, alien
Welt f (-en) world; **-all** n universe; **-alter** n age; **-ausstellung** f international exhibition; **-berühmt** far-famed; **-gericht** n last judgment; **-geschichte** f universal history; **-kugel** f terrestrial globe; **-mann** m man of the world; **-meer** n ocean; **-postverein** m International Postal Union; **-sprache** f universal language; **-teil** m continent
weltlich secular; **-gesinnt** wordly
Wendekreis m (-e) tropic
Wendeltreppe f (-n) spiral stairs
wenden, sich - turn; **sich - an** apply to
Wendepunkt m (-e) turning-point
Wendung f (-en) turn
wenig little; **-er** less; **-ste** least; **-stens** at least
wenn if; when
wer da? who goes there?
werben court, woo; enlist, recruit

werden become; grow; turn
werfen throw; **sich -** warp (wood)
Werft f (-en) wharf
Werg n tow
Werk n (-e) work; **-statt** f workshop; **-tag** m working-day; **-tisch** m working table; **-zeug** n tool
Wermut m wormwood, vermouth
wert worth; **der Mühe -** worth the trouble
Wert m (-e) value; **-brief** m registered letter; **-papiere** n pl securities; **-schätzen** esteem; **-voll** precious
Wesen n being; essence
wesentlich essential
weshalb, weswegen why
Wespe f (-n) wasp
Weste f (-n) waistcoat
West(en) m west
westlich west(ern)
Westwind m west wind
Wette f (-n), **wetten** bet, wager
Wett-eifer, **-streit** m emulation; **-eifern** emulate; **-kampf** m contest; **-lauf** m, **-rennen** n race; **-rudern** n boat-race
Wetter n weather; **schlagende-firedamp**; **-fahne** f, **-hahn** m weather-cock; **-leuchten** n sheet lightning; **-bericht** m weather forecast; **-warte** f meteorological observatory; **-wechsel** m, **-umschlag** m change of weather **-wendisch** fickle
wetzen whet
Wichse f blacking
wichsen black, polish
Wicht m (-e) wight, wretch
wichtig important
Wichtigkeit f importance
wickeln wind; wrap up
Widder m (-) ram
wider against; **-fahren** befall; **-haken** m barb; **-halt** m hold; **-lager** n abutment; **-legen** refute; **-natürlich** unnatural; **-raten** dissuade; **-rechtlich** unlawful; **-rede** f contradiction; **-ruf** m revocation; **-rufen** revoke; **-sacher** m

adversary; **sich -setzen** resist; **-setzlich, -spenstig** refractory, obstinate; **-sinnig** absurd; **-sprechen** contradict; **-spruch** *m* contradiction; **-stand** *m* resistance; **-stehen, -steben** resist; **-strebend** reluctant; **-wärtig** disgusting; **-wille** *m* disgust; **-willig** reluctant

widmen dedicate

Widmung *f* (**-en**) dedication

widrig adverse; contrary

wie how ?; as

Wiede *f* (**-n**) withe

wieder again; **-beleben** revive; **-erkennen** recognize; **-erlangen** recover; **-erstatten, -geben** restore, return; **-genesen** recover; **-genesung** *f* recovery; **-hall** *m* echo; **-herstellen** restore; **-holen** repeat; **-holung** *f* repetition; **käuer** *m* ruminant; **-kehr** *f*, **-kehren, -kommen** return; **-täufer** *m* anabaptist; **-vergelten** retaliate; **wahl** *f* re-election; **-wählen** re-elect

Wiege *f* (**-n**) cradle

wiegen weigh; rock

wiehern neigh

Wien Vienna

Wiese *f* (**-n**) meadow

Wiesel *n* (**-**) weasel

wieviel how much?; **-Uhr ist es?** what is the time; **der wievielste ist es?** what day of the month?

wild wild; savage

Wild *n* game; **-bret** *n* venison; **-dieb** *m* poacher; **-schwein** *n* wild boar

Wildnis *f* wilderness

Wilhelm William

Wille *m* will

willenlos irresolute

willfahren comply with

willig willing

Willkomm(en) *m*, **willkommen** welcome

willkürlich arbitrary

wimmeln swarm

wimmern whine

Wimpel *m* (**-**) pennant

Wimper *f* (**-n**) eyelash

Wind *m* (**-e**) wind; **-beutel** *m* swaggerer; **-büchse** *f* air-gun; **-hund** *m* greyhound; **-mühle** *f* windmill; **-pocken** *f pl* chicken-pox; **-still, -stille** *f* calm; **-stoss** *m* gust; squall; **-zug** *m* draught

Winde *f* (**-n**) windlass, bindweed

winden wind; twist

windig windy

Windung *f* (**-en**) turning

Wink *m* (**-e**), **winken** nod; hint

Winkel *m* (**-**) angle

Winker *m* (**-**) indicator

winklig angular

winseln whine

Winter *m* winter; **-garten** *m* conservatory; **-kurort** *m* winter resort

winterlich wintry

Winzer *m* (**-**) vintager

winzig very small

Wipfel *m* (**-**) top (tree)

Wirbel *m* (**-**), **wirbeln** whirl; crown; roll; **-säule** *f* spine; **-wind** *m* whirlwind

wirken act; weave

wirklich real; **Wirklichkeit** *f* reality; **wirksam** efficient; **Wirkung** *f* effect

wirr confused

Wirrwarr *m* confusion

Wirsingkohl *m* (**-e**) savoy

Wirt *m* (**-e**) landlord; **-in** *f* landlady; **-schaften** manage; **-schafterin** *f* housekeeper; **-schaftlich** economical; **-shaus** *n* public-house

wischen wipe; rub

Wischlappen *m* (**-**) dish-cloth

wissen know; **Wissen** *n* knowledge; **meines -s** as far as I know; **-schaft** *f* science; **-schaftlich** scientific; **-tlich** wilful, deliberate

Witterung *f* scent; weather

Witwe(r) *f* (**-n**) (*m*) widow(er)

Witz *m* (**-e**) wit, joke; **witzig** witty

wo, -bei, -hin where; **-fern** if; **-für** for what; **-her** whence; **-rauf** whereupon

Woche *f* (**-n**) week; **-nbett** *n*
child-bed; **-nblatt** *n* weekly
(paper); **-ntag** *m* week-day
wöchentlich weekly
Wöchnerin *f* (**-nen**) lying-in
woman
Woge *f* (**-n**), **wogen** wave
wohl well; **Wohl** *n* welfare;
-befinden *n*, **-behalten** safe;
-bekannt well known; **-beleibt**
corpulent; **-ergehen** *n* welfare;
-fahrt *f* welfare; **-feil** cheap;
-gefällig agreeable; **-gemut**
cheerful; **-geruch** *m* perfume;
-geschmack *m* flavour; **-ha-
bend** wealthy; **-riechend** fragrant;
-sein *n* good health;
-stand *m* wealth; **-tat** *f*
benefit; **-täter** *m* benefactor;
-tätig charitable; **-tätigkeit
(sanstalt)** *f* charity (institution);
-weislich wisely; **-wollen** *n* benevolence; **-wollend**
benevolent
wohnen live; dwell
wohnhaft living; **Wohnhaus** *n*
dwelling-house
Wohnsitz *m* domicile
Wohnung *f* (**-en**) residence,
house; lodgings, flat; **-swechsel**
m removal
Wohnzimmer *n* (**-**) sitting-
room
wölben, **Wölbung** *f* (**-en**) vault
Wolf *m* (**-̈e**) wolf
Wolke *f* (**-n**) cloud
wolkig cloudy
Wolle *f* wool; **wollen** woollen;
wollig woolly
wollen will, wish
wollüstig voluptuous
Wonne *f* delight; rapture
wonnig delightful
Wort *n* (**e** or **-̈er**) word; **-bruch**
m breach of promise; **-führer** *m*
spokesman; **-karg** taciturn;
-laut *m* wording; **-spiel** *n*,
-witz *m* pun; **-streit**, **-wechsel**
m dispute
Wörterbuch *n* (**-̈er**) dictionary
wörtlich literal
Wrack *n* (**-e**) wreck
wringen wring

Wucher *m* usury; **-er** *m* usurer;
-isch usurious
Wuchs *m* growth; stature
Wucht *f* (**-en**) weight, pressure
wühlen stir, rummage
Wulst *m* (**-̈e**) roll; pad
wund sore
Wundarzt *m* (**-̈e**) surgeon
Wunde *f* (**-n**) wound
Wunder *n* (**-**) wonder; **-kind,
-tier** *n* prodigy; **-kur** *f* miraculous
cure; **-lampe** *f* magic
lantern; **-tat** *f*, **-werk** *n* miracle
wunder-bar, **-voll**, **-schön** wonderful;
-lich strange; **-tätig**
miraculous
wundern astonish; **sich -** wonder
Wunsch *m* (**-̈e**) wish, desire
wünschenswert desirable
Würde *f* dignity
würdig worthy
würdigen deign; appreciate
Würdigkeit *f* worth, merit
Wurf *m* (**-̈e**) throw, litter; **-ges-
choss** *n* projectile
Würfel *m* (**-**) dice; cube
Würfelbecher *m* (**-**) dice-box
würfeln play at dice
würgen strangle
Wurm *m* (**-̈er**) worm; **-mittel** *n*
vermifuge; **-stich** *m* worm-hole;
-stichig worm-eaten
Wurst *f* (**-̈e**) sausage
Würze *f* (**-n**) seasoning, spice
Wurzel *f* (**-n**) root, stump
würzen season
würzig aromatic
Wust *m* chaos
wüst deserted; waste
Wüste *f* (**-n**) desert
Wüstling *m* (**-e**) rake, libertine
Wut *f*, **wüten** rage
wütend furious
Wüterich *m* tyrant

X

Xanthippe *f* termagant
Xaver *m* Xavier
X-beine knock-knees

Xerswein *m* sherry
X-Strahlen *m pl* X-rays
Xylograph *m* (-en) xylographer

Y

Yacht *f* (-en) yacht
Ypsilon *n* letter Y
Ysop, Isop *m* hyssop

Z

Zacke *f* (-n) scallop, prong; cog; tooth (of comb)
zacken jag
zackig indented; toothed
zaghaft timid; timorous
zähe tough; sticky
Zähigkeit *f* tenacity
Zahl *f* (-en) number; figure
zahlbar payable
Zähler *m* (-) numerator
zahlen pay
zählen count
zahllos innumerable
zahlreich numerous
Zahlung *f* (-en) payment
zahlungs(un)fähig (in)solvent
zahm, zähmen tame
Zahn *m* (-e) tooth; **-arzt** *m* dentist; **-bürste** *f* toothbrush; **-fäule** *f* caries; **-fleisch** *n* gums; **-lücke** *f* gap; **-pasta** *f* toothpaste; **-rad** *n* cog-wheel; **-radbahn** *f* rack railway; **-schmerz** *m*, **-weh** *n* toothache; **-stocher** *m* toothpick
Zähneknirschen *n* gnashing of teeth
zahnen cut teeth
Zange *f* (-n) tongs
Zank *m* (-e), **zanken** quarrel
zänkisch quarrelsome
Zäpfchen *n* uvula
Zapfen *m* (-) peg; tap; cone
zapfen tap
Zapfenstreich *m* tattoo
zappeln sprawl, struggle
Zar *m* (-en) czar; **-in** *f* czarina
zart tender; delicate; **-gefühl**

n delicacy; **zärtlich** tender; **Zärtlichkeit** *f* tenderness
Zauber *m* (-), **-mittel** *n* charm; **-ei** *f* witchcraft; **-er** *m* magician; **z-haft** magic; **-laterne** *f* magic lantern
zaudern hesitate
Zaum *m* (-e) **zäumen** bridle
Zaun *m* (-e) fence; **-könig** *m* wren; **-pfahl** *m* fence-pole
Zebra *n* (-s) zebra
Zeche *f* (-n) score; mine
zechen drink hard
Zecher *m* (-) tippler
Zeder *f* (-n) cedar
Zehe *f* (-n) toe; **auf den Zehenspitzen** on tiptoe
zehn ten
Zehnt *m* tithe
zehren live on (off); be wasting
Zeichen *n* (-) sign; **-papier** *n* drawing-paper; **-tinte** *f* marking-ink
zeichnen draw; mark; sign; subscribe
Zeichner *m* (-) draughtsman
Zeichnung *f* (-en) drawing
Zeidler *m* (-) bee-keeper
Zeigefinger *m* (-) forefinger
zeigen show
Zeiger *m* (-) hand; pointer
Zeile *f* (-n) line
Zeit *f* (-en) time; **zur -** at the time; **zur rechten -** in good time; **von - zu -**, **-weise** from time to time; **-alter** *n* age; **-gemäss** opportune; **-genosse** *m* contemporary; **-rechnung** *f* era; **-schrift** *f* periodical; **-verlust** *m* loss of time; **-verschwendung** *f* waste of time; **-vertreib** *m* pastime; **-weilig** temporary
zeitig early; in good time
zeitlich temporal
Zeitung *f* (-en) newspaper; **-sschreiber** *m* journalist; **-sträger** *m* newsman, newsboy
Zelle *f* (-n) cell; cabin
Zelluloid *n* celluloid
Zelt *n* (-e) tent
Zement *m* cement
Zenit *m* zenith
zensieren censure; review

Zensur f (-en) censure; certificate

Zensus m census

Zentner m (-) hundredweight

zentral(isieren) central(ize)

Zentrum n (-en) centre

Zepter n (-) sceptre

zer-brechen break to pieces; **-brechlich** fragile; **-drücken** crush; **-fallen** decay, fall out; **-fliessen, -gehen** melt; **-knirscht** contrite; **-knittern** crumple; **-kratzen** scratch; **-legen** carve, decompose; **-lumpt** tattered; **-malmen** crush; **-quetschen** bruise; **-reiben** pulverize; **-reissen** rend, tear; **-rütten** derange; **-schlagen** break; **-schmettern** dash to pieces; **-setzen** decompose; **-splittern** shiver; **-springen** burst, crack; **-stören** destroy; **-störung** f destruction; **-stossen** pound; **-streuen** disperse, divert; **-streut** absent; **-streutheit** f absence of mind; **-streuung** f diversion; **-stückeln** dismember; **-teilen** divide; **-treten** trample; **-trümmern** demolish

Zerrbild n (-er) caricature

zerren pull

Zerstäuber m (-) spray-diffuser

Zeter schreien raise an outcry

Zettel m (-) bill; note, label

Zeug n (-e) stuff; nonsense; **-haus** n arsenal

Zeuge m (-n) witness; **zeugen** testify, beget; **-naussage** f evidence

Zeugnis n (-se) certificate

Zeugung f generation

Zichorie f chicory

Zickzack m zigzag

Ziege f (-n) goat

Ziegel m (-) brick, tile; **-brennerei** f brickworks

Ziegelofen m (⸚) brick-kiln

Ziegenpeter m mumps

Ziehbrunnen m (-) draw-well

ziehen draw, move, raise

Ziehharmonika f accordion

Ziehung f (-er) drawing (lots)

Ziel n (-e), **zielen** aim

Zielscheibe f (-n) target; mark

ziemen become, suit

ziemlich pretty; tolerably

Zier f (-en), **-rat** m, **-de** f ornament

zieren adorn

Ziererei f affection

zierlich nice; neat

Ziffer f (-n) figure; **-blatt** n dial

Zigarette f (-n) cigarette

Zigarre f (-n) cigar

Zigeuner m (-) gipsy

Zimmer n (-) room; **-decke** f ceiling; **-mädchen** n chambermaid; **-mann** m carpenter

zimperlich prim

Zimt m cinnamon

Zink n zinc

Zinke f (-n) prong

Zinn n tin; pewter

Zinne f (-n) battlement

Zinnober m cinnabar

Zinsen m pl interest

Zinsfuss m rate of interest

Zipfel m (-) tip

Zipperlein n gout

Zirkel m (-) (pair) compasses

zirpen chirp

Zirkus m (-se) circus

zischen hiss

zischeln whisper

ziselieren chase, carve

Zisterne f (-n) cistern

Zitadelle f (-n) citadel

Zitat n (-e) quotation

Zither f (-n) zither

zitieren cite; quote

Zitrone f (-n) lemon

zittern tremble

Zitz m chintz

Zitze f (-n) nipple

zivil civil

zivilisieren civilize

Zivilist m (-en) civilian

Zobel m (-) sable

Zofe f (-n) chambermaid

zögern hesitate

Zögerung f (-en) delay, hesitation

Zögling m (-e) pupil

Zoll m inch; custom, duty; **-amt** n custom-house; **-beamte** m custom-house officer; **-frei** free of duty; **-krieg** *m* tariff war; **-pflichtig** liable to duty

Zone *f* (**-n**) zone

Zoologie *f* zoology

zoologisch zoological

Zopf *m* (ˊˊe) pigtail, tress, plait

Zorn *m* anger

zornig angry

Zote *f* (**-n**) obscenity

zotig obscene

zottig shaggy

Zuber *m* (**-**) tub

zubereiten prepare

Zubereitung *f* (**-en**) preparation

zubinden tie up

zubringen pass

Zucht *f* (**-en**) breeding; discipline; **-haus** *n* convict prison; **-häusler** *m* convict

züchten breed

Züchter *m* (**-**) breeder

züchtig chaste

züchtigen chastise

Züchtigung *f* (**-en**) chastisement

zucken wince

zücken draw

Zucker *m*, (**zuckern**) sugar; **-bäcker** *m* confectioner; **-dose** *f* sugar-box; **-hut** *m* sugar-loaf; **-krankheit** *f* diabetes; **-plätzchen** drop; **-rohr** *n* sugar-cane; **-rübe** *f* sugar-beet; **-sachen** sweetmeats; **-sieder(ei)** *m* (*f*) refiner(y); **-zange** *f* sugar-tongs

Zuckung *f* (**-en**) convulsion

zudecken cover up

zudem besides, moreover

Zudrang *m* throng

zudrehen shut (off)

zudringlich importunate

zueignen attribute; dedicate

Zueignung *f* (**-en**) dedication

zuerkennen award

zuerst at first, first

Zufall *m* (ˊˊe) accident; chance

zufällig accidental

Zuflucht *f* (**-en**) refuge

zufolge according to

zufreiden contented; satisfied

Zufriedenneit *f* satisfaction

zufrieren freeze up

zufügen add; cause

Zufuhr *f* (**-en**) supply

Zug *m* (ˊˊe) traction; march; procession; feature; train; campaign; draught; move; **-brücke** *f* drawbridge; **-führer** *m* conductor, chief guard; **-luft** *f* draught; **-mittel** *n* attraction; **-pferd** *n* draught-horse; **-pflaster** *n* blister; **-vogel** *m* bird of passage

Zugabe *f* (**-en**) supplement, surplus

Zugang *m* (ˊˊe) access; approach

zugänglich accessible

zugeben grant; admit; add

zugegen present

zugehen close; happen; go towards

zugehören belong

Zügel *m* (**-**) bridle

zügellos unbridled

zügeln bridle; curb

Zugeständnis *n* (**-se**) concession

zugestehen grant; admit

zugetan attached

zugig draughty

zugleich at the same time

zugreifen help oneself

zugunsten in favour of

zuhören listen

Zuhörer *m* hearer

Zuhörerschaft *f* audience

zuknöpfen button

Zukunft *f*, **zukünftig** future

Zulage *f* (**-n**) increase, addition

zulangen help oneself

zulassen admit; permit

zulässig admissible

Zulassung *f* (**-en**) admission

Zulauf *m* concourse, run

zuletzt at last

zumachen shut

zumal especially

Zumutung *f* strange demand

zunächst next; first

Zunahme *f* (**-n**) increase

Zuname *m* (**-n**) family name; surname

Zünden catch fire; inflame

Zunder *m* (**-**) tinder

Zünder *m* fuse; lighter

Zünd-holz *n* match; **-nadelgewehr** needle-gun; **-schnur** *f* quick-match

zunehmen increase
Zuneigung *f* affection
Zunft *f* (¨e) guild
Zunge *f* (-n) tongue
Zungenfertigkeit *f* volubility
Zungenspitze *f* tip of the tongue
zupfen pull, tug
zurechtfinden (**sich**) find one's way
Zurechtweisung *f* (-en) reprimand
zureden exhort
zureiten break in
zuriegeln bolt
zürnen be angry
zurück back; **-bleiben** remain behind; **-bringen** bring back; **-fordern** reclaim; **-gehen** go back; **-gezogen** retired; **-gezogenheit** *f* retirement; **-haltend** reserved; **-haltung** *f* reserve; **-kehren**, **-reisen** return; **-lassen**, **-legen** leave behind, put by; **-schrecken** frighten; **-setzen**, **-setzung** *f* slight; **-stossen** repulse; **-strahlen** reflect; **-weisen** reject; **-ziehen** retire
Zuruf *m* (-e) call; acclamation
Zusage *f* (-n), **zusagen** promise, assent
zusammen together; **-berufen** convoke; **-brechen** break down; **-bruch** *m* collapse; **-fassen** sum up; **-fluss** *m* confluence; **-hang** *m* connection; **hängend** connected; **-häufen** accumulate; **-kommen** meet; **-kunft** *f* meeting; **-laufen** coagulate; **-legen** club together; **-rechnen** sum up; **-schrumpfen** shrink; **-setzen** compose; **-setzung** *f* compound; **-stellen** combine; **-stoss** *m* collision; **-stossen** collide; **-stürzen** collapse; **-treffen** meet; **-zählen** sump up; **-ziehen** contract, concentrate
Zusatz *m* (¨e) addition
Zuschauer *m* (-) spectator
Zuschlag *m* (¨e) adjudication; additional payment
zuschlagen knock down, slam

zuschliessen lock up
Zuschneider *m* (-) cutter-out
Zuschnitt *m* (-e) cut
zuschnüren tie up
zuschreiben attribute
Zuschrift *f* (-en) letter
Zuschuss *m* (¨e) extra allowance
zuschütten fill up
zusehen look on
zusehends visibly
zusenden send
zusetzen lose; urge
zusichern assure
Zuspruch *m* (¨e) custom; consolation
Zustand *m* (¨e) condition
zuständig competent
zustehen belong, become
zustellen deliver
zustimmen agree, assent
Zustimmung *f* (-en) assent
zustossen, zutragen (**sich**) occur
Zutaten *f pl* ingredients; trimmings
zuträglich useful; wholesome
zutrauen think capable
Zutrauen *n* confidence
zutraulich confiding
zutreffen prove right
Zutritt *m* (-e) admission
zuverlässig trustworthy
Zuversicht *f* confidence
zuversichtlich confident
zuvor before; **-kommen** anticipate; **-kommend** obliging; **-tun** surpass
Zuwachs *m* increment
zuwege bringen bring about
zuweilen sometimes
zuweisen assign
zuwenden turn to; bestow
zuwerfen bang, slam
zuwider contrary, repugnant; **-handeln** act contrary to
zuziehen draw; consult; **sich zuziehen** catch
Zwang *m* constraint; **-los** without constraint; **-sarbeit** *f* hard labour; **-sjacke** *f* straitjacket
zwangsweise by force
zwanzig twenty

zwar indeed
Zweck *m* (-e) aim; end; -essen *n* public dinner; -los useless; -mässig suitable
Zwecke *f* (-n) tack, peg
zwei two; -fach twofold; -mal twice; -te(ns) second(ly)
zwei-deutig ambiguous; Zwei-deutigkeit *f* ambiguity; -fach double; -kampf *m* duel; -rad *n* bicycle; -reihig double-breasted; -schneidig double-edged; -sitzer *m* tandem;-spänner *m* carriage and pair
Zweifel *m*, zweifeln doubt; -sfall *m* case of doubt
zweifelhaft doubtful
zweifellos doubtless
zweifelsohne doubtless
Zweig *m* (-e) branch; -bahn *f* branch line; -geschäft *n* branch office
Zwerchfell *n* diaphragm
Zwerg *m* (-e) dwarf
Zwetsch(g)e *f* (-n) plum
zwicken pinch
Zwicker *m* (-) pince-nez
Zwieback *m* biscuit, rusk
Zwiebel *f* (-n) onion; bulb
Zwie-gespräch *n* dialogue; -licht *n* twilight; -spalt *m*, -tracht *f* discord
Zwillich *m* (-e) ticking

Zwilling *m* (-e) twin; -sbruder *m* twin brother
Zwinge *f* (-n) ferrule
zwingen force, compel
Zwinger *m* (-) cage, dungeon, bearpit
zwinkern twinkle
Zwirn *m* (-e) thread
zwirnen twist
zwischen between
Zwischenakt *m* entr'acte
Zwischendeck *n* (*m*) steerage (-passenger)
Zwischen-fall *m* incident; -gericht *n* entremets; -handel *m* intermediate trade; -raum *m* interval; -station *f* intermediate station; -stock *m* mezzanine; -stunde *f* interval; -träger *m* tell-tale; -wand *f* partition wall; -zeit *f* interval
Zwist *m* (-e) dispute, quarrel
zwitschern twitter; chirp
Zwitter *m* (-) hybrid, bastard
zwölf twelve
zwölffach twelvefold
zwölfte twelfth
Zyklon *m* (-e) cyclone
Zyklus *m* (-en) cycle; series
Zylinder *m* (-) cylinder; glass, chimney; silk hat
zylindrisch cylindrical
Zyniker *m* (-) zynisch cynic(al)
Zypresse *f* (-n) cypress

APPENDIX A

LIST OF PRINCIPAL GERMAN STRONG AND IRREGULAR VERBS

Verbs marked with an asterisk are conjugated with *sein*.

Infinitive	3rd Sing. Pres. Indic.	1st and 3rd Sing. Impf. Indic.	Past Participle	English
backen	bäckt	buk	gebacken	bake
befehlen	befiehlt	befahl	befohlen	command
beginnen	beginnt	begann	begonnen	begin
beissen	beisst	biss	gebissen	bite
bergen	birgt	barg	geborgen	hide
betrügen	betrügt	betrog	betrogen	deceive
bewegen	bewegt	bewog	bewogen	induce
biegen	biegt	bog	gebogen	bend
bieten	bietet	bot	geboten	offer
binden	bindet	band	gebunden	bind
bitten	bittet	bat	gebeten	request
blasen	bläst	blies	geblasen	blow
*bleiben	bleibt	blieb	geblieben	remain
brechen	bricht	brach	gebrochen	break
brennen	brennt	brannte	gebrannt	burn
bringen	bringt	brachte	gebracht	bring
denken	denkt	dachte	gedacht	think
*dringen	dringt	drang	gedrungen	press
empfehlen	(as befehlen)			recommend
*erlöschen	erlischt	erlosch	erloschen	get extinguished
erschrecken	erschrickt	erschrak	erschrocken	be terrified
essen	isst	ass	gegessen	eat
*fahren	fährt	fuhr	gefahren	go
*fallen	fällt	fiel	gefallen	fall
finden	findet	fand	gefunden	find
*fliegen	fliegt	flog	geflogen	fly
fressen	frisst	frass	gefressen	eat (of animals)
frieren	friert	fror	gefroren	freeze
geben	gibt	gab	gegeben	give
*gehen	geht	ging	gegangen	go
*gelingen	gelingt	gelang	gelungen	succeed
gelten	gilt	galt	gegolten	be worth
*genesen	genest	genas	genesen	recover
geniessen	geniesst	genoss	genossen	enjoy
*geschehen	geschieht	geschah	geschehen	happen
gewinnen	gewinnt	gewann	gewonnen	win
giessen	giesst	goss	gegossen	pour
gleichen	gleicht	glich	geglichen	resemble
*gleiten	gleitet	glitt	geglitten	glide
graben	gräbt	grub	gegraben	dig
greifen	greift	griff	gegriffen	grasp
halten	hält	hielt	gehalten	hold

Infinitive	3rd Sing. Pres. Indic.	1st and 3rd Sing. Impf. Indic.	Past Participle	English
hangen	hängt	hing	gehangen	hang
heben	hebt	hob	gehoben	lift
heissen	heisst	hiess	geheissen	to be named
helfen	hilft	half	geholfen	help
kennen	kennt	kannte	gekannt	know
klingen	klingt	klang	geklungen	sound
*kommen	kommt	kam	gekommen	come
laden	lädt	lud	geladen	load
lassen	lässt	liess	gelassen	let, allow
*laufen	läuft	lief	gelaufen	run
leiden	leidet	litt	gelitten	suffer
leihen	leiht	lieh	geliehen	lend
lesen	liest	las	gelesen	read
liegen	liegt	lag	gelegen	lie
lügen	lügt	log	gelogen	tell a lie
meiden	meidet	mied	gemieden	avoid
messen	misst	mass	gemessen	measure
nehmen	nimmt	nahm	genommen	take
nennen	nennt	nannte	genannt	name
preisen	preist	pries	gepriesen	praise
raten	rät	riet	geraten	advise
reiben	reibt	rieb	gerieben	rub
reissen	reisst	riss	gerissen	tear
*reiten	reitet	ritt	geritten	ride
*rennen	rennt	rannte	gerannt	run
riechen	riecht	roch	gerochen	smell
ringen	ringt	rang	gerungen	wrestle
*rinnen	rinnt	rann	geronnen	flow
rufen	ruft	rief	gerufen	call
schaffen	schafft	schuf	geschaffen	create
scheiden	scheidet	schied	geschieden	separate
scheinen	scheint	schien	geschienen	shine, seem
schieben	schiebt	schob	geschoben	push
schiessen	schiesst	schoss	geschossen	shoot
schlafen	schläft	schlief	geschlafen	sleep
schlagen	schlägt	schlug	geschlagen	beat
schliessen	schliesst	schloss	geschlossen	shut
schneiden	schneidet	schnitt	geschnitten	cut
schreiben	schreibt	schrieb	geschrieben	write
schreien	schreit	schrie	geschrieen	cry
*schreiten	schreitet	schritt	geschritten	stride
schweigen	schweigt	schwieg	geschwiegen	be silent
*schwellen	schwillt	schwoll	geschwollen	swell
*schwimmen	schwimmt	schwamm	geschwommen	swim
schwingen	schwingt	schwang	geschwungen	swing
schwören	schwört	schwor	geschworen	swear
sehen	sieht	sah	gesehen	see
senden	sendet	sandte	gesandt	send
singen	singt	sang	gesungen	sing
*sinken	sinkt	sank	gesunken	sink

Infinitive	3rd Sing. Pres. Indic.	1st and 3rd Sing. Impf. Indic.	Past Participle	English
sitzen	sitzt	sass	gesessen	sit
sprechen	spricht	sprach	gesprochen	speak
*springen	springt	sprang	gesprungen	spring
stehen	steht	stand	gestanden	stand
stehlen	stiehlt	stahl	gestohlen	steal
*steigen	steigt	stieg	gestiegen	ascend
*sterben	stirbt	starb	gestorben	die
stossen	stösst	stiess	gestossen	push
streichen	streicht	strich	gestrichen	stroke
streiten	streitet	stritt	gestritten	quarrel
tragen	trägt	trug	getragen	carry
treffen	trifft	traf	getroffen	hit, meet
treiben	treibt	trieb	getrieben	drive
*treten	tritt	trat	getreten	tread
trinken	trinkt	trank	getrunken	drink
tun	tut	tat	getan	do
verderben	verdirbt	verdarb	verdorben	spoil
vergessen	vergisst	vergass	vergessen	forget
verlieren	verliert	verlor	verloren	lose
*verschwinden	verschwindet	verschwand	verschwunden	disappear
verzeihen	verzeiht	verzieh	verziehen	forgive
*wachsen	wächst	wuchs	gewachsen	grow
wägen	wägt	wog	gewogen	weigh
waschen	wäscht	wusch	gewaschen	wash
*weichen	weicht	wich	gewichen	yield
weisen	weist	wies	gewiesen	point
wenden	wendet	wandte	gewandt	turn
werben	wirbt	warb	geworben	woo
werfen	wirft	warf	geworfen	throw
wiegen	wiegt	wog	gewogen	weigh
winden	windet	wand	gewunden	wind
wissen	weiss	wusste	gewusst	know
ziehen	zieht	zog	gezogen	draw
zwingen	zwingt	zwang	gezwungen	force

APPENDIX B
LIST OF COMMONLY USED GERMAN ABBREVIATIONS

a.a.O.	am angeführten Ort, at place quoted, loc. cit.	**ev.**	eventuell, if need be; evangelisch, Protestant
Abs.	Absender, sender	**FD-Zug**	Fernschnellzug, long distance express
Abt.	Abteilung, department, dept.	**ff.**	fein-fein, super, A1
a.D.	ausser Dienst, retired	**g.**	Gramm, gramme
A.G.	Aktiengesellschaft, limited company, Ltd.	**geb.**	geboren, born, née; gebunden, bound
a.o.	ausserordentlich, (professor) extraordinary	**Gebr.**	Gebrüder, brothers, Bros.
A.T.	Altes Testament, Old Testament, O.T.	**gef.**	gefälligst, please
Bd., Bde.	Band, Bände, volume(s)	**geh.**	geheftet, stitched, in sheets (of books); geheim, privy (councillor)
betr.	betreffs, concerning	**gest.**	gestorben, deceased
Bez.	Bezirk, district	**gez.**	gezeichnet, signed
bez.	bezahlt, paid, pd.	**G.m.b.H.**	Gesellschaft mit beschränkter Haftung, limited liability co.
Bl.	Blatt, leaf, sheet		
Br.	Bruder, brother		
b.w.	bitte wenden, please turn over	**Hbf.**	Hauptbahnhof, main station
bzw.	beziehungsweise, as above	**H.O.**	Handelsorganisation, Trade Organization
C.	Celsius, centigrade		
ca.	circa, about, more or less	**Hl.**	heilig, holy, saint
Cie.	Compagnie, company, Co.	**i.allg.**	im allgemeinen, in general
cmm.	Raumillimetre, cubic centimetre	**i.J.**	im Jahre, in the year, per annum
d.Ä.	der Ältere, the elder, senior	**i.R.**	im Ruhestande, retired
d.h.	das heisst, that is to say, i.e.	**Kfz.**	Kraftfahrzeug, motor vehicle
d.J.	der Jüngere, the younger, junior; dieses Jahres, this year	**km.**	Kilometer, kilometre
		l.B.	laut Bericht, as per advice
D.M.	Deutsche Mark	**Lkw.**	Lastkraftwagen, lorry
Dipl.-Ing.	Diploma der Ingenieurwissenschaften, B.Sc. (Eng.)	**L.-Z.**	Lazarettzug, hospital train
Einw.	Einwohner, inhabitant(s)	**m.**	Meter, metre
		M.	Mark, mark
erg.	ergänze, supplement, fill in, complete	**m.A.n.**	meiner Ansicht nach, in my opinion

m.E.	**meines Erachtens,** in my estimation	**t.**	Tonne, ton
MEZ.	**mitteleuropäische Zeit,** Central European Time	**u.**	**und,** and, &
		u.a.	**und andere,** and others; **unter anderem,** amongst other things, inter alia
M.-G.	**Maschinengewehr,** machine-gun		
Nachf.	**Nachfolger,** successor	**u.ä.**	**und ähnliche,** and similar things, and the like
n.Chr.	**nach Christus,** after Christ		
n.J.	**nächsten Jahres,** next year	**u.a.m.**	**und andere mehr,** and others besides, and so on
nachm.	**nachmittags,** afternoon, p.m.		
		u.dgl.	**und dergleichen,** and the like
n.M.	**nächsten Monats,** next month, prox.		
N.N.	**nomen nescio,** So-and-so, Mr. X	**u.E.**	**unseres Erachtens,** in our view
		ü.M.	**über Meeresspiegel,** above sea-level
Nr.	**Nummer,** number, No.		
N.T.	**Neues Testament,** New Testament, N.T.	**usw.**	**und so weiter,** and so on, etc.
		u.ü.V.	**unter üblichem Vorbehalt,** with the usual reservation, proviso
p.A.	**per Adresse,** care of, c/o		
PKW.	**Personenkraftwagen,** motor car	**u.zw.**	**und zwar,** and indeed, and what is more
p.p.	**per procura,** by proxy (added to signature)	**v.**	**von,** of, from
		v.Chr.	**vor Christus,** B.C.
P.S.	**Pferdestärke,** horsepower, h.p.	**Verw.**	**Verwaltung,** management, board
qm.	**Quadratmeter,** square metre	**vgl.**	**vergleiche,** compare, cf.
Reg. Bez.	**Regierungsbezirk,** administrative district	**v.H.**	**vom Hundert,** per cent.
		v.J.	**vorigen Jahres,** last year
resp.	**respektive,** respectively	**v.M.**	**vorigen Monats,** last month, ult.
S.	**Seite,** page, p.		
s.	**siehe,** see, vide, v.	**vorm.**	**vormittags,** in the morning, a.m.
Sa.	**Summa,** amount		
sek.	**Sekunde,** second, sec.	**z.B.**	**zum Beispiel,** for example, e.g.
s.o.	**siehe oben,** see above, vide supra		
		z.T.	**zum Teil,** partly
sog.	**sogennant,** so-called	**Ztr.**	**Zentner,** hundredweight, cwt.
SP.	**Siedepunkt,** boiling point, b.p.		
st.	**Stunde,** hour, hr.	**z.Z.,**	**zur Zeit,** at the time, for the time being, at the present time
s.u.	**siehe unten,** see below, vide infra	**z.Zt.**	

AN ENGLISH-GERMAN DICTIONARY

ABBREVIATION
ABKÜRZUNG

pl = plural   = Mehrzahl

A

a ein, eine, ein
aback rückwärts; überrascht
abaft nach hinten
abandon aufgeben, verlassen;
-ment das Aufgeben, die Ver-
lassenheit
abase erniedrigen; -ment die Er-
niedrigung
abash beschämen
abbey die Abtei
abbot der Abt
abbreviate abkürzen
abbreviation die Abkürzung
abdicate abdanken
abdication die Abdankung
abdomen der Unterleib
aberration die Abirrung
abet anstiften; -tor der Anstifter
abeyance, in - unentschieden
abhor verabscheuen; -rent abstossend
abide bleiben
ability die Fähigkeit
abject verworfen
abjure abschwören
able fähig
ablution die Waschung
abnegate ableugnen
aboard an Bord
abode der Aufenthalt
abolish abschaffen; -ment die
Abschaffung
abolition die Abschaffung
abominable abscheulich
abomination der Abscheu
aborigines die Ureinwohner p

abortion die Fehlgeburt
abortive zu früh geboren
abound im Überfluss vorhanden
sein
about um, umher, über, ungefähr
above über, oben, darüber
abrasion die Abschabung
abreast nebeneinander
abridge kürzen
abroad draussen, im Ausland
abrogate abschaffen
abrupt steil, plötzlich -ness die
Steilheit, Schroffheit
abscess das Geschwür
abscond flüchtig werden
absent abwesend; -ee der Ab-
wesende; -minded zerstreut
absolute absolut, unbeschränkt
absolution die Lossprechung
absolve lossprechen
absorb aufsaugen
abstain sich enthalten
abstemious enthaltsam
abstention die Enthaltung
abstinence die Enthaltsamkeit
abstract abstrakt, der Auszug,
ablenken
abstruse dunkel, schwerver-
ständlich
absurd albern, sinnwidrig
abundance der Überfluss; die
Fülle
abundant reichlich
abuse missbrauchen, beschimpfen, der Missbrauch
abusive schmähend
abut grenzen
abyss der Abgrund

acacia die Akazie
academic akademisch
accede beistimmen
accelerate beschleunigen
acceleration die Beschleunigung
accent, der Akzent, die Betonung; -uate betonen
accept annehmen; -able annehmbar; -ance die Annahme
access der Zugang; -ible zugänglich
accessory hinzukommend
accessories das Zubehör
accident der Unfall; das Unglück;
der Zufall (= chance); -al zufällig
acclamation der Beifall
acclimatize akklimatisieren
accommodate anpassen
accommodation die Anpassung,
die Unterkumft
accompaniment die Begleitung
accompany begleiten
accomplice der Mitschuldige
accomplish vollenden; -ed aus-
gebildet; -ment die Vollendung
accord übereinstimmen, gewähren, der Einklang
accordance die Übereinstimmung
according gemäss; -ly folglich
accost anreden
accouchement die Entbindung
accoucheur der Geburtshelfer
account die Rechnung, Berechnung; das Konto; der Bericht;
on - of wegen; on no - auf keinen
Fall; Keep -s Buch führen;
-able verantwortlich
accountant der Bücherrevisor
accredit beglaubigen
accretion der Zuwachs
accrue erwachsen; auflaufen
accumulate (sich) (an)häufen;
-ion die Anhäufung
accuracy die Genauigkeit
accurate genau
accursed verflucht
accuse anklagen; -ation die Anklage
ace das As
ache schmerzen, der Schmerz
achieve ausführen, vollenden;
-ment die Ausführung, die
Grosstat, die Leistung

aching schmerzhaft
acid sauer, herb
acknowledge anerkennen, bestätigen; -ment die Anerkennung
acme der Gipfel, der Höhepunkt
acorn die Eichel
acquaint bekanntmachen; -ance
die Bekanntschaft; -ed bekannt
acquiesce sich beruhigen, einwilligen; -nce die Einwilligung
acquire erwerben
acquisition die Erwerbung
acquit freisprechen; -tal die
Freisprechung
acre der Acker
acrimony die Schärfe
across quer, durch
act handeln, spielen, die Tat, das
Gesetz, der Akt, der Aufzug
action die Handlung, der Prozess
active tätig; -ity die Tätigkeit
actor der Schauspieler
actress die Schauspielerin
actual wirklich
acumen der Scharfsinn
acute scharf
adapt anpassen; -able anwendbar; -ation die Anwendung, die
Anpassung
add hinzufügen
adder die Natter
addict ergeben
addle unfruchtbar machen
address anreden, die Anrede;
die Anschrift
adduce anführen
adept erfahren
adequacy die Zulänglichkeit
adequate angemessen, hinrei-
chend
adhere anhangen; -nt der Anhänger
adhesion das Anhaften; der
Anschluss
adjacent anliegend
adjoin beifügen
adjourn (sich) vertagen
adjudicate zuerkennen
adjure beschwören; -ation die
Beschwörung
adjust ordnen, einstellen
administer verwalten

administration die Verwaltung
admirable herrlich
admiration die Bewunderung
admire bewundern
admissible zulässig
admission die Zulassung, der Eintritt
admit zulassen; -tance der Einlass
admixture die Beimischung
admonish mahnen
admonition die Ermahnung
ado die Mühe, das Getue
adolescence das Jünglingsalter
adolescent der Jüngling
adopt annehmen, adoptieren
adorable anbetungswert
adoration die Anbetung
adore anbeten
adorn schmücken; -ment der Schmuck, die Zierde
adrift treibend
adroit gewandt
adulation die Schmeichelei
adult erwachsen, der Erwachsene
adulterate verfälschen
adulterer der Ehebrecher
advance vorrücken, vorschiessen; -ment die Beförderung
advantage der Vorteil
advantageous vorteilhaft
adventure das Abenteuer
adventurer der Abenteurer
adventurous abenteuerlich
adversary der Gegner
adverse widrig
adversity die Not
advertise anzeigen; -isement die Anzeige, die Reklame; -iser der Anzeiger
advice der Rat, der Bericht
advisable ratsam
advise raten, benachrichtigen
adviser der Ratgeber
advocacy die Verteidigung
advocate der Anwalt, verteidigen
aerated kohlensauer
aerial die Antenne; (adj.) Luft-
aerodrome der Flugplatz
aeroplane das Flugzeug
æsthete der Ästhet, ästhetisch
afar fern, weit
affable leutselig

affair die Angelegenheit, das Geschäft, die Sache
affect gern haben, vorheucheln, angreifen
affectation die Affektiertheit, die Heuchelei
affected geziert, angegriffen
affection die Zuneigung, die Liebe; -ate liebevoll
affidavit die eidesstattliche Erklärung
affiliate sich angliedern
affiliation die Angliederung
affinity die Verwandtschaft
affirm behaupten; -ation die Behauptung, die Bejahung; -ative bejahend
affix anheften; befestigen
afflict betrüben; quälen; -ion das Leiden
affluence der Reichtum
affluent wohlhabend, reich
afford bieten, sich leisten
affront beleidigen, die Beleidigung
afield im Felde
afloat im Gang; schwimmend
afoot zu Fuss, im Gang
afraid furchtsam, bange
afresh von neuem
aft hinter
after nach
afterwards nachher, später
afternoon der Nachmittag
again wieder
against gegen
agate der Achat
age das Alter; of age mündig
aged alt
agency die Agentur, die Wirkung
agenda die Tagesordnung
agent der Agent, die wirkende Kraft
agglomeration die Anhäufung
aggrandize vergrössern; -ment die Vergrösserung
aggravate verschlimmern
aggregate anhäufen, die Anhäufung, gehäuft
aggression der Angriff
aggressive angreifend
aggressor der Angreifer

aggrieve bekümmern
aghast bestürzt
agile behende, flink
agility die Behendigkeit
agio das Aufgeld
agitate aufregen
agitation die Agitation, die Bewegung, die Aufregung
ago vor(her)
agonize martern; quälen
agony der Todeskampf
agree übereinstimmen, zugeben, sich einigen; **-able** angenehm; **-ment** die Übereinstimmung, der Vertrag
agriculture die Landwirtschaft
aground gestrandet
ague der Fieberfrost
ahead voraus, vorwärts
aid helfen, die Hilfe
ail schmerzen; **-ing** leidend; **-ment** das Leiden
aim zielen, das Ziel, die Absicht; **-less** ziellos
air die Luft, lüften, das Aussehen, das Lied; **- forces** die Luftstreitkräfte *pl*; **-man** der Flieger; **-raid-shelter** der Luftschutzraum; **-tight** luftdicht; **-y** luftig
aircraft, das Flugzeug; **-carrier** das Flugzeugmutterschiff
aisle das Seitenschiff
ajar halboffen
akin verwandt
alacrity die Bereitwilligkeit
alarm der Alarm, die Unruhe, der Wecker; **- clock** die Weckuhr; **-ist** der Bangemacher
alas ach! leider!
albeit obgleich
albumen das Eiweiss
alcove der Alkoven, die Nische
alder die Erle
alderman der Ratsherr
ale das engl. Bier
alert wachsam; **on the -** auf der Hut; **- (air raid)** der Alarm; **-ness** die Wachsamkeit
alias andersgenannt
alibi das Alibi
alien fremd, der Ausländer; **-ate** entfremden
alight brennend; aussteigen

align (aus)richten
alike gleich, ähnlich
aliment die Nahrung
alimony die Alimente *pl*
alive lebendig, lebhaft
all all, ganz, jeder; **above -** vor allem; **not at -** gar nicht; **- the better** um so besser; **- but** fast; **- clear (air raid)** Alarm aus!
allay lindern, beruhigen
allegation die Angabe
allege behaupten
allegiance die Ergebenheit
allegory die Allegorie
alleviate erleichtern
alleviation die Erleichterung
alley die Allee, das Gässchen; **blind-** die Sackgasse
alliance der Bund
allocate zuteilen; anweisen
allocation die Zuteilung
allot zuteilen, anweisen; **-ment** der Anteil, die Parzelle
allow erlauben, bewilligen; **-ance** die Genehmigung, das Taschengeld, der Rabatt
alloy die Legierung
allude anspielen
allure locken, ködern; **-ment** die Verlockung
alluring verlockend
allusion die Anspielung
alluvial angeschwemmt
ally (sich) verbinden; der Verbündeter
almighty allmächtig; der Allmächtige
almond die Mandel
almoner der Almosenpfleger
almost fast, beinahe
alms das Almosen; **-house** das Armenhaus
aloft oben, empor
alone allein, einsam
along längs, entlang; **-side** Seite an Seite; längsseits
aloof fern, abseits
aloud laut
alphabet das Alphabet
already schon
Alsace das Elsass
also auch
altar der Altar

alter (ver)ändern; sich ändern; **-ation** die Änderung

altercation der Zank; der Wortwechsel

alternate abwechselnd; **on - days** einen Tag um den andern

alternation die Abwechslung

alternative abwechselnd; die Alternative

although obgleich

altitude die Höhe

altogether zusammen; gänzlich

alum der Alaun

always immer

amalgamate verschmelzen

amalgamation die Verschmelzung; die Fusion

amass (auf)häufen

amateur der Liebhaber, der Dilettant

amaze erstaunen; **-ment** das Erstaunen

ambassador der Botschafter

amber der Bernstein

ambiguity die Zweideutigkeit

ambiguous zweideutig

ambition der Ehrgeiz

ambitious ehrgeizig

amble im Passgang gehen

ambulance der Krankenwagen

ambush der Hinterhalt; im Hinterhalt liegen

ameliorate verbessern

amenable verantwortlich, willfährig

amend verbessern; **-ment** die Verbesserung; **-s** *pl* die Vergütung; der Ersatz

amiable liebenswürdig

amicable freundschaftlich

amid mitten unter, inmitten

amiss verkehrt; übel; **take -** übelnehmen

amity die Freundschaft

ammonia das Ammoniak

ammunition die Munition

amnesty die Amnestie; begnadigen

among(st) unter

amorous verliebt

amortization die Tilgung

amount der Betrag; betragen

ample weit, reichlich

amplification die Erweiterung, die Verstärkung

amplify erweitern

amputate amputieren, abnehmen

amputation die Amputation

amuse amüsieren, unterhalten

amusement die Unterhaltung; der Zeitvertreib

amusing ergötzlich

analogous analog, ähnlich

analogy die Analogie; die Ähnlichkeit

analyse analysieren; zerlegen

analysis die Analyse

analytic analytisch

anarchist der Anarchist

anarchy die Anarchie

anatomist der Anatom

anatomy die Anatomie

ancestor der Vorfahr

ancestral angestammt

ancestry die Abstammung

anchor der Anker; ankern; **-age** der Ankergrund

ancient alt, ehemalig

and und

anecdote die Anekdote

anew von neuem

angel der Engel; **-ic** engelhaft

anger der Zorn; ärgern

angle der Winkel; die Angel; angeln; **-r** Angler *m*

angry zornig; böse

anguish die Angst; die Pein

angular winkelig; eckig

animal das Tier; tierisch

animate beleben; anregen; munter; **-d** lebhaft

animation die Belebung

animosity die Feindseligkeit

aniseed der Anis

ankle der Enkel

annals *pl* die Jahrbücher *pl*

annex anhängen; einverleiben; der Nachtrag; das Nebengebäude

annexation die Einverleibung

annihilate vernichten

annihilation die Vernichtung

anniversary der Jahrestag

annotate mit Anmerkungen versehen

announce ankündigen; **- ment**

die Ankündigung; die Bekanntmachung
annoy ärgern; plagen; **-ance** die
Plage; der Ärger
annual jährlich; die einjährige
Pflanze
annuity die Jahresrente
annul ungültig machen; tilgen
anoint salben
anomalous unregelmässig
anomaly die Unregelmässigkeit
anonymous namenlos
another ein anderer; noch einer
answer die Antwort; antworten,
entsprechen; **- for** bürgen
ant die Ameise
antagonism die Feindschaft
antagonist der Gegner; **-ic** geg-
nerisch
antarctic antarktisch
antecedent vorhergehend; **-s** das
Vorleben
antedate zurückdatieren
anterior vorhergehend
anteroom das Vorzimmer
anthem die Hymne
antic possierlich, komisch; die
Posse
anti-aircraft gun die Flak
anticipate vorausnehmen; zuvorkommen, vorhersagen
anticipation die Vorwegnahme;
die Vorahnung
antidote das Gegengift
antipathy die Abneigung
antiquarian antiquarisch
antiquary der Altertumsforscher
antique antik; die Antike
antiquity das Altertum
antiseptic antiseptisch
anvil der Amboss
anxiety die Angst; die Besorgnis
anxious ängstlich
any irgend ein
anybody irgend jemand; jedermann
anyhow irgendwie
anything irgend etwas
anywhere irgendwo
apart beiseite; **-from** abgesehen
von; **-ment** das Zimmer; die
Wohnung
apathy die Gleichgültigkeit

ape der Affe
aperture die Öffnung
apex der Gipfel
apiece pro Stück; für jeden
apish affisch; närrisch
apologetic verteidigend; ent-
schuldigend
apologize sich entschuldigen
apology die Entschuldigung
apostle der Apostel
appal erschrecken
apparatus der Apparat
apparel das Gewand
apparent offenbar
apparition die Erscheinung; das
Gespenst
appeal anrufen; flehen; appellieren; der Anruf; die Appella-
tion
appear (er)scheinen; **-ance** die
Erscheinung; der Schein; das
Aussehen
appease versöhnen; stillen
appellant der Appellant
append anhängen; **-age** der Anhang
appendicitis die Blinddarm-
entzündung
appertain gehören zu
appetite der Appetit
appetizing appetitlich
applaud beklatschen; preisen
applause der Beifall
apple der Apfel
appliance die Anwendung; das
Mittel
applicable anwendbar
application die Anwendung; der
Fleiss; die Bewerbung
applied angewandt
apply anwenden, anlegen; **- oneself to** sich widmen
appoint festsetzen, ernennen;
-ment die Ernennung; die Verabredung
apportion verteilen
apposite passend
apposition die Beifügung
appraise abschätzen
appreciable merklich
appreciate schätzen; würdigen
appreciation die Schätzung; die
Würdigung

apprehend verhaften; begreifen; befürchten
apprehension die Verhaftung; die Fassungskraft; die Befürchtung
apprehensive besorgt
apprentice der Lehrling; in die Lehre geben; **-ship** die Lehre; die Lehrzeit
approach (sich) nähern; die Annäherung; Zugang
approbation die Genehmigung
appropriate sich aneignen; angemessen; **-ness** die Angemessenheit
appropriation die Aneignung
approval die Billigung
approve billigen
approximate annähernd; nahe kommen
approximation die Annäherung
appurtenance das Zubehör
apricot die Aprikose
apron die Schürze
apt geneigt, geschickt
aptitude, aptness die Geneigtheit; die Begabung
aqueduct die Wasserleitung
arable pflugbar
arbiter der Schiedsrichter
arbitrary willkürlich
arbitrate entscheiden
arbitration der Schiedsspruch
arbour die Laube
arc der Bogen
arch der Bogen; wölben
archbishop der Erzbischof
architect der Architekt
ardent heiss, glühend
ardour der Eifer
arduous mühsam
area die Fläche
argue streiten; erörtern
arid dürr, trocken
arise aufsteigen; sich erheben
arm der Arm; die Waffe; (sich) bewaffnen
armament die Rüstung
armistice der Waffenstillstand
armour der Panzer
armoury das Zeughaus
army das Heer; die Armee
army A.A. die Flugabwehr

around um, herum
arouse wecken
arrange (an)ordnen
arrears die Rückstände *pl*
arrest verhaften; die Verhaftung
arrival die Ankunft
arrive ankommen; geschehen
arrow der Pfeil
arson die Brandstiftung
art die Kunst; die Verschlagenheit
artful schlau
artificial künstlich
artisan der Handwerker
artist der Künstler; **artistic** künstlerisch
as als, da, so; **as to** was betrifft; **as it were** sozusagen
ascend aufsteigen
ascension das Aufsteigen; **- Day** der Himmelfahrtstag
ascertain sich erkundigen
ash die Asche; die Esche (tree); **-tray** der Aschenbecher; **Ash-Wednesday** Aschermittwoch
ashamed beschämt
ashore am Ufer
aside beiseite
ask (question) fragen; **(demand)** fordern; **(request)** bitten
asleep schlafend; eingeschlafen
asparagus der Spargel
aspect das Ansehen; die Lage
asperity die Rauheit
aspirant der Bewerber
aspiration das Streben
aspire streben
ass der Esel
assail anfallen; **-lant** der Angreifer
assassin der Meuchelmörder; **-ate** ermorden; **-ation** der Meuchelmord
assault angreifen; der Angriff
assemble (sich) versammeln
assembly die Versammlung
assent zustimmen; die Zustimmung
assert behaupten; **-ion** die Behauptung
assess abschätzen; **-ment** die Schätzung

assets die Aktiva *pl*

assiduous emsig

assign anweisen; **-ation, -ment** Anweisung

assist beistehen; **-ance** der Beistand; die Hilfe; **-ant** der Gehilfe

associate der Teilhaber; sich gesellen

association die Verbindung; die Gesellschaft

assort sortieren; **-ment** die Auswahl

assuage lindern

assume übernehmen; annehmen

assumption die Annahme

assurance die Versicherung

assure versichern

astern achteraus

astonish in Erstaunen setzen; **-ment** das Erstaunen

astray irre

astute verschlagen; **-ness** die Verschlagenheit

asunder auseinander

at an, in, bei, auf, zu; **-last** zuletzt; endlich; **- least** wenigstens

atone büssen; **-ment** die Busse

atrocious grässlich

atrocity die Greueltat

attach anheften; beifügen; **-ment** die Anhänglichkeit

attack angreifen; der Angriff

attain erreichen; **-ment** die Erreichung; die Errungenschaft

attempt versuchen; der Versuch

attend bedienen; beiwohnen; aufmerksam sein; **-ance** die Bedienung; die Anwesenheit

attendant der Wärter

attention die Aufmerksamkeit

attentive aufmerksam

attest bezeugen

attic die Dachstube

attire kleiden; die Kleidung

attitude die Haltung

attorney der Anwalt

attract anziehen; **-ion** die Anziehung; **-ive** anziehend

attribute zuschreiben; die Eigenschaft

attune (ab)stimmen

auburn nussbraun

auction versteigern; die Versteigerung

audacious verwegen

audacity die Verwegenheit; die Frechheit

audible hörbar

audience die Zuhörerschaft; die Audienz

audit Rechnungen prüfen; die Rechnungsprüfung; **-or** der Rechnungsprüfer

aught etwas

augment vermehren; **-ation** die Vermehrung

August der August

august erhaben

aunt die Tante

austere streng

austerity die Strenge

authentic verbürgt, echt

author der Verfasser, der Urheber; **-ize** ermächtigen

autobus der Omnibus

autumn der Herbst

avail nützen; **- oneself (of)** benützen

available verfügbar

avalanche die Lawine

avarice der Geiz

avenge rächen

average der Durchschnitt; **on an - im Durchschnitt**

averse abgeneigt

aversion die Abneigung

avert abwenden

avidity die Gier

avoid meiden; vermeiden

avow offen bekennen

await erwarten

awake wecken

award zuerkennen; der Preis

aware unterrichtet; gewahr

away weg, fort

awe die Ehrfurcht

awful furchtbar; schrecklich

awhile eine Weile

awkward ungeschickt

awry schief

axe die Axt; das Beil

axis die Achse

axle die Achse

B

baby der Säugling; das Baby
bachelor der Junggesell
back der Rücken, die Ruckseite; zurück; verteidigen; wetten auf
backdoor die Hintertür
background der Hintergrund
backward zurück; langsam; spät; rückwärts
bacon der Speck
bad schlecht; schlimm; böse
badge das Abzeichen
badger der Dachs
baffle vereiteln
bag der Beutel; der Sack; die Handtasche; die Tasche; die Tüte
baggage das Gepäck
bail die Bürgschaft; auf Bürgschaftentlassen
bait der Köder; die Lockung
bake backen
baker der Bäcker
bakery die Bäckerei
balance die Waage, die Bilanz; das Gleichgewicht; wägen
bald kahl; -ness die Kahlheit
bale der Ballen
ball der Ball; die Kugel
ball point pen der Kugelschreiber
ban der Bann; verbieten
band das Band, die Musikkapelle
bandage der Verband
bandmaster der Kapellmeister
bank das Ufer, die Bank; eindämmen
bankrupt bankrott
banner die Fahne
banquet das Festmahl
baptism die Taufe
bar die Barre, das Gericht, die Schranke, der Schenktisch, die Bar; sperren; riegeln
barbed wire der Stacheldraht
barber der Friseur
bare bloss, dürftig; -ly kaum
barefaced unverschämt
bareness die Dürftigkeit; die Blösse
bargain der Gelegenheitskauf; handeln; feilschen
barge der Schleppkahn
bark die Rinde, das Gebell; bellen

barley die Gerste
barmaid das Schenkmädchen
barn die Scheune
baron der Baron
barrack(s) Kaserne
barrel das Fass; der Lauf (**firearm**)
barren unfruchtbar; -ness die Unfruchtbarkeit
barrier die Grenze; die Schranke
barrister der Rechtsanwalt
barter der Tausch; (ver)tauschen
base die Grundlage, die Basis; gründen; gemein; niedrig
basin das Becken; die Schüssel
bask sich sonnen
basket der Korb
bat die Fledermaus; der Schläger (**sports gear**)
batch der Schub, der Stoss
bath das Bad; baden
bathe baden
bathing costume der Badeanzug
battle die Schlacht
bay die Bucht
bay window das Erkerfenster
be sein
beach das Gestade; der Strand
bead die Glasperle
beak der Schnabel
beam der Balken, der Strahl; strahlen
bean die Bohne
bear der Bär
bear tragen, gebären
beard der Bart
bearer der Träger
beast das Tier; das Vieh
beastly scheusslich, viehisch
beat schlagen, klopfen
beautiful schön; **beauty** die Schönheit
beaver der Biber
because weil; - of wegen
become werden; anstehen
becoming passend
bed das Bett; das Beet (**flowers**)
bed clothes das Bettzeug
bedroom das Schlafzimmer
bee die Biene
beech die Buche
beef das Rindfleisch
beer das Bier

beetle der Käfer
beetroot die Runkelrübe
befall zustossen; widerfahren
before vor, bevor, ehe, früher
beg bitten, betteln
beget erzeugen
beggar der Bettler
begin anfangen
beginning der Anfang; der Beginn
begrudge missgönnen
behalf of (on) im Namen
behave sich betragen; **behaviour** das Benehmen
behead enthaupten
behind hinten; zurück; hinter
behindhand im Rückstande
behold erblicken
being das Dasein; das Wesen; das Geschöpf
belief der Glaube
believable glaublich
believe glauben
bell die Glocke; die Klingel; die Schelle
bellow brüllen
belly der Bauch
belong gehören; **belongings** die Habe; das Eigentum
beloved geliebt; der Geliebte
below unter; unten
belt der Gürtel
bench die Bank; der Arbeitstisch
bend beugen; sich biegen
beneath unter; unten
benediction der Segen
benefactor der Wohltäter; **beneficence** die Wohltätigkeit
benefice die Pfründe
benefit die Wohltat, der Vorteil; Vorteil bringen
benevolence das Wohlwollen
bent gebogen; die Neigung
bequest das Vermächtnis
berry die Beere
berth die Koje
beseech anflehen
beside neben; ausser
besides ausserdem
besiege belagern
best best; am besten
bestow schenken
bet die Wette; wetten
betimes beizeiten; bald; früh

betray verraten; **-al** der Verrat
betroth verloben; **-al** die Verlobung
better besser, lieber; (ver)bessern
between zwischen; dazwischen
beware sich hüten
bewilderment die Verwirrung; **bewilder** verwirren
bewitch behexen
beyond jenseits, über, darüber hinaus
bias das Vorurteil; die Neigung
bicycle das Fahrrad; radeln
bid befehlen, bieten
big gross, stark, dick
bile die Galle
bill der Schnabel; die Rechnung; **- of exchange** der Wechsel; **- of lading** der Frachtbrief
billet einquartieren; das Quartier
bin der Kasten; der Behälter
bind binden; **-ing** der Einband; verpflichten
birch die Birke, die Rute; züchtigen
bird der Vogel
birth die Geburt; **-day** der Geburtstag; **-place** der Geburtsort
bishop der Bischof; der Läufer (**chess**)
bit das Bissen; das Stückchen
bite beissen; der Biss
bitter bitter
bitterness die Bitterkeit
black schwarz, dunkel
blackberry die Brombeere
blackbird die Amsel
blackmail die Erpressung; erpressen
blackness die Schwärze
blacksmith der Grobschmied
bladder die Blase
blade der Halm (**grass**); die Klinge (**knife etc.**); **shoulder-blade** das Schulterblatt
blame der Tadel; tadeln
blank unbeschrieben; leer
blanket die Wolldecke
blaspheme lästern
blast der Windstoss; verfluchen;
blast-furnace der Hochofen

blaze die Flamme, lodern
bleach bleichen
bleak öde; kalt
bleed bluten
blend vermischen; die Mischung
bless segnen; **blessing** der Segen; **blessed** gesegnet
blight der Meltau
blind blind; **blindness** die Blindheit
bliss die Wonne
blister die Blase
blood das Blut; **bloody** blutig
bloom, blossom die Blüte; blüten
blot der Fleck, der Klecks; beflecken; löschen
blotting-paper das Löschpapier; **blotter** der Löscher
blow der Schlag; blasen
blue blau
blunder der Fehler; Fehler machen
blunt stumpf; stumpf machen
blush das Erröten; erröten
board das Brett; **boarding-school** das Internat; **-house** die Pension; **on board** an Bord
boast prahlen; die Prahlerei; **boaster** der Prahler
boat das Boot; das Schiff
bobbin die Spule
body der Körper; der Leib
bog der Sumpf
boil kochen
boil das Geschwür
boiler der Kessel
bold kühn
bolt der Bolzen; verriegeln
bomb die Bombe
bond das Band; der Schuldschein
bone der Knochen, die Gräte
bonfire das Freudenfeuer
bonus die Prämie
book das Buch; **-case** der Bücherschrank; **-seller** der Buchhändler; **-shop** der Buchladen **-ing office** die Fahrkartenausgabe
boot der Stiefel
booty die Beute
border der Rand, die Grenze; angrenzen

bore die Bohrung; der langweilige Schwätzer; bohren; langweilen
born geboren
borrow borgen
bosom der Busen
both beide; **both - and** sowohl - als auch
bother belästigen; die Plage
bottle die Flasche; auf Flaschen ziehen
bottom der Boden
bough der Zweig; der Ast
boulder der Steinblock
bound gebunden; begrenzen; springen; die Grenze; der Sprung
boundary die Grenze
bounty die Freigebigkeit
bout der Kampf; das Gelage
bow der Bogen, der Bug, die Verbeugung; verbeugen
bowel(s) die Eingeweide *pl*
box die Büchse; die Kiste; der Koffer; **- on the ear** die Ohrfeige
boy der Knabe; der Junge
brace das Paar
bracelet das Armband
braces die Hosenträger *pl*
bracket der Wandarm die Klammer
bracken das Farnkraut
brag prahlen
braid die Borte, die Flechte; flechten
brain das Gehirn
brake die Bremse; bremsen
bran die Kleie
branch der Ast, der Zweig; abzweigen; **branchless** zweiglos; **branch-line (rail)** die Zweigbahn; **branch-office** die Zweigstelle
brand der Brand; die Marke; brandmarken
brandy der Branntwein
brass das Messing
brave tapfer; **bravery** die Tapferkeit
brawl der Krawall; zanken
breach der Bruch
bread das Brot
breadth die Breite
break brechen; bersten; der

Bruch; der Absatz; die Lücke; die Pause

breakfast das Frühstück; frühstücken

breast die Brust

breath der Atem; **breathe** atmen; **breathless** atemlos

breeches die Kniehose

breed die Rasse; die Herkunft; erzeugen

breeze die Brise; **breezy** windig

brew das Gebräu; brauen; **brewery** die Brauerei

bribe die Bestechung; bestechen

brick der Backstein; **bricklayer** der Maurer

bride die Braut; **bridegroom** der Bräutigam; **bridesmaid** die Brautjungfer

bridge die Brücke; überbrücken

bridle der Zaum; zäumen

brief kurz; **brief-case** die Aktentasche

bright hell, glänzend

brighten hell machen

brightness die Klarheit; die Helle

brilliant glänzend

brim der Rand

brine das Salzwasser

bring bringen

brink der Rand

brisk lebhaft; munter; frisch

bristle die Borste

brittle zerbrechlich

broad breit

broadcast funken; senden; **-ing station** die Rundfunkstation

broaden breiter machen

broken gebrochen; **-hearted** betrübt

broker der Makler

brooch die Brosche

brood brüten; die Brut

brook der Bach

broom der Besen; der Ginster

brother der Bruder; **-in-law** der Schwager

brow die Stirn

brown braun

bruise die Quetschung; quetschen

brush die Bürste; die Pinsel; bursten

brute das Tier; der Unmensch

bucket der Eimer

buckle die Schnalle; schnallen

bud die Knospe; knospen

bug die Wanze

build bauen

builder der Baumeister

building das Gebäude

bulb die Knolle

bulk die Grösse; die Masse

bull der Stier

bullet die Kugel

bulletin der Tagesbericht

bump der Stoss; die Beule; stossen

bunch der Bund; der Strauss

bunk die Schlafkoje

buoyant heiter; schwimmend

burden die Last; belasten

burglar der Einbrecher; **burglary** der Einbruch

burial das Begräbnis

burn (ver)brennen

burrow der Bau; sich eingraben

burst der Bruch; bersten

bury begraben

bush der Busch

business das Geschäft; die Sache

busy geschäftigt

but aber; sondern; nur

butcher der Metzger; der Fleischer; schlachten

butler der Diener

butter die Butter; mit Butter bestreichen

butterfly der Schmetterling

buttock das Hinterteil

button der Knopf; zuknöpfen

buy kaufen; **buyer** der Käufer

by von, zu, nach, neben, bei; vorbei; **by heart** auswendig; **by all means** auf jeden Fall

by-election die Ersatzwahl

bystander der Zuschauer

C

cab die Droschke

cabbage der Kohl

cabin die Kajüte; die Hütte

cabinet das Kabinett; der Schrank

cabinet-maker der Kunst-
tischler
cable das Kabel; kabeln
cackle gackern
caddy das Teekästchen
cage der Käfig; einsperren
cajole schmeicheln
cake der Kuchen
calamitous unheilvoll
calamity das Unglück
calculable berechenbar
calculate berechnen
calculation die Berechnung
calendar der Kalender
calf das Kalb; die Wade (leg)
calico der Kattun
call rufen, nennen, besuchen;
der Ruf, der Besuch
caller der Besucher
calling der Beruf
callous hart; schwielig
calm die Ruhe; ruhig
calumniate verleumden
calumny die Verleumdung
calvary Golgotha
cambric der Batist
camel das Kamel
camp das Lager; lagern; zelten
campaign der Feldzug
camphor der Kampfer
can die Kanne; in Büchsen einmachen
canal der Kanal
canary der Kanarienvogel
cancel (to) durchstreichen
cancer der Krebs
candid aufrichtig; ehrlich
candidate der Kandidat; der
Bewerber
candidature die Kandidatur
candidness die Ehrlichkeit
candle die Kerze
candlestick der Leuchter
candour die Ehrlichkeit
candy das Zuckerwerk
cane das Rohr; der Stock
canine Hunds-; hündisch
canister die Blechbüchse
canker der Krebs
cannon die Kanone
canny vorsichtig
canoe das Kanu; das Paddleboot
canon der Domherr; der Kanon

canonize heiligsprechen
canopy der Baldachin
cantankerous streitsüchtig
canteen die Kantine
canto der Gesang; -s Gesänge
canvas das Segeltuch
canvass werben
cap die Mütze
capability die Fähigkeit
capable fähig
capacious geräumig
capacitate befähigen
capacity die Fähigkeit; der Inhalt
cape das Vorgebirge; das Kap
capital die Hauptstadt, das
Kapital, der Grossbuchstabe
capitulate kapitulieren
caprice die Laune
capsize kentern
captain der Kapitän; der Haupt-
mann
captious zänkisch
captivate fesseln
captive gefangen
capture die Beute, der Fang; fangen; gefangennehmen
car der Wagen; das Auto; - park
der Parkplatz
caravan die Karawane; der
Wohnwagen
caraway der Kümmel
carbine der Karabiner
carbolic (acid) die Karbolsäure
carbon der Kohlenstoff
carbuncle der Karbunkel
carburettor der Vergaser
carcass der Kadaver
card die Karte
cardboard der Pappdeckel
care die Sorge, die Pflege, die
Vorsicht; sorgen; sich kümmern
care of (c/o) per Adresse
career die Laufbahn
careful vorsichtig
carefulness die Sorgfalt
careless sorglos
carelessness die Sorglosigkeit
caress die Liebkosung; liebkosen
caretaker der Wächter
careworn abgehärmt
cargo die (Schiffs) ladung
caricature die Karikatur

carman der Fuhrmann
carnage das Blutbad
carnal unzüchtig
carnation die Nelke
carnival der Karneval
carnivorous fleischfressend
carol das Lied; das Weihnachts- lied
carousal das Trinkgelage
carp der Karpfen
carpenter der Zimmermann
carpet der Teppich
carriage der (Eisenbahn)wagen; die Fracht; die Haltung
carrier der Träger; der Fuhr- mann
carrion das Aas
carrot die Mohrrübe; die Möhre
carry fahren; führen; tragen
cart der Karren
cartage der Fuhrlohn
cartilage der Knorpel
cartoon dei Karikatur
cartridge die Patrone; **blank -** die Platzpatrone
carve schneiden; schnitzen; aushauen
cascade der Wasserfall
case das Futteral; das Gehäuse; das Scheide; das Fach; die Kiste; der Fall; das Etui; die Tasche
cash die Kasse, das Bargeld; einkassieren, einlösen
cash book das Kassabuch
cashier der Kassierer; entlassen
cask das Fass
casket das Schmuckkästchen
cast werfen; giessen
cast der Wurf; der Guss; die Rol- lenbesetzung (**theatre**)
caste die Kaste
casting vote die entscheidende Stimme
cast iron das Gusseisen
castle das Schloss; die Burg
castor oil das Rizinusöl
casual zufällig
casualty der Verlust; der Unfall
cat die Katze
cataclysm die Überschwemmung
catalogue der Katalog
cataract der Wasserfall; der Star
catarrh der Katarrh

catastrophe die Katastrophe
catch fangen, fassen; der Fang, der Haken; **catch a cold** sich erkälten
catchword das Schlagwort
caterpillar die Raupe
catgut die Darmsaite
cathedral der Dom
catholic der Katholik; katholisch
catkin das Kätzchen
cattle das (Rind) Vieh
cauldron der Kessel
cauliflower der Blumenkohl
cause die Ursache; verursachen
causeless grundlos
causeway der Dammweg
caustic ätzend
cauterize ausbrennen
caution die Warnung, die Vor- sicht; warnen
cautious vorsichtig
cavalry die Reiterei
cave die Höhle
cavity die Höhlung
caw schreien, krächzen
cease aufhören
ceaseless unaufhörlich
cedar die Zeder
cede nachgeben, abtreten
ceiling die Zimmerdecke
celebrate feiern
celebrated berühmt
celebration die Feier
celebrity die Berühmtheit
celerity die Geschwindigkeit
celery der Stangensellerie
celestial himmlisch
celibacy die Ehelosigkeit
celibate unverheiratet
cell die Zelle
cellar der Keller
cellulose der Zellstoff
Celtic keltisch
cement der Zement; zementieren
cemetery der Friedhof
cenotaph das Ehrengrabmal
censor der Zensor; zensieren
censure der Tadel; tadeln
census die Volkszählung
centenary die Hundertjahrfeier
central zentral
centre der Mittelpunkt
century das Jahrhundert

ceremonial förmlich
ceremonious umständlich
ceremony die Feierlichkeit
certain sicher; gewiss
certainly allerdings; gewiss
certainty die Gewissheit
certificate das Zeugnis; die Bescheinigung
certify (**to**) bescheinigen
cessation das Aufhören
cession die Abtretung
chafe abreiben, aufregen
chaff die Spreu
chagrin der Ärger
chain die Kette; anketten
chair der Stuhl; der Lehrstuhl
chair (**to be in the**) den Vorsitz führen
chairman der Vorsitzende
chalice der Kelch
chalk die Kreide
challenge herausfordern; die Herausforderung
chamber das Zimmer; die Kammer
chambermaid das Zimmermädchen
chamberpot das Nachtgeschirr
chamois die Gemse; das Wildleder
champion der Meister
championship die Meisterschaft
chance der Zufall, die Möglichkeit; wagen
chancellery die Kanzlei
chancellor der Kanzler
chandelier der Kronleuchter
change der Wechsel, der Tausch; das Kleingeld, die Veränderung; wechseln, tauschen, ändern; sich verändern; **change train** umsteigen
changeable veränderlich
channel der Kanal; die Rinne
Channel (**the**) der Armelkanal
chaos das Chaos
chap der Kerl; der Bursche
chapel die Kapelle
chaplain der Kaplan
chapter das Kapitel
char verkohlen
character der Charakter; das Zeugnis; der Buchstabe

charcoal die Holzkohle
charge laden, tragen, beschuldigen, angreifen; die Ladung, die Last; die Verwahrung
chargé d'affaires der Geschäftsträger
charitable wohltätig
charity die Nächstenliebe
charlatan der Marktschreier
charm der Zauber, der Reiz; bezaubern, entzücken
charming reizend
chart die Seekarte, die Tabelle
charter (**deed**) die Urkunde, der Freibrief; verfrachten, mieten
charwoman die Scheuerfrau
chary sorgsam
chase die Jagd; jagen, verfolgen
chasm die Kluft
chassis das Fahrgestell
chaste keusch
chastise züchtigen
chat die Plauderei; plaudern, schwatzen
chatterbox das Plappermaul
chatty geschwätzig
cheap billig; wohlfeil
cheapen verbilligen
cheapness die Billigkeit
cheat der Betrüger; betrügen
check die Kontrollmarke, das Hindernis; (**chess**) Schach kontrollieren, hemmen
checkmate Schachmatt
cheek die Backe; die Wange
cheeky unverschämt
cheer der Frohsinn; trösten; anspornen; erheitern
cheerful heiter, lustig
cheerless freudlos
cheese der Käse
chemical chemisch
chemicals die Chemikalien *pl*
chemist der Apotheker
chemistry die Chemie
chequered karriert; bunt
cherish pflegen; hegen
cherry die Kirsche
chess das Schach
chess-board das Schachbrett
chest die Brust; (**box**) die Kiste
chest of drawers die Kommode
chestnut die Kastanie

chew kauen
chicken das Huhn
chickenpox die Windpocken *pl*
chide schelten
chief(ly) hauptsächlich
chief of staff der Generalstabs-chef
chieftain der Häuptling
chilblain die Frostbeule
child das Kind
childbirth die Niederkunft
childhood die Kindheit
childish kindisch
childless kindlos
chill die Kälte; die Erkältung
chilly frostig
chime das Glockenspiel; Glocken läuten
chimney der Schornstein
chimney-sweep der Schornstein-feger
chin das Kinn
china das Porzellan
Chinaman der Chinese
chink die Ritze; klimpern
chintz der Kattun
chip (a) der Span; schnitzeln
chirp zirpen
chirrup zwitschern
chisel der Meissel; meisseln
chivalrous ritterlich
chivalry die Ritterlichkeit
chlorine das Chlor
chloroform das Chloroform
chocolate die Schokolade
choice die Wahl, die Auswahl; auserlesen
choir der Chor
choke ersticken; würgen; ver-stopfen
choose (aus)wählen
chop das Kotelett
chop zerhauen
chopper das Hackmesser
chord die Saite; der Akkord
chorus der Chor; der Refrain
Christ der Christus
christen taufen
Christendom die Christenheit
Christian christlich
Christian name der Vorname
Christianity das Christentum
Christmas Weihnachten

Christmas box das Weihnachts-geschenk
Christmas eve der Weihnachts-abend
chronic chronisch
chronic die Chronik; aufzeichnen
chrysalis die (Insekten) Puppe
chuckle kichern
chum der Stubengenosse; der Kamerad
church die Kirche
churchman der Geistliche
churchyard der Kirchhof
churl der Kerl; der Bauer
churlish grob
churn buttern; das Butterfass
cider der Apfelwein
cigar die Zigarre
cigarette die Zigarette
cinder die Schlacke; die ausgeg-lühte Kohle
Cinderella das Aschenbrödel
cinema das Kino; das Lichtspiel
cinnamon der Zimt
cipher die Ziffer; die Null
circle der Kreis, der Ring; um-kreisen
circuit die Rundreise; der Strom; short-c der Kurzschluss
circular kreisförmig; das Rund-schreiben
circulate umlaufen
circulation der Umlauf; (blood-) der Kreislauf
circumference der Umfang
circumnavigate umschiffen
circumscribe umschreiben
circumscription die Umschrei-bung
circumstance der Umstand
circumstantial umständlich
circus der Zirkus
citadel die Zitadelle
citation die Vorladung
cite vorladen
citizen der Bürger
citizenship das Bürgerrecht
citron die Zitrone
city die Stadt
civic bürgerlich
civil höflich, bürgerlich
civilian der Zivilist
civility die Höflichkeit

civilization die Zivilisation; die Kultur
civilize zivilisieren
claim der Anspruch, die Forderung; Anspruch machen, fordern
claimant der Anspruchmacher
clairvoyant der Hellseher
clamber klettern
clammy klebrig
clamour das Geschrei; lärmen
clamp die Klampe; verklammern
clan der Stamm
clandestine heimlich
clang der Klang, der Schall; schallen
clap der Schlag; klatschen
claret der Rotwein; der Bordeaux-wein
clarify abklären
clash zusammenstossen; nicht harmonieren
clash das Geklirr; der Widerstreit
clasp der Haken
clasp (to) umfassen; festhalten
class die Klasse; klassifizieren
classic klassisch; der Klassiker
clatter (a) das Getöse, das Gerassel; rasseln, klappern
clause die Klausel; der Satz
claw die Klaue; kratzen
clay der Ton
clean sauber; rein; säubern; reinigen
cleanliness die Reinlichkeit
cleanse säubern; reinigen
clear klar, hell; deutlich; aufklären; abräumen
clearance die Freilegung
clearance die Ausräumung; die Verzollung; **(sale)** der Ausverkauf
clear-headed klardenkend
clearing-house die Abrechnungsstelle
clearness die Klarheit
cleave spalten
cleft die Spalte
clemency die Gnade
clench zusammenballen; zusammendrücken
clergy die Geistlichkeit
clergyman der Geistliche

clerk der Büroangestellte; der Schreiber
clever klug
click ticken; knacken
client der Kunde; der Klient
cliff die Klippe; der Felsen
climate das Klima
climax der Höhepunkt
climb klimmen; klettern
climber der Kletterer; der Bergsteiger
climbing-plant die Schlingpflanze
cling ankleben; anhängen
clinical klinisch
clip beschneiden; die Zwicke
clippings die Abfälle *pl*
cloak bemänteln; der Mantel
cloakroom die Garderobe, die Gepäckabgabe
clock die Uhr
clockwork das Uhrwerk
clod der Erdklumpen
clog (to) hemmen, verstopfen; der Holzschuh
cloister der Kreuzgang; das Kloster
close schliessen; verschlossen, eng, genau; der Schluss, das Ende
close by dicht bei
closet das Kabinett; **water-** der Abort; die Toilette
closure der Schluss; verschliessen
clot gerinnen; das Klümpchen
cloth das Tuch
clothe bekleiden
clothes die Kleider *pl*; die Kleidung
clothes-brush die Kleiderbürste
clothes-press der Kleiderschrank
clothing die Kleidung
cloud die Wolke; bewölken, verdunkeln
cloudless wolkenlos
cloudy wolkig; bedeckt
clove die Gewürznelke
clover der Klee; **in-** üppig
clown der Clown; der Tölpel
club die Keule, der Knüttel, das Treff, der Verein; knüppeln
clue der Anhaltspunkt
clump der Klumpen

clumsy plump; ungeschickt
cluster die Traube; der Büschel
clutch greifen; die Kuppelung, der Griff
coach die Kutsche; einpauken; der Einpauker; der Trainer
coachman der Kutscher
coagulate gerinnen
coal die Kohle
coal-dust der Kohlenstaub
coal-mine die Kohlengrube
coalition die Vereinigung
coarse roh; grob; gemein
coarseness die Grobheit
coast die Küste
coat der Rock, der Mantel, der Überzug; die Haut, der Anstrich; überziehen, überstreichen
coating der Anstrich
coax schmeicheln
cob der Kolben
cobbler der Schuhflicker; der Schuster
cobweb das Spinngewebe
cock das Hahn
cockerel der junge Hahn
cockroach die Schabe
cocoa der Kakao
coco-nut die Kokosnuss
cod der Kabeljau
code das Gesetzbuch, der Schlüssel; chiffrieren
codliver oil der Lebertran
coerce zwingen
coercion der Zwang
coffee der Kaffee
coffee-pot die Kaffeekanne
coffer der Geldkasten
coffin der Sarg
cog der Radzahn
cogitate nachdenken
cognate verwandt
cognizance die Kenntnis
cogwheel das Zahnrad
cohabit beisammenwohnen
coherence der Zusammenhang
coherent zusammenhängend
coil die Rolle, die Spule; aufwickeln
coin die Münze; münzen, prägen
coinage das Gepräge
coincide zusammentreffen
coke der Koks

cold kalt, gefühllos; der Schnupfen, die Kälte; **catch -** sich erkälten
cold-blooded kaltblütig
colic die Kolik
collaborate mit-, zusammenarbeiten
collaboration die Mitarbeit
collaborator der Mitarbeiter
collapse zusammenbrechen, einfallen; der Einsturz, der Zusammenbruch
collar beim Kragen fassen; der Kragen
collar-bone das Schlüsselbein
colleague der Kollege; der Amtsgenosse
collect sammeln; einkassieren
collection die Sammlung
collector der (Steuer) Einnehmer; der Sammler
college das Kollegium; die Höhere Schule
collide zusammenstossen
collier der Kohlenarbeiter
colliery die Kohlengrube
collision der Zusammenstoss
colloquial familiär
collusion das heimliche Einverständnis
Cologne Köln
colonel der Oberst
colonial kolonial
colonist der Ansiedler; der Kolonist
colonize kolonisieren
colony die Kolonie
colour die Farbe; färben
colours die Fahne
colouring die Färbung
colourless farblos
colour-blind farbenblind
colt das Füllen
column die Kolonne; die Säule
coma der Scheintod
comb der Kamm; kämmen
combat der Kampf; bekämpfen
combination die Verbindung
combine verbinden
combustible der Brennstoff; brennbar
combustion die Verbrennung
come (to) kommen (sein); **- about**

zutragen; - **for** abholen; - **to pass, happen** geschehen

comedian der Schauspieler, der Komiker

comedy das Lustspiel

comely anständig, anmutig

comestibles die Nahrungsmittel *pl*

comet der Komet

comfort der Trost, die Bequemlichkeit; trösten; erquicken

comfortable bequem, behäbig

comforter der Tröster; der Schal

comic(al) komisch

command der Befehl, die Herrschaft; befehlen

commander der Befehlshaber; **-in-chief** der Oberbefehlshaber

commemorate gedenken; feiern

commemoration die Gedächtnisfeier

commence anfangen

commencement der Anfang

commend loben, empfehlen

commendable löblich, empfehlenswert

comment die Anmerkung, die Auslegung; auslegen, erläutern

commerce der Handel

commercial kaufmännisch

commiserate bemitleiden

commiseration das Mitleid

commissariat die Militärintendantur

commission das Offizierspatent, die Kommission, der Auftrag; beauftragen

commissioner der Bevollmächtigte

commissionaire der Dienstmann

commit (to) begehen; übergeben; **- oneself** sich bloss-stellen

committal das Überweisen

committee der Ausschuss

commode der Nachtstuhl

commodious geräumig

commodity die Ware

common gemein; das Gemeindeland

commoner der Bürger

commonly gewöhnlich

Commons (House of) das Unterhaus

commonplace gewöhnlich

commonwealth das Gemeinwesen; die Republik

commotion die Erschütterung; der Aufruhr

communicate mitteilen

communication die Verbindung; die Mitteilung

communicative mitteilsam

communion die Gemeinschaft; das Abendmahl

communism der Kommunismus

community die Gemeinde

commute umwandeln

compact der Vertrag

compact dicht; fest

companion der Gefährte

companionable gesellig

companionship die Gesellschaft

company die Gesellschaft

comparable vergleichbar

comparative relativ, vergleichend; der Komparativ

compare vergleichen

comparison der Vergleich

compartment die Abteilung; das Abteil; das Fach

compass der Umfang, der Kompass; umgeben

compasses (pair of) der Zirkel

compassion das Mitleid

compassionate mitleidig

compatible vereinbar

compatibility die Verträglichkeit

compatriot der Landsmann

compel zwingen

compensate ersetzen; entschädigen

compensation der Ersatz

compete konkurrieren

competence die Befähigung; die Kompetenz

competent zuständig

competition die Konkurrenz

competitor der Mitbewerber

compile zusammentragen

complacent selbstzufrieden

complain sich beklagen

complaint die Klage; die Krankheit

complement die Ergänzung

complete vollenden; vollständig; vollendet

completion die Vollendung
complex verwickelt
complexion die Gesichtsfarbe
compliance die Einwilligung
complicate verwickeln
complication die Verwicklung
complicity die Mitschuld
compliment der Gruss, das Kompliment; beglückwünschen
comply willfahren
component der Bestandteil
compose zusammensetzen; verfassen
composed beruhigt, gefasst
composer der Komponist
composition die Zusammensetzung; der Aufsatz
composure die Gemütsruhe
compound zusammengesetzt; die Mischung
comprehend begreifen
comprehensible begreiflich
comprehension die Fassungskraft
comprehensive umfassend
compress (to) zusammendrücken
compression die Zusammendrückung
comprise enthalten
compromise der Kompromiss; übereinkommen
compulsion der Zwang
compulsory zwingend
compute berechnen
comrade der Kamerad
concave konkav
conceal verbergen
concede einräumen; gestatten
conceit die Eitelkeit; die Einbildung
conceited eingebildet
conceivable denkbar; begreiflich
conceive (to) sich denken; begreifen; empfangen
concentrate (sich) konzentrieren
conception der Begriff; die Empfängnis
concern betreffen
concern die Angelegenheit; das Geschäft
concerned bekümmert; beteiligt
concerning betreffs
concert (music) das Konzert

concession das Zugeständnis
conciliate versöhnen
conciliation die Versöhnung
conciliatory versöhnlich
concise bündig
conciseness die Kürze; die Bündigkeit
conclude beschliessen
conclusion (ending) der Schluss; (decision) der Beschluss
conclusive entscheidend
concord die Eintracht
concrete der Beton; konkret
concur zusammentreffen
concurrence die Übereinstimmung
concussion die Erchütterung
condemn verdammen; verurteilen
condemnation die Verurteilung
condense verdichten; abkürzen
condescend sich herablassen
condescension die Herablassung
condiment die Würze
condition die Lage; der Zustand; die Bedingung
conditional bedingt
conditionally bedingungsweise
condole kondolieren
condolence das Beileid
condone vergeben
conduct die Führung, das Betragen; führen, leiten
conductor der Führer; der Schaffner
cone der Kegel; der Zapfen
confectioner der Konditor
confederacy das Bündnis
confederate der Bundesgenosse; verbündet
confer verleihen, beratschlagen
conference die Konferenz
confess bekennen; beichten
confession die Beichte
confidant, der Vertraute
confide vertrauen
confidence das Vertrauen
confident zuversichtlich
confidential vertraulich; privat
confine die Grenze; begrenzen
confinement die Haft; das Wochenbett
confirm bestätigen; konfirmieren

confirmation die Bestätigung;
die Konfirmation
confiscate beschlagnahmen
confiscation die Beschlagnahme
conflagration der Brand
conflict der Streit; streiten
conflicting widersprechend
confluence der Zusammenfluss
conform ubereinstimmen
conformity die Übereinstimmung
confound (to) verwechseln; verwirren
confuse (to) verwirren
confusion die Verwirrung
confute widerlegen
congeal gefrieren
congenial sympatisch
congestion (medical) der Blutandrang; **(population)** die Übervölkerung; **(traffic)** die Verkehrsstockung
congratulate gratulieren
congregate sich versammeln
congregation die Gemeinde; die Versammlung
congress der Kongress
conjecture die Mutmassung; mutmassen
conjugal ehelich
conjugate konjugieren
conjugation die Konjugation
conjunction die Verbindung; das Bindewort
conjure beschwören
conjurer der Zauberer
connect verbinden
connection die Verbindung
connoisseur der Kenner
conquer erobern
conqueror der Sieger; der Eroberer
conquest die Eroberung
conscience das Gewissen
conscience-struck reuig
conscientious gewissenhaft
conscientiousness die Gewissenhaftigkeit
conscious bewusst
consciousness das Bewusstsein
conscript ausheben
conscription die Zwangsaushebung
consecrate weihen

consecration die Einsegnung
consecutive aufeinander, folgend
consent die Zustimmung
consent (to) einwilligen
consequence die Folge
consequently folglich
conservation die Erhaltung
conservative konservativ
conservatory das Treibhaus
conserve bewahren
consider erwägen; betrachten; halten für
considerable beträchtlich
considerate rücksichtsvoll
consideration die Rücksicht; die Betrachtung
consignment die Übersendung
consign zusenden
consignee der Empfänger
consist bestehen
consistent fest; gemäss
consolation der Trost
console trösten
consolidate festigen
consort der Gatte; die Gattin
conspicuous auffallend
conspiracy die Verschwörung
conspirator der Verschwörer
conspire sich verschwören
constable der Schutzmann
constancy die Beständigkeit
constant standhaft; beständig
constipate verstopfen
constipation die Verstopfung
constituency der Wahlkreis
constituent der Wähler
constitute ausmachen
constitution die Verfassung
constitutional verfassungsmässig
constrain zwingen
construct bauen; errichten
construction der Bau; die Konstruktion
constructive aufbauend
consul der Konsul
consult um Rat fragen
consultation die Konsultation; die Beratschlagung
consume verzehren
consumer der Verzehrer; der Abnehmer
consummate vollenden

consumption der Verbrauch; (**medical**) Schwindsucht
consumptive schwindsüchtig
contact die Berührung
contagion die Ansteckung
contagious ansteckend
contain enthalten; umfassen
container der Behälter
contaminate verunreinigen
contamination die Befleckung
contemplate betrachten
contemplation die Betrachtung
contemplative nachdenklich
contemporary zeitgenössisch; der Zeitgenosse
contempt die Verachtung
contemptible verächtlich
contemptuous geringschätzend
contend streiten, behaupten
content zufrieden
contentment die Zufriedenheit
contention die Behauptung; der Streit
contents der Inhalt
contest der Streit; bestreiten
context der Zusammenhang
contiguous anstossend
continent das Festland
continual fortwährend
continuance die Fortdauer
continuation die Fortsetzung
continue fortsetzen; fortfahren
continuous ununterbrochen
contour der Umriss
contortion die Verzerrung
contraband die Schmuggelware
contract der Vertrag
contract (**to**) (sich) zusammenziehen, sich zuziehen
contractor der Unternehmer
contradict widersprechen
contradiction der Widerspruch
contradictory widersprechend
contrary entgegengesetzt; das Gegenteil
contrary (**on the**) im Gegenteil
contrast der Gegensatz; gegenüberstellen
contravene zuwiderhandeln
contravention die Übertretung
contribute beitragen
contribution der Beitrag
contributor der Mitarbeiter

contrite zerknirscht
contrition die Zerknirschung
contrivance (**invention**) die Vorrichtung
contrive (**to**) gelingen; erfinden; ersinnen
control (**to**) kontrollieren; beherrschen; die Aufsicht, die Kontrolle, die Gewalt
controversy der Streit
convalescence die Genesung
convalescent genesend
convene zusammenberufen
convenience die Bequemlichkeit; die gelegene Zeit
convenient bequem; passend
convent das Nonnenkloster
convention die Versammlung; die Konvention
conventional herkömmlich
converge zusammenlaufen
conversation die Unterhaltung; das Gespräch
converse sich unterhalten
conversion die Verwandlung; die Bekehrung
convert der Bekehrte; verwandeln, bekehren
convertible umwechselbar
convex konvex
convey führen; senden
conveyance die Übermittlung; das Fuhrwerk
convict der Zuchthäusler; überführen; überzeugen
conviction die Überführung; die Überzeugung
convince überzeugen
convivial festlich
conviviality die Geselligkeit
convoke (**to**) berufen
convoy geleiten; das Geleit
convulsion die Zuckung; der Krampf; Erschütterung
coo girren
cook der Koch, die Köchin; kochen
cookery die Kochkunst
cool kühl; kühlen; abkühlen
coolie der Kuli
coolness Kühle
coop der Hühnerkorb
cooper der Küfer

co-operate mitwirken
co-operation die Mitwirkung
co-operative society der Konsumverein
cope sich messen mit
copious reichlich
copiousness die Fülle
copper das Kupfer
copy die Abschrift, das Exemplar; kopieren
copy-book das Schreibheft
copyright das Verlagsrecht
coquet kokettieren
coquetry die Gefallsucht
coquettish kokett
coral die Koralle
cord der Strick
cordial herzlich
cordiality die Herzlichkeit
core der Kern
cork der Kork; verkorken
corkscrew der Korkzieher
corn das Korn; das Hühnerauge
corner der Winkel; die Ecke
corner-seat der Eckplatz
corner-stone der Eckstein
cornflower die Kornblume
coronation die Krönung
corporation die Körperschaft
corporal körperlich; der Korporal
corps das Korps
corpse die Leiche
corpulent wohlbeleibt
Corpus Christi das Fronleichnamsfest
correct richtig; - berichten, verbessern
correction die Berichtigung; die Verbesserung
correctness die Richtigkeit
correspond entsprechen
correspondence der Briefwechsel
correspondent der Korrespondent
corridor der Gang; der Korridor
corroborate bestätigen
corroboration die Bestätigung
corrode (to) zerfressen
corrosive ätzend
corrugated-iron das Wellblech
corrupt verderben; bestechen; verderbt; bestechlich

corruption das Verderbnis; die Bestechung
corset das Korsett
cosmopolitan weltbürgerlich
cost die Kosten pl, der Preis; kosten
costermonger der Strassenhändler
costly kostbar
costume das Kostüm
cosy behaglich
cot die Wiege; das Kinderbett
cottage die Hütte; das Landhäuschen
cotton die Baumwolle
cotton-wool die Watte
couch das Ruhebett; das Lager
cough husten; der Husten
council der Rat
councillor der Ratsherr
counsel der Rat, der Anwalt; raten
count der Graf; zählen, rechnen
countenance das Gesicht, die Miene; begünstigen
counter der Ladentisch
counteract zuwiderhandeln
counterbalance aufwiegen
counterfeit nachmachen; nachgemacht
counterfoil das Kontrollblatt
countermand (to) abbestellen
counterpart das Gegenstück
countersign gegenzeichnen
countless unzählbar
country das Land; die Gegend; das Vaterland
countryman der Landsmann
county die Grafschaft
couple das Paar; koppeln, (sich) paaren
courage der Mut; die Tapferkeit
courageous mutig; tapfer
course der Lauf
course (meal) der Gang
course (exchange) der Wechselkurs
in due - zur gehörigen Zeit
of course natürlich
court der Hof, der Gerichtshof; den Hof machen
courteous höflich
courtesy die Höflichkeit

courtier Höfling	**creature** das Geschöpf
court-martial das Kriegsgericht	**credentials** das Beglaubigungs-
courtyard der Hof	schreiben
cousin der Vetter; die Kusine	**credibility** die Glaubwürdigkeit
covenant der Vertrag	**credible** glaubwürdig
cover die Decke, der Deckel;	**credit** der Kredit; das Guthaben
bedecken, schützen	**credit (to)** glauben; kreditieren
covet begehren	**creditable** achtbar
covetous begehrlich; habsüchtig	**creditor** der Gläubiger
cow die Kuh; einschüchtern	**credulous** leichtgläubig
coward der Feigling	**creed** das Glaubensbekenntnis
cowardice die Feigheit	**creek** die Bucht
cowardly feige	**creep** kriechen; schleichen
cower kauern	**creeper** die Schlingpflanze
cowslip die Schüsselblume	**creepy** gruselich
coy spröde	**cremate** einäschern
crab die Krabbe	**cremation** die Leichenverbren-
crab(apple) der Holzapfel	nung
crack der Knall, der Krach, der	**crescent** der Halbmond
Sprung; springen, knacken, knal-	**cress** die Kresse
len	**crest** der Kamm
crackle knistern	**crestfallen** niedergeschlagen
cradle die Wiege; wiegen	**crevasse (crevice)** die Spalte
craft das Handwerk, die List	**crew** die Mannschaft
craftsman der Handwerker	**crib** die Krippe
crafty schlau	**cricket** die Grille
crag die Klippe; die Felsspitze	**crier** der Ausrufer
cram einstopfen; einpauken	**crime** das Verbrechen
cramp der Krampf; einschränken	**criminal** der Verbrecher; ver-
crane der Kranich, der Kran;	brecherisch
- **one's neck** den Hals recken	**crimson** das Karmesin
crank die Kurbel; der verdrehte	**crimson** karmesinrot
Mensch	**cringe** sich krümmen
cranky überspannt	**crinkle** die Falte; sich falten
cranny der Spalt	**cripple** verkrüppeln; der Krüppel
crape der Krepp	**crisis** die Krise
crash der Krach; krachen	**crisp** knusperig; kraus
crass grob	**critic** der Kritiker
crate der Packkorb; die Latten-	**critical** kritisch
kiste	**criticize** kritisieren
crater der Krater	**criticism** die Kritik
crave verlangen; erflehen	**croak** krächzen
craving das Verlangen	**crochet** die Häkelarbeit; häkeln
crawl kriechen	**crockery** die Töpferware; das
crayfish der Krebs	Geschirr
crayon der Buntstift	**crocodile** das Krokodil
crazy verrückt; baufällig	**crook** der Haken, der Hirtenstab;
creak knarren	krümmen
cream die Sahne; der Rahm	**crooked** krumm
crease die Falte; falten	**crop** die Ernte, der Kropf (**birds**);
create erschaffen; ernennen	stutzen, schneiden
creation die Schöpfung	**cross** das Kreuz; böse, mürrisch;
creator der Schöpfer	durchkreuzen, überschreiten

crossing der Übergang; die Überfahrt

cross-examination das Kreuzverhör

cross-bow die Armbrust

crouch sich ducken

crow die Krähe; krähen

crowd die Menge; (sich) drängen

crown die Krone, der Scheitel, der Gipfel; krönen

crucial entscheidend

crucifix das Kruzifix

crucifixion die Kreuzigung

crucify kreuzigen

crude roh

cruel grausam

cruelty die Grausamkeit

cruise kreuzen; die Seefahrt

cruiser der Kreuzer

crumb die Krume; krümeln, zerbröckeln

crumple zerknittern

crunch (to) zerknirschen

crusade der Kreuzzug

crusader der Kreuzfahrer

crush zerquetschen, unterdrücken; das Gedränge

crust die Kruste

crutch die Krücke

cry schreien, weinen; das Geschrei

crypt die Gruft

crystal der Kristall

crystallize kristallisieren

cub der Junge

cube der Würfel

cuckoo der Kuckuck

cucumber die Gurke

cuddle herzen

cue das Stichwort

cuff die Manschette; puffen; **hand-** die Handfessel

cuff-link der Manschettenknopf

culinary kulinarisch

culprit der Schuldige

cult der Kultus

cultivate anbauen; pflegen

cultivation der Ackerbau; die Pflege

culture die Kultur

cumbersome lästig; schwerfällig

cunning verschlagen, schlau; die List

cup die Tasse; der Becher; der Pokal

cupboard der Schrank

cupidity die Begierde

curate der Hilfsgeistliche

curb zügeln

curd die dicke Milch

cure die Kur; das Heilmittel

cure heilen

curfew die Abendglocke, das Ausgehverbot

curiosity die Neugierde

curious neugierig; merkwürdig

curl die Locke; kräuseln

curly lockig

currant die Johannisbeere; die Korinthe

currency der Umlauf; die Währung

current (um)laufend; der Strom, die Strömung

curse der Fluch; verfluchen

cursory flüchtig

curt kurz

curtail abkürzen; beschränken

curtain der Vorhang; die Gardine

curve biegen, krümmen; die Krümmung; die Kurve

curved gebogen

cushion das Kissen

custodian der Hüter;

custody die Haft; die Verwahrung

custom der Gebrauch; die Gewohnheit; die Kundschaft

custom(s) der Zoll

customs-house das Zollamt

customary gebräuchlich

customer der Kunde

cut schneiden; der Schnitt; **- off** abschneiden; **- through** durchschneiden; **- teeth** Zähne bekommen

cute schlau

cutlass der Hirschfänger

cutler der Messerschmied

cutlery die Bestecke *pl*

cutlet das Kotelett

cutter der Zuschneider; die Schneidemaschine

cutting scharf; schneidend

cycle das Fahrrad, der Zyklus; radfahren

cyclist der Radfahrer
cyclone der Wirbelsturm
cylinder der Zylinder; die Walze
cynic der Zyniker
cynical zynisch
cypress die Zypresse
czar der Zar

D

dab betupfen; der Klaps
dabble bespritzen; plätschern;
  sich einmischen
dabbler der Pfuscher
daddy der Papa
daffodil die Osterglocke
dagger der Dolch
daily täglich
daily paper die Tageszeitung
daintiness die Feinheit
dainty die Leckerei; lecker, fein
dairy die Molkerei
daisy das Gänseblümchen
dale das Tal
dally tändeln
dam der Damm; (ab)dämmen
damage der Schaden; beschädigen
damask der Damast
damn verdammen
damnable verdammenswert
damnation die Verdammung
damp befeuchten, feucht; der
  Dunst, die Feuchtigkeit
damper der Dämpfer; die Ofen-
  klappe
damsel das Mädchen
dance tanzen; der Tanz
dancer der Tänzer; die Tänzerin
dandelion der Löwenzahn
dandruff die Kopfschuppen *pl*
dandy der Stutzer
danger die Gefahr
dangerous gefährlich
dangle baumeln
Danube die Donau
dank dunstig; nasskalt
dapper flink; nett
dare dürfen; wagen; herausfordern
daring kühn; die Kühnheit

dark dunkel; finster
dark-room die Dunkelkammer
darken verdunkeln
darkness die Dunkelheit; die
  Finsternis
darling der Liebling
darn stopfen; die Stopfstelle, der
  Wurfspiess
dart schleudern, werfen
dash der Strich
dashing schneidig; flott
date das Datum; datieren; die
  Dattel
date (out of) aus der Mode; veraltet
date (up to) zeitgemäss; modern
daub überschmieren
daughter die Tochter; -in-law
  die Schwiegertochter
daunt entmutigen
dauntless unerschrocken
dawdle schlendern; Zeit vergeuden
dawn die Dämmerung; däm-
  mern
day der Tag; to-day heute
daybreak der Tagesanbruch
daze betäuben
dazzle blenden
dead tot; matt
dead-beat totmüde
deadlock die Stockung; der
  Stillstand
deaf taub
deafen betäuben
deafness die Taubheit
deal der Teil; - cards Karten
  geben; handeln; austeilen; - (a
  great) sehr viel
dealer der Händler
dear lieb; teuer
dearth der Mangel
death der Tod
death-duty die Erbschaftssteuer
death-penalty die Todesstrafe
debar ausschliessen
debase erniedrigen
debate erörtern; die Debatte
debauch(ery) die Ausschweifung
debenture die Obligation
debility die Schwäche
debit belasten; das Debet
debt die Schuld; in - verschuldet

debtor der Schuldner
decadence der Verfall
decanter die Karaffe
decapitate enthaupten
decay der Verfall; verfallen
decease das Ableben
deceit der Betrug; die Täuschung
deceitful (be)trügerisch
deceive betrügen; täuschen
decency der Anstand
decent anständig
deception die Täuschung; der Betrug
decide entscheiden
deciduous wood der Laubwald
decipher entziffern
decision der Entschluss
decisive entscheidend
deck das (Ver-) Deck; schmücken
declaim deklamieren
declaration der Erklärung
declare (sich) erklären
decline verweigern; ablehnen, abnehmen; die Abnahme, der Niedergang
decode entziffern
decompose zerlegen; verwesen
decorate zieren; schmücken
decoration die Verzierung
decorous anständig
decoy ködern; der Köder
decrease die Abnahme; abnehmen, vermindern
decree das Dekret, der Erlass; beschliessen; verordnen
decrepit abgelebt; altersschwach
decry in Verruf bringen
dedicate widmen
dedication die Widmung
deduce folgern; ableiten
deduct abziehen
deduction der Abzug
deed die Tat; die Urkunde
deem halten für
deep tief
deep(ness) die Tiefe
deepen vertiefen
deer das Reh; das Rotwild
deface entstellen
defamation die Verleumdung
defamatory verleumderisch
defame verleumden
default der Mangel

defeat die Niederlage; schlagen, besiegen
defect der Fehler; der Mangel
defection der Abfall
defective mangelhaft; schadhaft
defence die Verteidigung
defend verteidigen
defendant der Beklagte
defer verschieben
deference die Ehrerbietung
defiance der Trotz
deficiency der Mangel
defile beflecken, schänden; der Engpass
define erklären; bestimmen
definit(iv)e bestimmt
definition die Erklärung; die Definition
deflect ablenken; abweichen
deform verunstalten; entstellen
deformity die Verunstaltung
defraud betrügen
defray bezahlen; bestreiten
deft geschickt
defunct verstorben
defy herausfordern; trotzen
degenerate entarten
degeneration die Entartung
degrade herabsetzen; entwürdigen
degree die Stufe; der Grad
degrees (by) allmählich
deign geruhen
deity die Gottheit
dejected entmutigt; niedergeschlagen
dejection die Niedergeschlagenheit
delay verzögern, hindern; der Aufschub
delectable ergötzend
delegate der Abgeordnete, der Beauftragte; beauftragen
deliberate überlegen, erwägen; bedachtsam, wohlerwogen
deliberation die Überlegung
delicacy der Leckerbissen; die Delikatesse; die Zartheit; das Zartgefühl
delicate zart; fein; schwächlich
delicious köstlich
delight das Vergnügen; ergötzen
delightful entzückend

delinquent der Verbrecher
delirious wahnsinnig; irre
deliver befreien; abliefern; ausführen
deliverance die Befreiung
delivery die Lieferung
delude täuschen
deluge die Flut; überschwemmen
delusion die Täuschung
delve graben
demand fordern, fragen, verlangen; die Nachfrage, das Verlangen
demeanour das Benehmen
democracy die Demokratie
democratic demokratisch
demolish niederreissen; demolieren
demonstrate beweisen
demonstration der Beweis; die Demonstration
demoralize demoralisieren
demur Einwendungen machen
demure zimperlich
den die Höhle; die Bude
denial die Verneinung
denomination die Benennung; die Sekte
denote bedeuten
denounce anzeigen; androhen
dense dicht; dumm
densify die Dichtheit
dent die Beule; einbeulen
dentist der Zahnarzt
denude entblössen
deny verneinen; verleugnen
depart abreisen; weggehen
department die Abteilung; der Bezirk
departure die Abreise
depend abhängen; sich verlassen
dependable zuverlässig
dependence die Abhängigkeit
dependent abhängig
depict schildern
deplete entleeren
deplorable bejammernswert
deplore beweinen; bejammern
depopulate entvölkern
depopulation die Entvölkerung
deport deportieren
deportment das Verhalten
depose absetzen

deposit niederlegen, einzahlen; die Einlage, der Niederschlag; die Ablagerung, das Pfand
depot das Lagerhaus; das Depot
deprave verderben
depravity die Verderbtheit
deprecate missbilligen
depreciate herabsetzen; entwerten; im Wert sinken
depreciation die Entwertung
depress niederdrücken
depression die Niedergeschlagenheit, die Senkung, das Tief; die Flauheit
deprivation die Beraubung
deprive berauben
depth die Tiefe
deputy der Abgeordnete; der Stellvertreter
deracinate entwurzeln
derail entgleisen
derailment die Entgleisung
derange stören
derelict herrenlos; verlassen
deride verlachen
derision die Verspottung
derisive spöttisch
derivation die Ableitung
derive ableiten
derogatory beeinträchtigend
descend herkommen; herabsteigen; abstammen
descendant der Nachkomme
descent das Herabsteigen; die Abstammung
describe beschreiben
description die Beschreibung
desecrate entweihen
desecration die Entweihung
desert die Wüste; öde, verlassen
deserter der Fahnenflüchtige
deserve verdienen
deserving verdienstvoll
design bestimmen, beabsichtigen, entwerfen; der Entwurf, die Zeichnung
designate bezeichnen; ernennen
desirable wünschenswert
desire begehren, verlangen; der Wunsch, das Begehren
desirous begierig
desist abstehen
desk das Pult; der Schreibtisch

desolate einsam; öde
desolation die Verwüstung; das Elend
despair die Verzweiflung; verzweifeln
desperate verzweifelt
despicable verächtlich
despise verachten
despite trotz
despoil plündern
despond verzagen
despondency die Verzagtheit
despot der Despot
despotism die Gewaltherrschaft
dessert der Nachtisch
destination die Bestimmung; das Ziel
destine bestimmen
destiny das Schicksal
destitute hilflos
destitution die Not
destroy zerstören; vernichten
destruction die Zerstörung
destructive zerstörend
desultory planlos; oberflächlich
detach absondern
detachable abtrennbar
detachment die Absonderung
detail die Einzelheit
detain zurückhalten; festhalten
detect entdecken
detective der Geheimpolizist
detention die Vorenthaltung; die Haft
deter abschrecken
deteriorate verschlechtern
deterioration die Verschlechterung
determination die Entschlossenheit
determine festsetzen; sich entschliessen
detest verabscheuen
detestable abscheulich
dethrone entthronen
detour der Umweg
detract vermindern; herabsetzen
detriment der Nachteil
detrimental nachteilig
devastate verwüsten
develop entwickeln
development die Entwicklung
deviate (to) abweichen

deviation die Abweichung
device die Erfindung; der Wahlspruch
devil der Teufel
devilish teuflisch
devise erfinden
devoid bar; ohne
devote widmen; weihen
devoted ergeben
devotion die Andacht; die Ergebenheit
devour verschlingen
devout fromm
dew der Tau
dexterity die Gewandtheit
dexterous gewandt
diagnosis die Diagnose
dial das Zifferblatt
dialect die Mundart
dialogue das Zwiegespräch
diameter der Durchmesser
diamond der Diamant
diarrhœa der Durchfall
diary das Tagebuch
dice der Würfel
dictate diktieren
dictation das Diktat
dictator der Diktator
dictatorship die Diktatur
dictionary das Wörterbuch
die sterben; der Stempel
diet die Diät
differ sich unterscheiden; anderer Meinung sein
difference der Unterschied; der Streit
different verschieden; ander
difficult schwierig
difficulty die Schwierigkeit
diffidence die Schüchternheit
diffuse verbreiten
dig graben
digest verdauen
digestion die Verdauung
dignified würdevoll
dignitary der Würdenträger
dignity die Würde
digress abschweifen
digression die Abschweifung
dike der Deich; eindämmen
dilapidated baufällig
dilapidation der Verfall
dilatory aufschiebend

diligence der Fleiss
diligent fleissig
dilute verdünnen
dilution die Verdünnung
dim trübe; verdunkeln; trüben
dimension die Dimension; das Ausmass
diminish vermindern
diminutive winzig
dimple das Grübchen
din das Getöse
dine speisen
dinghy das Dingi; das Schlauchboot
dingy schmutzig
dining-car der Speisewagen
dining-room das Speisezimmer
dinner das Mittagessen; das Festmahl
dint (by - of) kraft
dip eintauchen
diploma das Diplom
diplomacy die Diplomatie
diplomat der Diplomat
dire grässlich
direct gerade; unmittelbar; richten; lenken; weisen
direction die Richtung; die Leitung; die Anordnung; die Anweisung
director der Direktor
directory das Adressbuch
dirge der Grabgesang
dirt der Schmutz
dirty schmutzig; beschmutzen
disability die Unfähigkeit
disable unfähig machen
disabled körperbehindert; kriegsbeschädigt
disadvantage der Nachteil
disadvantageous nachteilig
disaffection die Abneigung
disagree nicht übereinstimmen; streiten; nicht bekommen
disagreeable unangenehm
disagreement die Meinungsverschiedenheit
disallow nicht gestatten
disappear verschwinden
disappearance das Verschwinden
disappoint enttäuschen
disappointment die Enttäuschung

disapprobation, disapproval die Missbilligung
disapprove missbilligen
disarm entwaffnen
disarmament die Entwaffnung; die Abrüstung
disarrange in Unordnung bringen
disaster das Unglück
disastrous unheilvoll
disband entlassen; auflösen
disbelief der Unglaube
disbelieve nicht glauben
disburse auszahlen
discard ablegen
discern unterscheiden
discernible sichtbar; erkennbar
discerning scharfsichtig
discernment der Scharfsinn
discharge entladen, entlassen, abfeuern; die Entlassung, die Entladung
disciple der Jünger; der Schüler
discipline die Zucht
disclaim leugnen
disclose enthüllen
disclosure die Enthüllung
discolour entfärben
discomfort die Unbehaglichkeit
disconcert beunruhigen
disconnect ausschalten; trennen
disconsolate trostlos
discontent die Unzufriedenheit
discontented unzufrieden
discontinue unterbrechen; aufhören
discontinuance die Unterbrechung; das Aufhören
discord die Uneinigkeit
discordant missklingend
discount diskontieren; der Abzug, der Diskont
discourage abraten; entmutigen
discourse die Rede; reden
discourtesy die Unhöflichkeit
discover entdecken
discoverer der Entdecker
discovery die Entdeckung
discredit in schlechten Ruf bringen
discreditable schimpflich
discreet vorsichtig; verschwiegen

discretion das Gutdünken; die Besonnenheit

discriminate unterscheiden

discrimination die Unterscheidung

discuss erörtern; besprechen

discussion Erörterung

disdain verschmähen, verachten; die Verachtung

disdainful geringschätzig

disease die Krankheit

disembark ausschiffen

disengage befreien; losmachen

disengaged frei; unbeschäftigt

disentangle entwirren

disfavour die Ungnade

disfigure entstellen

disgorge ausspeien

disgrace die Schande; die Ungnade

disgraceful schimpflich

disguise verkleiden; die Verkleidung

disgust der Ekel; anekeln

disgusting ekelhaft; widrig

dish die Schüssel; das Gericht

dishearten entmutigen

dishonest unehrlich

dishonesty die Unredlichkeit

dishonour die Schande; verunehren

dishonourable ehrlos

disillusion enttäuschen

disinclination die Abneigung

disinclined abgeneigt

disinfect desinfizieren

disinherit enterben

disinterested uneigennützig

disk die Scheibe; die Platte

dislike der Widerwille; nicht mögen

dislocate verrenken

dislodge vertreiben

disloyal treulos

disloyalty die Treulosigkeit

dismal düster; traurig

dismay die Bestürzung; erschrecken

dismiss entlassen

dismissal die Entlassung

dismount absteigen

disobedience der Ungehorsam

disobedient ungehorsam

disobey nicht gehorchen

disobliging unhöflich; ungefällig

disorder die Unordnung

disorderly unordentlich

disorganize zerrütten

disown verleugnen

disparage herabsetzen

dispatch die Abfertigung; die Depesche; abfertigen, absenden

dispel zerstreuen

dispensary die Apotheke

dispense erlassen; austeilen

disperse zerstreuen

displace absetzen; verlegen

displacement die Absetzung; die Wasserverdrängung

display entfalten, ausstellen; die Schaustellung, der Prunk

displease missfallen

displeasure das Missfallen

disposal die Verfügung, der Verkauf

dispose anordnen, verfügen

disposed geneigt

disposition die Neigung; die Anordnung

disprove widerlegen

disproportion das Missverhältnis

dispute der Streit; (be)streiten

disqualification der Ausschluss

disqualify ausschliessen

disregard die Nichtachtung; unbeachtet lassen

disreputable gemein; schimpflich

disrepute der üble Ruf

disruption die Zerreissung

dissatisfaction die Unzufriedenheit

dissatisfy nicht befriedigen

dissect zergliedern; sezieren

dissection die Zergliederung; die Sezierung

dissemble sich verstellen

dissension der Zwist

dissent anderer Meinung sein; die Meinungsverschiedenheit

dissimilar ungleichartig

dissipate verschwenden

dissipated ausschweifend

dissolution die Auflösung

dissolve auflösen

dissuade abraten

distance die Entfernung; die Ferne
distant entfernt, fern
distaste der Widerwille
distasteful widerwärtig
distil destillieren
distillery die Brennerei
distinct verschieden; deutlich
distinction die Auszeichnung; der Unterschied
distinguish unterscheiden; auszeichnen
distort verdrehen
distortion die Verdrehung
distract ablenken; zerstreuen
distraction die Zerstreutheit
distress das Elend, die Not; peinigen
distressing schmerzlich
distribute austeilen; verteilen
distribution die Verteilung
district der Bezirk; die Gegend
distrust misstrauen; das Misstrauen
disturb stören
disturbance die Störung; die Unruhe
disunite (sich) trennen
disuse der Nichtgebrauch
ditch der Graben
dive tauchen
diver der Taucher
diverse verschieden
diversion die Ablenkung; die Umleitung
divert ablenken
divest entkleiden; berauben
divide (ein)teilen
divine göttlich; weissagen
diving-bell die Taucherglocke
divinity die Theologie; die Gottheit
divisible teilbar
division die Teilung; die Abstimmung; die Division
divorce die Scheidung; scheiden
divulge verbreiten
dizziness der Schwindel
dizzy schwindelig
do tun; aufführen
docile gelehrig
dock das Dock, die Anklagebank, in ein Dock bringen (kommen)

dockyard die Schiffswerft
doctor der Arzt; der Doktor
doctrine die Lehre
document die Urkunde
documentary urkundlich
dodge ausweichen
dodge der Kniff
doff abnehmen; ausziehen; ablegen
dog der Hund
dog nachspüren
dogged hartnäckig; störrig
doggedness die Hartnäckigkeit
dogma das Dogma; der Glaubenssatz
dogmatic dogmatisch
dole die Arbeitslosenunterstützung
doleful kläglich
doll die Puppe
dolphin der Delphin
domain die Domäne; das Gebiet
dome die Kuppel
domestic häuslich
domicile der Wohnsitz
domiciled wohnhaft
dominate (be)herrschen
domination die Herrschaft
dominion die Herrschaft
don anziehen
donation die Schenkung
done getan; gar gekocht
donkey der Esel
doom das Urteil, das Schicksal; verurteilen
doomsday der jüngste Tag
door die Tür
doors (out of) draussen
doorkeeper der Pförtner
doorway die Türöffnung
dormant schlafend; unbenutzt
dormitory der Schlafsaal
dose die Dosis
dot der Punkt; punktieren
dote vernarrt sein
double doppelt, verdoppeln; das Ebenbild
doubt der Zweifel; (be)zweifeln
doubtful zweifelhaft
doubtless ohne Zweifel
dough der Teig
doughty tapfer
dove die Taube

down die Daune; nieder, unten, herab
downcast niedergeschlagen
downfall der Untergang
downhearted niedergeschlagen
downstairs (nach) unten
downwards abwärts
dowry die Mitgift
doze schlummern; das Schläfchen
dozen das Dutzend
draft entwerfen; der Entwurf, die Tratte
drag schleppen
dragon der Drache
drain der Abfluss; der Abzugsgraben; entwässern; austrocknen
drainage die Entwässerung
drake der Enterich
drama das Drama
dramatic dramatisch
dramatist der Dramatiker
drape hüllen
draper der Tuchhändler
draught der Zug; der Schluck; der Tiefgang; die Zugluft
draughts das Damenspiel
draughtsman der Zeichner
draw ziehen; zeichnen
drawbridge die Zugbrücke
drawer die Schublade
drawers (underclothes) die Unterhose
drawing die Zeichnung
drawing-room der Salon
dread fürchten; die Furcht
dreadful furchtbar; schrecklich
dream der Traum; träumen
dreamy träumerisch
dreary traurig; öde
dredge ausbaggern
dredger der Bagger
dregs (sediment) der Bodensatz; der Hefe
drench durchnässen
dress der Anzug; die Kleidung; das Kleid; sich kleiden
dress-coat der Frack
dressing der Verband
dressing-gown der Morgenrock
dressing-room das Ankleidezimmer
dressing-table der Frisiertisch
dressmaker die Schneiderin

drift treiben; die Trift, die Wehe, der Lauf
drill bohrer; exerzieren
drill (tool) der Bohrer
drink trinken, saufen; das Getränk
drinkable trinkbar
drip tröpfeln
dripping das Bratenfett
drive treiben, fahren; der Fahrweg, die Fahrt
drivel geifern
driver der Treiber; der Fahrer
driving licence der Führerschein
drizzle rieseln; der Sprühregen
droll drollig
dromedary das Dromedar
drone die Drohne, der Faulenzer; brummen; das Summen
droop hängen; sinken lassen
drop fallen lassen
drop der Tropfen
dropsy die Wassersucht
dross die Schlacke
drought die Dürre
drown ertränken
drowned (to get) ertrinken
drowning das Ertrinken
drowsiness die Schläfrigkeit
drowsy schläfrig
drudge (to) sich placken
drudge der Knecht; der Packesel
drudgery die Plackerei
drug die Droge
druggist der Drogist
drum die Trommel; trommeln
drummer der Trommler
drunk betrunken
drunkard der Trunkenbold
drunkenness die Trunkenheit
dry trocken, dürr; trocknen
dubious zweifelhaft; ungewiss
ducal herzoglich
duchess die Herzogin
duchy das Herzogtum
duck die Ente; tauchen
due die Gebühr
due gebührend; fällig
duel das Duell; der Zweikampf
duet das Duett
duke der Herzog
dull dumm; matt; stumpf

dullness die Stumpfheit; die Mattheit
dumb stumm
dumbfounded sprachlos
dummy der Strohmann
dump die Abladestelle, das Munitionslager; umkippen
dumping-ground der Abladeplatz
dumpling der Mehlkloss
dunce der Dummkopf
dung der Dünger
dungeon der Kerker
dupe der Narr; der Betrogene
dupe anführen
duplicity die Doppelzüngigkeit
durability die Dauerhaftigkeit
durable dauerhaft
duration die Dauer
during während
dusk die Dämmerung
dust der Staub; stäuben
dustbin der Müllkasten
duster das Staubtuch
dusty staubig
dutiful pflichttreu
duty die Pflicht; der Zoll
dwarf der Zwerg
dwell wohnen
dwelling die Wohnung
dwindle vermindern
dye der Farbstoff; färben
dyer der Färber
dynamite das Dynamit
dynamo der Dynamo
dynasty die Dynastie
dysentery die Ruhr

E

each jeder, jede, jedes
each other einande
eager eifrig
eagerness der Eifer
eagle der Adler
ear das Ohr
earache der Ohrenschmerz
ear-ring der Ohrring
earl der Graf
early früh
earn verdienen
earnest ernst; der Ernst

earnings der Verdienst; der Lohn
earth die Erde
earthenware das Steingut
earthly irdisch
earthquake das Erdbeben
ease die Ruhe, die Bequemlichkeit; beruhigen
easel die Staffelei
easiness die Leichtigkeit
east der Osten
Easter Ostern
easterly östlich
easy leicht
easy chair der Lehnstuhl
eat essen; fressen
eatable essbar
eatables die Esswaren *pl*
eaves die Dachtraufe
eavesdropper der Horcher
ebb die Ebbe; ebben
ebony das Ebenholz
eccentric exzentrisch; überspannt
ecclesiastic geistlich, kirchlich; der Geistliche
echo das Echo; wiederhallen
eclipse die Verfinsterung; (sich) verdunkeln
economical sparsam; wirtschaftlich
economics die Volkswirtschaftslehre
economize sparen
economy die Sparsamkeit; die Wirtschaft
ecstasy die Verzückung
eddy der Wirbel; wirbeln
edge die Schärfe; die Schneide; der Rand; die Kante
edible essbar
edification die Erbauung
edifice das Gebäude
edify erbauen
edit herausgeben
edition die Ausgabe; die Auflage
editor der Herausgeber; der Redakteur
editorial der Leitartikel
educate erziehen; ausbilden
education die Erziehung, die Bildung
eel der Aal
efface ausstreichen; auslöschen

effacement die Auslöschung	**elevate** erhöhen; erheben
effect die Wirkung; bewirken	**elevation** die Erhöhung
effective wirksam	**elevator** der Fahrstuhl
effectuate bewerkstelligen	**eligible** wählbar
effeminacy die Verweichlichung	**eligibility** die Wählbarkeit
effeminate weibisch	**eliminate** entfernen
effervesce aufbrausen; schäumen	**elimination** die Ausscheidung
effete entkräftet	**elk** das Elentier
efficacious wirksam	**eil** die Elle
efficacy die Wirksamkeit	**elm** die Ulme
efficiency die Kraft; die Tüchtigkeit	**elocution** die Vortragskunst
efficient tüchtig; leistungsfähig	**elope** entlaufen
effigy das Bild(nis)	**eloquence** die Beredsamkeit
effort die Anstrengung; die Mühe	**eloquent** beredt
effrontery die Frechheit	**else** sonst; anders
effusion der Erguss	**elsewhere** anderswo
effusive überschwenglich	**elucidate** erläutern
egg das Ei	**elucidation** die Erläuterung
egg-cup der Eierbecher	**elude** ausweichen
egoist der Egoist	**elusive** ausweichend
egoism die Selbstsucht; der Egoismus	**emaciated** abgezehrt
egress der Ausgang	**emaciation** die Abmagerung
Egypt Ägypten	**emanate** ausstrahlen
eiderdown die Eiderdaune; die Daunendecke	**emanation** die Ausströmung
either einer von beiden; entweder	**emancipate** frei machen
eject ausstossen	**emancipation** die Befreiung
elaborate ausarbeiten; ausgearbeitet	**embalm** einbalsamieren
elapse verlaufen	**embankment** der Damm
elastic elastisch	**embargo** das Verbot
elastic das Gummiband	**embark** (sich) einschiffen; sich einlassen
elated in gehobener Stimmung	**embarrass** in Verlegenheit bringen
elbow der Ellbogen	**embarrassment** die Verlegenheit
elbow-room der Spielraum	**embassy** die Botschaft
elder älter; der Holunder	**embellish** verschönern
elderly ältlich	**embellishment** die Verschönerung
eldest älteste	**embers** die glühende Asche
elect erwählen	**embezzle** veruntreuen
election die Wahl	**embezzlement** die Unterschlagung
elector der Wähler; der Kurfürst	**embitter** verbittern
electorate die Wählerschaft	**emblem** das Sinnbild; das Emblem
electric elektrisch	**embodiment** die Verkörperung
electricity die Elektrizität	**embody** verkörpern
electrify elektrisieren	**embrace** umarmen; umfassen
elegance die Eleganz	**embroider** sticken
elegant elegant	**embroidery** die Stickerei
elegy die Elegie	**embroil** verwickeln
elementary elementar	**emerald** der Smaragd
elephant der Elefant	

emerge auftauchen
emergency der Notfall
emery der Schmirgel
emigrant der Auswanderer
emigrate auswandern
emigration die Auswanderung
eminence die Anhöhe; die Eminenz
eminent hervorragend
emissary der Bote
emit gussenden
emolument das Gehalt
emotion die Gemütsbewegung
emotional erregbar
emperor der Kaiser
emphasis der Nachdruck; die Betonung
emphatic nachdrücklich
emphasize betonen
empire das Reich
employ anwenden; anstellen
employee der Arbeitnehmer; der Angestellte
employer der Arbeitgeber
employment die Beschäftigung
empower ermächtigen
empress die Kaiserin
empty leer; leeren
emulate wetteifern
emulation der Wetteifer
enable befähigen
enact verfügen
enamel das Emaille, der Schmelz; emaillieren
enamoured verliebt
encamp sich lagern
encampment das Lager
enchant bezaubern
enchanting bezaubernd
encircle umringen
enclose einschliefsen; beilegen
enclosure die Einlage; die Einzäumung
encounter begegnen; das Zusammentreffen; das Gefecht
encourage ermutigen
encouragement die Ermutigung
encroach übergreifen
encroachment der Übergriff
encumber belasten
encumbrance die Last
encyclopædia die Enzyklopädie
end das Ende, das Ziel; (be)enden

endanger gefährden
endear teuer machen
endearment die Zärtlichkeit
endeavour sich bestreben, sich bemühen; die Bemühung
ending das Ende; der Schluss
endless endlos
endorse indossieren; bestätigen
endorsement die Indossierung; die Bestätigung
endow ausstatten; dotieren
endowment die Dotation; die Ausstattung
endurance die Ausdauer
endure aushalten
enemy der Feind
energetic energisch
energy die Tatkraft; die Energie
enervate entnerven
enfeeble schwächen
enforce erzwingen
engage (sich) verpflichten; sich einlassen; mieten; verloben
engagement die Verpflichtung; die Verlobung; das Gefecht
engaging einnehmend
engender erzeugen
engine die Maschine; die Lokomotive
engine-driver der Lokomotivführer
engineer der Ingenieur
engineering der Maschinenbau
English englisch
Englishman der Engländer
engrave gravieren
engraver der Graveur
engraving der Kupferstich
engross ganz in Anspruch nehmen
engulf verschlingen
enhance steigern
enigma das Rätsel
enigmatic rätselhaft
enjoy geniessen; - oneself sich gut unterhalten; sich erfreuen
enjoyment der Genuss
enlarge vergrössern; erweitern
enlargement die Erweiterung; die Vergrösserung
enlighten aufklären
enlist (sich) anwerben lassen; anwerben

enliven beleben
enmity die Feindschaft
ennoble adeln
enormity die Ungeheuerlichkeit
enormous ungeheuer
enough genug
enrage wütend machen
enrapture entzücken
enrich bereichern
enrol einschreiben
ensign die Fahne; der Fähnrich
enslave versklaven
ensue folgen
ensuing folgend; nächst
entail zur Folge haben
entangle verwickeln
enter (to) eintreten; einschreiben
enterprise die Unternehmung
entertain unterhalten; bewirten
entertainment die Unterhaltung
enthusiasm die Begeisterung
entice locken
enticement die Verlockung
entire ganz; vollständig
entitle (to) berechtigen; betiteln
entrails die Eingeweide *pl*
entrance der Eingang
entreat ersuchen
entreaty die Bitte
entrench mit Graben versehen
entrenchment die Verschanzung
entrust anvertrauen
enumerate aufzählen
enumeration die Aufzählung
enunciate aussagen
enunciation die Aussprache
envelop einwickeln
envelope der Briefumschlag
enviable beneidenswert
envious neidisch
environment die Umgebung
envisage ins Auge fassen
envoy der Gesandte
envy der Neid; beneiden
ephemeral eintägig; vergänglich
epic das Epos; episch
epidemic die Seuche
epilepsy die Fallsucht
epileptic fallsüchtig
epilogue das Nachwort
Epiphany das Dreikönigsfest
episcopal bischöflich

episode die Episode
epitaph die Grabschrift
epoch der Zeitabschnitt; die Epoche
Epsom salts das Bittersalz
equable ruhig
equal gleich; gleichen
equality die Gleichheit
equalization die Gleichmachung
equalize gleichmachen
equanimity der Gleichmut
equation die Gleichung
equator der Äquator
equestrian der Reiter
equilibrium das Gleichgewicht
equip ausrüsten
equipment die Ausrüstung
equitable billig
equity die Billigkeit
equivalent gleichwertig
equivocal zweideutig
equivocate zweideutig reden
era die Zeitrechnung; die Ära
eradicate ausrotten
erase ausradieren; ausstreichen
erasure die Rasur
ere bevor; ehe
erect aufrecht; errichten
erection die Errichtung
ermine das Hermelin
erosion die Zerfressung; die Erosion
erotic erotisch
err (sich) (ver)irren
errand der Auftrag
errand-boy der Laufbursche
erratum der Druckfehler
erroneous irrig
error der Irrtum
erudite gelehrt
erudition die Gelehrsamkeit
eruption der Ausbruch
escapade Seitensprung
escape entweichen, entrinnen; das Entweichen; das Entrinnen
escort das Geleit, die Bedeckung; geleiten
espalier das Spalier
especial besonder
espionage die Spionage
esplanade die Promenade
espouse (ver)heiraten
espy spähen

essay der Aufsatz, der Versuch; versuchen

essence die Essenz; das Wesen

essential wesentlich

establish einsetzen; festsetzen; gründen

establishment die Anstalt; die Errichtung; die Gründung

established church die Staatskirche

estate der Stand; das Landgut

esteem die Hochschätzung; achten

estimate schätzen; der Voranschlag

estimable schätzbar

estimation die Meinung; die Schätzung

estrange entfremden

estrangement die Entfremdung

estuary die Mündung

etching die Radierung

eternal ewig

eternity die Ewigkeit

ether der Äther

ethics die Ethik

eulogize loben

eulogy die Lobrede

Europe Europa

European europäisch

evacuate ausleeren; räumen

evacuation die Ausleerung; die Räumung

evade ausweichen

evaporate verdampfen

evasion die Ausflucht

evasive ausweichend

eve der Vorabend

even eben; gerade; sogar; glatt; **not** - nicht einmal

evening der Abend

evening-dress der Gesellschaftsanzug; das Abendkleid

event das Ereignis

events (at all) auf alle Fälle

eventful ereignisvoll

eventual etwaig; schliesslich

ever je; jemals; immer

evergreen das Immergrün

everlasting immerwährend

evermore immerfort

every jeder, jede, jedes

everybody jedermann

everything alles

everywhere überall

evict vertreiben

evidence der Beweis; das Zeugnis

evident augenscheinlich

evil übel; das Übel, das Böse

evoke hervorrufen

evolution die Entwicklung

ewe das Mutterschaf

exact genau

exact fordern; eintreiben; erpressen

exacting anspruchsvoll

exactness, exactitude die Genauigkeit

exaggerate übertreiben

exaggeration die Übertreibung

exalt erhöhen; erheben

exaltation die Erhöhung

examination die Prüfung; die Untersuchung

examine untersuchen

example das Beispiel; **for** - zum Beispiel

exasperate ärgern

exasperation der Ärger

excavate ausgraben

excavation die Ausgrabung

exceed überschreiten; übertreffen

exceedingly ausserordentlich

excel sich auszeichnen

excellence die Vortrefflichkeit

excellency die Excellenz

excellent vortrefflich

except ausnehmen; ausgenommen; ausser

exception die Ausnahme

exceptional aussergewöhnlich

excess das Übermass

excessive übermässig

exchange tauschen, wechseln; der Tausch, die Börse, der Wechsel, das Fernamt

exchequer der Staatsschatz; das Schatzamt

excise die Verbrauchssteuer

excitable erregbar

excite aufregen; reizen

excitement die Aufregung

exclaim ausrufen

exclamation der Ausruf

exclude ausschliessen

exclusion der Ausschluss
exclusive ausschliesslich; exklusiv
excretion die Absonderung
excruciating qualvoll
exculpate entschuldigen
excursion der Ausflug
excuse entschuldigen; verzeihen; die Entschuldigung; die Ausrede
execrable abscheulich
execration die Verwünschung
execute ausführen; hinrichten
execution die Ausführung; die Hinrichtung
executioner der Scharfrichter
executive die vollziehende Gewalt
executor (will) der Vollstrecker
exemplary vorbildlich
exempt befreit; befreien
exemption die Befreiung
exercise (sich) üben, exerzieren; die Übung
exert (sich) anstrengen
exertion die Anstrengung
exhale ausdünsten
exhalation die Ausdünstung
exhaust erschöpfen
exhaustion die Erschöpfung
exhaustive erschöpfend
exhibit ausstellen; vorzeigen
exhibition die Ausstellung
exhilarate erheitern
exhort ermahnen
exhortation die Ermahnung
exhume (to) ausgraben
exhumation die Wiederausgrabung
exigency das Bedürfnis
exile verbannen; der Verbannte, die Verbannung
exist sein; leben
existence das Dasein
existent vorhanden; lebend
existing vorhanden
exit der Ausgang
exonerate freisprechen
exorbitant übermässig
exotic exotisch
expand (sich) ausdehnen
expanse die Weite, die Breite
expansion die Ausdehnung
expansive ausgedehnt
expatriate verbannen

expatriation die Verbannung
expect erwarten
expectant erwartend
expectation die Erwartung
expediency die Zweckmässigkeit
expedient ratsam; das Mittel
expedition die Expedition
expedite beschleunigen
expeditious schnell
expel (to) vertreiben
expend ausgeben; aufwenden
expense die Ausgabe; die Kosten *pl*
expensive teuer; kostspielig
experience die Erfahrung; das Erlebnis; erfahren; erleben
experienced erfahren; bewandert
experiment der Versuch; Versuche anstellen
experimental erfahrungsmässig
expert erfahren, kundig; der Sachverständige, der Fachmann
expiate sühnen
expiation die Sühnung
expire sterben; ablaufen
explain erklären
explanation die Erklärung
explanatory erklärend
explicable erklärbar
explicit ausdrücklich
explode sprengen; explodieren
exploit die Tat; ausbeuten
exploitation die Ausbeutung
exploration die Erforschung
explore erforschen
explorer der Erforscher
explosion die Explosion; der Ausbruch
explosive der Sprengstoff; explosiv
export ausführen; die Ausfuhr
exporter der Exporteur
expose aussetzen; darlegen; (photo) belichten
exposition die Auslegung
express ausdrücken; äussern; der Schnellzug; der Eilbote
expression der Ausdruck
expressive ausdrucksvoll
expressly ausdrücklich
expropriate enteignen
expropriation die Enteignung

expulsion die Vertreibung
expurgate ausmerzen; reinigen
exquisite vorzüglich
extant noch vorhanden
extemporary unvorbereitet
extend ausdehnen; sich erstrecken
extension die Ausdehnung; die Erweiterung; die Verlängerung; der Anbau
extensive ausgedehnt
extent die Weite; die Ausdehnung
extenuate mildern
exterior, external äusserlich
exterminate vertilgen
extinct ausgestorben
extinction das Aussterben; die Tilgung
extinguish auslöschen
extirpate ausrotten
extirpation die Ausrottung
extol preisen
extort erpressen
extortion die Erpressung
extra extra; sonder
extract der Auszug; ausziehen
extraction das Ausziehen; die Gewinnung
extradite ausliefern
extradition die Auslieferung
extraordinary ausserordentlich
extravagance die Verschwendung
extravagant verschwenderisch
extreme das Extrem; äusserst, höchst
extremity das Äusserste; die höchste Not
extricate freimachen
exuberance der Überfluss
exuberant üppig
exude ausschwitzen
exult frohlocken
exultation das Frohlocken
eye das Auge, das Öhr; ansehen
eyeball der Augapfel
eyebrow die Augenbraue
eyelash die Augenwimper
eyelid das Augenlid
eyesight die Sehkraft
eyesore der hässliche Anblick
eye-witness der Augenzeuge

F

fable die Fabel; das Märchen
fabric das Gewebe; der Stoff
fabulous fabelhaft
façade die Fassade
face das Gesicht, die Fläche; ansehen, gegenüberliegen
facetious witzig
facilitate erleichtern
facile leicht
facility die Leichtigkeit
facing (opposite) gegenüber
facsimile die genaue Nachbildung
fact die Tatsache
faction die Partei
factory die Fabrik
faculty die Fähigkeit; die Fakultät
fade verwelken
fagged (out) erschöpft
faggot das Reisigbündel
fail fehlen; fehlschlagen
failing der Fehler
failure der Misserfolg
faint in Ohnmacht fallen; schwach
faint-hearted verzagt
fainting die Ohnmacht
fair hübsch; schön; blond; billig; der Jahrmarkt; die Kirmes
fairness die Blondheit; die Billigkeit
fairly ziemlich
fairy die Fee
faith der Glaube; das Vertrauen
faithful treu
faithfulness die Treue
faithless treulos
fake der Schwindel; fälschen
falcon der Falke
fall fallen
fall asleep einschlafen
fall due fällig werden
fall ill krank werden
fallacious trüglich
fallacy der Trugschluss
fallow brach
false falsch
falsehood die Lüge
falseness die Falschheit
falsification die Verfälschung
falsify fälschen

falter straucheln; stocken
fame der Ruhm
famed berühmt
familiar vertraut
familiarity die Vertraulichkeit
familiarize vertraut machen
family die Familie
famine die Hungersnot
famish aushungern
famous berühmt
fan der Fächer, der Ventilator; der Liebhaber; fächeln
fanatic der Fanatiker
fanatical fanatisch
fanciful phantastisch
fancy die Einbildung, die Phantasie; die Neigung; sich einbilden, lieb haben; begehren
fancy-goods die Modeartikel *pl*
fancy-work die feine Handarbeit
fancy-price der Liebhaberpreis
fang der Fang(zahn)
fantastic fantastisch
far weit; fern; entfernt; **by -** bei weitem
farce die Posse
farcical possenhaft
fare das Fahrgeld, die Speise; sich befinden
fare (bill of) die Speisekarte
farewell der Abschied; das Lebewohl
farm der Bauernhof; bebauen
farmer der Bauer
far-sighted weitsichtig
farther weiter
farthest am weitesten
fascinate bezaubern
fascination der Reiz
fashion die Form, die Mode; gestalten
fashionable modisch
fast schnell; fest; fasten
fasten befestigen
fastener der Verschluss
fastidious wählerisch
fat das Fett; fett, dick
fatal tötlich; verhängnisvoll
fatalist der Fatalist
fate das Schicksal
fateful verhängnisvoll
father der Vater

father-in-law der Schwiegervater
fatherless vaterlos
fatherly väterlich
fathom der Faden; ergründen
fathomless unergründlich
fatigue die Müdigkeit; ermüden
fatness die Fettigkeit
fatten mästen
fatty fettig
fault der Fehler; die Schuld
faultless fehlerfrei; tadellos
faulty mangelhaft
favour die Gunst, der Gefallen; begünstigen
favour (in - of) zu Gunsten
favourable günstig
favourite der Günstling; der Liebling; Lieblings-
fawn das Rehkalb; schmeicheln
fear die Furcht; fürchten
fearful furchtbar
fearless furchtlos
feasible möglich
feast das Fest; schmausen
feat (action) die Tat
feather die Feder
feature der Gesichtszug, das Merkmal; beschreiben
February der Februar
fecundity die Fruchtbarkeit
federation der Bund
fee der Lohn; das Honorar
feeble schwach
feeble-minded geistesschwach
feebleness die Schwäche
feed fütter, sich nähren; das Futter, die Nahrung
feel (sich) fühlen
feeling das Gefühl
feign heucheln
feigned verstellt
feint die Verstellung; die Finte
felicitate beglückwünschen
felicitation die Beglückwünschung
felicity die Glückseligkeit
fell fällen
fellow der Bursche, der Kerl
fellow-citizen der Mitbürger
fellow-creature der Mitmensch
fellowship die Gesellschaft; die Gemeinschaft

felony das Kapitalverbrechen
felt der Filz
female weiblich
feminine weibisch; weiblich
fen das Moor; der Sumpf
fence der Zaun; einzäunen, fechten
fencing die Fechtkunst
fend abwehren
fender der Kaminvorsetzer
ferment gären
fermentation die Gärung
fern das Farnkraut
ferocious wild
ferret das Frettchen; durchsuchen
ferrule die Zwinge
ferry die Fähre; übersetzen
fertile fruchtbar
fertility die Fruchtbarkeit
fertilization die Befruchtung
fertilize befruchten
fervent inbrünstig
fervour die Inbrunst; die Glut
festival das Fest
festive festlich
festivity die Festlichkeit
festoon die Girlande
fetch holen
fetter die Fessel; fesseln
feud die Fehde
feudal feudal
fever das Fieber
few wenige
fiancé der Verlobte
fib lügen; die Lüge
fibre die Faser; die Fiber
fickle wankelmütig
fiction die Erdichtung; die Romanliteratur
fiddle die Geige
fidelity die Treue
fidget (to) unruhig sein
fidgets die nervöse Unruhe
field das Feld
field-glasses das Fernglas
fiend der Teufel
fiendish teuflich
fierce wild
fiery feurig
fig die Feige
fight der Kampf; das Gefecht

fighter der Kämpfer; das Jagdflugzeug; kämpfen, fechten
figurative bildlich
figure die Gestalt, die Figur, die Ziffer; bilden
filament die Faser
filch stehlen
file die Reihe, der Briefordner, die Feile; einordnen, feilen
filial kindlich
filings die Feilspäne *pl*
fill (sich) füllen
fillet (beef or fish) das Filet
film das Häutchen, der Film; verfilmen
filter der Filter; filtrieren
filth der Schmutz; der Kot
filthy schmutzig; kotig
fin die Flosse
final endlich; entgültig
finance das Finanzwesen; finanzieren
financial finanziell
finch der Fink
find (to) finden; der Fund
finder der Finder
finding der Wahrspruch
fine fein, schön; die Geldstrafe
fine zu einer Geldstrafe verurteilen
fineness der Feinheit
finger der Finger; betasten
finish endigen, aufhören; die Vollendung, der Schluss
fir (tree) die Fichte; die Tanne; die Kiefer
fire das Feuer; anzünden, feuern
fire alarm der Feuermelder
fire brigade die Feuerwehr
fire engine die Feuerspritze
fire escape die Rettungsleiter
fireman der Feuerwehrmann
fireplace der Kamin
fireproof feuerfest
firewood das Brennholz
firework das Feuerwerk
firm fest; die Firma
firmness die Festigkeit
first erst; zuerst; erstens
first (at) zuerst
first-rate erstklassig
fish der Fisch; fischen, angeln
fisherman der Fischer

fish-hook der Angelhaken
fishing-line die Angelschnur
fishing-tackle das Angelgerät
fishmonger der Fischhändler
fissure die Spalte
fist die Faust
fit der Anfall; der Sitz; (an)passen, tauglich, passend
fitful launisch
fitness die Tauglichkeit
fits (and starts) (by) ruckweise
fitting passend; schicklich
fix befestigen; einrichten
fixed festgesetz; fest
fizz zischen, sprudeln
flabby schlaff
flabbiness die Schlaffheit
flag die Flagge; die Fahne
flagrant offenkundig
flagstaff die Fahnenstange
flagstone die Steinplatte
flail der Dreschflegel
flake die Flocke
flame die Flamme; flammen
flank die Flanke, die Weiche, die Seite; grenzen
flannel der Flanell; der Waschlappen
flap die Klappe, die Krempe; schlagen
flare das Lichtsignal; flackern
flash aufblitzen; der Blitz
flashlight das Blitzlicht
flashy grell
flask die Flasche
flat platt, flach; die Etage, die Wohnung
flatten platt machen
flatter schmeicheln
flatterer der Schmeichler
flattery die Schmeichelei
flatulence die Blähsucht
flaunt prunken
flavour der Geschmack, der Wohlgeruch, die Würze; würzen
flaw der Riss; der Sprung; der Fehler
flawless fehlerlos
flax der Flachs
flaxen flachsen
flay schinden
flayer der Schinder
flea der Floh

flee fliehen
fleece das Vlies; scheren
fleecy wollig
fleet schnell; die Flotte
fleeting flüchtig
flesh das Fleisch
fleshy fleischig
flexibility die Biegsamkeit
flexible biegsam
flick schnippen; der Schneller
flicker flackern
flight die Flucht; der Flug
flighty leichtsinnig
flimsy dünn; nichtig
flinch zurückweichen; zucken
fling werfen; der Wurf
flint der Feuerstein; der Kiesel
flippancy die Leichtfertigkeit
flippant leichtfertig
flirt kokettieren; die Kokette
flirtation die Liebelei
flit flitzen; huschen
flitch (bacon) die Speckseite
flitter flattern
float das Floss; flössen, treiben, schwimmen
floating dock das Schwimmdock
flock die Herde; der Haufen
flock together sich scharen
flog peitschen
flogging die Prügelstrafe
flood die Flut; überschwemmen
floor der Fussboden; die Etage
florid blühend
flounder zappeln
flour das Mehl
flourish blühen; der Schnörkel; die Fanfare
flow der Strom; fliessen
flower die Blume, die Blüte; blühen
flower-pot der Blumentopf
fluctuate schwanken
fluctuation die Schwankung
flue der Rauchfang
fluency die Geläufigkeit
fluent fliessend
fluid flüssig; die Flüssigkeit
flurry die Unruhe
flush erröten
fluster aufregen
flute die Flöte
flutter flattern; die Unruhe

flux der Fluss
fly fliegen, fliehen; die Fliege
flying-boat das Flugboot
flywheel das Schwungrad
foal das Fohlen
foam der Schaum; schäumen
focus der Brennpunkt
fodder das Futter
foe der Feind
fog der Nebel
foggy nebelig
foible die Schwäche
foil (to) vereiteln
foil die Folie; das Florett
fold die Falte; falten; die Schaf-
hürde
folding-chair der Klappstuhl
folding-door die Flügeltür
folding-screen die spanische
Wand
foliage das Laub
folk die Leute *pl*
folklore die Volkskunde
follow folgen
follower der Anhänger
folly die Torheit
foment bähen
fomentation die Bähung
fond zärtlich
fond (to be - of) gern haben
fondle liebkosen
fondness die Vorliebe
font der Taufstein
food die Speise; die Lebensmittel
pl
fool der Tor; zum Narren halten
foolhardy tollkühn
foolish töricht
foot der Fuss
football der Fussball
footstep der Schritt
footman der Diener
footpath der Fussweg
footprint die Fuss-stapfe
footwear das Schuhwerk
fop der Geck
foppish geziert
for für; mit; nach; aus; auf; denn
forage fouragieren; umherstöbern
forbear sich enthalten
forbearance die Nachsicht
forbid verbieten
forbid (God) Gott bewahre!

force die Kraft, der Zwang, die
Gewalt; zwingen
forced landing die Notlandung
forceful wirkungsvoll
forceps die Zange
forces die Truppen
forcible gewaltsam
ford die Furt; durchwaten
forebode ahnen
forecast die Voraussage; voraus-
sagen
forefather der Vorfahr
foreground der Vordergrund
forehead die Stirn
foreign fremd; ausländisch
foreigner der Ausländer
foreland das Vorgebirge
foreman der Werkmeister
foremost vorderste; vornehmste
forenoon der Vormittag
forerunner der Vorbote; der Vorläufer
foresee vorhersehen
foresight die Vorsicht
forest der Forst; der Wald
forester der Förster
forestry die Forstwirtschaft
foretell vorhersagen
forethought der Vorbedacht
forewarn vorherwarnen
forfeit das Reugeld, das Pfand;
verwirken; verlieren
forge die Schmiede; schmieden,
fälschen
forger der Fälscher
forgery die Fälschung
forget vergessen
forgetful vergesslich
forgetfulness die Vergesslichkeit
forget-me-not das Vergissmeinnicht
forgive vergeben
forgiveness die Verzeihung
forgo aufgeben; verzichten
fork die Gabel; (sich) gabeln
forlorn verloren; verlassen
form die Gestalt, die Form, **das**
Formular, die Bank, die Klasse;
(sich) bilden; gestalten
formal förmlich
formality die Förmlichkeit
formation die Bildung
former früher; ehemalig

formerly ehemals; früher
formidable furchtbar; schrecklich
formula die Formel
forsake verlassen
forswear abschwören
fort das Fort
forth fort; vorwärts
forthcoming bevorstehend
forthwith sogleich
fortification die Befestigung
fortify befestigen; stärken
fortnight vierzehn Tage
fortress die Festung
fortunate glücklich
fortune das Glück; das Vermögen; das Schicksal
fortune-teller der Wahrsager; die Wahrsagerin
forward vorwärts; (nach-)senden; befördern
foster pflegen
foster-mother die Pflegemutter
foul unrein; schmutzig
foulness die Unreinigkeit
found gründen
foundation die Gründung; das Fundament
foundation-stone der Grundstein
founder der Gründer, der Giesser; scheitern
foundling das Findelkind
foundry die Giesserei
fountain die Quelle; der Springbrunnen
fountain-head der Urquell
fountain-pen die Füllfeder
fowl das Geflügel; das Huhn
fox der Fuchs
fox-hunting die Fuchsjagd
fraction der Bruchteil
fracture der Knochenbruch
fragile zerbrechlich; schwach
fragility die (Ge- or Zer) brechlichkeit
fragment das Bruchstück
fragrance der Duft; der Wohlgeruch
fragrant wohlriechend
frail schwach; gebrechlich
frame das Gestell; der Rahmen; die Einfassung
franchise das Wahlrecht

frank frei; offen
frankness die Offenheit
frantic wahnsinnig
fraternal brüderlich
fraternity die Bruderschaft
fraternize sich verbrüdern
fraud der Betrug
fraudulent betrügerisch
fray abreiben; durchscheuern
freak die Laune; das Monstrum
freckle die Sommersprosse
freckled sommersprossig
free frei; kostenlos; befreien
freedom die Freiheit
freeholder der Grundeigentümer
freemason der Freimaurer
freemasonry die Freimaurerei
free trade der Freihandel
freeze frieren
freight die Fracht; verfrachten
freighter das Frachtschiff
French französisch
Frenchman der Franzose
frenzy die Raserei
frequency die Häufigkeit
frequent häufig; oft besuchen
fresh frisch
freshness die Frische
fresh water das Süsswasser
fret sich grämen; ärgern
fretful ärgerlich
friar der Mönch
friction die Reibung
Friday der Freitag
Friday (Good) der Karfreitag
friend der Freund; die Freundin
friendly freundlich
friendship die Freundschaft
frieze der Fries
fright die Furcht; der Schreck
frighten erschrecken
frightful schrecklich
frigid frostig; kalt
frigidity die Kälte
frill die Krause; kräuseln
fringe die Franse; (**hair**) das Pony; (be)fransen
frisk hüpfen
friskiness die Lustigkeit
frisky lustig, munter; ausgelassen
fritter der Pfannkuchen
frivolous leichtfertig
frivolity die Leichtfertigkeit

frock das Kleid
frock-coat der Gehrock
frog der Frosch
frolic fröhlich; der Scherz; spassen
from von; aus
front die Stirn; die Vorderseite; die Front
front garden der Vorgarten
frontage die Vorderfront
frontier die Grenze
frontispiece das Titelbild
frost der Frost
frosty frostig
frost-bitten erfroren
froth der Schaum; schäumen
frown die Stirn runzeln
frozen gefroren
frugal mässig, genügsam
frugality die Genügsamkeit
fruit die Frucht; das Obst
fruiterer der Obsthändler
fruitful fruchtbar
fruitless fruchtlos
frustrate vereiteln
fry braten
fuel der Brennstoff
fugitive der Flüchtling; flüchtig
fulfil erfüllen
fulfilment die Erfüllung
full voll
full moon der Vollmond
full-stop der Punkt
fulminate blitzen; donnern
fulness die Fülle
fulsome widerlich
fumble umherfühlen
fume der Dampf, der Dunst; rauchen, erregt sein
fumigate ausräuchern
fun der Spass
function die Funktion; die Tätigkeit; funktionieren
functionary der Beamte
fund der Fonds; das Kapital
funeral das Begräbnis
fungus der Pilz
funk die Mordsangst
funk sich drücken vor
funnel der Trichter; der Schornstein
funny komisch; drollig
fur der Pelz

furbish polieren; putzen
furious wütend
furlough der Urlaub
furnace der Schmelzofen
furnish versehen; möblieren; einrichten
furniture die Möbel *pl*
furrier der Kürschner
furrow die Furche; furchen
further ferner; weiter; fördern
fury die Wut
fuse der Zünder, die Sicherung; schmelzen; durchbrennen
fusion die Verschmelzung
fuss das Getue; der Lärm
futile nutzlos
futility die Nutzlosigkeit
future die Zukunft; zukünftig
fuzz der feine Flaum
fuzzy flockig

G

gab das Geplauder
gabble schnattern; das Geschnatter
gable der Giebel
gadfly die Bremse
gag knebeln; der Knebel
gaiety die Fröhlichkeit
gaily fröhlich; munter
gain der Gewinn; gewinnen
gainings der Gewinn
gait der Gang
gaiter die Gamasche
gala das Galafest
gale der Sturmwind
gall die Galle; wund reiben, ärgern
gallant(ly) tapfer; galant
gallantry die Tapferkeit
gallery die Galerie
galley die Galeere
gallop der Galopp; galoppieren
gallows der Galgen
galvanic galvanisch
galvanism der Galvanismus
galvanize galvanisieren
gamble das Glücksspiel
gamble um Geld spielen
gambler der Spieler
game das Spiel; das Wild

gamekeeper der Wildhüter
gamut die Tonleiter
gander der Gänserich
gang die Bande
gangrene der Brand
gangway die Laufplanke; der Durchgang
gaol das Gefängnis
gaoler der Kerkermeister
gap die Lücke; die Spalte
gape gaffen
garage die Garage; die Tankstelle; die Wagenpflege
garb die Kleidung
garden der Garten
gardener der Gärtner
gardening der Gartenbau
garland die Girlande
garlic der Knoblauch
garnish schmücken
garret die Dachstube
garrison die Garnison; mit einer Garnison belegen
garrulous geschwätzig
garter das Strumpfband
gas das Gas
gash die klaffende Wunde
gasp keuchen
gate das Tor
gather sammeln
gathering die Versammlung
gaudy bunt; grell
gauge das Mass, die Spurweite; abschätzen
gaunt hager
gauze die Gaze
gay heiter
gear das Zeug; das Pferdegeschirr
gem der Edelstein
gender das Geschlecht
generalize verallgemeinern
generally im allgemeinen
generate erzeugen
generation die Erzeugung; die Generation
generosity die Grossmut, die Freigebigkeit
generous freigebig; grosszügig
genial munter
genius das Genie
Geneva Genf
Genoa Genua

gentle sanft; gütig
gentlemanly anständig; gebildet
gently mild; sanft
genuine echt
geographer der Geograph
geography Geographie; die Erdkunde
geologist der Geolig
geology die Geologie
germ der Keim
German deutsch
German der Deutsche
Germany Deutschland
germinate keimen
germination das Keimen
gesticulate gestikulieren
gesture die Gebärde
get bekommen; erhalten; verschaffen; gelangen; werden; holen
get in einsteigen
get out aussteigen
get up aufstehen
ghastly grässlich
gherkin die Pfeffergurke
ghost das Gespenst
giant der Riese
gibbet der Galgen
giblets das Gänseklein
giddy schwindelig
gift die Gabe; das Geschenk
gifted begabt
gigantic riesenhaft
giggle kichern; das Gekicher
gild vergolden
gilding die Vergoldung
gill die Kieme
gimlet der Handbohrer
gin der Wacholderbranntwein
ginger der Ingwer
gingerly sachte
gingerbread der Pfefferkuchen
gipsy der Zigeuner; die Zigeunerin
girder der Tragbalken
girdle umgürten; der Gürtel
girl das Mädchen
girth der Gurt
give geben; schenken
give in nachgeben
giver der Geber
glacier der Gletscher
glad froh
gladden erfreuen

glade die Lichtung
gladly gern
gladness die Freude
glance der Blick, der Schimmer; blicken, schauen
gland die Drüse
glare das blendende Licht, der Glanz; starr ansehen, glänzen
glass das Glas
glass (looking-) der Spiegel
glassy gläsern
glaze verglasen; die Glasur
glazier der Glaser
gleam der Schein; strahlen, glänzen
glean (auf) (nach)lesen
gleaner der Ährenleser
glee die Fröhlichkeit
glen die Bergschlucht
glib glatt; zungenfertig
glide gleiten
glider das Segelflugzeug; der Segelflieger
glimmer der Schimmer; glimmern
glimpse der flüchtige Blick; erblicken
glisten glitzern
glitter glänzen
globe die Kugel
globe trotter der Weltbummler
globular kugelförmig
gloom der Trübsinn; die Dunkelheit
gloomy traurig; duster
glorious glorreich, herrlich
glory der Ruhm; die Herrlichkeit
gloss der Glanz; glänzend machen
glossy glänzend
glove der Handschuh
glow die Glut; glühen
glow-worm das Glühwürmchen
glue der Leim; leimen
glum mürrisch
glutton der Vielfrass; der Schlemmer
gluttonous gefrässig
gluttony die Gefrässigkeit
glycerine das Glyzerin
gnarled knorrig
gnash knirschen
gnat die Mücke
gnaw nagen

go gehen; fahren; reisen; werden
go-between der Vermittler
goal das Ziel; das Tor
goat die Ziege
gobble gierig verschlingen
goblet der Becher
God der Gott
godchild das Patenkind
goddess die Göttin
godfather der Pate
godless gottlos
godliness die Frömmigkeit
godly fromm
godsend der wahre Segen
goitre der Kropf
gold das Gold
golden golden
goldsmith der Goldschmied
gone weg, fort
gong der Gong
good gut; wohl; recht
goods die Waren *pl*
good-for-nothing der Taugenichts
Good Friday der Karfreitag
goodbye das Lebewohl
goodly anmutig
good-natured gutmütig
goodness die Güte
goods train der Güterzug
goodwill das Wohlwollen; der Wert der Firma
goose die Gans
gooseberry die Stachelbeere
goose-step der Paradeschritt
gore das geronnene Blut
gorge die Kehle, die Schlucht; verschlingen
gorgeous prächtig
gorse der Stechginster
gospel das Evangelium
gossip der Klatsch; schwatzen; die Klatschbase
gourd der Kürbis
gout die Gicht
govern regieren; beherrschen
governess die Erzieherin
government die Regierung
governor der Herrscher; der Gouverneur
gown der Talar; das Frauenkleid
grab plötzlich greifen

grace die Gnade, die Anmut; das Tischgebet; schmücken
graceful anmutig
gracious gnädig
grade der Grad; einteilen
gradient die Steigung
gradual allmählich
graduate abstufen
graft pfropfen
grain das Korn
grammar die Grammatik
grammatical grammatisch
gramophone der Plattenspieler
granary der Kornspeicher
grand grossartig
grandchild der Enkel; die En-kelin
grand duke der Grossherzog
grandeur die Grösse; die Pracht
grandfather der Grossvater
grandmother die Grossmutter
grange die Scheune
granite der Granit
grant die Bewilligung; bewilligen
granular körnig
grape die Traube
graphic graphisch
grapple packen; ergreifen; rin-gen; entern
grasp der Griff; greifen
grasping gierig
grass das Gras
grasshopper die Heuschrecke
grate der Rost; schaben
grateful dankbar
gratify befriedigen
grating das Gitter
gratis unentgeltlich; umsonst
gratitude die Dankbarkeit
gratuity das Trinkgeld
grave das Grab; ernst
gravel der Kies
graveyard der Kirchhof
gravity der Ernst; die Schwere
gravy die Bratensosse
gray, grey grau
graze weiden
grease das Fett; die Schmiere; schmieren
greasy fettig; schmierig
great gross
great-grandfather der Urgross-vater

great-grandmother die Urgross-mutter
greatly sehr
greatcoat der Überzieher
greatness die Grösse
greed die Gier; die Habsucht
greedy gierig
green grün; der Rasenplatz
greengrocer der Gemüsehändler
greenhorn der Grünschnabel
greenhouse das Gewächshaus
greenish grünlich
greens das Gemüse
greet grüssen
greeting der Gruss
grey grau
greyhound der Windhund
grief der Gram; die Kummer
grievance die Beschwerde
grieve sich grämen
grievous schmerzlich
grill der Bratrost; auf dem Roste braten
grim grimmig
grimace die Fratze; die Grimasse
grime der Schmutz
grin Grinsen das; grinsen
grind mahlen; schleifen
grinder der Schleifer
grindstone der Schleifstein
grip der Griff; fest greifen
gripes das Bauchgrimmen
grisly scheusslich
grit der Griess; der Mut
gritty kiesig
groan stöhnen; das Stöhnen
grocer der Materialwarenhändler
grocery das Kolonialwarenge-schäft
groin die Leistengegend
groom der Stall- (Reit)knecht
groove furchen; die Rinne, die Nut
grope tasten
gross dick; grob; Brutto-
gross das Gros
grossness die Grobheit
grotesque grotesk
grotto die Grotte
ground der Grund, der Boden; gründen
ground-floor das Erdgeschoss
groundless grundlos

groundwork die Grundlage
group die Gruppe; gruppieren
grouse das Waldhuhn
grow wachsen; werden
growl knurren; brummen
grown-up erwachsen
growth der Wuchs; das Gewächs; das Erzeugnis
grub (insect) die Made
grudge der Groll; missgönnen
gruel der Haferschleim
gruesome grausig
gruff barsch
grumble murren
grumpy böse; mürrisch
grunt grunzen
guarantee die Bürgschaft; verbürgen
guard die Wache, der Schaffner; der Zugführer; bewachen
guardian der Vormund
guards die Garde
guardsman der Gardist
guerilla-warfare der Kleinkrieg
guess erraten; die Vermutung
guest die Gast
guidance die Leitung
guide der Führer; leiten, führen
guild die Innung; die Gilde
guile die Arglist
guilt die Schuld
guilty schuldig
guinea-fowl das Perlhuhn
guinea-pig das Meerschweinchen
guise die Gestalt; das Gewand; die Maske
guitar die Gitarre
gulf der Abgrund; der Meerbusen; der Golf
gull die Möwe
gullet der Schlund
gully die Schlucht
gulp der Schluck; schlucken
gum das Gummi, das Zahnfleisch; gummieren
gun die Kanone; das Gewehr; die Flinte
gunboat das Kanonenboot
gun-carriage die Lafette
gun-cotton die Schiessbaumwolle
gunner der Kanonier
gunpowder das Schiesspulver
gunsmith der Büchsenmacher

gush der Erguss; hervorströmen
gusset der Zwickel
gust der Windstoss
gut der Darm; ausweiden
gutter die Rinne; die Gosse
guttural der Kehllaut
guzzle saufen; fressen
gymnasium die Turnhalle
gymnastics das Turnen
gynæcologist der Frauenarzt
gypsum der Gips

H

haberdasher der Kurzwaren-händler
haberdashery die Kurzwaren *pl*
habit die Gewohnheit; die Lebensweise
habitable bewohnbar
habitation die Wohnung
habitual gewohnt; gewöhnlich
hack hacken; das Mietpferd
hackney die Lohnkutsche
hackneyed abgedroschen
haddock der Schellfisch
hæmorrhage der Blutsturz
hæmorrhoids die Hämorrhoiden *pl*
hag die Hexe; das alte Weib
haggard abgehärmt
haggle feilschen
hail der Hagel; hageln, anrufen
hailstone das Hagelkorn
hair das Haar
hairbrush die Haarbürste
hairdresser der Friseur
hairpin die Haarnadel
hairy haarig
half die halb; die Hälfte
half-caste der Mischling
halibut der Heilbutt
hall die Halle; der Saal; der Hausflur; die Diele
hallstand der Garderobenständer
hallow heiligen
Hallowmass das Allerheiligen-fest
hallucination die Sinnestäuschung
halo der Hof; der Heiligenschein

halt anhalten; der Halt
halter die Halfter
halve halbieren
ham der Schinken
hamlet das Dörfchen
hammer der Hammer; hämmern
hammock die Hängematte
hamper der Packkorb; hemmen
hand die Hand; der Uhrzeiger; der Arbeiter; reichen, händigen; **give a - helfen; at - zur Hand**
handbag die Handtasche
handcuff die Handfessel
handful die Handvoll
handicap hindern; das Hindernis
handicraft die Handarbeit; das Handwerk
handkerchief das Taschentuch
handle der Stiel, der Griff; handhaben; behandeln
handle-bar die Lenkstange
handrail das Geländer
handsome schön; hübsch
handwriting die Handschrift
handy geschickt; zur Hand
hang hangen; hängen
hangar die Flugzeughalle
hangman der Henker
hanker sich sehnen
haphazard der Zufall; zufällig
hapless unglücklich
happen geschehen; sich ereignen
happiness das Glück
happy glücklich
harangue die Ansprache; feierlich anreden
harass belästigen; quälen
harbour der Hafen; beherbergen
hard hart; gefühllos; mühsam; schwer
harden verhärten
hardhearted hartherzig
hardiness die Kühnheit; die Ausdauer
hardly kaum
hardness die Härte; die Schwierigkeit
hardship die Not
hard-up in Not
hardware die Eisenwaren *pl*
hardy kühn; abgehärtet
hare der Hase
harlot die Hure

harm der Schaden, das Unrecht; beschädigen, schaden verletzen
harmful schädlich
harmless harmlos
harness das Geschirr; anschirren
harp die Harfe
harpoon die Harpune
harrow die Egge; eggen, quälen
harsh streng; barsch
harshness der Strenge
hart der Hirsch
harvest die Ernte; ernten
hash das gehackte Fleisch
haste die Eile, die Hast; eilen beschleunigen
hasty eilig; voreilig; hitzig
hat der Hut
hatch die Luke
hatch die Brut; brüten
hatchet die Axt; das Beil
hate hassen; nicht gern tun
hateful verhasst; gehässig
hatred der Hass
hatter der Hutmacher
haughty hochmütig; stolz
haul ziehen; schleppen
haunch die Hüfte; der Schenkel
haunt (to) oft besuchen, spuken; der Aufenthalt, das Lager
have haben; lassen
hawk der Habicht
hawker der Hausierer; hausieren
hay das Heu
haystack der Heuschober
hazardous gefährlich; gewagt
haze der Dunst
hazelnut die Haselnuss
hazy dunstig; diesig
head der Kopf, das Haupt; anführen
headache das Kopfweh
head-dress der Kopfputz
heading die Überschrift
headland das Vorgebirge
headlight der Scheinwerfer
headlong unbesonnen
headmaster der Schuldirektor
headquarters das Hauptquartier
headstrong halsstarrig
headwaiter der Oberkellner
headway der Fortschritt
headwind der Gegenwind
heal heilen

health die Gesundheit
healthiness die Gesundheit
healthy gesund
heap der Haufen; die Menge; häufen
hear hören
hearing das Gehör
hearken horchen
hearsay das Hörensagen
hearse der Leichenwagen
heart das Herz; by - auswendig; take - Mut fassen
heart attack der Herzschlag
heartfelt herzlich; innig
hearth der Herd
heartiness die Herzlichkeit
heartless herzlos
heartrending herzzerreissend
hearty tüchtig; herzlich
heat die Hitze; erhitzen, heizen
heath die Heide
heather das Heidekraut
heathen der Heide
heave heben
heaven der Himmel
heavenly himmlisch
heaviness die Schwere
heavy schwer
Hebrew hebräisch
hectic hektisch
hedge die Hecke; einhegen
hedgehog der Igel
heed die Acht, die Aufmerksamkeit; beachten
heedful achtsam
heedless unachtsam
heel die Ferse; der Absatz
heifer die Färse
height die Höhe; der Gipfel
heighten erhöhen
heir der Erbe
heiress die Erbin
heirloom das Erbstück
hell die Hölle
hellish höllisch
helm das Steuer
helmet der Helm
helmsman der Steuermann
help die Hilfe; der Beistand; helfen
helpful hilfreich
helpless hilflos
helter-skelter holterdiepolter

helpmate der Gehilfe
hem säumen; der Saum
hemisphere die Halbkugel
hemp der Hanf
hen die Henne
hence von hier; von nun an; daher
henceforth von nun an
her sie, ihr
herb das Kraut
herbalist der Pflanzenkenner
herd die Herde
herdsman der Hirt
here hier; hierher
hereafter hiernach
hereby hiermit
hereditary erblich
heresy die Ketzerei
heretic der Ketzer
heritage das Erbgut; die Erbschaft
hermetic luftdicht; hermetisch
hermit der Einsiedler
hernia der Bruch
hero der Held
heroic heldenmütig
heroine die Heldin
heroism der Heldenmut
heron der Reiher
herring der Hering
hesitate zögern
hesitation die Unschlüssigkeit
hew hauen
hibernate überwintern
hide die Haut; das Fell
hide (sich) verbergen
hideous scheusslich
high hoch
high-explosive bomb die Sprengbombe
highland das Hochland
highness die Hoheit
high pressure der Hochdruck
high road die Landstrasse
high treason der Hochverrat
hilarity die Fröhlichkeit
hill der Hügel
hillock der kleine Hügel
hilly hügelig
hilt das Heft; der Griff
him ihn, ihm
hind die Hirschkuh; hinterer
hinder hindern

hindrance das Hindernis
hinge die Türangel
hint der Wink; (an)deuten
hip die Hüfte
hire die Miete, der Lohn; mieten
hireling der Mietling
hire-purchase die Ratenzahlung
his sein
hiss zischen
historian der Geschichtschreiber
historical geschichtlich
history die Geschichte
hit der Schlag, der Treffer;
schlagen, treffen
hit song der Schlager
hitch der Haken; fest machen,
haken
hither hierher
hitherto bisher
hive der Bienenstock
hoard der Vorrat; aufhäufen
hoar-frost der Reif
hoarse heiser
hoarseness die Heiserkeit
hoax die Fopperei, der Scherz;
foppen
hobble humpeln
hobby das Steckenpferd
hock der Rheinwein
hock das Sprunggelenk
hoe die Hacke; hacken
hog das Schein
hoggish schweinisch; gefrässig
hogshead das Oxhoft
hoist hissen
hold der Halt, die Gewalt, der
Griff, der Raum; halten, besitzen
hold-all der Koffer
holder der Hälter; der Inhaber;
der Besitzer
holding das Pachtgut
hole das Loch
holiday der Feiertag; -s die
Ferien pl
holiness die Heiligkeit
hollow die Höhle; hohl
holly die Stechpalme
holy heilig
holy-week die Karwoche
home die Heimat; das Haus;
des Heim, die Wohnung; (at) - zu
Hause
home-bred einheimisch

homeless heimatlos
homeliness die Schlichtheit
homely einfach; gemütlich
home-sickness das Heimweh
homewards heimwärts
homicide der Totschlag
honest ehrlich
honesty die Ehrlichkeit
honey der Honig
honeycomb die Honigwabe
honeymoon die Flitterwochen pl
die Hochzeitsreise
honeysuckle das Geissblatt
honorary ehren . . .
honour die Ehre; (be)ehren
honourable ehrenvoll
hood die Haube; die Kapuze
hoof der Huf
hook der Haken; haken
hooked krumm
hoop der Reif; der Reifen
hoot das Geschrei; schreien,
hupen
hooter die Hupe
hop das Hüpfen; hüpfen
hop der Hopfen
hope hoffen; die Hoffnung
hopeful hoffnungsvoll
hopeless hoffnungslos
horde die Gorde
horizon der Horizont
horizontal waagerecht
horn das Horn
hornet die Hornisse
horny hornig
horrible, horrid schrecklich;
entsetzlich
horrify entsetzen
horror das Entsetzen
horse das Pferd
horseback (on) zu Pferde
horseman der Reiter
horsemanship die Reitkunst
horsepower die Pferdestärke
(PS)
horserace das Pferderennen
horse-radish der Meerrettich
horticulture der Gartenbau
hose der Strumpf; der Schlauch
hosier der Strumpfwarenhändler
hosiery die Strumpfwaren pl
hospitable gastfrei
hospital das Krankenhaus

hospitality die Gastfreundschaft	**hurt** verletzen, schaden, weh tun;
host der Wirt; das Heer; die	die Verletzung
Hostie	**hurtful** schädlich; schmerzhaft
hostage der Geisel (die)	**husband** der Mann; der Ehemann
hostess die Wirtin	**husbandman** der Landwirt
hostile feindlich	**husbandry** die Landwirtschaft
hostility die Feindseligkeit	**hush** stillen; die Stille
hot heiss	**husk** die Hülse
hotel der Gasthof; das Hotel	**huskiness** die Rauheit
hothouse das Treibhaus	**husky** rauh; heiser
hound der Jagdhund; hetzen	**hustle** (sich) drängen
hour die Stunde	**hut** die Hütte; der Schuppen
hourly stündlich	**hutch** der Kasten
house das Haus	**hydrogen** der Wasserstoff
housebreaker der Einbrecher	**hydrophobia** die Wasserscheu
household der Haushalt	**hygiene** die Hygiene
householder der Hausbesitzer	**hymn** die Hymne; das Kirchen-
housekeeper die Haushälterin	lied
hovel die Hütte	**hyphen** der Bindestrich
hover schweben	**hypnotism** der Hypnotismus
how wie	**hypnotize** hypnotisieren
however wie auch immer; jedoch;	**hypocrisy** die Heuchelei
trotzdem	**hypocrite** der Heuchler
howl das Gehaul; heulen	**hypochondriac** schwermütig
hub die Nabe	**hypothesis** die Hypothese
hubbub der Lärm	**hysteria** die Hysterie
huddle sich drängen	**hysterical** hysterisch
hue die Farbe	
hug liebkosen; die Umarmung	
huge ungeheuer	**I**
hull der Rumpf	
hum summen	**I** ich
human menschlich	**ice** das Eis; kühlen
humanity die Menschheit	**iceberg** der Eisberg
humble demütig; bescheiden;	**icebound** eingefroren
demütigen	**icebox** der Eisschrank
humid feucht	**icebreaker** der Eisbrecher
humidity die Feuchtigkeit	**ice-cream** das Speiseeis
humiliation die Demütigung	**Iceland** Island
humming-bird die Kolibri	**icicle** der Eiszapfen
humour die Laune; der	**icy** eisig
Humor	**idea** der Begriff; die Idee
hump der Buckel; der Höcker	**ideal** das Ideal; ideal
hunchback der Bucklige	**idealism** der Idealismus
hundred das Hundert	**identical** identisch
hundred-weight der Zentner	**identify** identifizieren
hunger der Hunger; hungern	**identity** die Identität
hungry hungrig	**identity card** der Personalaus-
hunt die Jagd; jagen, hetzen	weis
hunter der Jäger	**idiocy** der Blödsinn
hurl werfen; schleudern	**idiot** der Dummkopf; der Idiot
hurricane der Orkan	**idiotic** blödsinnig; idiotisch
hurry die Eile; eilen, sich beeilen	**idle** träge; müssig; faulenzen

idleness die Trägheit; der Müssiggang
idler der Müssiggänger
idol der Abgott
idolater der Götzendiener
idolize vergöttern
if wenn; ob
ignite (sich) entzünden
ignoble unedel
ignominious schändlich
ignoramus der Dummkopf
ignorance die Unwissenheit
ignorant unwissend
ignore nicht wissen; ignorieren
ill krank; - (evil) übel; das Übel
ill-advised schlecht beraten
illegal ungesetzlich
illegible unleserlich
illegitimate unehelich
illicit unerlaubt
ill-natured bösartig
illness die Krankheit
illuminate beleuchten
illumination die Beleuchtung
illusion die Täuschung
illustrate erläutern; erklären; illustrieren
illustration die Erklärung; das Beispiel; die Abbildung
illustrious berühmt
image das Bild(nis); das Ebenbild
imaginable denkbar
imagination die Einbildung; die Vorstellung; die Einbilungskraft
imaginary eingebildet
imagine sich vorstellen; sich einbilden
imbecile geistesschwach; der Geistesschwache
imbibe einsaugen
imbue durchtränken
imitable nachahmbar
imitate nachahmen
imitation die Nachahmung
imitator der Nachahmer
immaculate unbefleckt
immaterial unbedeutend
immature unreif
immeasurable unermesslich
immediate ummittelbar; unverzüglich
immediately sogleich; sofort

immemorial unvordenklich
immense unermesslich; ungeheuer
immerse eintauchen
immigrant der Einwanderer
immigration die Einwanderung
imminent drohend; bevorstehend
immodest unbescheiden
immoral unsittlich
immortal unsterblich
immortality die Unsterblichkeit
immovable unbeweglich
immune geschützt
immunity die Freiheit
impair verschlechtern; schwächen
impart verleihen
impartial unparteiisch
impartiality die Unparteilichkeit
impassable ungangbar
impatience die Ungeduld
impatient ungeduldig
impede verhindern
impediment das Hindernis
impel antreiben
impend nahe sein; bevorstehen
impenetrable undurchdringlich
imperative unbedingt notwendig
imperceptible unmerkbar
imperfect unvollendet, mangelhaft
imperial kaiserlich
imperialism der Imperialismus
imperil gefährden
imperious herrisch
imperishable unvergänglich
impermeable undurchlässig
impersonal unpersönlich
impertinent unverschämt
impetuosity die Heftigkeit
impetuous ungestüm
impious gottlos
implacable unerbittlich
implement das Gerät
implicate verwickeln
implicit inbegriffen; unbedingt
implore anflehen
imply in sich schliessen; andeuten
impolite unhöflich
import einführen, importieren; die Einfuhr, der Import, die Bedeutung
importance die Wichtigkeit

important wichtig; bedeutend
importunate lästig; aufdringlich
importune belästigen
impose auferlegen
imposing imposant; imponierend
imposition die Steuer; die Aufleg-
ung; die Strafarbeit
impossibility die Unmöglichkeit
impossible unmöglich
impostor der Betrüger
imposture der Betrug
impotent unfähig; impotent
impoverish verarmen
impracticable untunlich
impregnable uneinnehmbar
impregnability die Unüber-
windlichkeit
impregnate befruchten
impress einprägen; Eindruck
machen; eindrücken
impression der Eindruck; der
Abdruck
impressive eindrucksvoll
imprint einprägen; aufdrücken;
der Eindruck
imprison verhaften; einkerkern
improbability die Unwahr-
scheinlichkeit
improbable unwahrscheinlich
improper ungeeignet; unschicklich
improve (sich) verbessern
improvement die Verbesserung
improvidence die Unvorsichtig-
keit
improvident unvorsichtig
imprudence die Unklugheit
imprudent unklug
impudence die Unverschämtheit
impudent unverschämt
impulse der Antrieb; der Impuls
impulsive leidenschaftlich
impunity die Straflosigkeit
impure unrein
impurity die Unreinheit
impute beimessen; zuschreiben
in in; an; auf; bei
inability die Unfähigkeit
inaccessible unzugänglich
inaccessibility die Unzugäng-
lichkeit
inaccuracy die Ungenauigkeit
inaccurate ungenau

inaction die Untätigkeit
inactive untätig
inadequacy die Unzulänglichkeit
inadequate unzulänglich
inadmissible unzulässig
inane geistlos
inanimate leblos
inapplicable unanwendbar
inasmuch insofern
inattentive unaufmerksam
inattention die Unaufmerksam-
keit
inaudible unhörbar
inaugurate einweihen
inauspicious ungünstig
inborn angeboren
incalculable unberechenbar
incapable unfähig
incapacity die Unfähigkeit
incarnate leibhaftig
incarnation die Menschwerdung
incendiary der Brandstifter
incendiary bomb die Brand-
bombe
incense der Weihrauch
incentive der Antrieb
incessant unaufhörlich
incest die Blutschande
inch der Zoll
incident der Zwischenfall
incidental zufällig
incinerate einäschern
incineration die Einäscherung
incision der Einschnitt
incite anreizen
inclement unfreundlich; rauh
inclination die Neigung
incline (sich) neigen; der Abhang
include enthalten
inclusive einschliesslich
incognito unerkannt
incoherence die Zusammenhangs-
losigkeit
incoherent unzusammenhängend
income das Einkommen
income tax die Einkommen-
steuer; die Lohnsteuer
incomparable unvergleichlich
incompatibility die Unverträg-
lichkeit
incompatible unverträglich
incompetence die Unfähigkeit
incompetent unfähig

incomplete unvollständig
incomprehensible unbegreiflich
inconceivable unfassbar
inconsiderate rücksichtslos
inconsistent unvereinbar
inconsolable untröstlich
inconstant wankelmütig
incontestable unbestreitbar
inconvenience die Unbequem-
  lichkeit; belästigen
inconvenient unbequem
incorporate einverleiben
incorrect unrichtig
incorrigible unverbesserlich
incorruptible unverderblich;
  unbestechlich
increase wachsen, (sich) vergrössern; der Zuwachs
incredible unglaublich
incredulous ungläubig
incriminate beschuldigen
incubate ausbrüten
inculcate einprägen
inculpate beschuldigen
incumbent aufliegend; obliegend
incur sich zuziehen
incurability die Unheilbarkeit
incurable unheilbar
indebted verschuldet
indebtedness die Verschuldung
indecision die Unentschlossenheit
indecency die Unanständigkeit
indecent unanständig
indeed in der Tat
indefatigable unermüdlich
indefinite unbestimmt
indelible unauslöschlich
indemnify entschädigen
indemnity die Entschädigung
indent (to) einzähnen
indenture der Kontrakt
independence die Unabhängigkeit
independent unabhängig
indescribable unbeschreiblich
indestructibility die Unzerstör-
  barkeit
indestructible unzerstörbar
inden der Zeiger; der Index; das
  Verzeichnis
India Indien
Indian der Inder; der Indianer
india-rubber das Gummi

indicate anzeigen; hinweisen
indication die Anzeige; der Hin-
  weis
indict anklagen
indifference die Gleichgültigkeit
indifferent gleichgültig
indigestible unverdaulich
indigestion die Verdauungsstör-
  ung
indignant entrüstet
indignation die Entrüstung
indiscreet unbesonnen
indiscretion die Unbesonnenheit
indiscriminate unterschiedslos
indispensable unentbehrlich
indisposed unwohl; abgeneigt
indisposition die Unpässlichkeit
indisputable unbestreitbar
indissoluble unauflöslich
indistinct undeutlich; unklar
individual das Individuum; in-
  dividuell
indolence die Trägheit
indolent träge
indomitable unbezähmbar
indoors im Hause
indubitable unzweifelhaft
induce bewegen; verleiten
induction die Induktion
indulgence die Nachsicht; der
  Ablass
indulgent nachsichtig
industrious fleissig; arbeitsam
industry der Fleiss; das Gewerbe; die Industrie
inebriate betrunken
ineffable unaussprechlich
ineffective wirkungslos; unwirksam
inefficient unfähig; unwirksam
inefficiency die Unfähigkeit
ineligible unwählbar
inept untauglich
inertia die Trägheit; die Untätigkeit
inestimable unschätzbar
inevitable unvermeidlich
inexcusable unverzeihlich
inexhaustible unerschöpflich
inexorable unerbittlich
inexperience die Unerfahren-
  heit
inexperienced unerfahren

inexplicable unerklärlich
inexpressible unausprechlich
inextricable unentwirrbar
infallibility die Unfehlbarkeit
infallible unfehlbar
infamous schändlich; verrufen
infancy die Kindheit
infant der Säugling; das Klein-
kind
infantry die Infanterie
infatuate betören
infect anstecken
infection die Ansteckung
infectious ansteckend
infer schliessen; folgern
inference die Folgerung
inferior (lower) niedriger; min-
derwertig; geringer; untergeordnet
infernal höllisch
infest heimsuchen
infidel ungläubig
infidel der (die) Ungläubige
infinite unendlich
infirm kraftlos
infirmary das Krankenhaus
infirmity das Gebrechen
inflame (sich) entzünden
inflammation die Entzündung
inflate aufblähen; aufpumpen
inflation die Inflation
inflexible unbeugsam; unbiegsam
inflict auferlegen
influence der Einfluss; beein-
flussen
influenza die Grippe
inform benachrichtigen; mitteilen
information die Auskunft
informer der Angeber
infraction die Verletzung
infrequent selten
infringe übertreten; verletzen
infringement die Übertretung
infuse einflössen; aufgiessen
infusion der Aufguss
ingenious sinnreich
ingenuity der Scharfsinn
ingot der Barren
ingratiate einschmeicheln
ingratitude die Undankbarkeit
ingredient der Bestandteil
inhabit bewohnen

inhabitant der Bewohner; der
Einwohner
inhale einatmen
inherit erben
inheritance die Erbschaft
inhospitable unwirtlich
inhuman unmenschlich
inimical feindlich
inimitable unnachahmlich
iniquity die Schlechtigkeit
initial der Anfangsbuchstabe;
anfänglich
initiate einführen; einweihen;
anfangen
inject einspritzen
injection die Einspritzung
injunction die Einschärfung;
das Verbot
injure beschädigen; verletzen
injury der Schaden; die Verletzung
injustice die Ungerechtigkeit
ink die Tinte
inkpot das Tintenfass
inland binnenländisch
inlay einlegen
inlet der Einlass; die Bucht
inmate der Hausgenosse; der
Insasse
inmost innerst
inn der Gasthof; das Wirtshaus
innate angeboren
inner inner; innerlich
innkeeper der Gastwirt
innocence die Unschuld
innocent unschuldig
innovation die Neuerung
innumerable unzählbar
inoculate (ein)impfen
inodorous geruchlos
inoffensive harmlos
inopportune ungelegen
inquest die Untersuchung; die
Leichenschau
inquire nachfragen; (sich) erkundigen
inquiry die Nachfrage; die Untersuchung
inquisitive neugierig
inroad der Eingriff
insane wahnsinnig
insanity der Wahnsinn
insatiable unersättlich
inscribe einschreiben

inscription die Inschrift
inscrutable unerforschlich
insect das Insekt
insecure unsicher
insecurity die Unsicherheit
insensibility die Unempfindlichkeit
insensible unempfindlich
inseparable untrennbar
insert (to) einsetzen; einfügen
insertion die Einfügung
inside inwendig; innerhalb; das Innere
insight die Einsicht
insignificant unbedeutend
insincere unaufrichtig
insinuate (to) andeuten
insipid geschmacklos; fade
insist bestehen
insistent beharrend
insolence die Frechheit
insolent unverschämt; frech
insolvency die Zahlungsunfähigkeit
insolvent zahlungsunfähig
inspect besichtigen; nachsehen
inspection die Besichtigung
inspire begeistern; einflössen
instability die Unbeständigkeit
install einsetzen
instalment die Teilzahlung
instance das Beispiel
instant der Augenblick; sofortig
instantaneous sofortig
instead (of) statt; anstatt
instep der Spann
instigate anstiften
instigation die Anreizung
instinct der Naturtrieb; der Instinkt
instinctive instinktiv; unwillkürlich
institute anordnen; einsetzen
institution die Errichtung
instruct unterrichten
instruction der Unterricht
instruction die Vorschrift
instructive lehrreich
instrument das Instrument; das Werkzeug
insubordinate widersetzlich
insubordination die Widersetzlichkeit

insufficient ungenügend
insular Insel . . . ; insular
insulate isolieren; absondern
insulation die Isolierung
insult die Beschimpfung, die Beleidigung; beleidigen
insuperable unüberwindlich
insupportable unerträglich
insurance die Versicherung
insure (ver)sichern
insurgent der Aufrührer
insurrection der Aufstand
intact unberührt
integral ganz; vollständig
integrity die Redlichkeit; die Vollständigkeit
intellect der Verstand
intellectual intellektuell
intelligence die Intelligenz; der Verstand
intelligence (military) die Nachricht
intelligent intelligent
intelligible verständlich
intemperate unmässig
intend beabsichtigen
intense stark; heftig
intensity die Intensität
intensive intensiv
intent, intention die Absicht
intentional absichtlich
inter (to) beerdigen
intercede Fürbitte einlegen
intercept abfangen
intercession die Fürbitte; die Fürsprache
interchange der Austausch
interchangeable austauschbar
intercourse der Verkehr
interdict verbieten
interest die Interesse, die Zinsen *pl*, Anteil; der interessieren
interesting interessant
interfere sich einmischen
interim die Zwischenzeit
interior inner, innerlich
interior das Innere
interlace durchflechten
interlude das Zwischenspiel
intermediary der Vermittler
intermediate zwischen . . .
interment die Beerdigung
intermission die Unterbrechung

intern internieren
internal inner; innerlich
interpose vermitteln; einschieben
interpret dolmetschen; erklären
interpreter der Dolmetscher
interrogate befragen; verhören
interrogation das Verhör
interrupt unterbrechen
interruption die Unterbrechung
interval der Abstand: die Pause
intervene dazwischentreten
intervention das Dazwischentreten
interview die Unterredung
intestate ohne Testament
intestines die Eingeweide *pl*
intimacy die Vertraulichkeit
intimate intim; vertraut; andeuten
intimidate einschüchtern
into in
intolerable unerträglich
intolerance die Unduldsamkeit
intolerant unduldsam
intonation die Betonung
intoxicate berauschen
intrepid unerschrocken
intrepidity die Unerschrockenheit
intricate verwickelt
intrigue das Ränkespiel
introduce einführen; vorstellen
introduction die Einführung; die Vorstellung
intrude (sich) eindrängen; stören
intrusion das Eindrängen
intrust anvertrauen
intuition die Intuition
inundate überschwemmen
inure abhärten; gewöhnen
invade (ein), (über)fallen
invader der Eindringling
invalid ungültig, schwach; der Kranke
invalidity die Ungültigkeit
invaluable unschätzbar
invariable unveränderlich
invasion der Einfall
invective die Schmähung
invent erfinden
invention die Erfindung
inventive erfinderisch
inventor der Erfinder

inverse umgekehrt
invert umkehren
invest anlegen; einschliessen; bekleiden
investigate erforschen; untersuchen
investment die Geldanlage; die Einschliessung
inveterate eingewurzelt
invigorate stärken
invincible unbesiegbar
inviolable unverletzlich
invisible unsichtbar
invitation die Einladung
invite einladen
invoice die Faktura; die Rechnung
invoke anrufen
involuntary unfreiwillig
involve umfassen; verwickeln
invulnerable unverwundbar
invulnerability die Unverwundbarkeit
inward inner; innerlich
I.O.U. der Schuldschein
irascibility der Jähzorn
irascible reizbar; jähzornig
irate erzürnt
irksome lästig
iron das Eisen; plätten, bügeln
irons die Fesseln *pl*
iron-casting der Eisenguss
iron-foundry die Eisengiesserei
iron-ware die Eisenwaren *pl*
ironical ironisch
ironmonger der Eisenhändler
irony die Ironie
irreconcilable unversöhnlich
irrefutable unwiderleglich
irregular unregelmässig
irregularity die Unregelmässigkeit
irrelevant belanglos
irreparable unersetzlich
irreproachable untadelhaft
irresistible unwiderstehlich
irresolute unentschlossen
irresponsible unverantwortlich
irrevocable unwiderruflich
irrigate bewässern
irrigation die Bewässerung
irritable reizbar
irritate reizen

island die Insel
islander der Inselbewohner
islet das Inselchen
issue die Ausgabe, der Ausgang; der Nachkomme; herausgeben
isthmus die Landenge
italics die Kursivschrift
itch das Jucken; jucken
item der Artikel
itinerary der Reiseplan
ivory das Elfenbein
ivy der Efeu

J

jabber schwatzen
jack der Hebel; die Zwinge; der Stiefelknecht
jackal der Schakal
jackdaw die Dohle
jacket die Jacke
jade die Schindmähre; ermüden
jag kerben; die Kerbe
jail das Gefängnis
jailer der Gefängniswärter
jam die Marmelade
jam pressen; klemmen
janitor der Pförtner
January der Januar
Japan Japan; lackieren
jar der Krug, das Glas; knarren, stören
jargon das Kauderwelsch
jasmine der Jasmin
jaundice die Gelbsucht
jaw der Kiefer
jealous eifersüchtig
jealousy die Eifersucht
jeer höhnen; spotten; der Spott
jelly die Gallerte; das Gelee
jemmy das Brecheisen
jeopardize (to) gefährden
jeopardy die Gefahr
jerk der Ruck; zucken
jersey die Wolljacke
jest der Scherz; scherzen
jestingly im Spass
jester der Spassmacher
Jesuit der Jesuit
jet der Strahl; (vor)springen
jet-black pechschwarz

jet-plane das Düsenflugzeug
jettison über Bord werfen
jetty der Landungsplatz
Jew der Jude
jewel das Juwel
jeweller der Juwelier
jewelry die Juwelen *pl*
Jewess die Jüdin
Jewish jüdisch
Jewry das Judentum
jilt sitzen lassen
jingle klingeln; das Geklingel
job die Arbeit
job-lot die Ramschware
jobber der Makler
jockey der Jockei; prellen
jocular spasshaft
join verbinden
joiner der Tischler
joint das Gelenk, der Braten; gemeinsam
joke der Spass; spassen
jollity die Lustigkeit
jolly lustig
jolt (to) rütteln, stossen; der Stoss
jot das Jota
journal die Zeitschrift; die Zeitung
journalist der Journalist
journey reisen; die Reise
journeyman der Geselle
jovial jovial, lustig
joviality der Frohsinn
joy die Freude
joyful, joyous fröhlich; freudig
joyless freudlos
jubilant jubelnd; frohlockend
jubilation der Jubel
jubilee das Jubiläum
Judaism das Judentum
judge der Richter, der Kenner; richten, beurteilen
judgment das Urteil; die Meinung
judicial gerichtlich
judicious verständig
jug der Krug
juggle gaukeln
juggler der Gaukler
juice der Saft
juicy saftig
juiciness die Saftigkeit
jump der Sprung; springen

junction der Knotenpunkt; die Verbindung
juncture das Gelenk
jungle das Sumpfdickicht; die Dschungel
junior jünger
juniper der Wacholder
jurisdiction die Gerichtsbarkeit
juror, juryman der Geschworene
jury die Geschworenen
just gerecht; richtig; gerade
justice die Gerechtigkeit
justification die Rechtfertigung
justify rechtfertigen
justness die Gerechtigkeit
jut hervorragen; hervorspringen
jute die Jute
juvenile jugendlich
juxtaposition die Nebeneinanderstellung

K

kale der Krauskohl; der Grünkohl
kaleidoscope das Kaleidoscop
kangaroo das Känguruh
keel der Kiel
keen scharf; eifrig
keenness die Schärfe; der Eifer
keep der Unterhalt, die Obhut; halten, bewahren, unterhalten
keeper der Hüter, der Aufseher; der Inhaber; der Wächter
keeping die Aufsicht
keepsake das Andenken
keg das Fässchen
kennel die Hundehütte
kerbstone der Randstein
kernel der Kern
kettle der Kessel
kettledrum die Kesselpauke
key der Schlüssel; die Tonart; die Taste
keyboard die Klaviatur
keyhole das Schlüsselloch
keynote der Grundton
keystone der Schluss-stein
khaki staubfarben
kick ausschlagen, treten; der Tritt
kid das Zicklein
kid glove der Glacéhandschuh
kidnap entführen

kidney die Niere
kill töten; schlachten
kill-joy der Spassverderber
kiln der Brennofen
kilt der Schottenrock
kin die Verwandtschaft
kind die Art; gütig, freundlich
kindle anzünden
kindly freundlich
kindness, kindliness die Freundlichkeit; die Güte
kindred die Verwandtschaft
king der König
kingdom das Königreich
kingly königlich
kinsman der (die) Verwandte
kipper der Räucherhering
kiss der Kuss; küssen
kit die Ausrüstung
kitchen die Küche
kite der Drache
kitten das Kätzchen
knack der Kunstgriff
knacker der Abdecker
knapsack der Tornister
knave der Schelm; der Bube
knavish schurkisch
knead kneten
knee das Knie
knee-cap die Kniescheibe
kneel knien
knell die Totenglocke
knick-knacks die Nippsachen *pl*
knickerbockers die Kniehosen *pl*
knife das Messer
knight der Ritter; der Springer
knit stricken
knitting das Strickzeug
knob der Knopf; der Knorren; der Griff
knobby knorrig
knock klopfen; das Anklopfen, der Schlag
knocker der Türklopfer
knot knoten; der Knoten, die Schleife
knotty knotig; schwierig
know wissen; kennen
knowing schlau; wissentlich; erfahren, klug
knowledge die Kenntnis; das Wissen

knuckle der Knöchel
knuckle-duster der Schlagring
knuckle under nachgeben
Koran der Koran
kudos der Ruhm

L

label der Zettel, das Etikett; bekleben, etikettieren
laboratory das Laboratorium
laboratory assistant der Laborant
laborious mühsam; arbeitsam
labour die Arbeit, die Mühe, die Wehen *pl*; **- exchange** der Arbeitsnachweis; (be)arbeiten
labourer der Arbeiter
laburnum der Goldregen
labyrinth das Labyrinth
lace die Schnur, die Spitze; (zu-) schnüren
lacerate zerreissen
laceration die Zerreissung
lack der Mangel; fehlen
lacquer (varnish) der Lack; lackieren
lad der Bursche
ladder die Leiter
laden beladen
ladle der Schöpflöffel
lady die Dame
lag zurückbleiben
lager das Lagerbier
lake der See
lamb das Lamm
lame lahm
lameness die Lahmheit
lament klagen; jammern
lamentable kläglich
lamentation die Wehklage
lamp die Lampe
lance die Lanze; aufschneiden
lance-corporal der Gefreite
lancet die Lanzette
land das Land; landen
landed begütert
landing die Landung
landing-stage die Landungsbrücke
landowner, landholder der Grundbesitzer
landlord der Wirt

landlady die Wirtin
landscape die Landschaft
landslide der Erdrutsch
lane die Gasse
language die Sprache
languid matt; schlaff
languish schmachten
languor die Mattigkeit
lank, lanky schlank; dünn
lantern die Laterne
lap der Schoss; lecken
lapse der Verlauf, der Fehltritt; verfallen, verfliessen
larch die Lärche
lard das Schmalz
larder die Speisekammer
large gross
largeness die Grösse
lark die Lerche; der Streich
larva die Larve
larynx der Kehlkopf
lash (whip) der Hieb; peitschen
lash (eye) die Wimper
lass das Mädchen
last letzte; dauern; der Leisten
latch die Klinke
late spät; verspätet; verstorben
lately kürzlich; in letzter Zeit
latent verborgen
lateral seitlich
lath die Latte
lathe die Drehbank
lather der Schaum; einseifen
Latin lateinisch; das Latein
latitude die Breite
latitude der Spielraum
latter letztere
latterly neuerdings
lattice das Gitter
laud loben
laudable löblich
laugh das Lachen; lachen
laughable lächerlich
laughing-stock der Gegenstand des Gelächters
laughter das Gelächter
launch der Stapellauf, die Barkasse; vom Stapel lassen
laundress die Wäscherin
laundry die Waschanstalt
laureate der Hofdichter
laurel der Lorbeer
lava die Lava

lavatory die Toilette
lavender der Lavendel
lavish verschwenderisch; verschwenden
law das Gesetz; das Recht
lawful gesetzlich
lawless gesetzlos
law-court der Gerichtshof
lawn der Rasenplatz
lawsuit der Prozess
lawyer der Anwalt
lax schlaff; lässig
laxative das Abführmittel
lay das Lied; legen; weltlich
layer die Schicht
layman der Laie
laziness die Faulheit
lazy faul
lead das Blei
lead die Führung, die Leitung; führen, leiten
leaden bleiern
leader der Führer
leading article der Leitartikel
lead-pencil der Bleistift
leaf das Blatt
leaflet das Blättchen; das Flugblatt
leafy belaubt
league der Bund; die Liga; sich verbünden; die Meile
leak lecken; das Leck
leakage die Leckage
leaky leck
lean (sich) lehnen; mager
leaning die Neigung
leanness die Magerkeit
leap springen; der Sprung
leap-frog das Bockspringen
leap-year das Schaltjahr
learn lernen; erfahren
learned gelehrt
learning die Gelehrsamkeit
lease die Pacht, die Miete; verpachten
leaseholder der Pächter
leash die Leine; koppeln
least wenigste; **at least** wenigstens; mindestens
leather das Leder
leathery lederartig
leave die Erlaubnis, der Urlaub; abreisen, (ver)lassen

leaven der Sauerteig; säuern
leavings die Überbleibsel *pl*
lecture die Vorlesung; Vorlesung halten
lecturer der Dozent
ledge das Sims
ledger das Hauptbuch
leech der Blutegel
leek der Lauch
left link(s)
leg das Bein
legacy das Vermächtnis
legal gesetzlich
legalize rechtstkräftig machen
legality die Gesetzlichkeit
legation die Gesandtschaft
legend die Legende; die Sage
legendary legendhaft; sagenhaft
leggings die Gamaschen *pl*
legible leserlich
legion die Legion
legislation die Gesetzgebung
legislative gesetzgebend
legislator der Gesetzgeber
legitimacy die Gesetzmässigkeit die eheliche Geburt
legitimate rechtmässig; ehelich
leisure die Musse
lemon die Zitrone
lemonade die Limonade
lend leihen; verleihen
length die Länge
lengthen (sich) verlängern
leniency die Milde
lenient mild
lens die Linse
Lent die Fastenzeit
lentil die Linse
leopard der Leopard
leper der Aussätzige
leprosy der Aussatz
less weniger; geringer
lessen vermindern
lesson die Lektion; die Stunde
lest damit nicht
let lassen; vermieten
lethal tödlich
lethargic lethargisch
lethargy die Schlafsucht
letter der Buchstabe; der Brief
letter-box der Briefkasten
letter-case die Brieftasche
letterpress der Druck

letter-weight der Briefbeschwerer
lettuce der Salat
level gleich, eben, waagerecht; das Niveau; ebnen
lever der Hebel
levy die Erhebung die Aushebung; erheben, ausheben
lewd unzüchtig; liederlich
liability die Verantwortlichkeit; die Haftpflicht
liable ausgesetzt; haftbar
liar der Lügner
libel die Schmähschrift, die Verleumdung; verleumden
liberal (ideas) freisinnig; - **(generous)** freigebig, liberal
liberality die Freigebigkeit
liberate befreien
libertine der Wüstling
liberty die Freiheit
librarian der Bibliothekar
library die Bibliothek; die Bücherei
lice die Läuse *pl*
licence berechtigt; die Erlaubnis, die Konzession, die Zügellosigkeit; **driving -** der Führerschein
licentious zügellos
lick lecken
lid der Deckel; **eye-** das Augenlid
lie die Lüge; lügen
lieu (in - of) statt; anstatt
lieutenant der Leutnant
life das Leben
life-annuity die Leibrente
lifeboat das Rettungsboot
lifebelt der Rettungsgürtel
lifeguard die Leibwache
life-insurance die Lebensversicherung
lifetime die Lebenszeit
lift der Aufzug, der Fahrstuhl; (er)heben
light leicht; das Licht; hell, anzünden
lighten erleichtern
light-hearted fröhlich
lighthouse der Leuchtturm
lighting die Beleuchtung
lightning der Blitz
lightning-conductor der Blitzableiter

lignite die Braunkohle
like gleich; gern haben
likelihood die Wahrscheinlichkeit
likely wahrscheinlich
likeness die Ähnlichkeit
likewise gleichfalls
liking der Gefallen
lilac der Flieder
lily die Lilie
lily of the valley das Maiglöckchen
limb das Glied
lime der Kalk
lime tree die Linde
limestone der Kalkstein
limit die Grenze, die Frist; begrenzen
limited mit beschränkter Haftung
limp schlapp
limpid klar; hell
line die Linie, die Zeile, die Reihe; linieren, füttern
linen die Leinwand; die Wäsche
liner der Überseedampfer
linger säumen; zögern
linguist der Sprachenkenner
liniment die Salbe
lining das Futter
link das Glied; verbinden
linnet der Hänfling
linoleum das Linoleum
linseed der Leinsamen
linseed-oil das Leinöl
lint der Flachs; die Scharpie
lion der Löwe
lioness die Löwin
lip die Lippe
lipstick der Lippenstift
liqueur die Likör
liquid flüssig; die Flüssigkeit
liquidate liquidieren
liquor die Flüssigkeit; der Alkohol
lisp lispeln
list die Liste, die Schlagseite; listen
listen (to) anhören; horchen; lauschen
listener der Horcher; der Hörer
listless träge
litany die Litanei

literal buchstäblich
literature die Literatur
Lithuania Litauen
litmus der Lackmus
litter die Streu; der Wurf; die Unordnung; der Abfall
little klein; wenig; gering
little by little nach und nach
live leben; wohnen; lebendig
livelihood der Unterhalt
liveliness die Lebhaftigkeit
lively lebhaft
liver die Leber
livid bleifarbig; fahl
living der Unterhalt; lebend
lizard die Eidechse
load die Ladung, die Last; (be)laden
loaf der Laib; das Brot
loafer der Müssiggänger
loam der Lehm
loamy lehmig
loan die Anleihe, das Darlehen; leihen
loath unwillig
loathe sich ekeln vor; verabscheuen
loathsome ekelhaft
lobby die Vorhalle
lobe das Ohrläppchen
lobster der Hummer
local örtlich
locality der Ort
localize lokalisieren; begrenzen
locate Ort bestimmen; finden
location der Standort
loch der See
lock das Schloss, die Locke, die Schleuse; schliessen
lockout die Aussperrung
locksmith der Schlosser
locomotive die Lokomotive
locust die Heuschrecke
lode die Erzader
lodge das Häuschen, die Loge; wohnen; beherbergen
lodger der Mieter
lodging die Wohnung
loft der Speicher
lofty hoch; erhaben
log der Klotz; das Log
logic die Logik
logical logisch

loin die Lende
loiter trödeln
loiterer der Faulenzer
loll sich lehnen; umherlungern
loneliness die Einsamkeit
lonely, lonesome einsam
long lang; lange; sich sehnen
longitude die Länge
long-suffering langmütig
look der Blick, das Aussehen; (aus)sehen; - **(for)** suchen
looker-on der Zuschauer
looking-glass der Spiegel
look-out die Wache; Acht geben
loom der Webstuhl
loop die Schlinge; die Schleife
loophole das Schlupfloch
loose los; lose; lösen
loosen losmachen
loot die Beute; plündern
loquacious geschwätzig
lord der Herr
Lord's prayer das Vaterunser
lordly stolz; vornehm
lose verlieren
loser der Verlierer
loss der Verlust
lot das Los; der Teil; das Stück; die Menge; viele
lotion das Waschmittel
lottery die Lotterie
loud laut
lounge lungern
lounger der Müssiggänger
lounge-suit der Jakettanzug
louse die Laus
lout der Lümmel
lovable liebenswert
love die Liebe; lieben; **in love** verliebt
love-affair der Liebeshandel
lovely herrlich; reizend
lover der Liebhaber
low niedrig; leise; niedergeschlagen; brüllen
lower abnehmen; erniedrigen; herablassen
lowland das Tiefland
lowliness die Demut
lowly demütig; niedrig
lowness die Niedrigkeit
loyal treu
loyalty die Treue

lozenge die Pastille
lubricant der Schmierstoff
lubricate schmieren
lubrication die Schmierung
lucid klar; durchsichtig
lucidity die Klarheit
luck das Glück
lucky glücklich
lucrative einträglich
ludicrous lächerlich
luggage das Gepäck
luggage-van der Gepäckwagen
lugubrious kläglich; traurig
lukewarm lauwarm
lull einlullen
lumbago der Hexenschuss
lumber das Gerümpel; das Bauholz
luminous leuchtend
lump der Klumpen; die Masse
lunacy der Irrsinn
lunatic wahnsinnig
lunatic-asylum die Irrenanstalt
lunch das Mittagessen; zu Mittag
essen
lung die Lunge
lure der Köder; ködern
lurid düster; finster
lurk lauern
luscious sehr süss; saftig
lust die Begierde; die Wollust
lustre der Glanz; der Kronleuchter
lusty rüstig; munter
luxurious, luxuriant üppig
luxury der Luxus
lying-in (childbirth) das
Wochenbett
lynch lynchen
lynx der Luchs
lyre die Leier
lyrical lyrisch

M

macaroni die Makkaroni *pl*
macaroon die Makrone
mace der Amtsstab
machination die Ränke *pl*
machine die Maschine
machinery die Maschinen *pl*
macintosh der Regenmantel

mackerel die Makrele
mad verrückt; wahnsinnig
madam gnädige Frau
madden (to) toll machen
madman der Verrückte
magazine das Magazin; die Zeitschrift
maggot die Made
magic die Zauberei; die Zauber-
kunst
magical magisch
magician der Zauberer
magistrate der Polizeirichter
magnanimous grossmütig
magnanimity die Grossmut
magnet der Magnet
magnetism der Magnetismus
magnificent prächtig; herrlich
magnify vergrössern
magnifying glass das Vergrösserungsglas
magnitude die Grösse
magpie die Elster
mahogany das Mahagoniholz
maid die Magd; das Dienstmädchen
maid (old) die alte Jungfer
maiden die Jungfrau; jungfräu-
lich
maiden-speech die Jungfernrede
mail die Post; absenden
mail-boat das Paketboot
mail-train der Postzug
maim verstümmeln; lähmen
main Haupt . . .
maintain erhalten; behaupten
maintenance die Erhaltung; der
Unterhalt
maize der Mais
majestic majestätisch
majesty die Majestät
major der Major, der Mündige;
grösser
majority die Mündigkeit; die
Mehrzahl
make machen; lassen; bewirken;
die Machart; das Fabrikat: die
Marke
maker der Fabrikant
makeshift der Notbehelf
malady die Krankheit
male der Mann, das Männchen;
männlich

malediction die Verwünschung
malevolence die Böswilligkeit
malice die Bosheit
malicious boshaft
malign verleumden
malignant boshaft; bösartig
malleable hämmerbar
mallet der Schlegel
malt das Malz; mälzen
mammal das Säugetier
mammoth riesig; das Mammut
man der Mann, der Mensch; bemannen
manacle fesseln
manage handhaben; leiten
management die Verwaltung
manager der Leiter; der Direktor
mane die Mähne
manful tapfer
mangle verstümmeln; die Mangel
manhood das Mannesalter
mania die Sucht; der Wahnsinn
maniac der Wahnsinnige
maniacal wahnsinnig
manifest offenbaren
manifestation die Offenbarung
manifesto das Manifest
manifold mannigfaltig
manipulate (to) behandeln
manipulation die Behandlung
mankind das Menschengeschlecht
manliness die Männlichkeit
manly männlich; mannhaft
manner die Weise; die Art
mannered gesittet
mannerly höflich
manœuvres das Manöver; manövrieren
man-of-war das Kriegsschiff
manor das Rittergut
mansion das herrschaftliche Wohnhaus
manslaughter der Totschlag
mantelpiece der Kaminsims
mantle der Mantel
manual Hand . . .; das Handbuch
manufacture die Fabrikation; fabrizieren
manufacturer der Fabrikant
manure der Dünger; düngen

manuscript das Manuskript
many viele
many a mancher, manche, manches
map die Landkarte
maple der Ahorn
mar stören; verderben
marauder der Plünderer
marble der Marmor
march der März, der Marsch; marschieren
mare die Stute
margarine die Margarine
margin der Rand; der Spielraum
marigold die Ringelblume
marine der Seesoldat
mariner der Matrose; der Seemann
maritime see . . .
mark die Mark, die Marke; bezeichnen
market der Markt
market-gardener der Handelsgärtner
market-place der Marktplatz
marksman der Meisterschütze
marmalade die Marmelade
marmot das Murmeltier
marriage die Heirat; die Ehe
married verheiratet
marry (ver)heiraten
marsh der Sumpf
marshal der Marschall
marshy sumpfig
mart der Markt
marten der Marder
martial kriegerisch
martial (court-) das Kriegsgericht
martial-law das Kriegsrecht
martyr der Märtyrer
martyrdom das Märtyrertum
marvel das Wunder; (sich) wundern
marvellous wunderbar
masculine männlich
mask die Maske; maskieren
mason der Maurer
masonry das Mauerwerk
mass die Messe; die Masse
massacre das Blutbad; niedermetzeln

massive massiv
mast der Mast
master der Herr, der Meister;
beherrschen
masterly meisterhaft
masterpiece das Meisterstück
mastery die Gewalt; die Meisterschaft
mastiff der Bullenbeisser
mat die Matte
match das Streichholz, das Gleiche,
der Wettkampf; zusammenpassen
matchless unvergleichlich
mate der Genosse, die Genossin,
der Maat; paaren; mattsetzen
material das Material; der Stoff
materialism der Materialismus
maternal mütterlich
mathematician der Mathematiker
mathematics die Mathematik
matrimony die Ehe
matrimonial ehelich
matron die Vorsteherin; die
Oberin
matter der Stoff, die Materie, die
Sache, der Inhalt; bedeuten
matter-of-course selbstver-
ständlich
matter-of-fact tatsächlich
matter (it does not) es schadet
nichts; es macht nichts
matter (what does it) was macht
das?
matter (what is the) was ist los?
mattress die Matratze
mature reif
mature (to) reifen
maturity die Reife; der Verfall
maudlin rührselig
maul zerreissen
maxim der Grundsatz
may der Mai; mögen, können,
dürfen
maybe vielleicht
may-fly die Eintagsfliege
mayor der Bürgermeister
maze das Labyrinth; der Irrgar-
ten
meadow die Wiese
meagre mager; dürr
meal die Mahlzeit; das Mehl
mealy mehlig

mean gemein, niedrig, geizig,
mittel; der Mittelpunkt, die
Mittelmässigkeit, das Mittel; die
Mitte; meinen; bedeuten
meander (sich) schlängeln
meaning die Bedeutung
meanness die Gemeinheit; der
Geiz
means das Vermögen; die Mittel
pl
means (by no) keinesfalls
meanwhile mittlerweile
measles die Masern pl
measure die Mass, die Massregel;
messen
meat das Fleisch
mechanic der Mechaniker; der
Handwerker
mechanical mechanisch
mechanics die Mechanik
mechanization die Motorisie-
rung
mechanize mechanisieren
medal die Medaille
meddle (to) (sich) abgeben
meddlesome aufdringlich
mediæval mittelalterlich
mediate vermitteln
mediation die Vermittlung
mediator der Vermittler
medical ärztlich
medical officer der Amtsarzt
medicament das Heilmittel
medicinal medizinisch
medicine die Medizin; die Arznei
mediocre mittelmässig
mediocrity die Mittelmässigkeit
mediate (to) nachdenken
Mediterranean das Mittelmeer
medium das Mittel; mittel
medley das Gemisch; das Pot-
pourri
meek sanftmütig; demütig
meet (sich) treffen; begegnen;
versammeln
meeting die Versammlung
melancholy die Schwermut;
schwermütig
mellow reif; sanft; weich
melody die Melodie
melon die Melone
melt schmelzen
member das Glied; das Mitglied

membership die Mitgliedschaft
memoir die Denkschrift
memorable denkwürdig
memorandum das Memorandum
memorial das Denkmal
memory das Gedächtnis
menace die Drohung; bedrohen
menagerie die Menagerie
mend (aus)bessern, reparieren
menial niedrig
mensuration die Messkunst
mental geistig
mention die Erwähnung; erwähnen
menu die Speisekarte
mercantile marine die Handelsflotte
mercenary feil; der Söldner
mercer der Schnittwarenhändler
merchandise die Ware
merchant der Grosshändler; der Kaufmann
merciful barmherzig
merciless unbarmherzig
mercury das Quecksilber
mercy die Barmherzigkeit
mere(ly) bloss; allein
merge verschmelzen; aufgehen in
merit der Verdienst; verdienen
merited wohlverdient
meritorious verdienstlich
mermaid die Seejungfer
merriment die Fröhlichkeit
merry lustig; fröhlich
mesh die Masche; umgarnen
mess der Schmutz; die Unordnung
message die Botschaft
messenger der Bote
metal das Metall
metallic metallisch
metamorphosis die Verwandlung
metaphor die Metapher
meteor das Meteor
meter das Meter; der Messer
method die Methode
metre das Versmass
metropolis die Weltstadt
mettle der Naturstoff; der Mut
mew miauen
mica der Glimmer
Michaelmas das Michaelisfest

microbe die Bakterie
microphone das Mikrophon
microscope das Mikroskop
mid mitten
mid-air (in) in freier Luft
mid-day der Mittag
middle die Mitte
middle-aged in mittlerem Alter
middle-ages das Mittelalter
middle-classes der Mittelstand
middling mittelmässig
midnight die Mitternacht
midshipman der Leutnant
midst die Mitte
midsummer der Hochsommer
midsummer-day der Johannistag
midway halbwegs
midwife die Hebamme
mien die Miene
might die Macht; die Kraft
mighty mächtig
migrate wandern
mild mild
mildew der Mehltau; der Brand
mile die Meile
mileage die Meilenzahl
militant kämpfend; streitend
military militärisch
milk die Milch; melken
milky-way die Milchstrasse
mill die Mühle; die Fabrik; mahlen
miller der Müller
millet die Hirse
milliner die Putzmacherin
millionaire der Millionär
mimic nachäffen
mimic der Nachäffer
mince hacken
mince(d)-meat das Hackfleisch
mind der Geist, der Sinn, die Absicht; die Lust; das Gedächtnis; sich kümmern um, achthaben; **I don't -** es ist mir egal
mind (never) es tut nichts
mindful eingedenk
mine der, die, das meinige
mine die Grube; das Bergwerk; die Mine
miner der Bergmann
mineral das Mineral
mingle (sich) mengen

miniature das Miniaturgemälde; Klein . . .
mining der Bergbau
minion der Günstling
minister der Priester, der Minister, der Gesandte; dienen, darreichen, helfen
ministry das Ministerium
Ministry of Labour das Arbeitsministerium
minor kleiner, geringer; der (die) Minderjährige; moll
minority die Minderheit
minstrel der Spielmann
mint die Minze, die Münze; münzen
minute sehr klein; der Minute, der Augenblick
miracle das Wunder
miraculous wunderbar
mirage die Luftspiegelung
mire der Kot
mirror spiegeln; der Spiegel
mirth die Fröhlichkeit
misadventure das Unglück
misanthrope der Menschenfeind
misbehave sich schlecht benehmen
misbehaviour das schlechte Betragen
miscarriage das Misslingen; die Fehlgeburt
miscarry misslingen
miscellaneous gemischt
mischief das Unheil; der Unfug
mischievous (wicked) boshaft; nachteilig
misconduct das schlechte Benehmen
misconstruction die Missdeutung
misdeed die Missetat
misdemeanour das Vergehen
miser der Geizhals
miserable elend
miserly geizig
misery das Elend
misfortune das Unglück
misgiving die Befürchtung
mishap der Unfall
misinterpret missdeuten
misjudge falsch beurteilen
mislay verlegen

mislead verleiten
mismanage schlecht verwalten
misplace verstellen
misprint der Druckfehler
miss das Fräulein
miss (ver)missen; (ver)fehlen
missile das Wurfgeschoss
mission die Sendung; die Gesandtschaft; der Beruf; die Mission
missionary der Missionar
misspell falsch schreiben
misstate falsch angeben
misstatement die falsche Angabe
mist der Nebel
mistake verwechseln, missverstehen; der Irrtum, der Fehler
mister der Herr
mistletoe die Mistel
mistress die Hausfrau; die Herrin; die Lehrerin; die Mätresse
mistrust misstrauen; das Misstrauen
mistrustful misstrauisch
misty nebelig
misunderstand missverstehen
misunderstanding das Missverständnis
misuse der Missbrauch; missbrauchen
mitigate mildern
mitten der Fausthandschuh
mix (sich) mischen
mixture die Mischung
moan stöhnen; das Stöhnen
moat der Graben
mob der Pöbel; anfallen
mobility die Beweglichkeit
mobilize mobil machen
mock (ver)spotten
mockery die Spötterei
mode die Mode; die Art und Weise
model das Modell; das Muster; das Vorbild
moderate mässig; mässigen
moderation die Mässigung
modern modern
modest bescheiden; sittsam
modesty die Bescheidenheit
modify abändern
moist feucht
moisten befeuchten
moisture die Feuchtigkeit
molar der Backenzahn

mole das Mal; der Maulwurf
mole-hill der Maulwurfshaufen
molest belästigen
mollify besänftigen
moment der Augenblick; die
Wichtigkeit
momentary augenblicklich
momentous wichtig
monarch der Monarch
monarchy die Monarchie
monastry das Kloster
Monday der Montag
money das Geld
money-order die Postanweisung
mongrel der Mischling
monk der Mönch
monkey der Affe
monogamy die Einehe
monogram das Monogramm
monopoly das Monopol
monotonous eintönig
monotony die Eintönigkeit
monster das Ungeheuer
monstrosity das Ungeheuer
month der Monat
monthly monatlich
monument das Denkmal
moo muhen
mood die Stimmung; die Laune;
moody launisch; mürrisch
moon der Mond
moor das Moor, der Maure; fest-
machen
mooring der Ankerplatz
mop der Scheuerlappen; wischen
mope betrübt sein
moral sittlich, moralisch; die
Moral
morality die Sittlichkeit
morass der Morast
morbid krankhaft
mordant beissend
more mehr, ferner; (once) - noch
einmal
more and more immer mehr
more or less mehr oder weniger
moreover überdies; ausserdem
morning der Morgen; this -
heute früh; heute morgen
morose mürrisch
morphine das Morphium
morrow morgen
morsel der Bissen; das Stückchen

mortal sterblich; tödlich
mortality die Sterblichkeit
mortar der Mörser; der Mörtel
mortgage die Hypothek; verpfänden
mortification die Kasteiung; der
Ärger; die Kränkung
mortify demütigen; kasteien
mortuary die Leichenhalle
mosque die Moschee
mosquito der Moskito
moss das Moos
mossy moosig
most meist; am meisten; meistens; höchstens
mostly meistens
moth die Motte
moth-eaten mottenzerfressen
mother die Mutter
mother-in-law die Schwieger-
mutter
mother-of-pearl die Perlmutter
mother-tongue die Mutter-
sprache
motherly mütterlich
motion die Bewegung; der Antrag
motionless bewegungslos
motive der Beweggrund
motley bunt
motor der Motor
motor-boat das Motorboot
motor-car das Auto; der Wagen
motor-cycle das Motorrad
motor-road die Autobahn; die
Autostrasse
motto der Wahlspruch; das
Motto
mould die Form; formen; der
Schimmel
mouldy schimmelig
moult (sich) mausern
mound der Erdhügel
mount der Berg; der Rahmen;
besteigen, einrahmen
mountain der Berg
mountains das Gebirge
mountainous gebirgig
mountain-range die Gebirgs-
kette
mourn (be)trauern
mourning die Trauer
mouse die Maus

moustache der Schnurrbart
mouth die Mund; das Maul; die Mündung
mouthpiece das Mundstück; der Wortführer
move (sich) bewegen; (um)ziehen; die Bewegung, der Zug
move (set in motion) in Bewegung setzen
moveable beweglich
movement die Bewegung
mow mähen
mower der Mäher
much viel; sehr
muck der Mist; der Dreck
mud der Schlamm
muddle die Unordnung; verwirren
muddy schlammig; schmutzig
muff der Muff; der Dummkopf
muffle unwickeln; einhüllen
muffler das Halstuch
mug der Becher
mulberry die Maulbeere
mule das Maultier
mulled wine der Glühwein
multiple vielfach
multiplication die Multiplikation
multiply (sich) vermehren
multitude die Menge
mumble (to) murmeln
mumps der Ziegenpeter
municipal städtisch
munificence die Freigebigkeit
murder der Mord; ermorden
murderer der Mörder
murderous mörderisch
murmur murmeln; das Murren; das Gemurmel
muscle der Muskel
muscular muskulös
muse (nach)sinnen; die Muse
museum das Museum
mushroom der Pilz
music die Musik
musical musikalisch
musician der Musiker
muslin der Musselin
mussel die Muschel
must müssen
mustard der Senf
muster mustern; aufbringen

musty muffig; dumpfig
mute stumm; der, die Stumme
mutilate verstümmeln
mutineer der Meuterer
mutiny die Meuterei; meutern
mutter murmeln; murren
mutton das Hammelfleisch
mutual gegenseitig
mutuality die Gegenseitigkeit
muzzle das Maul, die Mündung, der Maulkorb; Maulkorb anlegen
my mein, meine, mein
myopic kurzsichtig
myriad die Myriade
myrtle die Myrte
mysterious gehimnisvoll
mystery das Geheimnis
mystic mystisch; geheimnisvoll
mystify täuschen
myth die Mythe; die Sage
mythology die Mythologie
mythological mythologisch

N

nail der Nagel; nageln
naïve unbefangen; naiv
naked nackt, bloss; -ness die Nacktheit
name der Name, nennen; -less namenlos; -ly nämlich; -sake der Namensvetter
nap das Schläfchen
nape das Genick
napkin die Serviette; die Windel
narrate erzählen
narration die Erzählung
narrow eng, schmal; -minded engherzig; -ness die Enge
nasty eklig; widerlich
natal Geburts . . .
nation das Volk; die Nation
national national
nationality die Staatsangehörigkeit
native der, die Eingeborene; einheimisch
natural naturlich
naturalist der Naturforscher
naturalize einbürgern; naturalisieren

nature die Natur
naught nichts; die Null
naughty unartig
nautical nautisch
naval airman der Marineflieger
navigable schiffbar
navigate schiffen; steuern
navigation die Schiffahrt
navy die Flotte; die Marine
near nahe, in der Nähe; **-ly** beinahe, ungefähr
nearness die Nähe
neat nett; sauber
neatness die Sauberkeit
necessaries die Bedürfnisse *pl*
necessary notwendig; nötig
necessity die Notwendigkeit; das Bedürfnis
neck der Hals
necklace as Halsband
necktie die Krawatte
need die Not; nötig haben, brauchen
needful bedürftig
needle die Nadel
needy bedürftig; arm
nefarious schändlich
negative negativ; verneinend
neglect die Vernachlässigung, vernachlässigen; **neglectful** nachlässig; **negligence** die Nachlässigkeit
negotiate verhandeln; unterhandeln
negotiation die Unterhandlung
neigh wiehern
neighbour der Nachbar
neighbourhood die Nachbarschaft
neighbouring benachbart
neighbourly nachbarlich, freundlich
neither keiner; **neither . . . nor** weder . . . noch; auch nicht
nephew der Neffe
nerve der Nerv
nervous nervös
nest das Nest; nisten
nestle sich anschmiegen
net das Netz
nettle die Nessel
neutral neutral
neutrality die Neutralität

never niemals; nie
nevertheless trotzdem; dennoch; nichtsdestoweniger
new neu
news die Nachricht; die Neuigkeit
newspaper die Zeitung
New Year das Neujahr
New Year's Eve der Silvester
next nächst; zunächst
nib die Spitze
nibble knabbern
nice fein; nett; artig
nickel das Nickel
nickname der Spitzname
niece die Nichte
niggardly geizig
nigh nahe; beinahe
night die Nacht; **last -** gestern abend; **by -** nachts; **-ly** nächtlich
nightingale die Nachtigall
nightmare das Alpdrücken
nimble flink
nip zwicken
nipple die Brustwarze
nitric acid die Salpetersäure
nitrogen der Stickstoff
no nein; kein
nobility der Adel
noble adlig; edel
nobleman der Edelmann
nobody niemand
nod nicken
noise der Lärm; **noiseless** geräuschlos; **noisy** geräuschvoll
nominal namentlich; nominell
nominate ernennen
none keiner, keine, keines
nonsense der Unsinn
non-smoker der Nichtraucher
nook der Winkel
noon der Mittag
nor noch; auch nicht
normal normal
north der Norden, nördlich; **northerly** nördlich
nose die Nase; **-dive** der Sturzflug
nostril das Nasenloch
not nicht
notable bemerkenswert
notch die Kerbe

note das Zeichen, die Note, der Ton, das Briefchen; bemerken, notieren
noted berühmt
note-paper das Briefpapier
nothing nichts
notice die Beobachtung, die Kündigung, die Notiz, die Anzeige, die Bekanntmachung; bemerken; **to give -** kündigen
notification die Meldung; die Anzeige
notify bekannt machen; anzeigen
notion der Begriff
notoriety die Offenkundigkeit
notorious allbekannt
nourish ernähren
nourishment die Nahrung
novel neu; der Roman
novelty die Neuheit
novice der Anfänger
now jetzt; nun; **nowadays** heutzutage; **now and then** dann und wann
nowhere nirgends
noxious schädlich
nude nackt
nudity die Nacktheit
nuisance die Plage; der Unfug
numb betäuben
number die Zahl, die Nummer; zählen
number-plate das Nummernschild
numerous zahlreich
nun die Nonne
nurse die Amme, die Pflegerin; pflegen
nursery die Kinderstube
nut die Nuss; die Mutter
nutcracker der Nussknacker
nutrition die Ernährung; **nutritious** nahrhaft
nylon das Nylon

O

oak die Eiche
oar das Ruder
oasis die Oase
oath der Schwur; der Eid
oats der Hafer
obdurate halsstarrig

obedience der Gehorsam; **obedient** gehorsam
obey gehorchen
object der Gegenstand, der Zweck; einwenden
objection der Einwand
obligation die Verpflichtung
oblige verpflichten; nötigen
obliging gefällig
obliterate auslöschen
oblivion die Vergessenheit
oblivious vergesslich
oblong länglich; das Rechteck
obnoxious anstößig
obscene unanständig
obscure dunkel; unbekannt
obscurity die Dunkelheit
observant aufmerksam
observation die Beobachtung; die Bemerkung
observe beobachten; bemerken
observer der Beobachter
obsolete veraltet
obstacle das Hindernis
obstinacy die Hartnäckigkeit
obstinate hartnäckig
obstruct hindern; aufhalten
obstruction das Hindernis
obtain erlangen; erhalten
obtrude sich aufdrängen
obvious deutlich; klar
occasion die Gelegenheit; **die** Veranlassung
occasional gelegentlich
occident der Westen
occult geheim; verborgen
occupant der Inhaber; der Bewohner
occupation die Beschäftigung; die Besetzung; der Besitz; der Beruf
occupy beschäftigen; bewohnen; besetzen
occur vorkommen
occurrence das Ereignis
ocean der Ozean
oculist der Augenarzt
odd ungerade; seltsam; einzeln
odious verhasst; abscheulich
odorous duftend; wohlriechend
odour der Duft; der Geruch
of von, aus, an, bei, über
off von; weg; fort; ab; auf der Höhe von

offal der Abfall
offence die Beleidigung; das Vergehen
offend beleidigen; verstossen
offensive anstossig; die Offensive
offer anbieten; das Angebot
offhand unvorbereitet; unhöflich
office das Büro; das Amt
officer der Beamte; der Offizier
official amtlich; der Beamte
often oft
oil das Öl; oily ölig
ointment die Salbe
old alt; oldish ältlich
old-fashioned altmodisch
omelet der Eierkuchen
omission die Auslassung; die Unterlassung
omit auslassen, versäumen
omnipotent allmächtig
omniscient allwissend
on auf; an; weiter
one ein; einzig; man
once einmal; einst
one-sided einseitig
onion die Zwiebel
onlooker die Zuschauer
only einzig; nur
onslaught der Angriff
onward vorwärts
open offen; (sich) öffnen
open-handed freigebig
opening die Öffnung; der Anfang
openness die Offenherzigkeit
opera die Oper
operate wirken; operieren
opinion die Meinung
opponent der Gegner
opportune gelegen
opportunity die Gelegenheit
oppose sich widersetzen; entgegenstellen
opposite entgegengesetzt, gegenüber; das Gegenteil
opposition der Widerstand; die Opposition
oppress bedrücken
oppression die Unterdrückung
oppressive (unter)drückend
option die Wahl
optional wahlfrei
opulence der Reichtum
opulent wohlhabend

or oder
orange die Apfelsine
oration die Rede
orator der Redner
orbit die Bahn
orchard der Obstgarten
orchestra das Orchester
orchid die Orchidee
ordain bestimmen; ordinieren
ordeal die Feuerprobe
order befehlen, bestellen; der Befehl, die Ordnung, die Bestellung
orderly ordentlich
ordinance die Verordnung
ordinary gewöhnlich
ore das Erz
organ das Organ; die Orgel
organize organisieren
organization die Einrichtung; die Organisation
orgy die Orgie
orient der Osten; der Orient
oriental östlich
orifice die Öffnung
origin der Ursprung; die Herkunft
original ursprünglich
originate hervorbringen; entstehen
ornament die Verzierung
ornate geziert
orphan das Waisenkind
oscillate schwingen
oscillation die Schwingung
ostensible angeblich
ostentatious prahlend
ostrich der Strauss
other ander; each - einander
otherwise anders; sonst
ought sollte; sollten
our unser
ourselves wir selbst, uns
oust ausstossen; vertreiben
out aus; hinaus; heraus
outbid überbieten
outbreak der Ausbruch
outburst der Ausbruch
outcast ausgestossen; der (die) Ausgestossene
outcome das Ergebnis
outcry der Aufschrei
outdo übertreffen
outer äusser

outfit die Ausrüstung
outhouse das Nebengebäude
outing der Ausflug
outlaw der Geächtete; ächten
outlay die Auslage
outlet der Ausgang; der Auslass
outline der Umriss; skizzieren
outlive überleben
outlook die Aussicht
outnumber an Zahl übertreffen
outpost der Vorposten
outrage schmählich behandeln, schänden; die Gewalttätigkeit, die gröbliche Beleidigung
outrageous abscheulich
outright gänzlich
outset der Anfang
outside ausser, äusserst; der Äussere; draussen
outsider der Aussenseiter
outskirt die Grenze
outspoken freimütig
outstrip überholen
outwards auswärts, äusserlich
outweigh überwiegen
outwit überlisten
ovation die Ovation
oven der Backofen
over über; übrig; vorüber
overawe einschüchtern
overbalance umkippen
overbearing herrisch
overboard über Bord
overburden überladen
overcast bedeckt
overcharge überteuern
overcoat der Mantel
overcome überwinden
overcrowded überfüllt
overdone übertrieben; übergar
overdraft die Überziehung
overdue überfällig
overexpose überbelichten
overflow (to) überfliessen; der Überfluss
overhead oben
overhear überhören
overjoyed hocherfreut
overlook übersehen
overpower (to) überwältigen
overrate überschätzen
overrun überschwemmen
overseas über See

overseer der Aufseher
overshadow verdunkeln
oversight das Versehen
oversleep (sich) verschlafen
overstrain überanstrengen
overt offen
overtake einholen
overthrow umstürzen; der Sturz; die Niederlage
overtime die Überstunden *pl*
overture die Ouvertüre; der Vorschlag
overturn umstürzen
overweight das Übergewicht
overwhelm überwältigen
overwork (sich) überarbeiten
owe schuldig sein; verdanken
owing to infolge
owl die Eule
own eigen; zugeben; besitzen
owner der Eigentümer; der Besitzer
ownership der Besitz
ox der Ochs
oxygen der Sauerstoff
oyster die Auster
ozone das Ozon

P

pace der Schritt, die Geschwindigkeit; das Tempo; schreiten
pacific friedlich
Pacific der Stille Ozean
pacify beruhigen
pack das Paket, der Pack, das Rudel; die Meute; packen
package Bündel
packer der Packer
packet das Päckchen
packing die Verpackung
pact der Vertrag
pad das Polster, der Schreibblock; polstern
paddle das Ruder; paddeln; planschen
paddock das Gehege
padlock das Vorhängeschloss
pagan der Heide; heidnisch
page der Page; die Seite
pageant das Festspiel
pageantry der Prunk

pall der Eimer
pain der quälen; der Schmerz
painful schmerzhaft; schmerzlich
painstaking arbeitsam
paint die Farbe, der Anstrich; malen, anstreichen
painter der Maler, die Malerin; der Anstreicher
painting das Gemälde; die Malerei
pair das Paar; paaren
palace der Palast
palatable schmackhaft
palate der Gaumen
palatinate die Pfalz
pale blass; bleich; erbleichen
paleness die Blässe
Palestine Palästina
paling der Pfahlzaun
pall das Bahrtuch
pallid blass; bleich
palm die Palme; die Handfläche
palpable offenbar; fühlbar
palpitate klopfen
palpitation das Herzklopfen
paltry armselig
pamper verzärteln
pamphlet die Flugschrift
pan die Pfanne
pancake der Pfannkuchen
pander fröhnen
pane die (Fenster)Scheibe
pang das Weh; die Angst
panic die Panik
panorama das Panorma
pansy das Stiefmütterchen
pant keuchen
panther der Panther
pants die Unterhose
papal päpstlich
paper das Papier; die Zeitung; der Zettel; tapezieren; **wall-** die Tapete
paper-clip die Heftklammer
paper-hanger der Tapezierer
parable das Gleichnis
parachute der Fallschirm
paradise das Paradies
paragraph der Absatz
parallel parallel
paralyze lähmen
paralysis die Lähmung
paralytic gelähmt

parapet die Brustwehr
parapet (**bridge**) das Geländer
parasol der Sonnenschirm
parcel das Paket
parch (aus)dörren
parchment das Pergament
pardon die Verzeihung; verzeihen
pardonable verzeihlich
pare beschneiden
parentage die Elternschaft
parenthesis die Parenthese; die Klammer
parents die Eltern *pl*
parish die Gemeinde
parishioner das Pfarrkind
park der Park; parken
parking das Parken
parking-meter die Parkuhr
parliament das Parlament
parlour das Wohnzimmer
parody die Parodie
parole das Ehrenwort; die Parole
parrot der Papagei
parsimonious sparsam
parsimony die Sparsamkeit
parsley die Petersilie
parsnip die Pastinake
parson der Pfarrer
part der Teil, die Rolle; (sich) trennen; scheiteln; **take -** teilnehmen
partake zu sich nehmen
partial teilweise; eingenommen
partiality die Vorliebe; die Parteilichkeit
participant der Teilnehmer
participate teilnehmen
particle das Teilchen
particular besonder
particularity die Seltsamkeit
particularly besonders
particulars die Einzelheiten *pl*
parting der Abschied; der Scheitel
partisan der Parteigänger
partition die Scheidewand; die Teilung
partly zum Teil
partner der Teilhaber
partnership die Teilhaberschaft
partridge das Rebhuhn
party die Partei; die Gesellschaft; die Partie

pass (ver) (durch)gehen, vorüber-
gehen, vorbeigehen; der Pass
passage der Durchgang; die
Durchfahrt; die Überfahrt; der
Korridor
passenger der Passagier; der (die)
Reisende
passenger-train der Personenzug
passer-by der Vorübergehende
passion die Leidenschaft
passionate leidenschaftlich
passive passiv
passport der Reisepass
password das Losungswort
past vorbei, nach; die Vergangenheit
paste die Paste, der Teig, der
Kleister; kleistern, kleben
pasteboard die Pappe
pastime der Zeitvertreib
pastry das Tortengebäck
pasture die Weide; weiden
pat der Klaps; klopfen
patch der Fleck; flicken
patent das Patent; offenbar
paternal väterlich
path der Pfad
patience die Geduld
patient geduldig; der Patient
patrimony das Erbgut
patriot der Patriot
patriotic patriotisch
patriotism der Patriotismus
patrol die Patrouille; patrouil-
lieren
patronize begünstigen
patronizing gönnerhaft
pattern das Muster
pauper der, die Arme
pause die Pause; pausieren
pave pflastern
pavement das Pflaster; der Bürgersteig
paw die Pfote
pawn das Pfand; verpfänden
pawnbroker der Pfandleiher
pawnshop das Leihhaus
pay bezahlen; die Bezahlung, der
Lohn; - **attention** achtgeben
payable zahlbar; fällig
payment die Zahlung
pea die Erbse

peace der Friede
peaceful friedlich; ruhig
peach der Pfirsich
peacock der Pfau
peahen die Pfauhenne
peak die Spitze; der Gipfel
peal das Geläute
pear die Birne
pearl die Perle
peasant der Bauer
peasant-woman die Bäuerin
peasantry das Landvolk
peat der Torf
pebble der Kieselstein
peck picken
pectoral Brust . . .
peculiar besonder; seltsam
peculiarly besonders
peculiarity die Eigentümlich-
keit
pedantic pedantisch
peddle hausieren
pedestrian der Fussgänger
pedigree der Stammbaum
pedlar der Hausierer
peel die Schale; schälen
peep gucken; der Blick
peerless unvergleichlich
peevish verdriesslich
peg der Pflock; der Haken; die
Klammer
pelican der Pelikan
pell-mell verworren
pelt das Fell; bewerfen
pen die Feder; **fountain-** die
Füllfeder; der Füller
penholder der Federhalter
penal Straf . . .; strafbar
penalty die Strafe
pencil der Bleistift
pendulum das Pendel
penetrate durchdringen; eindringen
peninsula die Halbinsel
penitent reuig; der Büsser
penitentiary das Zuchthaus
pennant der Wimpel
pension die Pension, die Rente;
pensionieren
pensive gedankenvoll
pent up eingeschlossen
penurious geizig
penury die Armut

people das Volk, die Leute *pl*; bevölkern
pepper der Pfeffer
peppermint die Pfefferminze
peppery gepfeffert
perambulator der Kinderwagen
perceive wahrnehmen; bemerken
perception Wahrnehmung
perch der Barsch, die Stange; sich setzen
perchance vielleicht
peremptory unbedingt
perfect vollkommen; ausbilden
perfection die Vollkommenheit
perfidious treulos
perfidy die Treulosigkeit
perforate durchlöchern
perform ausführen; aufführen
performance die Ausführung, die Leistung; die Aufführung; die Darstellung
perfume der Wohlgeruch; das Parfüm
perhaps vielleicht
peril die Gefahr
perilous gefährlich
period die Periode
periodical periodisch; die Zeitschrift
perish umkommen; sterben
perjure falsch schwören
perjurer der Meineidiger
perjury der Meineid
permanent fortdauernd
permission die Erlaubnis
permit erlauben; der Erlaubnisschein
pernicious verderblich
perpetrate verüben
perpetual fortwährend; ewig
perpetuity die Ewigkeit; für immer
persecute verfolgen
persecution die Verfolgung
perseverance die Beharrlichkeit
persevere beharren
person die Person
personal persönlich
personify verkörpern
perspective die Perspektive; die Aussicht
perspicacity die Scharfsichtigkeit

perspiration der Schweiss
perspire schwitzen
persuade überreden
persuasion die Überredung
persuasive überredend
pert naseweis; keck
peruse durchlesen
perverse verkehrt; verstockt
perversion die Verkehrung; die Verdrehung
pervert (to) verkehren; verdrehen; verderben
pervious durchlässig
pest die Pest; die Plage
pestilence die Pestilenz
pet hätscheln; der Liebling
petition die Bittschrift
petrify versteinern
petrol das Benzin
petroleum das Petroleum
petticoat der Unterrock
petty klein; kleinlich
petulant gereizt
pew der Kirchenstuhl
pewter das Zinn
phase die Phase
pheasant der Fasan
phial das Fläschchen
philanthropic menschenfreundlich
philanthropist der Menschenfreund
philatelist der Briefmarkensammler
philosopher der Philosoph
philosophy die Philosophie
phlegm der Schleim
phonetics die Phonetik
photograph photographieren; die Photographie
photographer der Photograph
phrase die Phrase; der Satz
physical physisch
physician der Arzt
physics die Physik
pianist der Klavierspieler
piano das Klavier; **grand-** der Flügel
pick picken, pflücken; die Auswahl
pickle pökeln; einmachen
picklock der Dietrich
pickpocket der Taschendieb

pictorial illustriert
picture schildern; die Bild
picturesque malerisch
pie die Pastete
piece das Stück; die Figur
piece together zusammensetzen
pier die Landungsbrücke
pierce durchstechen; durchbohren
piety die Frömmigkeit
pig das Schwein
pigeon die Taube
pigeon-hole das Fach
pig-iron das Roheisen
pigmy der Zwerg
pike der Hecht
pile der Pfahl; (heap) der Haufen; aufhäufen
pilfer stehlen; mausen
pilgrim der Pilger
pill die Pille
pillage die Plünderung; plündern
pillar der Pfeiler; die Säule
pillory der Pranger
pillow das Kopfkissen
pilot der Pilot, der Lotse, lotsen; der Flugzeugführer; führen
pimple der Pickel
pin heften; die Nadel
pincers die Kneifzange
pinch zwicken, kneifen; der Kniff, der Druck
pine die Kiefer; sich grämen, sich sehnen
pineapple die Ananas
pink die Nelke; rosa
pinnacle die Spitze; der Spitzturm
pint die Pinte; der Schoppen
pioneer der Pionier; der Bahnbrecher
pious fromm
pipe die Pfeife, die Röhre; das Rohr; pfeifen
piracy die Seeräuberei
pirate der Seeräuber
pistol die Pistole
piston der Kolben
piston-rod die Kolbenstange
pit die Grube; das Parterre
pitch verpichen; das Pech, der Standort; der Platz, die Tonhöhe, aufstellen, aufschlagen, stimmen

pitch-fork die Heugabel
pitcher der Krug
piteous kläglich
pith das Mark; die Kraft
pithy kernig
pitiful mitleidig; erbärmlich
pitman der Bergmann
pity das Mitleid
pity (it is a) es ist schade
pivot der Zapfen; der Angelpunkt
placard das Plakat
place der Ort, die Stelle, die Stätte, der Platz; legen, stellen, setzen
placid gelassen; ruhig
plague die Plage, die Seuche; die Pest; plagen
plain eben; einfach; die Ebene; ebnen
plainness die Klarheit
plaintiff der Kläger
plaintive kläglich
plait die Flechte, der Zopf; flechten
plan der Plan; planen
plane der Hobel, die Fläche; eben, flach; ebnen, hobeln; (-tree) die Platane
planet der Planet
plank die Planke; die Bohle
plant die Pflanze, die Anlage; pflanzen
plantation die Plantage
planter der Pflanzer
plaster das Pflaster, der Stuck, der Putz; bepflastern, tünchen; - of Paris der Gips
plasterer der Gipsarbeiter; der Stuckateur
plate das Blech, die Platte, die Tafel, der Teller, das Silbergeschirr; plattieren, versilbern
platform die Plattform; die Rednerbühne; der Bahnsteig; das Parteiprogramm
platinum das Platin
play das Spiel, das Schauspiel; spielen
player der Spieler
playground der Spielplatz; der Schulhof
plea die Ausrede; der Prozess; das Gesuch

plead plädieren; verteidigen
plead guilty sich schuldig bekennen
pleasant angenehm; freundlich
pleasantness die Freundlichkeit
pleasantry der Spass
please gefallen; befriedigen
please (if you) Bitte!
pleased zufrieden; erfreut
pleasure das Vergnügen; das Belieben
pledge das Pfand, die Bürgschaft, das Gelübde; verpfänden, verbürgen, zutrinken
plenipotentiary der Bevollmächtigte
plentiful reichlich
plenty die Fülle; der Überfluss
pleurisy die Brustfellentzündung
pliable, pliant biegsam
plight der Zustand; verpfänden, versprechen
plod mühsam gehen; sich abmühen
plodder der Büffler
plot der Platz, die Parzelle, der Anschlag, die Verschwörung; anzetteln
plough der Pflug; pflügen
pluck der Mut, pflücken
plug der Pflock, der Stecker; zustopfen
plum die Pflaume
plumage das Gefieder
plumber der Klempner
plume die Feder; (sich) putzen
plump beleibt; dick; fett
plum-pudding der Plum pudding
plunder die Beute; plündern
plunge tauchen
ply betreiben, regelmässig fahren; die Lage
pneumatic tyre der Luftreifen
poach wildern
poached eggs verlorene Eier
poacher der Wilddieb
pocket die Tasche; in die Tasche stecken
pod die Hülse; die Schote
poem das Gedicht
poet der Dichter
poetical poetisch
poetry die Poesie; die Dichtkunst

point die Spitze; der Punkt; spitzen, zeigen
pointed spitz
pointer der Zeiger; der Hühnerhund
poise das Gleichgewicht; die Haltung
poison das Gift; vergiften
poisonous giftig
poke stossen, schüren, stecken
poker der Feuerhaken
pole der Pol; die Stange
police die Polizei
policeman der Polizist; der Schutzmann
police-station die Polizeiwache
policy die Politik; die Klugheit; die Police
polish der Glanz, die Politur, die Wichse; polieren, wichsen
polite höflich
politeness die Höflichkeit
politic politisch; schlau
politician der Politiker
politics die Politik
poll der Kopf; die Person; (election) die Wahlliste
poll stutzen; Stimme abgeben
polling das Wählen; **-booth** die Wahlzelle
pollute beflecken; verunreinigen; schänden
pomatum die Pomade
pommel der Knauf; puffen
pomp der Prunk; der Pomp
pompous prunkvoll; pomphaft
pond der Teich
ponder erwägen
ponderous schwer
pontiff der Papst
pony das Pony; der Pferdeschwanz (**hair**)
pool der Pfuhl, zusammenlegen
poop das Heck
poor arm
pop der Puff, der Knall; puffen, knallen
poplar die Pappel
poppy der Mohn
populace der Pöbel
popular populär; volkstümlich
populate bevölkern
population die Bevölkerung

populous volkreich
porcelain das Porzellan
porch die Vorhalle
pore die Pore
pork das Schweinefleisch
porous porös
porpoise das Meerschwein
porridge der Haferbrei
port der Hafen; der Portwein; das Backbord
portable tragbar
portal das Portal
porter der Träger; der Pförtner
portfolio die Mappe
portion der Teil; teilen
portly beleibt
portmanteau der Koffer
portrait das Portät
portray abmalen; schildern
position der Stand; die Stellung; die Lage; der Standpunkt
positive bestimmt; sicher; positiv
possess besitzen
possession der Besitz
possessor der Besitzer
possibility die Möglichkeit
possible möglich
post der Pfahl, der Pfosten, die Post; absenden
postage das Porto
postage stamp die Briefmarke
postal-order die Postanweisung
postman der Briefträger
postmark der Poststempel
posterior später; hinter
posterity die Nachwelt
post-office das Postamt
postpone verschieben
postscript die Nachschrift
posture die Stellung; die Haltung
pot der Topf
potato die Kartoffel
potent stark
potential möglich
potion der Trank
pottery die Töpferware
pouch der Beutel
poulterer der Geflügelhändler
poultry das Geflügel
pound das Pfund; zerstossen
pour giessen
poverty die Armut

powder das Pulver, der Puder; pudern, streuen
power die Kraft; die Macht; die Gewalt; **-station** das Kraftwerk
powerful mächtig
powerless machtlos
practicable ausführbar
practical praktisch
practice die Praxis; die Ausübung; das Verfahren; der Brauch
practise (sich) üben; ausüben; einüben
prairie die Prärie
praise das Lob; loben
praiseworthy lobenswert
prank der Possen; der Streich
prate, prattle das Geschwätz; schwatzen
pray beten; bitten
prayer das Gebet
preach predigen
preacher der Prediger
preamble die Einleitung
precarious unsicher
precaution die Vorsicht
precedence der Vorrang; der Vortritt
precedent der Präzedenzfall
precept die Vorschrift
precinct der Bezirk; der Bereich
precious kostbar; edel
precipice der Abgrund
precipitate (herab)stürzen; übereilen; der Niederschlag
precise genau
precision die Genauigkeit
precocious frühreif
precocity die Frühreife
precursor der Vorläufer
predecessor der Vorgänger
predict vorhersagen
prediction die Weissagung
predilection die Vorliebe
predominance das Vorherrschen
predominant vorherrschend; überweigend
predominate vorherrschen
preface die Vorrede; einleiten
prefer vorziehen
preferable vorzuziehend
preference der Vorzug
preferment die Beförderung
pregnant schwanger

prejudice das Vorurteil
preliminary vorläufig
prelude das Vorspiel
premature vorzeitig; verfrüht
premeditate vorher überlegen
premeditation der Vorbedacht,
premier der Premierminister
premises das Grundstück
premium die Prämie
preparation die Vorbereitung,
die Zubereitung
prepare (sich) vorbereiten
prepay (to) vorausbezahlen;
frankieren
preponderance das Übergewicht
preponderant überwiegend
preponderate überwiegen
preposterous widersinnig
prerogative das Vorrecht
presage die Vorbedeutung, die
Ahnung; prophezeien
prescribe verschreiben
prescription das Rezept; die
Vorschrift
presence die Gegenwart
present gegenwärtig; die Gegenwart; das Geschenk; darstellen;
schenken
presentiment das Vorgefühl
presently sogleich; bald
preservation die Bewahrung
preservative das Schutzmittel
preserve bewahren; einmachen
preserves die Konserven pl
preside den Vorsitz führen
president der Präsident
press die Presse; pressen, drängen, drücken
pressing dringend
pressure der Druck
presume vermuten
presumption die Vermutung
presumptive mutmasslich
presumptuous anmassend
pretence der Vorwand
pretend vorgeben; beanspruchen
pretension der Ausspruch
pretext der Vorwand
pretty hübsch; niedlich; ziemlich
prevail (be)herrschen; vorherrschen
prevalence das Vorherrschen

prevalent überwiegend; vorherrschend; überall verbreitet
prevent zuvorkommen; verhindern
preventative das Schutzmittel
prevention die Verhinderung
previous vorhergehend
prey (booty) die Beute; rauben
prey (bird of) der Raubvogel
price der Preis
priceless unschätzbar
prick der Stich; stechen
prickle der Stachel; der Dorn
pride der Stolz; der Hochmut;
sich brüsten
priest der Priester
prim (demure) zimperlich
primary erst; Haupt . . .
prime vorzüglichst; hauptsächlich; erste
primer das Elementarbuch
primitive primitiv; ursprünglich
primrose die Primel
prince der Fürst; der Prinz
princely fürstlich
principal der Vorsteher, das
Kapital; hauptsächlich
principality das Fürstentum
principle Grundsatz
print drucken; der Druck
printer der (Buch)drucker
prior früher
priority der Vorzug
prison das Gefängnis
prisoner der (die) Gefangene
privacy die Zurückgezogenheit
private privat, persönlich; der
Gemeine
privation die Entbehrung
privilege das Vorrecht
Privy Council der Staatsrat
prize der Preis; schätzen
probability die Wahrscheinlichkeit
probable wahrenscheinlich
probation die Probezeit; die
Probe
probe sondieren; prüfen
problem das Problem
procedure das Verfahren
proceed fortfahren; hervorge-
hen; verfahren
proceedings das Verfahren

proceeds der Ertrag
process das Verfahren; die Methode; der Prozess
procession die Prozession
proclaim verkünden
procrastinate aufschieben
procreate (er)zeugen
procure beschaffen; erlangen; kuppeln
prodigal verschwenderisch
prodigality die Verschwendung
prodigious erstaundlich; ungeheuer
prodigy das Wunder
produce produzieren, hervorbringen, vorführen; das Erzeugnis, das Produkt
production die Erzeugung
productive produktiv; fruchtbar
profane gottlos; profan; entweihen
profess bekennen
profession der Beruf; die Erklärung; das Bekenntnis
professional Berufs . . .
professor der Professor
proffer anbieten
proficient tüchtig
profile das Profil
profit der Vorteil, der Gewinn; nutzen
profitable vorteilhaft
profligate verworfen; liederlich
profound tief; gründlich
profuse über mässig; überreich
profusion der Überfluss
progeny die Nachkommenschaft
program das Progamm
progress der Fortschritt; fortschreiten
prohibit verbieten
prohibition das Verbot
project der Plan; planen
projectile das Wurfgeschoss
projector der Projektionsapparat
prologue der Prolog
prolong verlängern
prolongation die Verlängerung
promenade der Spazierweg; der Spaziergang
prominence das Hervorragen
prominent hervorragend
promiscuous unterschiedlos

promise das Versprechen; versprechen
promontory das Vorgebirge
promote fördern
promotion die Beförderung; die Förderung
prompt prompt; schnell; pünktlich; veranlassen
prompter der Souffleur
promulgate bekanntmachen
promulgation die Verbreitung
prone geneigt
prong die Zinke
pronged zackig
pronounce aussprechen
pronunciation die Aussprache
proof die Probe; der Beweis
proof-sheet der Korrekturbogen
prop stützen; die Stütze
propagate fortpflanzen; erzeugen; verbreiten
propagation die Fortpflanzung; die Verbreitung
propel vorwärtsstreiben
propeller der Propeller; die Schiffsschraube
proper eigentlich, anständig, richtig
property das Eigentum; die Eigenschaft
prophecy die Prophezeiung; prophezeien
prophet der Prophet
proportion das Verhältnis; der Anteil
proportional verhältnismässig
proposal der Vorschlag; der Antrag
propose vorschlagen; Antrag machen
proposition der Vorschlag
proprietor der Eigentümer
prosaic prosaisch
prose die Prosa
prosecute (gerichtlich) verfolgen
prosecution die Verfolgung
prospect die Aussicht
prosper gedeihen
prosperity die Wohlfahrt
prosperous gedeihlich; glücklich
prostrate hingestreckt; entkräftet

protect (be)schützen
protection der Schutz
protest der Protest, der Einspruch; protestieren
protestant der Protestant
protract verzögern
proud stolz
prove prüfen; beweisen
proverb das Sprichwor
proverbial sprichwörtlich
provide versehen; versorgen
provided vorausgesetzt
providence die Vorsehung
province die Provinz
provision der Vorrat
provisions die Lebensmittel *pl*
provocation die Herausforderung
provoke reizen
prow der Bug
prowess die Tapferkeit
proximity die Nähe
proxy die Stellvertretung; die Vollmacht
prude die Spröde
prudence die Vorsicht
prudery die Ziererei
prune die Backpflaume; beschneiden
prussic acid die Blausäure
psalm der Psalm
public das Publikum; öffentlich
public-house das Wirtshaus
publican der Gastwirt
publish bekanntmachen; verlegen; herausgeben
publisher der Verleger
pudding der Pudding
puddle der Pfuhl; die Pfütze
puerile kindisch
puff der Hauch; schnaufen
puff up (sich) aufblähen
pull der Zug; ziehen
pulley die Rolle
pulmonary Lungen . . .
pulp der Brei; das Mark
pulpit die Kanzel
pulse der Puls
pumice der Bimsstein
pump die Pumpe; pumpen
pumpkin der Kürbis
pun das Wortspiel
punch die Bowle; der Faustschlag;

das Locheisen; schlagen, stossen, durchlochen
punctual pünktlich
punctuality die Pünktlichkeit
punctuate interpunktieren
punctuation die Interpunktion
puncture der Stich, das Loch, die Reifenpanne; stechen
pungent beissend; scharf
punish (be)strafen
punishable strafbar
punishment die Strafe
puny winzig; schwach
pupil der Schüler
puppet die Puppe
puppy der junge Hund
purchase der Einkauf; (ein)-kaufen
pure rein
pure (genuine) echt; lauter
purgative das Abführmittel
purgatory das Fegefeuer
purge die Reinigung; Abführmittel
purge (political or police) die Säuberungsaktion; - **(to)** abführen; purgieren
purify reinigen
purity die Reinheit
purloin entwenden
purple der Purpur; purpurfarben
purport der Inhalt, der Sinn; bedeuten
purpose der Zweck; die Absicht
purr (to) schnurren
purse die Börse; das Porte-monnaie
purser der Zahlmeister
pursue verfolgen
pursuit die Verfolgung
purvey versorgen; versehen
purveyor der Lieferant
pus der Eiter
push der Stoss, der Schub; stossen, drängen
puss die Mieze
put (to), place setzen; legen; stellen; stecken; **put aside** beiseitelegen; - **down** hinlegen; - **on (clothes)** anziehen, **(hat, glasses)** aufsetzen, **(weight)** zunehmen, **(light, radio)** anschalten; - **out (hand)** ausstreck

en, (light, radio) ausschalten;
- out of action ausser Betrieb
setzen
putrefaction die Fäulnis
putrefy (ver)faulen
putrid faul; verdorben
putty der Glaserkitt
puzzle das Rätsel; verwirren
pygmy der Zwerg

Q

quadrangle der Hof; das Viereck
quadruped der Vierfüsser
quadruple vierfach
quagmire der Sumpfboden
quail die Wachtel
quaint seltsam; -ness die Seltsamkeit
quake zittern; beben
qualification die Befähigung; die Einschränkung
qualify befähigen; einschränken
quality die Qualität; die Eigenschaft
qualm die Übelkeit
quantity die Anzahl; die Menge
quarrel der Streit, der Zank
quarrelsome zänkisch
quarry der Steinbruch
quarter das Viertel
quarterly vierteljährlich
quarters das Quartier
quash unterdrücken
quaver die Achtelnote; zittern
quay der Kai
queen die Königin
queer seltsam; wunderlich; unwohl
quench löschen
query die Frage; bezweifeln
quest das Suchen
question die Frage; (be)fragen, zweifeln; ask - eine Frage stellen
queue die Schlange
quick schnell; lebendig; lebhaft
quicken beschleunigen
quickness die Geschwindigkeit die Lebhaftigkeit
quicksilver das Quecksilber
quiet ruhig; die Ruhe

quilt die Steppdecke
quit verlassen; quitt; los
quite ganz, gänzlich
quittance die Quittung
quiver zittern
quotation das Zitat; die Anführung; die Preisangabe
quote berechnen, zitieren

R

rabbet die Fuge; die Nut
rabbi der Rabbiner
rabbit das Kaninchen
rabble der Pöbel
rabid wütend
rabies die Tollwut
race die Rasse
race das Wettrennen; rennen
race course die Rennbahn
racial rassisch
rack das Gestell; der Ständer; das Gepäcknetz; foltern; **to go to rack and ruin** zugrunde gehen
racket der Tennisschläger
racket der Lärm
racy kräftig
radar das Radar
radiance das Strahlen
radiant strahlend
radical ursprünglich, gründlich, radikal
radio das Radio
radish der Rettich
radius der Radius; der Strahl
raffle auslosen
raft das Floss
rafter der Sparren
rag der Lumpen
ragamuffin der Strassenbengel
rage die Wut; wüten
ragged zerlumpt
raid der Überfall, die Razzia; überfallen
rail der Riegel, die Schiene; **by -** mit der Eisenbahn
rail die Ralle (**bird**)
rail spotten; fluchen
railing das Geländer; die Reling
railroad, railway die Eisenbahn
rain der Regen; regnen

rainbow der Regenbogen
rainy regnerisch
raise aufheben, errichten, erhöhen, erwecken
raisin die Rosine
rake der Rechen, die Harke, die Wüstling; harken, scharren
rally (sich) wieder sammeln; die Versammlung; das Treffen
ram der Widder; rammen
ramble umherstreifen, herumschweifen
ramification die Verzweigung
rampant zügellos; wuchernd
rampart der Wall
ramshackle baufällig
rancid ranzig
rancorous erbittert
rancour der Groll; der Hass
random (at) aufs Geratewohl
range die Reihe, der Raum, der Bereich; die Bergkette, der Herd; die Auswahl, die Reichweite; ordnen, sich reihen, sich erstrecken
rank der Rang, die Reihe
rank üppig; ranzig; unanständig
ransack durchsuchen; plündern
ransom das Lösegeld
rap der Schlag; schlagen, klopfen
rapacious raubgierig
rape der Raub; die Notzucht; rauber
rapid schnell
rapidity die Schnelligkeit
rapids die Stromschnellen *pl*
rapt hingerissen
rapture die Entzückung
rare selten
rarefy (sich) verdünnen
rareness, rarity die Seltenheit
rascal der Schurke
rash rasch, hastig; der Hautausschlag
rasher die Speckscheibe
rashness Übereilung
rasp die Raspel; raspeln
raspberry die Himbeere
rat die Ratte
ratable steuerpflichtig
rate das Mass, der Satz, der Grad, die Steuer; schätzen, besteuern
rather eher, lieber, ziemlich

ratify bestätigen
ratio das Verhältnis
rational rational, vernunftsgemäss
rattle das Gerassel, die Klapper, das Röcheln; rasseln
rattlesnake die Klapperschlange
raucous heiser
ravage die Verwüstung; verwüsten
rave toben; schwärmen, rasen
ravel verwickeln
raven der Rabe
ravenous gefrässig
ravine der Hohlweg
ravish rauben, entzücken, schänden
ravishing hinreissend
raw roh
ray der Strahl
ray (fish) der Rochen
raze auskratzen, zerstören
razor das Rasiermesser
razor-blade die Rasierklinge
reach erreichen, einholen; die Reichweite, der Bereich
react gegenwirken, reagieren
reaction die Gegenwirkung; die Reaktion
read lesen
readable lesbar
reader der Leser, das Lesebuch
readily gern, leicht
readiness die Bereitwilligkeit
ready bereit, fertig
real wirklich, echt
real estate das Grundeigentum
reality die Wirklichkeit
realize verwirklichen; sich vergegenwärtigen; einsehen
realm das Königreich
ream das Ries (Papier)
reap ernten
reaper der Schnitter; die Mähmaschine
reappear wiedererscheinen
rear der Hintergrund;
reason die Vernunft, die Ursache; der Grund; urteilen
reasonable vernünftig
reasoning die Beweisführung
rebate der Rabatt
rebel der Rebell; rebellieren

rebellion die Empörung
rebellious rebellisch
rebound der Rückprall; zurückprallen
rebuke rügen
recall zurückrufen
recant widerrufen
recast umformen
recede zurückgehen
receipt der Empfang; die Quittung
receive empfangen; aufnehmen
recent neu
recently neulich
receptacle der Behälter
reception der Empfang; die Aufnahme
receptionist die Empfangsdame
recess die Vertiefung
recipe die Rezept
reciprocal wechselseitig
reciprocate erwidern
recital der Vortrag
recite vortragen; aufsagen
reckless sorglos
recklessness die Unbesonnenheit
reckon rechnen; denken
reclaim urbar machen; zurückfordern
recognition die Erkennung
recognize erkennen
recoil zurückspringen
recollect sich erinnern
recollection die Erinnerung
recommend empfehlen
recommendation die Empfehlung
recompense entschädigen; belohnen
reconcilable versöhnbar
reconcile versöhnen
reconciliation die Versöhnung
reconsider wieder erwägen
reconstruct wiederaufbauen
reconstruction der Wiederaufbau
record die Urkunde, der Bericht, der Rekord, die Schallplatte; aufzeichnen
recorder der Registrator
records das Archiv; die Akten
recourse die Zuflucht

recover wiederbekommen; wiedererlangen; sich erholen
recovery die Genesung; die Wiedererlangung
recreation die Erholung
recrimination die Gegenbeschuldigung
recruit der Rekrut; rekrutieren
rectangle das Rechteck
rectangular rechtwinklig
rectify berichtigen
rector der Pfarrer; der Rektor
rectory das Pfarrhaus
recur wiederkehren
recurrence die Wiederkehr
recurring wiederkehrend
red rot
redbreast das Rotkehlchen
redden rot werden; erröten
reddish rötlich
redeem zurückkaufen, einlösen, erlösen
redeemer der Erlöser
redemption die Erlösung
red-hot rotglühend
redistribute wiederverteilen
redistribution die Wiederverteilung
redouble verdoppeln
redoubtable furchtbar
redress die Abhilfe
red-tape die Bürokratie
reduce verkleinern; vermindern; bezwingen
reduction die Verminderung
reed das Ried; das Rohr
reef das Riff
reek dunsten, stark riechen, übel riechen; der Rauch
reel die Haspel, die Rolle; taumeln
re-elect wiederwählen
re-embark wiedereinschiffen
re-establish wiederherstellen
refectory der Speisesaal
refer (sich) beziehen
referee der Schiedsrichter
reference die Beziehung; die Referenz; **with - to** in Bezug auf
refine verfeinern; raffinieren
refined verfeinert
refinery die Raffinerie
refit ausbessern

reflect nachdenken; zurückwerfen; wiederspiegeln
reflection die Überlegung; die Wiederspiegelung
reform die Reform; (sich) bessern, reformieren
reformation die Reformation; die Besserung
reformer der Reformator
refraction die Brechung
refractory widerspenstig
refrain (sich) enthalten
refresh sich erfrischen; auffrischen
refreshment die Erfrischung
refrigerate abkühlen
refrigerator der Kühlschrank
refuge die Zuflucht
refugee der Flüchtling
refusal die Verweigerung
refuse verweigern; sich weigern
refuse der Abfall; der Ausschuss
refute widerlegen
regal königlich
regale bewirten; erquicken
regard der Blick, die Achtung, Rücksicht; ansehen, betreffen; **kind -s** herzliche Grüsse
regardless (of) unbekümmert
regatta die Regatta
regency die Regentschaft
regenerate wiedererzeugen
regent der Regent
regiment das Regiment
region die Gegend, das Gebiet;
register das Register; **- (to)** einschreiben, aufgeben
registrar der Standesbeamte
regret bedauern; das Bedauern
regular regelmässig
regularity die Regelmässigkeit
regulate regeln
regulation die Regulierung; die Ordnung; die Vorschrift
rehearsal die Probe
rehearse Probe halten
reign die Regierung; regieren
reimburse wiedererstatten; zurückzahlen; entschädigen
rein der Zügel
reindeer das Renntier
reinforce verstärken
reinforcement die Verstärkung

reinsurance die Rückversicherung
reinsure rückversichern
reissue die Neuausgabe; wiederausgeben
reiterate wiederholen
reject verwerfen
rejoice (to) (sich) erfreuen
rejoicing die Freude
rejoin wieder treffen, vereinigen
rejoinder die Erwiderung
relapse der Rückfall; zurückfallen
relate berichten; erzählen; sich beziehen
related verwandt
relation der (die) Verwandte; das Verhältnis
relative verhältnismässig, bezüglich; der (die) Verwandte
relax erschlaffen; mässigen; sich entspannen
relay wiederlegen; der Staffellauf; übertragen
release freilassen
relent sich erweichen lassen
relentless unbarmherzig
reliable zuverlässig
reliability die Zuverlässigkeit
reliance das Vertrauen
relic der Überrest; die Reliquie
relief die Erleichterung; die Unterstützung
relieve erleichtern; helfen; unterstützen
religion die Religion
relinquish aufgeben, verzichten
relish geniessen
reluctance das Widerstreben
reluctant unwillig; ungern
rely sich verlassen
remain bleiben
remainder der Rest
remains die Überreste *pl*
remark die Bemerkung; bemerken
remarkable bemerkenswert, merkwürdig
remarry wiederheiraten
remedy das Heilmittel, das Hilfsmittel; abhelfen
remember sich erinnern
remembrance die Erinnerung

remind erinnern

remiss nachlässig

remission die Vergebung, die Erlassung

remit übersenden

remittance die Geldsendung

remnant der Rest

remonstrance die Vorstellung

remonstrate Vorstellungen machen

remorse die Gewissenbisse *pl*

remorseless gefühllos

remorselessness die Gefühllosigkeit

remote entfernt

removal der Umzug; die Beseitigung

remove entfernen; beseitigen

remunerate belohnen

remuneration die Belohnung

rend zerreissen

render leisten; übersetzen; zurückgeben; erweisen

rendezvous das Stelldichein

renegade der Renegat

renew erneuern

renewal die Erneuerung

renounce verzichten; entsagen

renown der Ruhm

renowned berühmt

rent (house), die Miete; - (farm) die Pacht; der Riss; mieten

reopen wiederöffnen

reorganization die Neugestaltung

reorganize reorganisieren

repair die Ausbesserung; ausbessern; reparieren

reparation die Entschädigung

repast die Mahlzeit

repay zurückzahlen

repeal die Aufhebung, der Widerruf; abschaffen

repeat wiederholen

repel zurückstossen

repent bereuen; Busse tun

repentance die Reue

repetition die Wiederholung

replace ersetzen; zurückstellen

replenish wiederfüllen

replete gefüllt

reply die Erwiderung, die Antwort; antworten

report der Bericht, der Knall; berichten

reporter der Reporter; der Berichterstatter

repose die Ruhe; ruhen

reprehend tadeln

reprehensible tadelnswert

represent vorstellen; vertreten

representation die Vorstellung; die Vertretung

representative der Vertreter

repress unterdrücken

reprieve die Begnadigung; begnadigen

reprimand der Verweis; einen Verweis erteilen

reprint der Neudruck; wieder abdrucken

reprisal die Wiedervergeltung

reproach der Vorwurf; vorwerfen

reproduce wiedererzeugen, fortpflanzen

reproof der Tadel

reprove tadeln

reptile das Reptil

republic die Republik

repudiate verwerfen; nicht anerkennen

repudiation die Verwerfung

repugnance die Abneigung

repugnant zuwider

repulse zurücktreiben

repulsive abstossend

reputable angesehen; anständig

reputation der Ruf; das Ansehen

repute (by) vom Hörensagen

request das Gesuch; ersuchen

require verlangen, brauchen

requisite erforderlich; das Erfordernis

rescue die Rettung; retten

research die Forschung

resemblance die Ähnlichkeit

resemble gleichen

resent übelnehmen

resentful empfindlich, grollend

resentment der Groll

reservation der Vorbehalt; die Vorbestellung

reserve reservieren; die Reserve, die Zurückhaltung

reserved zurückhaltend

reside wohnen

residence der Wohnsitz; das Wohnhaus
resident wohnhaft
resident der Bewohner
residue der Rest
resign aufgeben; verzichten, sich ergeben
resignation die Ergebung; der Rücktritt
resigned ergeben
resin das Harz
resist widerstehen
resistance der Widerstand
resolute entschlossen
resolution der Entschluss
resolve beschliessen; der Entschluss
resolved entschlossen
resort die Zuflucht; Zuflucht nehmen; der Erholungsort
resource das Hilfsmittel
respect die Hinsicht, die Achtung; hochachten
respectable achtbar
respectful ehrerbietig
respecting in Bezug auf
respective betreffend
respiration das Atmen
respire atmen
respite der Aufschub
resplendent glänzend
respond antworten; reagieren
responsibility die Verantwortlichkeit
responsible verantwortlich
rest ruhen; die Ruhe, der Rest
restaurant das Restaurant, die Gaststätte
restive aufsässig
restless ruhelos
restlessness die Unruhe
restoration die Wiederherstellung
restore wiederherstellen
restrain zurückhalten; einschränken
restraint die Zurückhaltung
restrict einschränken
restriction die Einschränkung
result das Ergebnis; folgen
resume wieder aufnehmen
resumption die Wiederaufnahme
resurrection die Auferstehung

resuscitate wiedererwecken
retail der Kleinhandel; im kleinen verkaufen
retail-price der Kleinhandelspreis
retailer der Kleinhändler
retain zurückhalten
retaliate vergelten
retaliation die Vergeltung
retard verzögern, aufhalten
retardation die Verzögerung
retention das Zurückhalten
retina die Netzhaut
retinue das Gefolge
retire (sich) zurückziehen
retirement die Zurückgezogenheit
retort die Erwiderung; erwidern; die Retorte
retouch auffrischen
retrace zurückverfolgen
retreat der Rückzug, die Zurückgezogenheit; sich zurückziehen
retrench verschanzen; (sich) einschränken
retrenchment die Verschanzung; die Einschränkung
retribution die Vergeltung
retrograde rückgängig
retrospect der Rückblick
return die Rückgabe, die Rückkehr; zurückgeben, zurückkehren
return ticket die Rückfahrkarte
reunion die Wiedervereinigung
reunite sich wiedervereinigen
reveal offenbaren
revel schwelgen, schwärmen; die Lustbarkeit
revelation die Offenbarung; die Entdeckung
reveller die Schwelger
revenge die Rache; sich rächen
revengeful rachsüchtig
revenue das Einkommen
reverberate widerhallen
revere verehren
reverence die Ehrerbietung; die Ehrfurcht
reverend ehrwürdig
reverent ehrerbietig
reverse das Gegenteil, die Rückseite; umstossen, umkehren

revert zurückkommen; heimfallen

review der Überblick, die Rezension, die Revue; besprechen, mustern

reviewer der Rezensent

revile schmähen

revise revidieren

revision die Revision

revival die Erweckung; die Wiederbelebung

revive wieder beleben; wieder aufleben

revocable widerruflich

revoke widerrufen

revolt die Empörung; sich empören

revolution die Umdrehung; die Revolution

revolve umdrehen; sich drehen; überlegen

revolver der Revolver

reward die Belohnung; belohnen

rheumatic rheumatisch

rheumatism der Rheumatismus

rhinoceros das Nashorn

rhubarb der Rhabarber

rhyme reimen; der Reim

rhythm der Rhythmus

rib die Rippe

ribbon das Band

rice der Reis

rich reich

riches der Reichtum

rick der Schober

rickety rachitisch; baufällig

rid befreien; get - of loswerden

riddle das Rätsel; durchlöchern

ride der Ritt, die Fahrt; reiten, fahren

rider der Reiter

ridge der Rücken; der Grat

ridicule lächerlich machen; der Spott

ridiculous lächerlich

rifle die Büchse, das Gewehr; plündern

rig (to) auftakeln

rigging die Takelage

right recht; das Recht; gerade, richtig, rechts

righteous gerecht

rigid steif; unbeugsam

rigorous streng

rigour die Strenge

rim der Rand; der Radkranz

rind die Rinde

ring der Ring, der Kreis, der Klang; läuten, klingeln

ringleader der Rädelsführer

rink die Eisbahn; die Rollschuhbahn

rinse (aus)spülen

riot der Aufruhr; die Schwelgerei

rioter der Aufrührer

rip aufreissen; aufschneiden

ripe reif

ripen reifen

ripeness die Reife

ripple sich kräuseln; kräuseln

rise das Steigen, die Erhöhung, der Aufgang; die Steigerung; aufstehen, aufgehen, sich erheben

risible lächerlich

risk die Gefahr; wagen

risky gewagt; gefährlich

rite (ceremony) der Ritus

rival der Mitbewerber, der Nebenbuhler; wetteifern

rivalry der Wetteifer

river der Fluss

rivet das Niet; nieten

road die Strasse

roadway der Fahrdamm

roam umherstreifen

roar das Gebrüll; brüllen

roast der Braten; braten

roast beef der Rinderbraten

rob (be)rauben

robber der Räuber

robbery der Raub

robe die Robe; das Kleid

robin das Rotkehlchen

robust kräftig; rüstig

rock der Felsen; schaukeln

rocket die Rakete

rocking-chair der Schaukelstuhl

rod die Rute; der Stab; die Stange

roe der Rogen; das Reh

rogue der Schelm

roll die Rolle, das Brötchen; rollen

roller die Roll; die Walze

rollicking ausgelassen

romance der Roman; die Romanze

romantic romantisch
romp der Wildfang; herumtoben
roof das Dach; überdachen
rook die Saatkrähe; der Turm (chess)
room der Raum; das Zimmer; die Stube
roost die Sitzstange; sitzend schlafen
root die Wurzel; (ein)wurzeln
rope das Seil; der Strick; das Tau
rosary der Rosenkranz
rose die Rose
rosette die Rosette
rosy rosig
rot faulen; die Fäulnis
rotary drehend
rotate sich drehen
rotation die Drehung; der Kreislauf
rouge die Schminke
rough rauh; grob
roughness die Rauheit
round rund, rund herum; die Runde; runden
roundabout das Karussell; umständlich
rouse aufwecken; erwecken; erregen
rout die wilde Flucht; in die Flucht schlagen
route der Weg
rove umherwandern
row die Reihe; redern; der Lärm; zanken
rowdy lärmend; der Raufbold
royal königlich
royalty das Königtum; die Tantieme
rub reiben
rubber der Gummi
rubber-stamp der Stempel
rubbish der Schutt; der Abfall; der Schund; der Quatsch
ruby der Rubin
rudder das Steuerruder
ruddy rötlich
rude roh; grob
rudeness die Roheit
rudimentary Anfangs . . .
rudiments die Anfangsgründe *pl*
rue bereuen
ruff die Krause

ruffian der Raufbold
ruffle (to) zerknittern
rug die Decke; die Brücke
rugged rauh
ruin die Ruine, der Verfall; **zu** Grunde richten
rule die Regel, die Herrschaft; linieren, beherrschen
ruler das Lineal; der Herrscher
rum der Rum
ruminate wiederkäuen; grübeln
rummage (to) durchstöbern
rumour das Gerücht
rump der Steiss
rump-steak das Rumpfstück
rumple zerdrücken; runzeln
run der Lauf, die Fahrt; rennen, laufen
runaway der Flüchtling
rung die Sprosse
runner der Läufer
rupture der Bruch; brechen
rural ländlich
rush der Sturz, der Andrang, der Hochbetrieb; sich stürzen; die Binse
russet braunrot
rust der Rost; rosten
rustic ländlich
rustle rascheln
rusty rostig
rut das Geleise; die Brunst
ruthless unbarmherzig
ruthlessness die Unbarmherzigkeit
rye der Roggen

S

Sabbath der Sabbat
sable der Zobel
sabre der Säbel; niedersäbeln
sack der Sack; plündern
sackcloth die Sackleinwand
sacrament das Sakrament
sacred heilig
sacrifice das Opfer; opfern
sacristy die Sakristei
sacrilege die Gotteslästerung
sad traurig
sadden betrüben
saddle der Sattel; satteln

saddler der Sattler
sadness die Traurigkeit
safe der Geldschrank; sicher, unversehrt
safely wohlbehalten
safety die Sicherheit
sagacious scharfsinnig
sagacity der Scharfsinn
sage weise; die Salbei
sago der Sago
sail das Segel; segeln
sailor der Matrose
saint der (die) Heilige
salad der Salat
salad-bowl die Salatschüssel
salary das Gehalt; die Besoldung
sale der Verkauf; der Ausverkauf
saleable verkäuflich
salesman der Verkäufer
saline salzig; die Saline
saliva der Speichel
sallow gelblich
salmon der Lachs
saloon der Salon
salt das Salz; salzig, (ein)salzen
salt-cellar das Salzfässchen
saltpetre der Salpeter
salubrious gesund
salutary heilsam
salutation der Gruss
salute die Begrüssung; begrüssen; der Salut; salutieren
salvage die Bergung
salvation die Rettung
Salvation Army die Heilsarmee
salve die Salbe; retten
salver der Präsentierteller
same selb
same (all the) trotzdem
sample das Muster; die Probe
sanatorium das Sanatorium
sanctify heiligen
sanction die Bestätigung; bestätigen, genehmigen
sanctity die Heiligkeit
sanctuary das Heiligtum, die Freistätte
sand der Sand
sand-bank die Sandbank
sandy sandig
sandwich das belegte Brot
sane geistig, gesund

sanguine hoffnungsvoll
sanguinary blutig; (cruel) blutdürstig
sanitary Gesundheits . . .
sanitation die Gesundheitspflege; die sanitäre Anlage
sanity der gesunde Verstand
sap der Saft; untergraben
sapling der junge Baum
sapphire der Saphir
sarcasm der beissende Spott
sarcastic beissend; sarkastisch
sardine die Sardine
sardonic sardonisch
sash die Schärpe; die Binde
Satan der Teufel; der Satan
satanic satanisch
satchel die Mappe
satiate sättigen
satiation die Sättigung
satin der Atlas
satire die Satire
satirical satirisch
satisfaction die Befriedigung
satisfactory(ily) befriedigend
satisfy befriedigen
Saturday der Sonnabend; der Samstag
sauce die Tunke
saucer die Untertasse
saunter schlendern
sausage die Wurst
savage wild; der Wilde
save sparen, retten, erlösen; ausser
savings die Ersparnisse pl
savings bank die Sparkasse
saviour der Erlöser; der Heiland
savour der Geschmack; schmecken
savoury schmackhaft
saw die Säge; sägen
sawdust die Sägespäne pl
say sagen
saying das Sprichwort
scab der Grind
scabbard die Scheide
scaffold das Gerüst; das Schafott
scald die Brandwunde; verbrühen
scale die Schuppe, die Schale, der Mass-stab, die Tonleiter; ersteigen
scales die Waage

scalp die Kopfhaut
scaly schuppig
scan prüfen
scandal der Skandal, die Schmach
scandalize Ärgernis geben
scandalous schändlich
scant(y) knapp
scapegoat der Sündenbock
scar die Narbe; vernarben
scarce selten, knapp
scarcely kaum
scarcity der Mangel
scare (er)schrecken; scheuchen
scare der Schreck, die Panik
scarecrow die Vogelscheuche
scarf der Schal, die Halsbinde
scarlet scharlachrot
scarlet fever der Scharlach
scathing scharf
scatter (sich) zerstreuen
scavenger der Strassenkehrer
scene die Szene; die Bühne
scenery die Landschaft
scent das Parfüm, der Geruch, der Duft, die Witterung; wittern, riechen
sceptre das Zepter
schedule das Verzeichnis; aufzeichnen
scheme der Plan, das Schema; Pläne schmieden
scholar der Gelehrte; der Schüler
school die Schule; schulen
schooner der Schoner
science die (Natur) Wissenschaft
scientific wissenschaftlich
scientist der Wissenschaftler
scissors die Schere
scoff spotten
scold schelten
scoop die Schaufel; schöpfen
scooter der Roller
scope der Gesichtskreis; der Spielraum
scorch (ver)sengen
score die Kerbe, die Partitur, die Punktzahl; anmerken, markieren
scorn die Verachtung, der Spott; verachten
scornful verächtlich
scorpion der Skorpion
scoundrel der Schurke
scour scheuern; putzen

scourge die Plage, die Geissel; plagen, peitschen
scout der Späher; der Pfadfinder
scowl finster blicken
scramble klettern, sich reissen um; das Balgerei
scrambled egg das Rührei
scrap das Stückchen; der Ausschnitt; der Streit
scrape kratzen; scharren
scraper das Kratzeisen
scratch der Riss, die Schramme; kratzen
scrawl das Gekritzel; kritzeln
scream der Schrei; schreien
screech kreischen
screen der Schirm; schirmen
screw die Schraube; schrauben
scribble das Gekritzel; kritzeln
script die Schrift
Scripture die heilige Schrift
scrub scheuern, schrubben, das Gestrüpp
scruple der Skrupel; das Bedenken
scrupulous gewissenhaft
scrutinize untersuchen
scuffle die Balgerei; sich balgen
sculptor der Bildhauer
sculpture die Bildhauerkunst; meisseln, aushauen
scum der (Ab)Schaum
scurf die Haarschuppen *pl*
scurrilous gemein
scurvy der Skorbut; gemein
scuttle der Kohlenbehälter; versenken; eilen
scythe die Sense
sea die See; das Meer
seal die Robbe, der Seehund, der Stempel, das Siegel; siegeln
sealing-wax der Siegellack
seam der Saum; die Naht
seaman der Matrose; der Seeman
seamstress die Näherin
search das Suchen; suchen, untersuchen; -light der Scheinwerfer
season die Jahreszeit; würzen
seasonable zeitgemäss
seasoning die Würze
seat der Sitz, der Sessel; hinsetzen
second zweite; die Sekunde; unterstützen

secondary untergeordnet; sekundär

second-hand gebraucht

secondly zweitens

secrecy die Heimlichkeit

secret geheim, heimlich; das Geheimnis

secretary der Sekretär

Secretary (of State) der Minister

secrete verbergen, **(med.)** ausscheiden

secretion (med.) die Ausscheidung

sect die Sekte

section der Schnitt; der Teil

secular weltlich; hundertjährig

secure sicher; sichern

securities die Wertpapiere *pl*

security die Sicherheit

sedative das Beruhigungsmittel

sedentary sitzend

sediment der Bodensatz

seduce verführen

see sehen; einsehen

see der Bischofssitz

seed der Same; die Saat

seedy schäbig

seek suchen; begehren

seem scheinen

seemingly scheinbar

seemly schicklich

see-saw die Wippe

seethe sieden

seize ergreifen

seizure die Ergreifung; der Anfall, die Beschlagnahme

seldom selten

select auslesen; auswählen; auserwählt

selection die Auswahl

self selbst

self-conceit der Eigendünkel

self-conscious befangen

selfish selbstsüchig

selfishness die Selbstsücht

self-praise das Eigenlob

self-reliance das Selbstvertrauen

self-service shop der Selbstbedienungsladen **- restaurant** das Automatenrestaurant

self-will der Eigenwille

self-willed eigensinnig

sell verkaufen

seller der Verkäufer

semblance der Anschein

senate der Senat

senator der Senator

send (to) senden, schicken; **- for** holen, kommen lassen

sender der Absender

senile greisenhaft

senior älter

sensation die Empfindung; die Sensation

sensational sensationell

sense der Sinn, das Gefühl, der Verstand; fühlen

senseless sinnlos

sensibility die Empfindlichkeit

sensible vernünftig

sensitive empfindlich

sensual wollüstig; sinnlich

sensuous sinnlich

sentence der Satz, das Urteil; verurteilen

sentiment das Gefühl

sentimental empfindsam

sentry die Schildwache

separable trennbar

separate (sich) trennen; getrennt

separation die Trennung

septennial siebenjährig

septuagenarian der Siebzigjährige

sepulchre das Grab

sequel die Folge

sequence die Reihenfolge

serenade das Ständchen

serene heiter, ruhig

serenity die Heiterkeit; die Ruhe

serf der Leibeigene

serfdom die Leibeigenschaft

sergeant der Sergeant

serial periodisch; Reihen ...

series die Reihe

serious ernst

sermon die Predigt

serpent die Schlange

servant der Diener; das Dienstmädchen

serve dienen; bedienen

service der Dienst; der Gottesdienst

serviceable nützlich; dienlich

servile kriechend; sklavisch

session die Sitzung

set setzen, stellen, richten, untergehen, gerinnen, fassen; der Satz, die Reihe; - **about** daran gehen
set forth darlegen
set out abreisen
set up (sich) etablieren
settle festsetzen; versorgen; abmachen, abschliessen (sich) ansiedeln
settlement die Festsetzung; die Niederlassung; der Abschluss
settler der Ansiedler
sever (sich) trennen
several mehrere; verschieden; einzeln
severe strong
severity die Strenge
sew nähen
sewer der Abzugskanal
sewing-machine die Nähmaschine
sex das Geschlecht
sexton der Küster
sexual geschlechtlich
shabby schäbig
shackle fesseln; die Fessel
shade der Schatten; der Schirm; beschatten
shadow der Schatten
shady schattig
shaft der Schaft; der Stiel; die Deichsel; die Welle; der Strahl
shaggy zottig
shake schütteln; zittern
shaky wackelig
shallow die Untiefe; seicht
sham der Trug; falsch; heucheln
shame die Scham, die Schande, beschämen
shame-faced schamhaft
shameful schändlich
shameless schamlos
shampoo die Haare waschen
shape die Gestalt, der Umriss die Form; gestalten, bilden
share der Anteil, die Aktie; teilen
shareholder der Aktionär
shark der Haifisch
sharp scharf
sharpen schärfen; spitzen
sharpness die Schärfe
shatter zerschmettern
shave (sich) rasieren

shavings der Späne *pl*
shawl der Schal
sheaf die Garbe
shear scheren
sheath die Scheide
shed die Hütte, der Schuppen; vergiessen, abwerfen
sheep das Schaf
sheep-dog der Schäferhund
sheepish blöde
sheer (steep) steil; lauter
sheet die Fläche; das Blatt; das Bettuch; der Bogen
shelf das Brett; das Fach; das Regal
shell die Schale; schälen; die Muschel; die Hülse; aushülsen; die Granate; bombardieren
shelter das Obdach, der Schutz; schützen
shepherd der Schäfer; hüten
shepherdess die Hirtin
sherry der Sherry
shield das Schild; schirmen
shift die Veränderung, die Ausflucht, die Schicht; schieben, (sich) ändern, wechseln
shin das Schienbein
shine der Glanz; glänzen
shingle die Schindel; der Strandkies
shingles (medical) die Gürtelrose
ship das Schiff; verladen, verschiffen
shipbuilding der Schiffbau
shipment die Verladung
shipper der Verschiffer
shipwreck der Schiffbruch
shipyard die Werft
shire die Grafschaft
shirk ausweichen; sich drücken
shirt das Hemd
shirt-sleeve der Hemdärmel
shiver der Schauer; schauern, zittern
shoal die Untiefe; die Menge; der Schwarm
shock der Stoss, der Anstoss; der Schlag; (an)stossen
shocking anstössig; schrecklich
shoddy kitschig
shoe der Schuh; - **(of horse)** das Hufeisen; beschlagen

shoemaker der Schuhmacher

shoe-polish die Schuhwichse

shoot schiessen; (horticul.) sprossen; der Schössling

shooting die Jagd

shooting-star die Sternschnuppe

shop der Laden; einkaufen

shop assistant der Verkäufer

shopkeeper der Ladeninhaber

shore das Ufer, der Strand

short kurz

short-circuit der Kurzschluss

shortcoming der Fehler; der Mangel

shorten kürzer machen

shorthand die Stenographie; die Kurzschrift

shortly bald

shortness die Kürze

shortsighted kurzsichtig

shot der Schuss; die Kugel

shoulder die Schulter; schultern

shout das Geschrei; schreien

shovel die Schaufel

show zeigen; die Schau; die Ausstellung

shower die Schauer; der Regenguss

showy prahlend

shred der Fetzen, das Schnitzel; zerschneiden

shrew die Spitzmaus

shrewd scharfsinnig

shriek der Schrei; kreischen

shrill gellend; schrill

shrimp die Garnele

shrine der Schrein

shrink schrumpfen, einlaufen; - from zurückschaudern

shrivel einschrumpfen

shroud das Grabtuch; (ver)bergen

Shrove Tuesday die Fastnacht

shrub die Staude

shrug Achseln zucken

shudder der Schauder; schaudern

shuffle schieben; mischen; schlurfen

shun meiden

shunt rangieren

shut (sich) schliessen; zumachen

shutter der Fensterladen

shuttle das Schiffchen

shy scheu; schüchtern

shyness die Schüchternheit

sick krank; übel; überdrüssig

sicken krank werden

sickly kränklich

sickness die Krankheit

side die Seite

sidewalk der Bürgersteig

sideways seitwärts

siege die Belagerung

sieve das Sieb

sift sieben

sigh der Seufzer; seufzen

sight das Gesicht; die Sicht; der Anblick; das Schauspiel

sign das Zeichen, der Wink, das Schild; unterzeichnen

signal das Signal; ausgezeichnet, Signale geben

signal-box das Stellwerk

signalize auszeichnen

signature die Unterschrift

signet das Siegel

significance die Bedeutung

signification die Bedeutung

signify bedeuten

silence das Schweigen

silent still; schweigend

silk die Seide

silkworm die Seidenraupe

sill (window) das Fensterbrett

silly albern

silver das Silber; versilbern

similar ähnlich

similarity die Ähnlichkeit

similitude die Ähnlichkeit

simple einfach; einfältig

simplicity die Einfachheit; die Einfalt

simplification die Vereinfachung

simplify vereinfachen

simulate vorgeben; heucheln

simulation die Heuchelei

simultaneous gleichzeitig

sin die Sünde; sündigen

since seit; seitdem; da

sincere aufrichtig

sincerity die Aufrichtigkeit

sinful sündig

sing singen

singe sengen

singer der Sänger

single einzig; einzeln; unverheiratet

singular sonderbar; seltsam

singularity die Sonderbarkeit

sink der Ausguss; sinken, (sich) senken, versenken

sinner der Sünder

sip das Schlückchen; schlürfen

sir der Herr

siren die Sirene

sirloin das Lendenstück

sister die Schwester

sister-in-law die Schwägerin

sit sitzen; - **(down)** (sich) setzen

site die Lage; der Bauplatz

sitting sitzend; die Sitzung

sitting-room das Wohnzimmer

situated gelegen

situation die Lage; die Stellung

size die Grösse; das Format; die Nummer

skate der Schlittschuh; Schlittschuh laufen

skein der Strang

skeleton das Skelett; das Gerippe

sketch die Skizze; skizzieren

skewer der Speiler

ski der Ski; schilaufen

skid der Hemmschuh; ausrutschen

skilful geschickt

skill die Geschicklichkeit

skilled gelernt

skim abschäumen

skin die Haut, der Petz, die Schale; häuten

skip hüpfen; überspringen; der Sprung

skirt der Rock; der Saum

skittle der Kegel

skulk lauern; sich verstecken

skull der Schädel

skunk das Stinktier

sky der Himmel

skylight das Oberlicht

skylark die Lerche

skyscraper der Wolkenkratzer

slab die Platte; die Tafel

slack schlaff

slacken schlaff werden

slake löschen

slam zuschlagen; der Schlemm

slander die Verleumdung; verleumden

slanting schräg

slap der Klaps; klapsen

slate der Schiefer

slaughter das Schlachten; schlachten

slaughter-house der Schlachthaus

slave der Sklave

slavery die Sklaverei

slay erschlagen

sledge der Schlitten

sleek glatt

sleep der Schlaf; schlafen

sleeper der Schläfer; die Schwelle

sleepiness die Schläfrigkeit

sleepless schlaflos

sleepy schläfrig

sleet der Graupelregen

sleeve der Ärmel

sleigh der Schlitten

slender schlank

slice die Schnitte

slide (to) gleiten

slight schwach, gering; die Verachtung; geringschätzig behandeln

slighting geringschätzig

slim schlank

slime der Schleim

slimy schleimig

sling die Schlinge, die Binde; schleudern

slink schleichen

slip ausgleiten; der Fehltritt; schlüpfen; das Versehen; das Stückchen; der Zettel; der Unterrock

slipper der Pantoffel

slippery schlüpfrig

slit schlitzen; der Schlitz

sloe die Schlehe

sloop die Schaluppe

slope der Abhang; sich neigen

sloping abschüssig, schräg

slot der Schlitz

slovenly schlumpig

slow langsam

slowness die Langsamkeit

slug die Wegschnecke

sluggard der Faulenzer

sluggish träge

sluice die Schleuse	**snipe** die Schnepfe
slum das Elendsviertel	**sniper** der Scharfschütze
slumber der Schlummer; schlummern	**snob** der Grosstuer
slump der Preissturz	**snobbishness** die Vornehmtuerei
slur binden; der Schandfleck	**snore** scharchen
slush der Schlamm; der Matsch	**snort** schnauben
sly schlau; verschlagen	**snout** die Schnauze
slyness die Schlauheit	**snow** der Schnee; schneien
smack patschen; der Klaps, der Geschmack	**snowfield** das Schneefeld
small klein	**snub** die Zurechtweisung; abfertigen
small-pox die Pocken *pl*	**snub nose** die Stumpfnase
smart der Schmerz; weh tun; schmuck, schlau	**snuff** der Schnupftabak; schnupfen
smartness die Schärfe; die Eleganz; die Schlauheit	**snug** behaglich
smash zerschmettern	**so** so; also; daher
smattering die oberflächliche Kenntnis	**soak** einweichen
smear beschmieren; die Schmiererei; der Fleck	**soap** die Seife; (ein)seifen
smell riechen; der Geruch	**soar** aufsteigen, sich erheben
smelt schmelzen	**sob** schluchzen
smile das Lächeln; lächeln	**sober** nüchtern
smirk schmunzeln	**sociable** gesellig
smite schlagen	**social** gesellschaftlich
smith der Schmied	**socialism** der Sozialismus
smithy die Schmiede	**socialist** der Sozialist
smock der Arbeitskittel	**society** die Gesellschaft
smoke der Rauch; rauchen	**sock** die Socke; der Strumpf
smooth glatt; glätten	**socket** die Höhle; die Hülse
smother ersticken, bedecken	**soda** die Soda
smoulder schwelen	**sodium** das Natrium
smudge der Schmutzfleck; beschmutzen	**sofa** das Sofa
smuggle schmuggeln	**soft** weich; sanft; gelinde
smuggler der Schmuggler	**soften** erweichen; mildern
smut der Schmutz; die Zoten *pl*	**softness** die Weichheit; die Milde
snack der Imbiss	**soil** beschmutzen; der Boden
snail die Schnecke	**solace** der Trost; trösten
snake die Schlange	**solar** Sonnen . . .
snap at schnappen	**solder** das Lot; löten
snappish bissig	**soldier** der Soldat
snare die Schlinge; verstricken	**sole** besohlen; die Sohle, die Seezunge; einzig
snarl knurren	**solemn** feierlich
snatch erschnappen	**solemnity** die Feierlichkeit
sneak der Kriecher; schleichen	**solicit** dringend bitten; ersuchen
sneer das Hohnlächeln; hohnlächeln	**solicitor** der Anwalt
sneeze niesen	**solid** fest; dauerhaft; gediegen
sniff schnüffeln	**solidity** die Festigkeit
snip schnippen; das Schnitzel	**soliloquy** das Selbstgespräch
	solitary einsam; einzeln
	solitude die Einsamkeit
	soluble löslich
	solution die Lösung
	solve lösen

solvency die Zahlungsfähigkeit
solvent zahlungsfähig
sombre düster
some irgendein; irgendetwas; einige
somebody jemand
something etwas
sometime einmal; einst; ehemalig
sometimes manchmal
somewhat etwas
somewhere irgendwo
son der Sohn
son-in-law der Schwiegersohn
song der Gesang; das Lied
sonnet das Sonett
soon bald
soot der Russ
soothe beruhigen
soothsayer der Wahrsager
sooty russig
sop eintunken
soprano der Sopran; die Sopranistin
sorcerer der Zauberer
sorcery die Zauberei
sordid gemein; schmutzig
sore wund; empfindlich; die wunde Stelle
sorely schwer
sorrow der Kummer; trauern
sorrowful traurig
sorry bekümmert; I am - es tut mir leid
sort die Sorte; die Art
sort out sortieren
soul die Seele
sound erklingen; der Schall; tönen; der Ton; der Laut, das Geräusch; der Sund; sondieren; gesund, kräftig
soup die Suppe
sour sauer
source die Quelle; der Ursprung
south der Süden
southern südlich
sovereign allerhöchst, unfehlbar; der Herrscher
sow säen; die Sau
space der Raum
spacious geräumig
spade der Spaten; das Pik (cards)
span die Spanne; spannen

spare spärlich; übrig, überflüssig; sparen; schonen
spark der Funken
sparkle funkeln
sparrow der Sperling
spasm der Krampf
spatter bespritzen
spawn der Laich; laichen
speak sprechen
speaker der Sprecher; der Redner
spear der Speer; spiessen
special besonder; speziell
specialist der Spezialist
speciality die Spezialität; die Besonderheit
specially besonders
species die Art; - (human) die Gattung
specific bestimmt
specification die Spezifizierung
specify spezifizieren; genau angeben
specimen die Probe
speck der Fleck
speckle sprenkeln
spectacle das Schauspiel; der Anblick
spectacles die Brille
spectacular eindrucksvoll
spectator der Zuschauer
spectre das Gespenst
speculate nachsinnen; spekulieren
speech die Sprache; die Rede
speechday das Schulfest
speechless sprachlos
speed die Eile; eilen; die Geschwindigkeit
speedy schnell
spell der Zauber; buchstabieren
spelling die Rechtschreibung
spend ausgeben (money); verbringen (time)
spendthrift der Verschwender
sphere die Kugel; die Sphäre; der Bereich
spherical kugelförmig
spice das Gewürz; würzen
spider die Spinne
spider's web das Spinngewebe
spike der lange Nagel; (ver)nageln

spill verschütten; vergiessen; der Fidibus

spin spinnen; wirbeln; (sich) drehen

spinach der Spinat

spindle die Spindel

spine der Dorn; das Rückgrat

spinning-wheel das Spinnrad

spinster die alte Jungfer

spiral spiral . . .

spire die Turmspitze

spirit der Geist

spirited lebhaft

spirits die Spirituosen

spiritual geistig; geistlich

spirt spritzen

spit speien; der Speichel

spite der Groll; ärgern

spiteful boshaft

splash spritzen; bespritzen; planschen; der Spritzfleck

spleen die Milz; die üble Laune

splendid glänzend; prächtig

splendour die Pracht

splice splissen

splint die Schiene

splinter der Splitter; splittern

split der Spalt; (sich) spalten

splutter sprudeln

spoil die Beute; rauben, verderben

spoke die Speiche

spokesman der Wortführer

spoliation die Beraubung

sponge der Schwamm

spongy schwammig

spontaneous freiwillig; spontan

spool die Spule

spoon der Löffel

sport der Sport, das Spiel, der Scherz; sich belustigen, scherzen

sportive scherzhaft

spot der Flecken, die Stelle; sprenkeln, bemerken

spotless fleckenlos

spouse der Gatte; die Gattin

spout der Ausguss; die Tülle

sprain die Verrenkung; verrenken

sprat die Sprotte

sprawl sich spreizen

spray (branch) der Zweig

spray (perfume, etc.) der Zerstäuber; die Gischt; bespritzen

spread (to) (sich) ausbreiten

sprig der Spross; das Reis

sprightly lebhaft

spring der Frühling, die Quelle, der Sprung, die Feder; springen, zersprengen

springtime die Frühlingszeit

sprinkle besprengen; sprenkeln

sprout sprossen; die Sprosse

sprouts der Rosenkohl

spruce nett; geputzt

spume der Schaum

spur der Sporn; spornen

spurious falsch; unecht

spurn verschmähen

sputter sprudeln

spy der Spion; spionieren, erspähen

squabble der Streit; streiten

squadron die Schwadron; das Geschwader

squalid ärmlich; schmutzig

squall die Bö, der Schrei; schreien

squander verschwenden

squanderer der Verschwender

square viereckig; das Viereck, der Platz; ehrlich; viereckig machen, ausgleichen

squash zerquetschen; der Schlag

squat (sich) niederkauern

squatter der Ansiedler

squeak, squeal knarren; quieken

squeamish wählerisch

squeeze pressen; drücken

squint schielen

squire der Landjunker

squirm sich winden

squirrel das Eichhörnchen

squirt spritzen

stab der Stich; stechen

stability die Beständigkeit

stabilize stabilisieren

stable der Stall; beständig

stack der Schober; aufstapeln

staff der Stab

stag der Hirsch

stage die Bühne; die Stufe

stage-coach die Postkutsche

stagger taumeln; wanken; verblüffen

stagnant stagnierend; stillstehend; flau

stagnate stagnieren; stocken

staid gesetzt; ruhig

stain der Flecken; beflecken, färben

stainless unbefleckt; rostfrei

staircase das Treppenhaus

stairs die Treppe; **down** - unten; **up** - oben; **go down** - hinuntergehen; **go up** - hinaufgehen

stake der Pfahl, der Einsatz; pfählen, aufs Spiel setzen

stale schal; abgestanden; trocken; veraltet

stalk der Stengel, der Halm; einherschreiten, beschleichen

stall der Stand; die Bude; der Sperrsitz; der Stuhl

stallion der Hengst

stalwart kräftig; handfest

stammer stottern; stammeln

stamp der Stempel, die Briefmarke; stempeln, prägen, stampfen

stanch stillen; hemmen

stand der Stand, das Gestell, der Ständer; stellen, stehen

standard die Standarte; die Norm; die Muster; der Mass-stab; die Währung

standardize vereinheitlichen

standing (rank) der Rang

standstill der Stillstand

stanza die Strophe

staple die Krampe, der Hauptgegenstand

star der Stern

starboard das Steuerbord

starch die Stärke; stärken

stare starren

starling der Star

starry gestirnt

start der Start, der Ruck, der Aufbruch, das Auffahren, der Anfang, der Vorsprung; aufbrechen, anfangen

startle erschrecken

startling erschreckend

starvation das Verhungern

starve verhungern

state der Staat, der Zustand, die Lage, der Prunk; festellen, erklären, angeben

stately stattlich

statement die Feststellung; die Behauptung; die Angabe; der Auszug

statesman der Staatsmann

station der Bahnhof, die Stelle, die Stellung, der Rang, die Station; stellen

stationer der Schreibwarenhändler

statistical statistisch

statistics die Statistik

statue die Bildsäule

stature der Wuchs

statute das Gesetz; das Statut

staunch tüchtig, zuverlässig

stay der Aufenthalt; aufhalten, bleiben

steadfast standhaft

steady fest; gesetzt, beständig; festigen

steak das Steak

steal stehlen; schleichen

stealth die Heimlichkeit; die List

stealthy verstohlen

steam der Dampf; dampfen, dämpfen

steamboat das Dampfboot

steam-engine die Dampfmaschine; die Dampflokomotive

steamer der Dampfer

steed das Ross

steel der Stahl

steep eintauchen; steil

steeple der Glockenturm

steeple-chase das Hindernisrennen

steer steuern

steerage das Zwischendeck

steering das Steuer

steering-gear die Steuerung

steersman der Steuermann

stem der Stamm, der Vordersteven; eindämmen, stemmen, aufhalten

stench der Gestank

stenographer der Stenograph

step der Schritt, die Stufe; treten

sterile unfruchtbar

sterility die Unfruchtbarkeit

sterling echt

stern ernst, streng; das Heck

sternness die Strenge

stew langsam kochen; schmoren
steward der Verwalter
steward (ship) der Schiffskellner; der Aufwärter
stewardess die Aufwärterin
stick der Stock; stecken, stechen, anhängen, (an)kleben
sticky klebrig
stiff steif
stiffen steifen
stiffness die Steifheit
stifle ersticken
stigma der Schandfleck; das Brandmal
stigmatize brandmarken
stile der Zaunübergang
still still; die Stille; stillen; noch immer; doch
stillness die Stille
stilt die Stelze
stilted hochtrabend
stimulant das Reizmittel
stimulate (an)reizen
sting der Stich, der Stachel; stechen
stingy geizig
stink der Gestank; stinken
stipend die Besoldung
stipulate festsetzen
stipulation die Festsetzung; die Klausel
stir sich regen, rühren; die Bewegung, die Aufregung
stirrup der Steigbügel
stitch der Stich, die Masche; nähen, steppen
stock der Stock; der Stamm, die Familie, der Vorrat, die Levkoje, das Kapital; versorgen, aufspeichern
stockbroker der Börsenmakler
stock-exchange die Börse
stockholder der Aktionär
stocking der Strumpf
stocks die Aktien *pl*
stoic der Stoiker; stoisch
stoke schüren
stoker der Heizer
stomach der Magen
stone der Stein; steinern; steinigen
stone (fruit) entsteinen; der Kern
stony steinig

stool der Schemel; der Hocker
stoop sich bücken; sich herablassen
stop der Punkt, der Halt, die Pause; die Haltestelle; halten, stopfen, aufhören
stoppage die Verstopfung
stopper der Stopsel
storage das Lagern
store das Lager, der Vorrat; lagern, aufspeichern
storekeeper storey; der Stock; Ladenbesitzer
stork der Storch
storm der Sturm, das Gewitter; stürmen
story die Geschichte; das Märchen; die Erzählung
stout dick; stark; das Starkbier
stove der Ofen
stow (to) (ver)stauen
straggle umherschweifen; verstreut liegen
straggler der Landstreicher; der Nachzügler
straight gerade; stracks; aufrecht
straighten gerade machen; gerade werden
strain die Anstrengung, die Weise, die Spannung; (sich) anstrengen, verrenken, pressen, seihen
strainer das Sieb
strait eng, schmal
straits die Meerenge
strand der Strand, die Litze, die Strähne; stranden
strange fremd; seltsam
stranger der Fremde; der Neuling
strangle erwürgen
strangulation die Erwürgung
strap der Riemen
stratagem die (Kriegs)list
strategical strategisch
strategy die Strategie
stratosphere die Stratosphäre
stratum die Schicht
straw das Stroh
strawberry die Erdbeere
stray einzeln; verirrt (ab)schweifen
streak der Streifen, der Strich; streifen

streaky streifig
stream der Strom; strömen
street die Strasse
strength die Kraft; die Stärke
strengthen stärken; erstarken
strenuous eifrig; rastlos
stress der Nachdruck, die Betonung, betonen
stretch strecken, sich erstrecken, ausdehnen; die Strecke
stretcher die Tragbahre
strew (be)streuen
strict streng; genau
stride der Schritt; schreiten
strife der Streit
strike schlagen, auffallen, streiken; der Streik
striking auffallend
string die Schnur, die Saite; binden
strip der Streifen; abstreifen, entblössen, berauben
stripe der Streifen, der Striemen; streifen
strive streben; sich bemühen
stroke der Strich; der Schlag, der Zug; streicheln
stroll der Spaziergang; herumschlendern
strong stark
stronghold die Festung
struggle der Kampf; ringen, sich abmühen
strut der Strebebalken; stolzieren
stubble die Stoppel
stubborn hartnäckig
stud der Hemdenknopf; das Gestüt
student der Student
studious fleissig
study studieren; das Studium, das Studierzimmer
stuff der Stoff, das Zeug; füllen
stuffing die Füllung; die Polsterung
stumble stolpern
stumbling-block das Hindernis
stump der Stumpf
stun betäuben
stupefy verblüffen; verdummen
stupendous erstaunlich
stupid dumm
stupidity die Dummheit

stupor die Betäubung
sturdy stark; handfest
stutter stottern
sty der Schweinestall
style der Stil; benennen
stylish modisch
suave verbindlich
subdivide unterteilen
subdue unterwerfen; besiegen; dämpfen
subject der Untertan, der (die) Staatsangehörige, der Gegenstand, das Thema; unterwerfen, ausgesetzt
subjection die Unterwerfung
subjugate unterjochen
sublime erhaben
submarine das Unterseeboot
submerge untertauchen
submission die Unterwerfung
submit vorlegen; sich unterwerfen; sich fügen
subordinate untergeordnet
subscribe unterzeichnen; unterschreiben; beitragen; subskribieren
subscriber der Abonnent
subscription die Unterschrift; der Beitrag; das Abonnement
subsequent folgend
subsequently hernach
subside sich legen
subsidize mit Geld unterstützen
subsidy die Geldbeihilfe
subsist bestehen
subsistence das Dasein
substance der Stoff; die Substanz; die Hauptsache
substantial wirklich; kräftig
substitute der Stellvertreter, der Ersatz; ersetzen
subterfuge die Ausflucht
subterranean unterirdisch
subtle fein, hinterlistig
subtract abziehen
suburb der Vorort
suburban vorstädtisch
subvention die Hilfe
subversion der Umsturz
subvert umstürzen
subway die Unterführung
succeed nachfolgen; gelingen
success der Erfolg

successful erfolgreich
succession die Erbfolge; die Reihenfolge
successor der Nachfolger
successive einander folgend
succour die Hilfe; helfen
succinct kurz ; bündig
succulent saftig
succumb sich ergeben; unterliegen
such solch
suck saugen
suckle säugen
sudden plötzlich
sue verklagen
suet das Nierenfett
suffer leiden; erleiden
suffering das Leiden
suffice genügen
sufficient genügend
suffocate ersticken
suffrage das Stimmrecht; die Wahlstimme
sugar der Zucker; süssen
suggest eingeben; vorschlagen
suggestion die Eingebung; die Andeutung; der Vorschlag
suggestive anregend; andeutend
suicide der Selbstmord
suicidal selbstmörderisch
suit der Anzug, der Prozess, das Gesuch; passen, anpassen
suitable passend
suitcase der Handkoffer
suite das Gefolge; die Reihe; die Zimmereinrichtung
suitor der Bewerber
sulk (to) mürrisch sein; schmollen
sulky mürrisch
sulphur der Schwefel
sulphuric acid die Schwefelsäure
Sultan der Sultan
sultry schwül
sum die Summe, die Rechenaufgabe; zusammenfassen
summary der Hauptinhalt; summarisch
summer der Sommer
summit der Gipfel
summon auffordern; vorladen
summons die Vorladung
sumptuous prächtig

sun die Sonne; sich sonnen
Sunday der Sonntag
sundry verschiedene
sunshine der Sonnenschein
sunny sonnig
sunrise der Sonnenaufgang
sunset der Sonnenuntergang
sunstroke der Sonnenstich
sup zu Abend essen
superabundant überreichlich
superannuate pensionieren
superb herrlich
superficial oberflächlich
superfluous überflüssig
superhuman übermenschlich
superintend beaufsichtigen
superintendence die Oberaufsicht
superintendent der Oberaufseher
superior ober; höher; besser
superiority die Überlegenheit
superlative höchst; der Superlativ
supernatural übernatürlich
superscription die Aufschrift
supersede verdrängen, ersetzen
superstition der Aberglaube
superstitious abergläubisch
superstructure der Oberbau
supper das Abendessen
supplant verdrängen
supple geschmeidig
supplement die Beilage; die Ergänzung
supplementary Ergänzungs . . .
supplicate demütig bitten
supply versehen, verschaffen, liefern; der Vorrat
support die Stütze, die Unterstützung; stützen, unterstützen, ertragen
supportable erträglich
suppose vermuten; annehmen
supposition die Annahme; die Vermutung
suppress unterdrücken
suppression die Unterdrückung
supremacy die Obergewalt
supreme höchst
sure sicher
surely sicherlich
surety die Sicherheit; die Bürgschaft

surf die Brandung
surface die Oberfläche
surfeit die Übersättigung, der Ekel; verekeln
surge die hohe Welle
surgeon der Chirurg
surly mürrisch
surmise vermuten
surmount überragen; überwinden
surname der Familienname
surpass übersteigen; übertreffen
surplus der Überschuss
surprise überraschen, erstaunen; die Überraschung
surprising überraschend; erstaunlich
surrender die Übergabe; (sich) ergeben
surreptitious heimlich
surround umgeben
surroundings die Umgebung
survey besichtigen, vermessen; der Überblick
surveyor der Feldmesser
survival das Überleben; überleben
survivor der (die) Überlebende
susceptible empfänglich
suspect im Verdacht haben; misstrauen
suspected verdächtig
suspend suspendieren; aufschieben; einstellen; aufhängen
suspenders der Strumpfhalter
suspense die Ungewissheit
suspension die Aufschiebung
suspension bridge die Hängebrücke
suspicion der Verdacht; das Misstrauen
suspicious verdächtig; argwöhnisch
sustain stützen; ertragen; unterhalten
sustenance der Unterhalt
swagger prahlen
swallow die Schwalbe; verschlingen, schlucken
swamp der Sumpf; versenken
swampy sumpfig
swan der Schwan
swarm der Schwarm; wimmeln

swathe winden
sway schwanken
swear schwören; fluchen
sweat der Schweiss; schwitzen
sweep fegen, kehren; der Schornsteinfeger
sweet süss; reizend
sweeten süssen
sweetheart das Liebchen
sweetness die Süssigkeit
swell schwellen; die Dünung
swelling die Geschwulst
swift schnell
swiftness die Schnelligkeit
swim schwimmen
swindle (be)schwindeln
swindler der Schwindler
swine das Schwein
swing schwingen
swirl wirbeln
switch die Weiche, der Schalter; schalten
swivel der Drehring
swollen geschwollen
swoon in Ohnmacht fallen; die Ohnmacht
swoop niederschiessen
sword das Schwert
syllable die Silbe
symbol das Sinnbild
symmetrical symmetrisch; ebenmässig
symmetry die Symmetrie; das Ebenmass
sympathetic mitfühlend
sympathize mitfühlen
sympathy das Mitgefühl
symphony die Symphonie
symptom das Symptom
synagogue die Synagoge
synonymous sinnverwandt
synthetic künstlich; synthetisch
syringe die Spritze
system das System
systematic(al) systematisch

T

table der Tisch; die Tafel
table-cloth das Tischtuch
tablet das Täfelchen, die Tablette
tacit stillschweigend

taciturn schweigsam

tack der Stift; die Zwecke; **- (to) on to** anheften

tackle das Gerät; takeln, anfassen

tact das Feingefühl; der Takt

tactician der Taktiker

tadpole die Kaulquappe

tag der Zettel

tail der Schwanz; der Schweif

tailor der Schneider; schneidern

taint der Flecken; beflecken

take (to) (an)nehmen; bringen; **take about** umherführen; **- away** wegnehmen; **- down** herunternehmen, niederschreiben; **- for** halten für; **- in** einnehmen; **- off** abnehmen, ausziehen, aufsteigen; **- over** übernehmen; **- up** aufnehmen, ergreifen

tale die Erzählung

talent das Talent

talented begabt

talk das Gespräch; sprechen, reden; das Gerede; der Vortrag

talkative gesprächig; redselig

talker der Schwätzer

tall lang; hoch

tallness die Höhe

tally das Kerbholz; nachzählen, stimmen

talon die Kralle, die Klaue

tame zahm; zähmen

tameness die Zahmheit

tan die Lohe; gerben, bräunen

tangible fühlbar

tank die Zisterne; der Tank, der Panzer

tankard der Krug

tanker der Tankdampfer

tanner der Gerber

tap das Klopfen, klopfen; der Zapfen; der Hahn; anzapfen, tippen

tape das Zwirnband; **red -** die Bürokratie

tape-measure das Bandmass

tapering spitzig

tapestry die gewirkte Tapete; der Wandteppich

tape-worm der Bandwurm

tar der Teer; teeren

tardy langsam, spät

tare die Wicke

target die Scheibe; das Ziel

tariff der Tarif

tarnish trübe machen; matt werden

tarry zögern; verweilen

tart die Torte; scharf

tartar der Weinstein; der Zahnstein

task (scholastic) die Aufgabe

tassel die Troddel

taste der Geschmack, die Neigung; kosten, schmecken

tasteful geschmackvoll

tasteless geschmacklos

tasty schmackhaft

tatters die Lumpen *pl*

tattle schwätzen; das Geschwätz

tattler der Plauderer

tattoo tätowieren

taunt der Spott; spotten

taut straff

tavern die Schenke

tawny lohfarben

tax besteuern; die Steuer

taxi die Taxe

tea der Tee

tea-pot die Teekanne

tea-spoon der Teelöffel

teach lehren

teacher der Lehrer

team das Gespann; die Mannschaft

tear die Träne, der Riss; (zer)reissen

tease necken; hänseln

teat die Zitze; der Sauger

technical technisch

technique die Technik

tedious langweilig

teem wimmeln

teethe zahnen

teetotaler der Abstinenzler

telegram das Telegramm

telegraph telegraphieren; der Telegraph

telephone der Fernsprecher, das Telefon; telephonieren, anrufen; **- exchange** das Fernsprechamt

telescope das Fernrohr

tell sagen, erzählen

temerity die Verwegenheit

temper die Laune, die Stimmung; die Wut; mässigen, härten
temperance die Mässigkeit
temperate mässig; gemässigt
temperature die Temperatur
tempest der Sturm
tempestuous stürmisch
temple der Tempel; die Schläfe
temporal zeitlich
temporary zeitweilig; vorläufig
tempt versuchen
temptation die Versuchung
tempting verführerisch
tenacious zähe
tenacity die Zähigkeit; die Beharrlichkeit
tenant der Pächter; der Mieter
tend pflegen; sich richten; sich neigen
tendency die Neigung
tender das Angebot; anbieten; der Tender; zart
tenderness die Zärtlichkeit; die Weichheit
tendon die Sehne
tenement die Mietswohnung
tenor der Tenor; der Verlauf; der Inhalt
tense die Zeitform; straff, gespannt
tension die Spannung
tent das Zelt
tentative versuchend; Versuchs . . .
tepid lauwarm
term die Grenze; das Trimester; der Termin, der Ausdruck; nennen
terminate endigen; enden
termination das Ende
terminus die Endstation
terms die Bedingungen *pl*
terrace die Terrasse
terrestrial irdisch
terrible schrecklich; fürchterlich
terrific fürchterlich
terrify erschrecken
territory das Gebiet
terror der Schrecken
test prüfen; die Probe; die Prüfung
testament das Testament
testator der Erblasser

testicle die Hode
testify bezeugen
testimonial das Zeugnis
testimony das Zeugnis; der Beweis
tether anbinden
text der Text; die Bibelstelle
text-book das Lehrbuch
than als
thank danken
thankful dankbar
thankfulness die Dankbarkeit
thankless undakbar
thanks der Dank
thanksgiving die Danksagung
that jener, jene, jenes; dass
thatch das Strohdach; mit Stroh decken
thaw das Tauwetter; tauen
the der, die, das
theatre das Theater
theft der Diebstahl
their ihr, ihre
theirs der, die, das ihrige
them ihnen, sie
theme das Thema
then dann; damals; da; denn
thence daher
theology die Theologie
theorem der Lehrsatz
theoretical theoretisch
there da, dort
there is es gibt
thereafter danach
thereby damit; dadurch
therefore daher; folglich; deswegen
thereupon darauf
thermometer das Thermometer
these diese
they sie
thick dick; dicht
thicken (sich) verdicken
thicket das Dickicht
thickness die Dicke
thickset untersetzt
thief der Dieb
thievish diebisch
thigh der Schenkel
thimble der Fingerhut
thin dünn; verdünnen
thing das Ding; die Sache
think denken; meinen

thinker der Denker
thinness die Magerkeit; die Dünnheit
third dritte; das Drittel
thirdly drittens
thirst der Durst; dürsten
thirsty durstig
thistle die Distel
thither dorthin
thong der Riemen
thorn der Dorn
thorny dornig
thorough durchgehend; gänzlich; gründlich
thoroughfare der Durchgang
though obgleich
thought der Gedanke
thoughtful gedankenvoll; achtsam
thoughtless gedankenlos
thrash prügeln
thrashing eine Tracht Prügel
thread der Faden, der Zwirn; der Zusammenhang; einfädeln
threadbare fadenscheinig
threat die Drohung
threaten drohen
thresh dreschen
threshold die Schwelle
thrift die Sparsamkeit
thrifty sparsam
thrill (durch) schauern; der Schauer
thrive gedeihen
throat die Kehle
throb klopfen, schlagen; der Schlag
throne der Thron
throng das Gedränge; (sich) drängen
through durch
throughout hindurch; durchaus
throw der Wurf; werfen
thrush die Drossel
thrust der Stoss; stossen
thud der dumpfe Schlag
thumb der Daumen
thump der Schlag; der Stoss
thunder der Donner; donnern
thunderbolt der Donnerkeil
thunderclap der Donnerschlag
thunderstorm das Gewitter
Thursday der Donnerstag

thus so, also
thwart durchkreuzen
thyme der Thymian
tick die Zecke, der Überzug; ticken; das Ticken
ticket die Fahrkarte; der Fahrschein; der Zettel
ticket-office der Schalter
tickle kitzeln
tide die Ebbe; die Flut
tidings die Nachrichten *pl*
tidiness die Ordnung
tidy sauber; ordentlich; sauber machen
tie das Band, die Binde; die Krawatte; binden
tier die Reihe
tiger der Tiger
tight fest; dicht; eng
tighten enger machen
tile der Ziegel, die Steinplatte, die Kachel; Platten legen
till bis; die Geldschublade; ackern, pflügen
tiller der Pflüger
tilt kippen
tilt die Neigung; die Plane
timber das Bauholz
time die Zeit, der Takt, das Mal;
timepiece die Uhr
timetable der Fahrplan; der Stundenplan
timely rechtzeitig
timid furchtsam
timidity die Furchtsamkeit
tin das Zinn; eindosen
tin-opener der Dosenöffner
tin-plate das Weissblech
tincture die Tinktur
tinder der Zunder
tinge die Farbe, färben
tingle klingen, jucken
tint der Farbton; färben
tiny winzig
tip die Spitze, das Trinkgeld, der Wink; Trinkgeld geben, kippen
tipple zechen
tippler der Trinker
tipsy betrunken
tiptoe die Zehenspitze
tip-top ausgezeichnet
tire der Radreifen; ermüden
tired müde

tiresome langweilig
tissue das Gewebe
tissue-paper das Seidenpapier
titbit der Leckerbissen
title der Titel; - **(claim)** der Anspruch; - **(to)** betiteln, benennen
title-deed die Eigentumsurkunde
titter kichern
to zu; nach; an; für; um
to and fro hin und her
toad die Kröte
toast trinken auf; der Trinkspruch das geröstete Brot; rösten
tobacco der Tabak
tobacconist der Tabakhändler
toboggan der Rodelschlitten
to-day heute
toe die Zehe
together zusammen
together with samt
toil die schwere Arbeit; sich abarbeiten
toilet die Toilette
token das Zeichen
tolerable erträglich; leidlich
tolerance die Duldsamkeit
tolerant duldsam
tolerate dulden
toleration die Duldung
toll läuten
tomato die Tomate
tomb die Gruft; das Grab
tomboy der Wildfang
tomcat der Kater
tomfoolery die Albernheit
to-morrow morgen
ton die Tonne
tone der Ton
tongs die Zange
tongue die Zunge
tongue (language) die Sprache
tonic das Stärkungsmittel
to-night heute abend
tonnage der Tonnengehalt
tonsil die Mandel
too zu; gleichfalls; auch
tool das Werkzeug
tooth der Zahn
toothache das Zahnweh
toothbrush die Zahnbürste
toothless zahnlos
toothpaste die Zahnpasta
toothpick der Zahnstocher

top der Gipfel, der Wipfel, die Spitze; oberst
topic der Gegenstand; das Thema
topical aktuell
topsy-turvy kopfüber
torch die Fackel
torchlight procession der Fackelzug
torment die Qual; quälen, martern
torpedo der Torpedo; torpedieren
torpedo-boat das Torpedoboot
torpid erstarrt
torpor die Erstarrung
torrent der Giessbach; der Strom
tortoise die Schildkröte
tortuous gewunden
torture die Folter; foltern
torturer der Folterer
toss werfen; schleudern
total total, gänzlich; der Gesamtbetrag
totter wanken; wackeln
touch das Gefühl, die Berührung, der Tastsinn; berühren, befühlen
touchstone der Prüfstein
tough zäh
tour die Reise; die Rundreise
tourist der Tourist
tourist-office das Reisbüro
tournament das Turnier
tow das Werg; schleppen, bugsieren
towards gegen; nach; zu
towel das Handtuch
tower der Turm; überragen
town die Stadt
town clerk der Stadtdirektor
town council der Stadtrat
town hall das Rathaus
townsfolk die Städter *pl*
township die Stadtgemeinde
toy das Spielzeug
trace die Spur, die Fährte; zeichnen, nachspüren
track die Bahn, der Pfad, das Geleise; verfolgen
tract die Strecke; das Traktat
tractable lenksam
traction das Ziehen; der Zug
tractor der Traktor
trade der Handel, das Gewerbe, das Geschäft; Handel treiben

trade-mark die Schutzmarke
trader der Händler
tradesman der Handwerker
tradespeople die Handelsleute
  pl or Geschäftsleute
trade-union die Gewerkschaft
trade-wind der Passatwind
tradition die Überlieferung
traditional überliefert
traffic der Verkehr; handeln
tragedy die Tragödie; das Trauer-
  spiel
tragic(al) tragisch
trail die Fährte, der Pfad; nachspüren, schleppen
trailer der Anhänger
train der Zug, das Gefolge; trainieren, ausbilden, abrichten
trainer der Trainer; der Abrich-
  ter
training-college das Lehrer-
  seminar
trait der Zug
traitor der Verräter
traitorous verräterisch
tramp der Landstreicher, umherstreifen
trample trampeln
trance die Verzückung
tranquil ruhig
tranquillity die Ruhe
transact verhandeln
transaction das Geschäft; die
  Verhandlung
transatlantic transatlantisch
transcribe abschreiben
transfer übertragen; die Verset-
  zung
transferable übertragbar
transfix durchbohren
transform umgestalten
transformation die Umgestal-
  tung
transfuse umgiessen
transgress überschreiten; sich
  vergehen
transgression das Vergehen; die
  Überschreitung
transit der Durchgang
transition der Übergang
translate übersetzen
translation die Übersetzung
translator der Übersetzer

transmit übersenden
transparent durchsichtig
transpire verlauten
transplant verpflanzen
transport transportieren; der
  Transport
trap die Falle, fangen
trap-door die Falltür
trapper der Pelzjäger
trash der Plunder; der Unsinn
trashy wertlos
travail die Wehen *pl*
travel reisen; die Reise
traveller der (die) Reisende
traverse durchgehen
travesty die Travestie
trawl das Schleppnetz
trawler der Schleppnetzfischer
tray das Tablett
treacherous treulos
treachery die Treulosigkeit
tread der Tritt; treten
treason der Verrat
treasure der Schatz; wert-
  schätzen
treasurer der Schatzmeister
treasury die Schatzkammer; das
  Schatzamt
treat behandeln; bewirten
treatise die Abhandlung
treatment die Behandlung
treaty der Vertrag
treble dreifach; verdreifachen
tree der Baum
trellis das Gitter
tremble zittern
tremendous ungeheuer
trench der Graben
trenchant scharf
trend sich richten; die Richtung
trepidation die Angst
trespass übertreten, sich vergehen; das unbefugte Betreten
tress die Haarlocke; die Flechte
trestle das Gestell
trial der Versuch; die Prüfung;
  das Verhör; der Prozess
triangle das Dreieck
triangular dreieckig
tribe der Stamm
tribunal der Gerichtshof
tributary der Nebenfluss
tribute der Tribut; die Abgabe

trick betrügen; der Kniff, die List
trickle tröpfeln
trifle die Kleinigkeit; tändeln
trifling geringfügig
trigger der Drücker; der Abzug
trim putzen, stutzen, zurechtmachen; nett
trimming die Garnierung
trinity die Dreieinigkeit
trinket der Schmuck
trip straucheln; der Ausflug
tripe die Kaldaunen *pl*; die Flecke *pl*
triple dreifach
tripod der Dreifuss
trite abgedroschen
triumph siegen; der Triumph
triumphant siegreich
trivial bedeutungslos
trolley der Karren
trolley-bus der Obus
trombone die Posaune
troop die Truppe; die Schar
trooper der Soldat
troops die Truppen *pl*
trophy das Siegeszeichen
tropical tropisch
tropics die Tropen *pl*
trot der Trott; traben
trouble die Unruhe, die Sorge, die Mühe; stören, sich bemühen, sich kümmern
troublesome beschwerlich; lästig
trough der Trog
trousers die Hose
trousseau die Ausstattung
trout die Forelle
trowel die Kelle
truant der Schwänzer
truce der Waffenstillstand
truck der Güterwagen; der Handkarren; der Lastwagen; der Tausch(handel)
trudge sich fortschleppen
true wahr; treu; echt
trump der Trumpf; trumpfen
trumpet die Trompete
truncheon der Knüppel
trunk der Stamm; der Rüssel; der Koffer; der Rumpf
truss das Bündel, das Bruchband; aufbinden

trust das Vertrauen; die Obhut; der Ring; (anver)trauen
trustee der Treuhänder; der Bevollmächtigte
trustful vertrauensvoll
truth die Wahrheit
truthfulness die Wahrhaftigkeit
try versuchen; sich bemühen; verhören; prüfen
trying schwierig
tub das Fass; der Kübel
tube das Rohr; die Röhre; die Tube
tuck einwickeln
Tuesday der Dienstag
tuft der Büschel
tug ziehen; der Schlepper
tuition der Unterricht
tulip die Tulpe
tumble stürzen; der Sturz
tumbledown baufällig
tumbler das Trinkglas
tumour die Geschwulst
tumult der Lärm; der Aufruhr
tune stimmen; die Melodie
tuneful wohlklingend
tuning-fork die Stimmgabel
tunnel der Tunnel
turbid trübe
turbine die Turbine
turbot der Steinbutt
turbulent ungestüm
turf der Rasen; mit Rasen belegen
turkey der Truthahn
turn (sich) drehen, (sich) wenden; die Drehung, die Richtung; **in -** der Reihe nach; **take -s** miteinander abwechseln
turner der Dreher; der Drechsler
turning die Wendung
turning-point der Wendepunkt
turnip die Rübe
turnover der Umsatz
turnscrew der Schraubenzieher
turpentine der Terpentin
turquoise der Türkis
turret das Türmchen
turtle die Schildkröte
tusk der Fangzahn
tussle der Streit
tutor der Hauslehrer
twaddle das Geschwätz
twice zweimal

twig der Zweig
twilight die Dämmerung
twin doppelt; das Zwilling
twine der Bindfaden
twinkle blinken; blinzeln
twirl wirbeln
twist drehen; die Drehung
twitch zucken; zwicken
twitter zwitschern
two zwei
twofold zweifach
type der Typ, die Type; auf der Maschine schreiben
typewriter die Schreibmaschine
typhoon der Taifun
typhus der Flecktyphus
tyrannical tyrannisch
tyranny die Tyrannei
tyrant der Tyrann
Tyrol das Tirol
Tyrolese der Tiroler

U

U-boat das Unterseeboot
ugliness die Hässlichkeit
ugly hässlich
ulcer das Geschwür
ulterior jenseitig; ferner
ultimate letzt
umbrage der Schatten, der Anstoss
umbrella der Regenschirm
umpire der Schiedsrichter
unabashed frech; unbeschämt
unabated unvermindert
unable unfähig
unacceptable unannehmbar
unaccompanied unbegleitet
unaccustomed ungewohnt
unacquainted unbekannt
unaffected ungerührt
unaided ohne Hilfe
unalterable unveränderlich
unanimity die Einmütigkeit
unanimous einmütig
unanswerable unwiderleglich
unanswered unbeantwortet
unapproachable unzugänglich
unarmed wehrlos
unasked ungebeten
unassisted ohne Hilfe

unassuming anspruchslos
unavoidable unvermeidlich
unauthorized unberechtigt
unaware(s) unbewusst; unversehens
unbearable unerträglich
unbecoming unziemlich
unbelief der Unglaube
unbelieving ungläubig
unbidden friewillig
unbind losbinden
unblemished tadellos
unblushing schamlos
unbounded unbegrenzt
unbroken ungebrochen
unbuckle losschnallen
unburden entlasten
unbusinesslike unpraktisch
uncertain ungewiss
uncertainty die Ungewissheit
unchangeable unveränderlich
uncharitable lieblos
unclaimed unverlangt
uncle der Onkel
uncomfortable unangenehm
uncommon ungemein; ungewöhnlich
unconditional bedingungslos
unconfirmed unbestätigt
unconquerable unüberwindlich
unconscious bewusstlos
unconstrained ungezwungen
uncontested unbestritten
uncontrollable unbezwingbar
unconvincing nicht überzeugend
uncork entkorken
uncouth grob; ungeschlacht
uncover entblössen; aufdecken
uncrowned ungekrönt
unction die Salbung; extreme - die letzte Ölung
undamaged unbeschädigt
undaunted unerschrocken
undeceive einem die Augen öffnen
undecided unentschieden
undefined unbestimmt
undeniable unleugbar
under unter; unten; - age unmündig
underclothes die Unterwäsche
underdone nicht gar
underfed unterernährt

undergo sich unterziehen; erdulden
undergraduate der Student
underground unterirdisch; die Untergrundbahn
undergrowth das Unterholz
underhand heimtückisch
underline unterstreichen
undermine untergraben
underneath unter; unten
underrate unterschätzen
undersell billiger verkaufen
undersign unterzeichnen
undersigned der Unterzeichnete
understand verstehen; vernehmen
understanding der Verstand; die Vereinbarung, die Voraussetzung
undertake unternehmen
undertaker der Leichenbestatter
undertaking das Unternehmen
undervalue unterschätzen
underwood das Unterholz
undeserved unverdient
undesirable unerwünscht
undiminished unvermindert
undisturbed ungestört
undivided ungeteilt
undo aufmachen; ungeschehen machen; aufknöpfen
undoing das Verderben
undoubted zweifellos
undress (sich) auskleiden
undue übermässig
undulation die wellenförmige Bewegung
unduly ungebührlich, übermassig
undying unsterblich
unearthly unirdisch
uneasiness die Unruhe
uneasy unruhig; ängstlich
uneducated ungebildet
unemployed arbeitslos
unemployment die Arbeitslosigkeit
unequalled unvergleichlich
unerring unfehlbar
unexpected unerwartet
unexplained unerklärt
unfailing unfehlbar
unfair unredlich; unbillig
unfasten losmachen
unfathomable unergründlich

unfavourable ungünstig
unfeeling gefühllos
unfold (sich) entfalten
unforeseen unvorhergesehen
unfortunate unglücklich
unfounded grundlos; unbegründet
ungenerous unedel
ungentlemanly ungebildet; grob
ungovernable zügellos; unlenksam
unhappy unglücklich
unheard unerhört
unhoped for unverhofft
uniform einförmig; die Uniform
union die Union; die Vereinigung; der Bund; der Verein
unique einzig
unison der Einklang
unit die Einheit
unite (sich) vereinigen
unity die Eintracht; die Einheit
universal allgemein; Welt . . .
universe das Weltall
unjust ungerecht
unjustifiable unverantwortlich
unkind unfreundlich
unknown unbekannt
unladylike nicht damenhaft
unlearn verlernen
unless wenn nicht
unload ausladen
unlock aufschliessen
unmarried unverheiratet
unmentionable nicht zu erwähnen
unmerciful unbarmherzig
unmindful sorglos
unmistakable unverkennbar
unmolested unbelästigt
unmoved unbewegt
unnatural unnatürlich
unnecessary unnötig
unnoticed unbemerkt
unobtainable unerreichbar
unoccupied unbesetzt; unbeschäftigt
unopposed ohne Widerspruch
unpack auspacken
unpaid unbezahlt
unparalleled unvergleichlich
unpardonable unverzeihlich
unperceived unbemerkt
unpleasant unangenehm

unpleasantness die Unannehmlichkeit
unpopular nicht beliebt
unprecedented unerhört
unprejudiced vorurteilsfrei
unpremeditated unüberlegt
unprepared unvorbereitet
unprepossessing nicht einnehmend
unprofitable uneinträglich
unpromising nicht viel versprechend
unquestionable fraglos
unrelenting unbeugsam
unremitting unaufhörlich
unrepentant reuelos
unreserved rückhaltlos
unruly unbändig; unlenksam
unsatisfactory unzulänglich
unsatisfied unzufrieden
unscrupulous gewissenlos
unseat vom Sitze vertreiben
unseemly unziemlich
unseen unsichtbar; ungesehen
unselfish uneigennützig
unsettled ungewiss
unsightly hässlich
unskilful ungeschickt; unkundig
unskilled unerfahren
unsolicited unverlangt
unsolved ungelöst
unsound ungesund
unsparing freigebig; schonungslos
unspeakable unsagbar; unaussprechlich
unsteady unbeständig
unsuccessful erfolglos
unsuitable unstatthaft; unpassend
untamable unbezähmbar
untaught ungelehrt
untenable unhaltbar
unthinkable undenkbar
unthinking gedankenlos
untidy unordentlich
untie losbinden
until bis
untold ungezählt; unsagbar
untoward widrig; ungünstig
unusual ungewöhnlich
unutterable unaussprechlich
unvarying unveränderlich

unveil entschleiern
unwell unwohl
unwieldy schwerfällig
unwilling ungern; unwillig
unwind abwickeln
unworthy unwürdig
unwritten ungeschrieben
unyielding unbeugsam; unnachgiebig
up auf; hinauf; oben
upbraid tadeln; schelten
uphill (berg)auf
uphold erhalten
upholsterer der Tapezierer; der Mobelhändler
upholstery die Polstermöbel *pl*
upland das Hochland
uplift emporheben
upon auf, an
upper ober; höher
upright aufrecht; aufrichtig
uprightness die Aufrichtigkeit
uproar der Aufruhr
uproarious lärmend
uproot entwurzeln
upset umstürzen; aus der Fassung bringen
upside down umgekehrt; drunter und drüber
upstairs (nach) oben
upstart der Emporkömmling
up-to-date modern
upwards aufwärts
urge treiben, drängen; der Drang
urgency die Dringlichkeit
urgent dringend; eilig
urine der Urin
urn die Urne; die Teemaschine
usage der Gebrauch; die Gewohnheit
use der Gebrauch, der Nutzen, die Anwendung; gebrauchen, benutzen, verwenden
used to pflegte
useful nützlich
usefulness die Nützlichkeit
useless unnütz; unbrauchbar; nutzlos
usher anmelden; einführen
usual üblich; gebräuchlich
usurer der Wucherer
usurp sich anmassen
usury der Wucher

utensil das Gerät; das Geschirr
uterus die Gebärmutter
utility die Nützlichkeit
utilize nutzbar machen
utmost äusserst; höchst
utter äusserst; gänzlich; äussern
utterance die Äusserung
utterly durchaus
uvula das Zäpfchen

V

vacancy die Leere; die freie Stelle
vacant leer; unbesetzt; unbewohnt
vacate leeren; räumen
vacation die Ferien *pl*
vaccinate impfen
vaccination die Impfung
vaccine der Impfstoff
vacillate schwanken
vagabond der Landstreicher
vagary die Laune; die Grille
vagina die Scheide
vagrancy die Landstreicherei
vagrant wandernd
vague unbestimmt
vagueness die Unbestimmtheit
vain eitel
vain (in) vergebens
vainglorious ruhmredig
vale das Tal
valet der Diener
valiant tapfer
valid gültig
validity die Gültigkeit
valley das Tal
valour die Tapferkeit
valuable wertvoll
valuation die Schätzung
value der Wert; schätzen
valueless wertlos
valuer der Schätzer
valve das Ventil; die Röhre
van der Lieferwagen; die Vorhut
vanilla die Vanille
vanish verschwinden
vanity die Eitelkeit
vanquish besiegen
vapour der Dunst
variable veränderlich
variance die Uneinigkeit

variation die Veränderung; die Variation
variegated bunt
variety die Abart; die Mannigfaltigkeit
various verschieden
varnish der Firnis, der Lack; firnissen, lackieren
vary (sich) verändern; abwechseln
vase die Vase
vast ungeheuer; sehr gross; weit
vat das Fass
vault das Gewölbe; wölben
vaunt sich rühmen
vaunting prahlerisch
veal das Kalbfleisch
vegetable das Gemüse
vegetation die Vegetation
vehemence die Heftigkeit
vehement heftig
vehicle das Fuhrwerk
veil der Schleier; verschleiern
vein die Ader
vellum das Velin
velocity die Schnelligkeit
velvet der Samt
venal käuflich; feil
veneer das Furnier
venerable ehrwürdig
veneration die Verehrung
vengeance die Rache
venison das Wildbret
venom das Gift
venomous giftig
vent das Luftloch; die Öffnung
ventilate lüften
ventilation die Lüftung
ventilator der Ventilator
ventriloquist der Bauchredner
venture das Unternehmen, das Wagnis; wagen
venturesome kühn
veracious wahrhaft
veracity die Wahrhaftigkeit
verbal mündlich
verbatim wörtlich
verbose wortreich
verdict das Urteil
verdure das Grün
verge der Rand
verger der Küster
verify bestätigen; prüfen

verily wirklich
vermicelli die Fadennudeln *pl*
vermifuge das Wurmmittel
vermin das Ungeziefer
vernacular die Landessprache
versatile vielseitig
versatility die Vielseitigkeit
verse der Vers; die Strophe
versed bewandert
version die Version; die Über-setzung
versus gegen
vertical senkrecht
vertiginous schwindelig
vertigo der Schwindel
very sehr; - **best** allerbest
vessel das Schiff; das Gefäss
vest die Weste; das Unterhemd
vested verbrieft
vestibule die Vorhalle
vestige die Spur
vestry die Sakristei
veteran der Veteran
veterinary der Tierarzt
veto das Veto
vex ärgern; plagen
vexation die Plage
vexatious ärgerlich
viaduct die Bahnbrücke
vibrate schwingen
vibration die Schwingung
vicar der Pfarrer
vicarage das Pfarrhaus
vice das Laster; der Schraubstock
viceroy der Vizekönig
vicious bösartig; lasterhaft
vicissitude der Wechselfall
victim das Opfer
victor der Sieger
victorious siegreich
victory der Sieg
victuals die Lebensmittel *pl*
view die Aussicht, die Ansicht, die Absicht, der Anblick; besehen
vigilance die Wachsamkeit
vigilant wachsam
vigour die Stärke; die Kraft
vigorous kräftig; lebhaft
vile niedrig; verächtlich
villa die Villa
village das Dorf
villager der Dorfbewohner; der Dörfler

villain der Schurke
villainous abscheulich
villainy die Schändlichkeit
vindicate verteidigen; recht-fertigen
vindication die Rechtfertigung
vindictive rachsüchtig
vine der Rebstock; die Rebe
vineyard der Weinberg
vintage die Weinlese; der Jahr-gang
violate verletzen; schänden
violence die Gewalttätigkeit
violent heftig; gewaltsam
violet das Veilchen
violin die Violine; die Geige
violinist der Geiger
violoncello das Cello
viper die Viper
virgin die Jungfrau
virginity die Jungfräulichkeit
virtue die Tugend
virtuoso der Virtuose
virtuous tugendhaft
viscous klebrig
visible sichtbar
vision die Erscheinung; das Ge-sicht
visionary der Schwärmer; einge-bildet
visit besuchen; der Besuch
visitor der Besucher
vital Lebens . . .; wesentlich
vitality die Lebenskraft
vitriol das Vitriol
vivacity die Lebhaftigkeit
vivid lebhaft
vixen die Füchsin
vocal Stimm . . .
vocal chord das Stimmband
vocalist der Sänger
vocation der Beruf
vociferous schreiend
voice die Stimme
void leer
volatile flüchtig
volcanic vulkanisch
volcano die Vulkan
volley die Salve
voltage die Spannung
volubility die Zungenfertigkeit
volume der Inhalt; der Band
voluminous dick; umfangreich

voluntary freiwillig
volunteer der Freiwillige; freiwillig dienen; sich erbieten
voluptuous wollüstig
vomit sich erbrechen; kotzen
voracious gefrässig
voracity die Gefrässigkeit
vortex der Wirbel
vote die (Wahl)stimme; wählen, stimmen
voter der Wähler
vouch bezeugen; verbürgen
voucher der Beleg; die Unterlage
vouchsafe bewilligen
vow das Gelübde
vowel der Vokal
voyage die Seereise; reisen
voyager der Reisende
vulgar gemein
vulgarity die Gemeinheit
vulnerable verwundbar
vulture der Geier

W

wabble wackeln
wad der Bausch; das Bündel; ausstopfen
wadding die Watte
waddle watscheln
wade (durch)waten
wafer die Oblate; die Waffel
waft wehen; der Hauch
wag der Spassvogel; schütteln, wedeln
wage der Lohn
wage war Krieg führen
wager die Wette; wetten
waggish schalkhaft
waggon der Wagen
waggoner die Fuhrmann
wagtail die Bachstelze
wail die Klage; beklagen
wainscot die Getäfel
waist die Taille
waistcoat die Weste
wait warten
waiter der Kellner
waiting-room der Wartesaal
waive aufgeben
wake wecken; aufwachen
wakeful wachsam

walk spazieren gehen; der Spaziergang
walker der Fussgänger
walking-tour die Fusstour
wall die Wand; die Mauer
wallet die Tasche; die Brieftasche
wallflower der Goldlack
walnut die Wallnuss
waltz der Walzer; walzen
wan blass; bleich
wand der Stab
wander wandern
wanderer der Wanderer
wane abnehmen
want brauchen, bedürfen, wünschen, fehlen; die Not, das Bedürfnis, der Mangel
wanton mutwillig
wantonness der Mutwille
war der Krieg; Krieg führen
warble zwitschern; trillern
warbler der Singvogel
ward das Mündel, die Station; der Bezirk; wehren
warden der Aufseher; der Vormund
wardrobe der Kleiderschrank
warehouse das Warenlager
warfare die Kriegführung
warlike kriegerisch
warm warm; wärmen
warmth die Wärme
warn warnen
warning die Warnung
warp (sich) werfen; die Kette
warrant die Vollmacht, die Bürgschaft; gewährleisten
warren das Gehege
warrior der Krieger
wart die Warze
wary vorsichtig
wash (sich) waschen
wash-basin das Waschbecken
washer der Dichtungsring
washerwoman die Wäscherin; die Waschfrau
washing die Wäsche
washing-up das Spülen
wash-stand der Waschtisch
wasp die Wespe
waste (**desert**) die Einöde; die Wüste (**devastation**); die Verwüstung, die Vergeudung;

(**refuse**) der Abfall; (**to**) **squander**) verschwenden, verwüsten; wüst, unbenutzt
wasteful verschwenderisch
waste-paper basket der Papierkorb
watch die Uhr, die Wache; wachen, beobachten
watch-dog der Wachhund
watchful wachsam
watch-maker der Uhrmacher
watchman der Nachtwächter
watchword die Losung
water das Wasser; bewässern
water-closet der Abort; das Wasserklosett
water-colours die Aquarellfarben *pl*
waterfall der Wasserfall
watering-place der Badeort
water-level der Wasserstand
water-power die Wasserkraft
waterproof der Regenmantel; wasserdicht
water-shed die Wasserscheide
watertight wasserdicht
waterworks das Wasserwerk
watery wässerig
wave die Welle, die Woge; wehen, winken
waver schwanken
wax das Wachs; der Siegellack
waxy wächsern
way der Weg; die Weise; **- out** der Ausgang
wayfarer der Wanderer
waylay auflauern
wayward mürrisch; launisch
we wir
weak schwach
weaken schwächen
weakling der Schwächling
weakness die Schwäche
wealth, riches der Reichtum
wealthy wohlhabend; reich
wean entwöhnen
weapon die Waffe
wear tragen; die Tracht
wear out abtragen
wearable tragbar
wear and tear die Abnutzung
weariness die Müdigkeit
wearisome ermüdend

weary müde; ermüden
weasel das Wiesel
weather das Wetter; **- forecast** der Wetterbericht
weave weben
weaver der Weber
web das Gewebe
wed (sich) (ver)heiraten; trauen
wedding die Hochzeit
wedding-ring der Trauring
wedge der Keil; keilen
wedlock die Ehe
Wednesday der Mittwoch
weed das Unkraut; jäten
week die Woche
week-day der Wochentag
weekly wöchentlich
weep weinen
weigh wägen; wiegen
weight das Gewicht
weighty gewichtig
weir das Wehr
weird seltsam; unheimlich
welcome willkommen; bewillkommnen
weld schweissen
welfare die Wohlfahrt; die Fürsorge
well die Quelle, der Brunnen; wohl, gut, gesund
wellbeing das Wohlsein
wellbred wohlerzogen
well off wohlhabend
well-wisher der Freund
welter sich wälzen; der Wirrwarr
wench das Mädchen; die Dirne
wend (sich) wenden; gehen
west der Westen
western, westerly westlich
westwards westwärts
wet nass; nass machen; die Nässe
wetness die Feuchtigkeit
wet nurse die Amme
whack tüchtig schlagen; prügeln
whale der Walfisch
whalebone das Fischbein
whaler der Walfischfänger
whale oil der Tran
wharf der Kai
wharfinger der Kaimeister
what was
whatever was auch immer
wheat der Weizen

wheedle schmeicheln
wheel das Rad; drehen, radeln
wheelbarrow der Schubkarren
wheelwright der Stellmacher
wheeze schnaufen; keuchen
when wann; als; wenn
whence woher; von wo
whenever so oft als; allemal
  wenn
where wo; wohin
whereabouts der Aufenthalt
wherefore weshalb
wherein worin
whereupon worauf
whet wetzen, schärfen
whether ob
whetstone der Schleifstein
whey der Molken
which welcher, welche, welches
whiff der Zug, der Hauch
while die Weile; während; verbringen; weilen
whim die Laune
whimsical launisch; grillenhaft
whine wimmern; winseln
whip die Peitsche; peitschen
whip-hand die Oberhand
whir schwirren
whirl wirbeln; der Wirbel
whirlpool der Strudel
whirlwind der Wirbelwind
whisk der Wisch; schnell wegtun,
  wischen, schlagen
whiskers der Backenbart
whisky der Whisky
whisper flüstern; das Geflüster
whistle pfeifen; die Pfeife
white weiss
whiten weissen
whiteness die Weisse; die Blässe
whitewash tünchen
whither wohin
Whit Sunday der Pfingstsonntag
whittle schnitzen
whiz zischen; sausen
who wer; der, die, das
whoever wer auch
whole ganz; das Ganze
wholesale der Grosshandel; im
  grossen
wholesome gesund
wholly gänzlich; völlig
whoop schreien; das Geschrei

whooping-cough der Keuch-
  husten
whortleberry die Heidelbeere
why warum
wick der Docht
wicked böse; gottlos
wickedness die Gottlosigkeit;
  die Bosheit
wicker der Weidenzweig
wicker-work das Flechtwerk
wide breit; weit
wide awake wach
widen erweitern
widow die Witwe
widowed verwitwet
widower der Witwer
width die Weite; die Breite
wield schwingen; handhaben
wife die (Ehe-) Frau; das Weib
wig die Perücke
wild wild
wildness die Wildheit
wilderness die Wildnis; die
  Wüste
wildfire das Lauffeuer
wilful eigensinnig; vorsätzlich
wiliness die Verschlagenheit; die
  Arglist
will der Wille, das Testament;
  wollen
willing willig; gern
willingness die Bereitwilligkeit
willow die Weide
willy-nilly wohl oder übel
wily listig; schlau
win gewinnen; siegen
wince zucken
winch die Kurbel; die Winde
wind der Wind, der Atem; blasen,
  (sich) wenden
wind up aufziehen
windfall das Fallobst; der Glücks-
  fall
windlass die Winde
windmill die Windmühle
window das Fenster
windpipe die Luftröhre
wine der Wein
wing der Flügel; beflügeln
wink blinzeln, winken; der Wink
winner der Gewinner; der Sieger
winter der Winter; überwintern
wintry winterlich

wipe wischen; putzen
wire der Draht; telegraphieren
wireless drahtlos
wireless message der Funkspruch
wireless operator der Funker
wisdom die Weisheit
wise weise
wish wünschen; der Wunsch
wishful sehnlich
wisp der Wisch; das Bündel
wistful nachdenklich; sehnsüchtig
wit der Witz; der Verstand
witch die Hexe
witchcraft die Hexerei
with mit
withdraw (sich) zurückziehen
withdrawal die Zurücknahme; der Rückzug; die Abhebung
wither (ver)welken
withhold zurückhalten; vorenthalten
within innerhalb; drinnen
without ausserhalb; ohne; draussen
withstand widerstehen
witness das Zeugnis, der Zeuge; bezeugen
witness-box die Zeugenbank
witticism die Witzelei
wittiness die Witzigkeit
witty geistreich
wizard der Zauberer
wizened schrumpelig
woe das Weh; das Leid
woeful traurig; jämmerlich
wolf der Wolf
wolfish gefrässig; wölfisch
woman die Frau; das Weib
womanly weiblich
womb die Gebärmutter
wonder das Wunder; sich wundern
wonderful wunderbar
wondrous wunderbar
wont(ed) gewöhnt
woo freien; werben
wood der Wald; das Holz
woodbine das Geissblatt
woodcut der Holzschnitt
wooded waldig
wooden hölzern

woodland die Waldung
woodman der Holzhacker; der Förster
woody waldig; holzig
wool die Wolle
woollen wollen
woolly wollig
word das Wort
wordy wortreich
work die Arbeit, **das Werk;** arbeiten, wirken
worker der Arbeiter
workhouse das Armenhaus
workman der Arbeiter
workmanship die Kunstfertigkeit
workshop die Werkstatt
world die Welt
wordly weltlich
world-wide weitverbreitet
worm der Wurm; sich krümmen
worm-eaten wurmstichig
wormwood der Wermut
worn out abgenutzt
worry plagen, quälen, sorgen; die Sorge
worse schlimmer; schlechter
worship anbeten, verehren; der Gottesdienst, die Anbetung, die Verehrung
worst schlimmste; schlechteste
worsted das Kammgarn
worth der Wert
worthless wertlos
worthwhile der Mühe wert
worthy würdig
wound die Wunde; verwunden
wrangle der Zank; streiten
wrap (ein)wickeln
wrapper die Hülle
wrath der Zorn
wrathful zornig; grimmig
wreath der Kranz
wreathe winden
wreck der Schiffbruch; das Wrack
wreckage die Trümmer *pl*
wren der Zaunkönig
wrench heftig ziehen, entwinden; die Verrenkung, der Ruck, der Schraubenschlüssel
wrest winden; verdrehen
wrestle ringen

wrestler der Ringer
wretch der Elende
wretched elend
wriggle sich biegen; sich schlängeln; sich winden
wrinkle die Runzel; (sich) runzeln
wrist das Handgelenk
wristband die Armelpriese; die Manschette
writ die Schrift; der Befehl
write schreiben
writer der Schreiber; der Schriftsteller
writing die Schrift; das Schreiben
writing-desk der Schreibtisch
writing-paper das Schreibpapier
wrong unrecht, falsch; das Unrecht, unrecht tun, kränken
wrong-headed verschroben
wrought gearbeitet
wrought-iron das Schmiedeeisen
wry krumm

X

X-rays die Röntgenstrahlen *pl*
xylographer der Holzschneider
xylography die Holzschneidekunst
xyster das Schabemesser
xystus der Säulengang

Y

yacht die Jacht
yap kläffen
yard der Hof; die Werft; die Elle; die Rahe
yarn das Garn
yawn gähnen
year das Jahr
yearly jährlich
yearn sich sehnen
yeast die Hefe
yell der Schrei; gellen, schreien

yellow gelb
yellowish gelblich
yelp bellen; kläffen
yeoman der Freisasse
yeomanry die (berittene) Miliz
yes ja
yesterday gestern
yet doch; aber; noch; sogar; **(as)** - bisher; **(not)** - noch nicht
yew die Eibe
yield aufgeben, nachgeben, hervorbringen; der Ertrag
yoke das Joch; ins Joch spannen
yokel der Tölpel
yolk der Dotter
yonder jener, jene, jenes; da, drüben
yore ehemals
you Sie, du, ihr, euch, Ihnen
young jung
youngster der Junge
your euer, Ihr, dein
yours der, die, das Deinige, Eurige, Ihrige
yourself (selves) ihr selbst; Sie selbst; du selbst
youth die Jugend; der Jüngling
youthful jugendlich
youthfulness die Jugend
yule Weihnachten *pl*

Z

zeal der Eifer
zealot der Eiferer
zealous eifrig
zebra das Zebra
zenith der Zenit
zero die Null
zest die Würze; die Lust
zigzag das Zickzack
zinc das Zink
zone die Zone
zoology die Zoologie; die Tierkunde
zoom der plötzliche Aufstieg

A CONCISE
GERMAN GRAMMAR

CONTENTS

INTRODUCTORY ADVICE

HERE you have a Concise German Grammar and a Concise German Dictionary to guide you in your study of the language. What difficulties lie in your path?

PRONUNCIATION

This Grammar concentrates on Accidence and Syntax, dealing with pronunciation briefly in the preliminary section. Your best way to learn the pronunciation is, apart from living in the country, to study gramophone records and to listen to the radio in German. That will do more for you than the printed page possibly can.

Get records giving the separate sounds and then the sounds combined in words and sentences, and listen to them every day, repeating them until you have them perfect. This will give you not only a correct pronunciation of the sounds but, what is just as important, the rhythm of the language, the stress on the syllables, the lilt, the rise and fall of intonation. It is not enough to listen once or twice: you must go on listening for months.

SPELLING

German has the very great advantage of having a spelling which pretty faithfully represents the pronunciation. Not for you the dull labour of having to memorize spellings like *vin, vins, vint, vint, vain, vains, vingt,* all of which spell exactly the same sound in French; nor need you burn the midnight oil like the foreigner who has to memorize *plough, though, enough, trough, cough, hiccough, through,* all of which are pronounced differently though all contain the same combination of letters, "ough". If you know the pronunciation of the German alphabet, you can pronounce practically any German word correctly.

STRESS

Like English, German has a strong stress on one syllable: im*póss*-ible—un*mög*lich. There is none of that shifting, delicate stress that makes French so difficult to speak smoothly. This strong stress makes the German words easy to say and easy to memorize. German is a rough-and-ready language as compared with French, and however badly you may speak it, you will never feel that you are murdering it, as is so often the case with French!

PRINT AND SCRIPT

The Gothic type is only a variant of the Roman, and though it looks strange at first, very little practice will make you a fluent reader, the words little by little becoming familiar and friendly. Most German books were once printed in Gothic, but the future will probably see it replaced by the Roman. However, as many books, inscriptions, signs, etc., still exist which were printed or written in the old type, it is useful to read Gothic until it becomes second nature.

Need you learn to write the Gothic script? No, there is no need to write it as all Germans can read Roman. Since the war, too, the Gothic script is no longer taught in German schools.

VOCABULARY

German has many words, like *Haus, Vater, Mutter, Garten, Fleisch, Freund, Kuh, Kalb, Hund,* which are so like the English — house, father, mother, garden, flesh (meat), friend, cow, calf, hound (dog) — that we recognize them at once. They will not, however, take you very far in German. In French there are literally thousands of words met with in books which are common to the two languages; *arriver, beauté, fraternité, consolation, observation, intime, probable, possibilité,* etc. This makes French so attractive to us, especially when we are beginning the language. Nevertheless, if you study your German vocabulary the right way, you will find that it is much easier and more familiar than seemed to be the case.

German is built up out of its own native elements, not, like English, containing a vast vocabulary borrowed from French, Latin, and Greek. German has, of course, a large number of such words, but in the last forty years they were often frowned on officially and were sometimes replaced by pure German words: *die Photographie* by *das Lichtbild* — "light-picture"; *das Telefon* by *der Fernsprecher* — "far-speaker".

Let us take a typical German word to pieces and see what we get out of it. *Die Eigenschaft* means "quality, attribute, property (in the sense that 'hardness is a property of iron'), character." You find all that in your dictionary and you try to memorize *Eigenschaft* as a block on its own. If you take it to pieces, its meaning becomes clearer and you attach it to a whole family of words which group themselves together in your memory. *Eigenschaft* falls into *eigen,* our word "own," as in "my own work," and the suffix *-schaft,* like our "-ship" in "friendship"; *Eigenschaft* then means "ownship" or "ownness," that which belongs especially to anything, just as "hardness" belongs especially to iron.

Now there is, I said, a family of words which group themselves round *eigen;* here they are: *das Eigentum* — "owndom" — is property in the sense of what you possess, what belongs to you; *der Eigentümer* is the proprietor; *der Eigensinn* — "own sense" — is obstinacy; *der Eigenwille* — "own will" — is wilfulness; *der Eigenname* — "own name" — is proper name or noun. Then there are some useful verbs: *sich eignen,* to be suitable, appropriate; *sich aneignen,* to appropriate (note how the "proper" comes in the English); *enteignen,* to expropriate. That is a small group, but it will serve as an example of how to dig round in your dictionary so as to group words in families and thus help your memory.

There is a further point: German likes to make compound words which look very long and clumsy but are in fact useful and often neat. English likes compound words too, but, unlike German, prints them separately. Thus our "Life Insurance Company" is just as much one word as the German *Lebensversicherungsgesellschaft,* which consists of the words *Leben,* "life," *Versicherung,* "making sure, or insuring," and *Gesellschaft,* "company or companionship," joined together by two *s*'s. Do not be frightened of these long words: break them down into their component parts and the meaning will shell out like peas from a pod.

GRAMMAR

Is German grammar really so difficult? No, it is not: the verb is easy, very much easier than the French with its *-é, -ée, -és, -ées, -er, -ez, -ai, -ais, -ait, -aient*, all of which have to the uninitiated ear the same sound and are horribly confusing. And then the French irregular verbs!   German is simplicity itself compared with them : *singen, ich singe, ich sang, ich habe gesungen* fall at once into place alongside the English — to sing, I sing, I sang, I have sung. The Pronouns are straightforward, whether personal, relative, or inter-rogative. Your difficulties will lie mainly with the declension of the Articles, Nouns, and Adjectives, and the use of the Cases, whilst the order of words will also prove a stumbling-block. Once you have mastered these, German is yours; but you *must* master them. No half-measures will do, no slovenly *thinking* you know : you must give your whole mind to the job of learning these basic facts. Re-member that this little Grammar will give you the materials to build with, but YOU YOURSELF must do the building, i.e. the learning. Nobody and no book can teach you a foreign language, they can only show you how to learn it.

READING

Grammar is a mere scaffolding and words mere bricks ; it is up to you to build the house. That means that you must drench yourself not merely in the grammar and the vocabulary, but in the living language : you must read, read, read and, if you have the oppor-tunity, speak, speak, speak. From the beginning of your studies you should tackle continuous texts and never allow a day to pass without some reading of German, either at home, in the train, the tube, the bus, or on the seat in the park.

THE GERMAN ALPHABET

English	German Characters		
	Printed	Written	
A a (ä)	𝔄 𝔞 (ä)	*A*	*a*
B b	𝔅 𝔟		
C c	ℭ c		
D d	𝔇 𝔡		
E e	𝔈 𝔢		
F f	𝔉 𝔣		
G g	𝔊 𝔤		
H h	ℌ 𝔥		
I i	ℑ 𝔦		
J j	ℑ 𝔧		
K k	𝔎 𝔨		
L l	𝔏 𝔩		
M m	𝔐 𝔪		

	German Characters	
English	Printed	Written
N n	𝕹 n	
O o (ö)	𝕺 o (ö)	
P p	𝕻 p	
Q q	𝕼 q	
R r	𝕽 r	
S s	*𝕾 ſ ß s	
T t	𝕿 t	
U u (ü)	𝖀 u (ü)	
V v	𝖁 v	
W w	𝖂 w	
X x	𝖃 x	
Y y	𝖄 y	
Z z	3 ʒ	

See Note on p. 262

* NOTE.—The capital letter Ꞩ is, of course, only used initially and is pronounced like our z in zeal.

The ſ is used initially, as in ſonnig, ſehen, and in the interior of a word between vowels, as in leſen, weiſe. In both cases it is pronounced like our z. It is also used in the interior of a word before consonants, as in Liſte, Erbſe, and is then pronounced like our s in soap. It is used in combination with p and t belonging to the stem of the word, and is pronounced shp and sht when initial, as in ſpät, ſtimmen; when in the interior of a word, as in Knoſpe, Kaſten, it is pronounced sp and st as in English.

The s is used at the end of a word or a stem syllable, as in Gans, Hänschen, and in compound words like Vaterlandsliebe, being pronounced like our s in both cases.

The ß is always pronounced like our s; it is used in the interior of a word after a long vowel, as in grüßen, reißen, and at the end of a word or stem syllable and before a t, as in Gruß, Fluß, mußt.

The ſſ is always pronounced as our s in soap and is found only in the interior of a word after a short vowel, as in Flüſſe, Gaſſe, Hinderniſſe.

In our *Concise Grammar* we have printed the German examples in Roman characters and we have used " s " and " ss " instead of the various letters given above.

GERMAN PRONUNCIATION

We give below a short simple guide to German pronunciation, giving the nearest English sound to the German one in order to help the beginner. It should be remembered that this is only an approximation as no two sounds in different languages are really exactly alike, e.g. the German t is much more " breathy " than the usual English t. The learner should, as advised in the " Introductory Advice," study the sounds on gramophone records.

There is one point which must be stressed, namely that German vowels when initial are pronounced with an explosion of the breath which is suddenly released. This is called the Glottal Stop and is a striking feature of German, giving it a sort of sergeant-major hammer-beat as the explosion bites off the words. In English we run the words together, as in oneandall or oneanall; in German the Glottal Stop separates the words and einundachtzig is pronounced ˀeinˀundˀachtzig, the ˀ representing the Glottal Stop. This Stop is found in many English and Scottish dialects, e.g. the Glasgow buter for butter.

Letters	Description
a	As *a* in father.
ai, ay	As *i* in fine.
au	As *ow* in fowl.
ä	Short, as *e* in get; long, as *a* in gate.
äu	As *oy* in coy.

Letters	Description
b	As in English, but pronounced *p* when final.
c	As *ts* in waits before i, e, ü, ö, ä; as *k* elsewhere.
ch	As *ch* in Scottish loch after a, o, u, au; as an exaggerated *h* in hue before i, e, ü, ö, ä.
d	As in English, but pronounced *t* when final.
e	When short, as *e* in get; when long (also spelt **eh** and **ee**), like the long close *é* in French *passé* or like Northern English and Scottish *a* in cake; when unaccented, like *a* in about.
ei, ey	Same value as **ai** and **ay** above.
eu	Same value as **äu** above.
f	As in English.
g	As *g* in English gape; when final, it is pronounced like the *ch* in Scottish loch after a, o, u, au and like *h* in hue elsewhere.
h	Aspirated as the *h* in half.
	When short, as *i* in fit; when long (also spelt **ih, ie, ieh**), as *i* in machine.
j	As *y* in you.
k	As in English. **ck** = *kk*. In **kn** the *k* is pronounced.
l	As *l* in long; never as the second *l* in little.
m	As in English.
n	As in English.
o	When short, as *o* in not; when long, as Northern English and Scottish *o* in no.
ö	When short, like *eu* in French *leur*, i.e. the *ir* sound in sir pronounced with the lips pouted; when long, like *eu* in French *feu*, i.e. a close *e* pronounced with the lips pouted.
p	As in English; in **pf** both the *p* and the *f* are sounded; **ph** = *f*.
qu	As *kv*.
r	Rolled on the tongue as in Scotland or on the uvula as in the Northumbrian " burr."
s	See under " Alphabet."
sch	As *sh* in shoot.
sp and st	As *shp* and *sht* (see under " Alphabet ") when initial.
t, th, dt	As *t* in English.
tz	As *ts* in waits.
u	When short, as *u* in put; when long (spelt also **uh**), as *oo* in rood.
ü	As French *u* in *lu*, i.e. pronounce lee with the lips well pouted.
w	As *f* in English.
v	As *v* in English.
x	As English *x* in wax.
y	As German ü in words loaned from Greek; as German i in other words.
z	As *ts* in waits.

1. THE CASES

Before we tackle the declension of the Articles we had better explain the use of the Cases in German. English nouns have only one case with a definite form of its own, the Genitive, as in " the man's son," where the " 's " is the Genitive ending. Our pronouns, however, have a Nominative form —" I," " he," " they "; an Accusative (or Dative)—" me," " him," " them," and a sort of Genitive—" mine," " his," " their ". In English we know whether a noun is Nominative, Accusative, or Dative only by its position in the sentence. In " The father sees the son," the father is the doer of the action of seeing, the subject of the sentence, and is Nominative. The son is the object or extent of the action of seeing and is the object of the sentence, the Accusative. We reverse the meaning if we reverse the positions of the nouns; " The son sees the father."

In German the noun, or more frequently the Article, shows by its form whether it is Nominative, Accusative, Genitive, or Dative. *Der Vater sieht den Sohn* can mean only " The father sees the son," and the order of the words cannot change the meaning, since the Nominative is marked out by *der* and the Accusative by *den*. Thus word-order is much freer in German than in English: all the following are possible. 1. *Der Vater sieht den Sohn.* 2. *Den Sohn sieht der Vater.* 3. *Sieht der Vater den Sohn?* 4. *Sieht den Sohn der Vater?* 5. *Der Vater den Sohn sieht.* 6. *Den Sohn der Vater sieht.* They all mean the same basically, but the emphasis is different.

This distinction between Nominative and Accusative, however, applies only to the Masculine Singular, not to the Fem., Neuter, and Plural.

The German cases are: Nominative (*der Werfall* = who-case), Accusative (*der Wenfall* = whom-case), Genitive (*der Wesfall* = whose-case), and the Dative (*der Wemfall* = to-whom-case). We shall set them out in that order, although grammars made in Germany use the order: Nom., Gen., Dat., Acc. Prepositions may govern any of the cases except the Nom.

Let us examine the cases one by one:

NOMINATIVE

The Nominative is the case of the doer of the action, the subject of the verb, and is used also as a Vocative as in : *Vater! hier kommt Mutter!* As in English, there is no special form in German for this case of " calling ".

ACCUSATIVE

The Accusative is the case which shows the extent or scope of the action. In *Der Mann sieht den Mond*, " The man sees the moon," the moon is the extent of the action of seeing. This is the most general use, viz. to indicate the object of the verb. In *Der Mann bleibt einen Monat*, " The man remains a month," a month is the extent in time of his remaining and is in the Accusative, though it is not the object of the verb. In *Der Sack wiegt einen Zentner*, " The bag weighs a hundredweight," the hundredweight is the extent of the weighing and is in the Accusative, but is not the object of the verb.

Certain Prepositions require the Accusative: *Das Buch ist für den Sohn*, "The book is for the son." Lists are given on p. 289.

GENITIVE

This case is mainly used to show the relationship between nouns: *Das Haus des Mannes*, "The man's house," *Die Häuser der Stadt*, "The houses of the town." The Genitive is also required by certain verbs and prepositions.

DATIVE

The Dative is closely related to the Accusative in that it comes within the scope of the action of the verb, but more indirectly. It indicates generally the person—rarely the thing—indirectly affected by or interested in the action. In *Der Vater gibt dem Sohn das Buch*, "The father gives the son the book," the book is the gift, the thing given, most closely related to the action of giving, and is in the Accusative; the son is indirectly affected by the giving and the gift, and is in the Dative case. In English we can show this by a preposition: "The father gives the book to the son."

The Dative is required by a number of verbs and prepositions.

II. DECLENSION OF THE ARTICLES

DEFINITE ARTICLE

	SINGULAR			PLURAL
	Masc.	*Fem.*	*Neut.*	*All genders*
Nom.	der	die	das	die
Acc.	den	die	das	die
Gen.	des	der	des	der
Dat.	dem	der	dem	den

Learn those sixteen words so that you can say them in your sleep. KNOW them! Let us now set them out in two groups, Masc. plus Neuter and Fem. plus Plural, as that will bring out similarities and help your memory.

	Masc.	*Neut.*	*Fem.*	*Plural*
Nom.	der	das	die	
Acc.	den	das	die	
Gen.		des	der	
Dat.		dem	der	den

Words declined like the above are: *dieser, diese, dieses* (this, this one); *jener, jene, jenes* (that, yon); *welcher, welche, welches* (which?); *solcher* (such); *mancher* (many a); *jeder* (each); *alle* (all).

INDEFINITE ARTICLE

	SINGULAR			PLURAL
	Masc.	*Fem.*	*Neut.*	*All genders*
Nom.	ein	eine	ein	keine*
Acc.	einen	eine	ein	keine
Gen.	eines	einer	eines	keiner
Dat.	einem	einer	einem	keinen

You will note that the endings of the Indef. are the same as those of the Def. Article except: Nom. Masc. *der — ein*; Nom. Neut. *das — ein*, and Acc. Neut. *das — ein*. If you have learnt the one, you know the other.

Words declined like *ein, eine, ein* are: *kein* (no, not any); *mein* (my); *dein* (thy); *sein* (his); *ihr* (her); *unser* (our); *Euer* and *Ihr* (your); *ihr* (their).

* As *ein, eine, ein* has no plural, we use *kein* (no, not any) instead.

III. DECLENSION OF THE NOUN

A. SINGULAR

FEMININE NOUNS

1. Feminine nouns have no case endings in the singular:

N. die Frau   A. die Frau   G. der Frau   D. der Frau
N. die Zeit   A. die Zeit   G. der Zeit   D. der Zeit

MASCULINE AND NEUTER NOUNS

2. A group of Masc. nouns, mostly ending in -e and denoting living creatures, add -n or -en to form the Acc., Gen., and Dat., e.g. *der Knabe* (boy), *der Fürst* (prince), *der Herr* (lord, master, Mr.):

N. der Knabe   A. den Knaben   G. des Knaben   D. dem Knaben
N. der Fürst   A. den Fürsten   G. des Fürsten   D. dem Fürsten
N. der Herr   A. den Herrn   G. des Herrn   D. dem Herrn

NOTE.—These Masc. nouns make the plural also by adding -n or en:

N. die Knaben   A. die Knaben   G. der Knaben   D. den Knaben
N. die Herren   A. die Herren   G. der Herren   D. den Herren

All other Masc. and Neuter nouns are declined as follows:

(a) The Nom. and Acc. are of the same form : *der Tisch—den Tisch ; der Führer — den Führer ; der König — den König ; das Haus — das Haus ; das Dach — das Dach.*

(b) In the Gen. they add -es or -s.
They always add -es if they end in a sibilant (= hissing sound) : -s, -ss, -z, -tz, -sch, -x, e.g. *das Haus — des Hauses ; der Tisch — des Tisches ; der Platz — des Platzes.* Nouns ending in -el, -er, -en, -chen, and -lein always add -s only : *der Führer — des Führers ; das Mädchen — des Mädchens.*

All Masc. and Neuter nouns other than (a) and (b) above may add either -es or -s, but -s is nowadays more usual, especially in the spoken language : *der König — des König(e)s ; der Tag — des Tag(e)s.*

(c) In the Dat., Masc. and Neuter nouns ending in -el, -er, -en, -chen and -lein have the same form as the Nom. : *der Führer — dem Führer ; das Mädchen — dem Mädchen.*
The Dat. ending -e may be added to all other Masc. and Neuter nouns, but it is becoming old-fashioned and is frequently omitted : *der König — dem König(e) ; der Monat — dem Monat(e).* It is more usual with monosyllables : *der Tag — dem Tag(e) ; das Haus — dem Haus(e),* but is very seldom heard in spoken German.

Examples of the above :

N. das Haus   A. das Haus   G. des Hauses   D. dem Haus(e)
N. der Vater A. den Vater G. des Vaters   D. dem Vater
N. der Tag   A. den Tag   G. des Tag(e)s D. dem Tag(e)

B. PLURAL

NOTE.—The vowel sounds *a*, *o*, *u*, and *au* tend to change into *ä*, *ö*, *ü*, and *äu* when an "*e*" or "*i*" sound is in a neighbouring syllable. This change of vowel sound is called modification (*der Umlaut*) and frequently occurs in the plural of nouns. Thus, *der Hut* adds *-e* and becomes *die Hüte*; *das Haus* adds *-er* and becomes *die Häuser*. There are, however, a number of exceptions.

Here are some useful rules for the Plural:

1. The great majority of Fem. nouns add *-n* or *-en*.
2. The Nom., Acc., and Gen. of all Plurals are alike.
3. The Dat. Plural always ends in *-n*.

We can classify our Plurals into:

I. Those which add *-n* or *-en*: *die Frau — die Frauen*; *der Knabe — die Knaben*.
II. Those which add nothing: *der Gürtel — die Gürtel*; *das Mädchen — die Mädchen*.
III. Those which add *-e*: *der König — die Könige*; *der Tag — die Tage*; *die Stadt — die Städte*.
IV. Those which add *-er*; *das Glass — die Gläser*.

The following table shows how Masc., Fem., and Neuter nouns are spread over the four classes:

I. PLURAL ENDING: *-n* OR *-en*

Masculine	Feminine	Neuter
Those ending in *-e* denoting living creatures.	Most Fem. nouns.	See below, "Mixed Declension."
None modify.	None modify.	None modify.
der Knabe — die Knaben.	**die Zeit — die Zeiten.**	**das Bett — die Betten.**

II. PLURAL ENDING: NONE

Masculine	Feminine	Neuter
Those ending in *-el*, *-er*, *-en*. Most do not modify; a few do.	Only two; both modify.	Those ending in *-el*, *-er*, *-en*, *-chen*, and *-lein*, and those with prefix *Ge-* ending in *-e*.
der Wagen — die Wagen; der Vater — die Väter.	**die Mutter — die Mütter; die Tochter — die Töchter.**	Only one modifies; **das Kloster — die Klöster** (convent)
NOTE: **der Käse — die Käse.**		**das Mittel — die Mittel; das Lager — die Lager; das Glöcklein — die Glöcklein; das Gebäude — die Gebäude.**

III. Plural Ending: -e

Most monosyllables.	Some 30 common monosyllables.	A small number of monosyllables.
The majority modify.	All modify.	None modify.

Most monosyllables. The majority modify. **der Baum — die Bäume; der Ast — die Äste;** but **der Hund — die Hunde.** Those ending in *-ig, -ing, -ling.*: **der König — die Könige.** None modify.

Some 30 common monosyllables. All modify. **die Hand — die Hände; Stadt — die Städte; Brust — die Brüste.** Also a few in *-nis* and *-sal*; they do not modify: **die Bedrängnis — die Bedrängnisse; die Trübsal — die Trübsale.**

A small number of monosyllables. None modify. **das Jahr — die Jahre; das Schaf — die Schafe.** Also those ending in *-nis* and *-sal*: **das Zeugnis — die Zeugnisse; das Schicksal — die Schicksale.**

IV. Plural Ending: -er

Some 11 common words and all Masc. in *-tum*.	None.	Most monosyllables and all Neuters in *-tum*.

Some 11 common words and all Masc. in *-tum*. All modify. **der Mann — die Männer; der Gott — die Götter; der Wald — die Wälder; der Reichtum — die Reichtümer.**

None.

Most monosyllables and all Neuters in *-tum*. All modify. **das Haus — die Häuser; das Glas — die Gläser; das Gras — die Gräser; das Eigentum — die Eigentümer.**

Here are some examples of the declensions, Sing. and Plural:

Class I

Sing. N. der Rabe	A. den Raben	G. des Raben	D. dem Raben
Plur. N. die Raben	A. die Raben	G. der Raben	D. den Raben
Sing. N. die Zeit	A. die Zeit	G. der Zeit	D. der Zeit
Plur. N. die Zeiten	A. die Zeiten	G. der Zeiten	D. den Zeiten

Class II

Sing. N. der Wagen	A. den Wagen	G. des Wagens	D. dem Wagen
Plur. N. die Wagen	A. die Wagen	G. der Wagen	D. den Wagen
Sing. N. der Vater	A. den Vater	G. des Vaters	D. dem Vater
Plur. N. die Väter	A. die Väter	G. der Väter	D. den Vätern
Sing. N. die Mutter	A. die Mutter	G. der Mutter	D. der Mutter
Plur. N. die Mütter	A. die Mütter	G. der Mütter	D. den Müttern
Sing. N. das Lager	A. das Lager	G. des Lagers	D. dem Lager
Plur. N. die Lager	A. die Lager	G. der Lager	D. den Lagern

Class III

Sing. N. **der Ast**	A. **den Ast**	G. **des Astes**	D. **dem Ast(e)**
Plur. N. **die Äste**	A. **die Äste**	G. **der Äste**	D. **den Ästen**
Sing. N. **der Arm**	A. **den Arm**	G. **des Arm(e)s**	D. **dem Arm(e)**
Plur. N. **die Arme**	A. **die Arme**	G. **der Arme**	D. **den Armen**
Sing. N. **die Gans**	A. **die Gans**	G. **der Gans**	D. **der Gans**
Plur. N. **die Gänse**	A. **die Gänse**	G. **der Gänse**	D. **den Gänsen**
Sing. N. **das Jahr**	A. **das Jahr**	G. **des Jahr(e)s**	D. **dem Jahr(e)**
Plur. N. **die Jahre**	A. **die Jahre**	G. **der Jahre**	D. **den Jahren**

Class IV

Sing. N. **der Mann**	A. **den Mann**	G. **des Mann(e)s**	D. **dem Mann(e)**
Plur. N. **die Männer**	A. **die Männer**	G. **der Männer**	D. **den Männern**
Sing. N. **das Glas**	A. **das Glas**	G. **des Glases**	D. **dem Glas(e)**
Plur. N. **die Gläser**	A. **die Gläser**	G. **der Gläser**	D. **den Gläsern**

C. NOTES ON THE TABLE OF PLURALS

Masculines in Class I declined like *Knabe* or *Rabe* are : *der Affe* (ape) ; *der Bote* (messenger) ; *der Bube* (lad) ; *der Erbe* (heir) ; *der Hase* (hare) ; *der Heide* (heathen) ; *der Junge* (boy) ; *der Löwe* (lion) ; *der Neffe* (nephew) ; *der Riese* (giant) ; *der Zeuge* (witness). The following have lost their *-e* and are declined like *Fürst* : *der Bär* (bear) ; *der Christ* (Christian) ; *der Graf* (count) ; *der Mensch* (human being) ; *der Narr* (fool) ; *der Held* (hero) ; *der Herr*, which makes *die Herren* in the plural.

Nouns of foreign origin accented on the last syllable also belong to Class I : *der Student — die Studenten ; der Philosoph — die Philosophen*, and are declined like *Knabe*.

Masculines in Class II mostly do not modify ; the following DO modify : *der Acker* (field) ; *der Bruder* (brother) ; *der Garten* (garden) ; *der Graben* (ditch) ; *der Hammer* (hammer) ; *der Hafen* (harbour) ; *der Handel* (trade) ; *der Mangel* (lack) ; *der Nagel* (nail) ; *der Ofen* (stove) ; *der Sattel* (saddle) ; *der Schnabel* (beak) ; *der Schwager* (brother-in-law) ; *der Vater* (father) ; *der Vogel* (bird).

Masculines in Class III mostly modify ; the following common words do NOT modify : *der Arm* (arm) ; *der Hund* (dog) ; *der Laut* (sound) ; *der Pfad* (path) ; *der Schuh* (boot, shoe) ; *der Tag* (day) ; *der Zoll* (inch). Class III also contains some foreign words such as *der General*, plural *die Generäle* or *Generale*. A number of these end in *-eur* : *der Redakteur* (editor) — *die Redakteure*.

Masculines in Class IV declined like *der Mann* are : *der Gott* (God) ; *der Abgott* (idol) ; *der Geist* (spirit) ; *der Leib* (body) ; *der Rand* (edge) ; *der Wald* (wood) ; *der Wurm* (worm) ; *der Strauch* (shrub) ; and the masculines in *-tum* : *der Irrtum* (error) and *der Reichtum* (riches).

The common Feminines in Class III which add *-e* and modify are : *die Angst* (fear) ; *die Axt* (axe) ; *die Bank* (bench) ; *die Braut* (bride) ; *die Faust* (fist) ; *die Frucht* (fruit) ; *die Gans* (goose) ; *die Hand* (hand) ; *die Kraft* (power) ; *die Kuh* (cow) ; *die Kunst* (art) ; *die Luft* (air) ; *die Lust* (desire) ; *die Macht* (might, power) ; *die Magd* (maid) ; *die Maus* (mouse) ; *die Nacht* (night) ; *die Nuss* (nut) ; *die Schnur* (string) ; *die Stadt* (town) ; *die Wand* (wall) ; *die Wurst* (sausage).

Neuter Monosyllables in Class III which add *-e* and do not modify are : *das Beil* (axe) ; *das Bein* (leg) ; *das Boot* (boat) ; *das Ding* (thing) ; *das Erz* (ore) ; *das Fell* (skin, pelt) ; *das Gift* (poison) ; *das Haar* (hair) ; *das Heer* (army) ; *das Jahr* (year) ; *das Knie* (knee) ; *das Kreus* (cross); *das Mass* (measure); *das Meer* (sea); *das Pferd* (horse); *das Recht* (right, law); *das Schaf* (sheep); *das Schiff* (ship); *das Schwein* (pig); *das Seil* (rope); *das Spiel* (game); *das Tier* (animal); *das Werk* (work); (*das Wort* (word) has two plurals: *Worte*, spoken words, and *Wörter*, words in general); *das Zelt* (tent); *das Ziel* (aim).

Neuter Monosyllables in Class IV which add *-er* and modify are: *das Amt* (office); *das Bad* (bath); *das Band* (ribbon); *das Blatt* (leaf, page); *das Buch* (book); *das Dach* (roof); *das Dorf* (village); *das Fass* (vat); *das Grab* (grave); *das Gras* (grass); *das Gut* (estate, commodity); *das Haupt* (head); *das Holz* (wood); *das Horn* (horn); *das Huhn* (hen); *das Kalb* (calf); *das Lamm* (lamb); *das Land* (land); *das Loch* (hole); *das Mahl* (repast); *das Rad* (wheel); *das Schloss* (castle, lock); *das Tuch* (cloth); *das Volk* (people).

D. THE MIXED DECLENSION

There are a few Masculine and Neuter nouns which take *-s* or *-es* in the Genitive but make the Plural in *-n* or *-en*. They are:

Der Dorn (thorn) — *des Dorn(e)s* — *die Dornen* or *Dörner;* *der Schmerz* (pain) — *des Schmerzes* — *die Schmerzen;* *der See* (lake; *die See* = sea) — *des Sees* — *die Seen;* *der Sporn* (spur) — *des Sporns* — *die Sporen* or *Spornen;* *der Staat* (state) — *des Staat(e)s* — *die Staaten;* *der Strahl* (beam, ray) — *des Strahl(e)s* — *die Strahlen;* *der Vetter* (cousin) — *des Vetters* — *die Vettern;* *der Nachbar* (neighbour) — *des Nachbars* — *die Nachbaren.* Also most loan words in *-or;* *der Doktor* — *des Doktors* — *die Doktoren.*

Der Funke (spark) has two declensions: (a) *der Funke* — *des Funken* — *die Funken* and (b) *der Funken* — *des Funkens* — *die Funken.* So also *der Friede(n)* (peace); *der Gedanke(n)* (thought); *der Glaube(n)* (belief); *der Name(n)* (name); *der Schade(n)* (hurt, damage).

The following Neuters also belong to the Mixed Declension: *das Auge* (eye) — *des Auges* — *die Augen;* *das Bett* (bed) — *des Bettes* — *die Betten;* *das Ende* (end) — *des Endes* — *die Enden;* *das Hemd* (shirt) — *des Hemdes* — *die Hemden;* *das Ohr* (ear) — *des Ohres* — *die Ohren;* *das Insekt* (insect) — *des Insektes* — *die Insekten;* *das Herz* (heart) — *des Herzens* — *die Herzen.*

E. SOME ODD PLURALS

The following are used only in the Plural: *die Eltern* (parents); *die Ferien* (holidays); *die Geschwister* (brothers and sisters); *die Kosten* (cost); *die Leute* (people).

The following have two plurals with different meanings:

Das Band has *die Bänder* (ribbons) and *die Bande* (chains).

Die Bank has *die Bänke* (benches) and *die Banken* (banks for money).

Das Ding has *die Dinge* (things) and *die Dinger* (wretched things or people).

Das Gesicht has *die Gesichte* (apparitions) and *die Gesichter* (faces).

Das Licht has *die Lichte* (candles) and *die Lichter* (lights).

Der Ort has *die Orte* (districts) and *die Örter* (towns, places).

Das Tuch has *die Tuche* (kinds of cloth) and *die Tücher* (pieces of cloth).

Das Wort has *die Worte* (connected words) and *die Wörter* (words as units).

Der Laden has *die Läden* (shops) and *die Laden* (shutters).

NOTE.—Words compounded with *-mann* have mostly the Plural in *-leute*: *der Kaufmann* (merchant), *die Kaufleute*; but *Staatsmann* makes *Staatsmänner*.

F. DECLENSION OF PROPER NOUNS

Proper nouns, Masc. and Fem., form their Genitive in *-s*: *Karls; Goethes; Bertas; Maries*. If they end in a sibilant *-ens* is used; *Hans — Hansens; Fritz — Fritzens*. If preceded by the Def. Art. the Genitive ending disappears: *des Karl; des Schiller; des jungen Goethe.*

IV. GENDER OF NOUNS

We give below some rule-of-thumb notes on gender, but the Golden Rule is to learn the German noun *with* its Definite Article: learn *der Tisch; die Zeitung; das Dach*. Do not try to memorize *Tisch*, m., *Zeitung*, f., *Dach*, n., and when you learn *der Tisch*, etc., say it aloud so that you use the natural linguistic channels to the memory, the ear and the organs of speech.

Masculines. All males: *der Mann, der Fürst*. A large number of nouns in *-er* denoting the doer of an action: *der Reiter*, horseman, *des Führer*, leader, driver.

The days of the week: *des Montag*; months: *der Juli*; seasons: *der Sommer*; points of the compass: *der Norden* or *Nord*.

Words of two syllables in *-en*: *der Garten, der Ofen*; a number of nouns in *-e* denoting living creatures: *der Rabe*; nouns derived directly from the stem of strong verbs: *der Fall, der Trunk*; nouns ending in *-ig*: *der König*; *-ich*: *des Fittich*; *-ling*: *der Findling*.

Feminines. Females: *die Frau*, but *das Weib, das Fräulein, das Mädchen*.

All nouns ending in *-ei*: *die Reiterei*; *-heit*: *die Kindheit*; *-keit*: *die Dankbarkeit*; *-ung*: *die Trennung*; *-schaft*: *die Freundschaft*; *-ie*; *die Familie*; *-ion*: *die Ration*; *-tät*: *die Universität*; *-ik*: *die Fabrik*; *-in*, corresponding to our *-ess*: *die Fürstin, die Herrin, die Freundin* (pl. *Herrinnen, Freundinnen*).

Nouns ending in *-e* denoting inanimates: *die Bluse, die Länge*; nouns ending in *-t* derived from strong verbs: *die Macht, die Tat*.

Neuters. All diminutives ending in *-chen* and *-lein*: *das Männlein, das Hütchen*. All other parts of speech used as nouns: infinitives: *das Singen*; adjectives used as abstract nouns: *das Schöne*, beauty, the beautiful; prepositions: *das Für und das Wider* ("for and against"; pros and cons). Names of metals, except *der Stahl*: *das Eisen, das Gold*. Names of countries: *das alte England*. (*Die Schweiz*, Switzerland, and *die Türkei*, Turkey, are feminine.) Most nouns ending in *-nis*: *das Begräbnis*; *-sal*: *das Schicksal*; *-sel*: *das Rätsel*; *-tum*: *das Königtum*, royalty.

NOTE—Compound nouns take the gender of the last component: *das Weinglas*, wineglass; *die Weinkaraffe*, wine-decanter. *Der Mut*, courage, makes *die Sanftmut*, gentleness; *die Schwermut*, melancholy, but *der Gleichmut*, equanimity; *der Hochmut*, pride, etc.

V. DECLENSION OF THE ADJECTIVE

The adjective is invariable when it forms part of the predicate : *der Mann ist alt ; die Frau ist alt : das Haus ist alt.*

If the adjective qualifies the noun directly — attributively — it is inflected : *der alte Mann, ein alter Mann ; die alte Frau, eine alte Frau ; das alte Haus, ein altes Haus.*

There are three declensions : **I. Weak,** when the adjective is preceded by the Definite Article or any of the following limiting words — *dieser, jener, welcher, jeder* (sing.), *alle* (pl.), *solcher, mancher.* **II. Mixed,** when the adjective is preceded by the Indefinite Article, a Possessive Adjective or *kein.* **III. Strong,** when the adjective precedes a noun without any article or other limiting word, e.g. red wine, modern music, good fruit. This declension is very common in the plural : young men, interesting books, high mountains. When found in the singular it is used chiefly with names of substances.

I. Weak

Endings of the adjective before *der, dieser, jener, jeder* (sing.), *alle* (pl.), *welcher, solcher, mancher.*

	Masc.	Fem.	Neut.	Plural
N.	-e	-e	-e	-en
A.	-en	-e	-e	-en
G.	-en	-en	-en	-en
D.	-en	-en	-en	-en

Note—There are only two endings, *-e* and *-en.*

Examples :

der rote Wein, die moderne Musik, dieses gute Obst, jenen alten Mann (acc.), *jedes kleinen Kindes* (gen.), *auf dem braunen Tisch* (dat.), *alle schönen Frauen* (nom. & acc. pl.).

II. Mixed

Endings of the adjective before *ein, kein, mein, dein, sein, ihr, unser, euer, Ihr.*

	Masc.	Fem.	Neut.	Plural
N.	-er	-e	-es	-en
A.	-en	-e	-es	-en
G.	-en	-en	-en	-en
D.	-en	-en	-en	-en

Note—Where the article or possessive adjective does not indicate gender, i.e. masc. nom. and neut. nom. and acc. cases, the adjective must do so.

The ending *-en* occurs in exactly the same cases as in Table I (separated from the other endings by the dividing line).

Examples:

ein weisser Wein, eine schwarze Tinte, ein dunkles Bier. meines besten Freundes, seinem alten Vater, Ihre schönen Bilder.

III. STRONG

Endings of the adjective where there is no article or possessive adjective.

	Masc.	Fem.	Neut.	Plural.
N.	-er	-e	-es	-e
A.	-en	-e	-es	-e
G.	-en	-er	-en	-er
D.	-em	-er	-em	-en

NOTE—The endings in this table are the same as those in the table for the declension of the definite article (cf. p. 266), except for the masc. and neut. genitive singular endings.

Examples:

roter Wein, moderne Musik, gutes Obst, der Geschmack guten Weins, junge Männer, hohe Berge.

Adjectives ending in *-el, -er, -en* generally drop the *-e* when decline, as *edel*, noble, but *ein edles Gebäude*, a noble building. *Hoch*, high, changes *ch* to *h* before *-e*: *der Berg ist hoch*, but *ein hoher Berg*, a high mountain, Present and Past Participles of verbs are adjectives and declined as such: *ein spannendes Buch*, a thrilling book; *der gejagte Hase*, the hunted hare. With numeral adjectives in the plural such as *viele*, many; *wenige*, few; *einige*, some; *andere*, other, the strong endings are used. With *alle*, all and *manche*, many, the weak endings are used.

Adjectives can be used as nouns, in which case they have a capital letter: *der Blinde*, the blind man; *die Blinde*, the blind woman; *die Blinden*, the blind; *ein Blinder*, a blind man; *eine Blinde*, a blind woman. The noun is declined exactly as if it were an adjective. The Neuter is also used in a general sense: *das Geschehene*, what has happened; *das Schöne in der Natur*, the beautiful in nature.

VI. COMPARISON OF ADJECTIVES

In English we have two ways of comparing Adjectives: " long,
longer, longest " and " beautiful, more beautiful, most beautiful."
In German there is only one way : add -er to the Positive for the
Comparative and -st or -est for the Superlative. The commonest
monosyllables also modify the vowel if it is a, o, or u. Adjectives
ending in a sibilant or in -d or -t, add -est for the Superlative, all others
adding -st.

Adjectives ending in -er, -el, or -en may drop the -e when adding
the -er for the Comparative, e.g. edel, noble, ed(e)ler ; heiser, hoarse,
heis(e)rer ; offen, open, off(e)ner.

A word about the Superlative. There are two kinds : (a) when we
compare one thing or person with others—called the Relative Superlative—as in " This river is the deepest," where " This river " is
compared with other rivers, Dieser Fluss ist der tiefste ; (b) the
Absolute Superlative, when a thing or person is compared with itself,
as in " The river is deepest here," Hier ist der Fluss am tiefsten, literally
" Here the river is at its deepest." Am is a fusion of an, at, and the
dative neuter dem.

Here are some examples of the comparison of Adjectives given
in the most convenient form for learning, viz. with als after the
Comparative, e.g. länger als, longer than :

Positive	Comparative	Rel. Superlative	Abs. Superlative
lang, long	länger als	der, die das längste	am längsten
kurz, short	kürzer als	der, die, das kürzeste	am kürzesten
alt, old	älter als	der, die, das älteste	am ältesten
einfach, simple	einfacher als	der, die, das einfachste	am einfachsten

The following monosyllables do not modify : klar, clear ; sanft,
gentle ; schlank, slender ; stolz, proud ; voll, full ; starr, stiff.

Irregular forms are :

> gut, good, besser, best
> hoch, high, höher, höchst
> nah, near, näher, nächst
> gross, big, grösser, grösst
> viel, much, mehr, meist

When declined, the Comparative and Superlative forms add on the
case inflexions exactly as does the Positive : der alte Mann, der ältere
Mann, der älteste Mann ; kein alter Mann, kein ält(e)rer Mann, kein
ältester Mann, etc.

VII. THE ADVERB

In English we generally form the Adverb from the Adjective by adding *-ly* e.g. beautiful, beautifully. In German the Adverb has the same form as the Adjective, but it is not declined: *Marie ist schön*, Mary is beautiful; *Marie singt schön*, Mary sings beautifully.

COMPARISON OF ADVERBS

The Adverb is compared in the same way as the Adjective, by adding *-er* and *-st* or *-est* to the Positive, and there are two Superlatives: (*a*) the Relative Superlative with *am*: *Er singt am schönsten von allen*, he sings the most beautifully of all, and *Er singt am schönsten, wenn er glücklich ist*, he sings most beautifully when he is happy; (*b*) the Absolute Superlative with *aufs* or *auf das*: *Er singt aufs schönste*, he sings most (very) beautifully, i.e. in the highest degree beautifully.

There are some few Adverbs which use the Superlative without *am* or *aufs*, e.g. *höchst*: *Ich bin höchst erfreut*, I am very (highly) delighted; *höflichst*, very politely, and *möglichst*, from *möglich*, possible: *Ich bitte Sie höflichst, möglichst bald zu schreiben*, I beg you (very politely) to write as soon as ever possible; *innigst*, very deeply: *Ich liebe sie innigst*, I love her very deeply.

Here are some examples of Adverbs compared:

Positive	Comparative	Rel. Superlative	Abs. Superlative
schön	**schöner als**	**am schönsten**	**aufs schönste**
schnell	**schneller als**	**am schnellsten**	**aufs schnellste**

The following are irregular:

gut (wohl), well	**besser**	**am besten**
gern, willingly	**lieber**	**am liebsten**
bald, soon	**eher**	**am ehesten**
viel, much	**mehr**	**am meisten**

VIII. NUMERALS

The Cardinal numbers are:

0 **null**	10 **zehn**	20 **zwanzig**
1 **ein, eine, ein**	11 **elf**	21 **einundzwanzig**
2 **zwei**	12 **zwölf**	22 **zweiundzwanzig**
3 **drei**	13 **dreizehn**	23 **dreiundzwanzig**
		30 **dreissig**
4 **vier**	14 **vierzehn**	40 **vierzig**
5 **fünf**	15 **fünfzehn**	50 **fünfzig**
(**funf**)	(**funfzehn**)	(**funfzig**)
6 **sechs**	16 **sechzehn**	60 **sechzig**
7 **sieben**	17 **siebzehn**	70 **siebzig**
	(**siebenzehn**)	(**siebenzig**)
8 **acht**	18 **achtzehn**	80 **achtzig**
9 **neun**	19 **neunzehn**	90 **neunzig**
		100 **hundert**
		101 **(ein) hundertundeins**
		102 **(ein) hundertundzwei**
		200 **zweihundert**
		1,000 **tausend**
		1,001 **(ein) tausendundeins**
		10,000 **zehntausend**
		100,000 **hunderttausend**
		1,000,000 **eine Million**

NOTES.—In counting, 1 is *eins*. To distinguish between the Indefinite Article *ein, eine, ein* and the numeral, e.g. " I have a book " and " I have one book," the numeral is printed with spaced letters (*gesperrt gedruckt*): *Ich habe ein Buch*, and *Ich habe e i n Buch*. In telephoning and in wireless 2 is prounced *zwo*.

The Ordinals are formed by adding *-t* to the Cardinals from 2 to 19 and *-st* from 20 onwards, except for first, third, and eighth.

1st	**der, die, das erste**		20th	**der, die, das zwanzigste**	
2nd	"	**zweite**	21st	"	**einundzwanzigste**
3rd	"	**dritte**	100th	"	**hundertste**
4th	"	**vierte**	101st	"	**hundertunderste**
8th	"	**achte**	1,000th	"	**tausendste**

Fractions are formed by adding *-tel* (from *das Teil*, part) to the ordinals but suppressing the *-t* of the stem, e.g. *dritt, Drittel*: *das Drittel*, the third; *ein Viertel*, a fourth, quarter; *ein Hundertstel*, one hundredth. *Halb*, half, is used for *ein Zweitel*: *eine halbe Stunde*, half an hour, or *die Hälfte* as in *Die Hälfte meines Vermögens*, half my fortune.

Other useful forms derived from the cardinals are those in *-erlei*: *einerlei*, of one kind; *zweierlei*, of two kinds; *allerlei*, of all kinds. They are uninflected. By adding *-mal* we get *eihmal*, once; *zweimal*, twice; *dreimal*, three times. By adding *-fach* we get *einfach*, one-fold, single, simple; *zweifach*, twofold; *dreifach*, threefold. By adding *-ens* to the ordinal we get *erstens*, in the first place; *zweitens*, in the second place, etc.

IX. DATES AND THE TIME

The names of the days of the week are: *der Montag, der Dienstag, der Mittwoch, der Donnerstag, der Frietag, der Samstag* or *Sonnabend, der Sonntag.*

The months: *der Januar, Februar, März, April, Mai, Juni, Juli, August, September, Oktober, November, Dezember.*

The seasons: *der Frühling, der Sommer, der Herbst, der Winter.*

Useful expressions are: *am Montag,* on Monday; *er kommt jeden Montag,* he comes every Monday; *sie besucht uns Montags,* she visits us on Mondays. *Im Frühling ist das Wetter kühl,* in spring the weather is cool; *im August ist es oft schwül,* in August it is often sultry.

For dates we ask: *Der wievielte ist heute?* or *Den wievielten haben wir heute?* What is the date (day of the month) today? The answer runs: *Es ist heute der zwanzigste Juli, neunzehnhundertfünfundvierzig* or *Wir haben heute den zwanzigsten Juli,* etc. Dates on a letter are in the Accusative: *Berlin, den vierten August.* To express " On Monday, the sixth of June," we say: *Am Montag, dem sechsten Juni.* To say " That took place in 1940," we have either *Das fand im Jahre 1940 statt* or *Das fand 1940 statt,* but we never use *in* alone before the year as we do in English. *Im* is a fusion of the preposition *in* and the dative *dem.*

To ask the time, we use *Wieviel Uhr ist es?* What time is it? We tell the time as follows:

Es ist neun Uhr. It is nine o'clock.

Es ist fünf (Minuten) nach neun. It is five past nine.

Es ist viertel nach neun ; es ist ein Viertel nach neun ; es ist ein Viertel zehn. It is a quarter past nine.

Es ist halb zehn. It is half-past nine.

Es ist zwanzig (Minuten) vor zehn. It is twenty to ten.

Es ist viertel vor zehn ; es ist ein Viertel vor zehn ; es ist dreiviertel zehn. It is a quarter to ten.

Um is used for " at " when telling the time: *Ich komme morgen um elf Uhr,* I shall come tomorrow at eleven. A.M. is *vormittags* ; P.M. is *nachmittags,* the parts of the day being: *der Morgen* or *der Vormittag, der Mittag, der Nachmittag, der Abend, die Nacht.* They all make adverbs by adding -s : *morgens, abends, nachts.*

Other useful time-words are: *heute,* today; *morgen,* tomorrow; *übermorgen,* the day after tomorrow; *gestern,* yesterday; *vorgestern,* the day before yesterday; *heute vor acht Tagen,* a week ago today; *heute über acht Tage,* a week from today. *Acht Tage,* like " huit jours " in French, is usual for " a week " : *Ich blieb acht Tage in Berlin,* I remained a week in Berlin, but *Eine Woche hat sieben Tage,* a week has seven days.

SUMMARY OF THE ADVERBIAL USES OF THE OBLIQUE CASES

The Accusative is used for time: *Er kommt nächsten Donnerstag,* he is coming next Thursday; *Jedes Jahr am 11ten August ist eine Feier,* there is a celebration every year on the 11th August; for measures: *Das Brett ist einen Fuss lang,* the board is a foot long;

for value: *Es ist keinen Heller wert*, it is not worth a red cent; *es kostet eine Mark*.

The Dative is used for time in: *Am Abend wenn wir im Bett sind*, in the evening when we are in bed; *im Sommer, im Winter, am Samstag*.

The Genitive is used for customary or repeated time: *Sonntags gehe ich nicht in die Schule*, I don't go to school on Sundays; similarly: *sommers, nachts, tags, morgens*. Indefinite Time is also in the Genitive: *Eines Tages als ich ins Konzert ging*, one day when I was going to the concert. Place is shown in: *Er ging seines Weges*, he went on his way; manner in: *guten Mutes sein* to be of good cheer; *der Meinung sein*, to be of the opinion; *meines Erachtens*, in my judgment, opinion; *stehenden Fusses*, on the spot, forthwith; *festen Schrittes*, with firm step.

We might mention here what was a Genitive but is now treated as the Neuter of the adjective used as a substantive: *Nichts Neues*, nothing new; *Ich habe etwas Interessantes für Sie*, I have something interesting for you; *Er kommt immer mit etwas Neuem*, he's always got something new.

X. PERSONAL PRONOUNS

DECLENSION

SINGULAR
Personal

	1st Pers.	2nd Pers.	3rd Pers.		
			er	sie	es
N.	ich	du, Sie	er	sie	es
A.	mich	dich, Sie	ihn	sie	es
G.	meiner	deiner, Ihrer	seiner	ihrer	seiner
D.	mir	dir, Ihnen	ihm	ihr	ihm

Reflexive

	1st Pers.	2nd Pers.	3rd Pers.
A.	mich	dich, sich	sich
D.	mir	dir, sich	sich

PLURAL

	1st Pers.	2nd Pers.	3rd Pers.
N.	wir	ihr, Sie	sie
A.	uns	euch, Sie	sie
G.	unser	euer, Ihrer	ihrer
D.	uns	euch, Ihnen	ihnen

Reflexive

	1st Pers.	2nd Pers.	3rd Pers.
A.	uns	euch, sich	sich
D.	uns	euch, sich	sich

NOTES—*Du* is used when speaking to an intimate friend, a relative, a child, an animal, or in angry insult to a stranger. *Ihr*, the plural of *du*, is used in the same way to friends, relatives, children, and in solemn speech. For all ordinary purposes you will never use either *du* or *ihr*, but will be content with the more formal *Sie* which is both singular and plural. When using *du* in a letter it is spelt with a capital: *Du*. *Sie*, you, is always spelt with a capital; *ich*, never except when commencing a sentence.

The Reflexive forms are used as in English: *Ich wasche mich*, I wash myself; *Ich schmeichle mir*, I flatter myself (the Dative is used with *schmeicheln* because this verb governs the Dative case). In such cases as: He has a book in front of him, the German uses the Reflexive, since "him" refers back to the subject "he": *Er hat ein Buch vor sich.*

Note that *sie* may mean: she, her, they, them, and when spelt with a capital also: you. You will have to be careful with these words at first.

The 3rd Pers. Neuter *es* is rather tricky. If it refers to a living being, e.g. *das Mädchen*, *das Weib*, it is declined as above; if it refers to an inanimate object, the Genitive becomes *dessen* and the Dative *demselben* (the same) or a compound of *da* with a preposition. An example or two will make this clear:

Sprachen Sie mit dem Mädchen?   Ja, ich sprach mit ihm (or *mit ihr* in spite of grammar!).   Did you speak to the girl?   Yes, I spoke to her.   *Liegt Ihr Buch auf dem Pult?   Ja, es liegt darauf (auf demselben).*   Is your book lying on the desk?   Yes, it is lying on it (thereon).   This applies to all inanimate objects whether Masc., Fem., or Neut., e.g.; *Schreiben Sie mit dieser Feder?   Ja, ich schreibe damit.* Are you writing with this pen?   Yes, I'm writing with it.   If the Preposition begins with a vowel—*an, auf, unter, über,* etc.—an " *r* " is inserted to make it easier to pronounce—*daran, darauf, darunter, darüber,* etc.—otherwise *da* is used : *dabei, damit, davon.*

XI. POSSESSIVE ADJECTIVES AND PRONOUNS

The Possessive Adjectives are **mein, meine, mein**, my; **dein, deine, dein**, thy; **sein, seine, sein**, his; **ihr, ihre, ihr**, her; **sein, seine, sein**, its; **unser, uns(e)re: unser**, our; **euer, eu(e)re, euer**, your; **Ihr, Ihre, Ihr**, your; **ihr, ihre, ihr**, their. They are declined like *ein, eine, ein*.

The Possessive Pronouns in English are; mine, thine, his, hers, its, ours, yours, theirs. German has no special form for " its," *sein* being used for both " his " and " its."

German has four different forms of the Possessive Pronouns, one uninflected and three inflected. The uninflected form can be used only as part of the predicate to indicate simple possession; the three inflected forms, which have all exactly the same meaning and uses, may be used in all circumstances.

These four forms are as follows:

1. The uninflected Possessive Pronouns are: **mein, dein, sein, unser, euer.** They can be used only as part of the predicate to indicate possession, e.g. *Dieser Hut (diese Feder, dieses Haus) ist mein (dein, sein, unser, euer)*, this hat(pen, house) is mine (thine, his, ours, yours). Note that **ihr** (hers, theirs) and **Ihr** (yours) cannot be so used; we must use one of the inflected forms given below, e.g. *Dieser Hut ist ihrer (der ihre, der ihrige)*; *Diese Feder ist ihre (die ihre, die ihrige)*.

2. The three inflected forms are:

(a)
meiner	**meine**	**meines**
deiner	**deine**	**deines**
seiner	**seine**	**seines**
ihrer	**ihre**	**ihres**
uns(e)rer	**uns(e)re**	**uns(e)res**
eu(e)rer	**eu(e)re**	**eu(e)res**
Ihrer	**Ihre**	**Ihres**
ihrer	**ihre**	**ihres**

These are declined like *dieser, diese, dieses*.

(b)
der deine	**die meine**	**das meine**
der deine	**die deine**	**das deine**
der seine	**die seine**	**das seine**
der ihre	**die ihre**	**das ihre**
der uns(e)re	**die uns(e)re**	**das uns(e)re**
der eu(e)re	**die eu(e)re**	**das eu(e)re**
der Ihre	**die Ihre**	**das Ihre**
der ihre	**die ihre**	**das ihre**

These are declined like an Adj. with the Def. Art.

(c)
der meinige	**die meinige**	**das meinige**
der deinige	**die deinige**	**das deinige**
der seinige	**die seinige**	**das seinige**
der ihrige	**die ihrige**	**das ihrige**
etc.	*etc.*	*etc.*

These are also declined like an Adj. with the Def. Art.

The plurals of the above are: (a) *meine*, etc.; (b) *die meinen*, etc.; (c) *die meinigen*, etc.

Examples of the use of the Possessive Pronouns are: *Dieser Hut ist mein (meiner, der meine, der meinige)*, this hat is mine; *Diese Feder ist unser (unsre, die unsre, die unsrige)*, this hat is ours; *Dieses Haus ist sein (seines, das seine, das seinige)*, this house is his; *Diese Bücher sind Ihre (die Ihren, die Ihrigen)*, these books are yours. *Frau Schmidt liebt ihre Kinder, kann aber meine (die meinen, die meinigen) nicht leiden*, Mrs. Smith loves her children but she cannot stand mine.

XII. DEMONSTRATIVE ADJECTIVES AND PRONOUNS

1. **Der, die, das** is used as a Demonstrative Adj., as in : *Ist DIE Dame Ihre Mutter?* Is *that* lady your mother? It is emphatic and is stressed in speech. It is declined like the Def. Art.

2. **Dieser, diese, dieses,** this ; **jener, jene, jenes,** that, yon ; **solcher, solche, solches,** such ; **derjenige, diejenige, dasjenige,** that (emphatic) ; **derselbe, dieselbe, dasselbe,** the same, are used as Adjectives and Pronouns. *Derjenige* and *derselbe* are declined as if they were separated into the Def. Art. and the Adjectives *jenige* and *selbe*. " Such a man " is *ein solcher Mann*, or an uninflected form can be used : *solch ein Mann ; solch eine Frau ; solch ein Kind*. *Derjenige* is used in solemn style : *Ich sehe denjenigen Mann dem ich so lange gesucht habe*, I see that man whom I have so long sought for. *Derselbe* presents no difficulties : *Wir haben denselben Namen*, we have the same name.

3. **Der, dieser, uener, solcher, derjenige, derselbe** are also used as pronouns : *Ist DER der Kaiser?* Is that the Emperor? *Ist DIE deine Tante?* Is she your aunt?* *Ein solcher ist gefährlich*, such a man is dangerous. *Derjenige, der das sagt, lügt*, he who says that, lies. *Er ist derselbe, den ich gestern traf*, he is the same man I met yesterday. All the preceding are declined like *dieser, diese, dieses* except *der, die, das* which, instead of the Genitive Masc. *des*, Fem. *der*, Neut. *des*, Plur. *der*, has Masc. *dessen*, Fem. *deren*, Neut. *dessen*, Plural *deren* (*derer*). This is also true of *der, die, das* used as a Relative Pronoun (see next chapter).

Das referring to a noun which is part of the predicate, e.g. That (this) is my father ; that is my mother ; that is my child ; these are my books, is uninflected : *Das ist mein Vater ; das ist meine Mutter ; das ist mein Kind ; das sind meine Bücher.*

* Note how emphatic the *der* and the *die* are.

XIII. RELATIVE PRONOUNS

English has three Relative Pronouns: who, which, that, as in:
1. The man, who was old, stepped forward. 2. The man that was
old stepped forward. 3. The book, which was lying on the table,
was open. 4. The book that was lying on the table was open.

In very correct English, "who" and "which" merely add some
information about the Antecedent (i.e. the word to which the Relative
Pronoun relates, as "man" and "book" above) and are preceded
by a comma; "that" is restrictive, i.e. it picks out one special
"man" or "book" from others, and is not preceded by a comma.
German has no such distinctions, nor has it special forms for persons
and things like our "who" and "which."

German has two Relatives: der, die, das and welcher, welche,
welches, both meaning "who," "which," or "that". They are
ALWAYS preceded by a comma and ALWAYS throw the verb to the
end of the Relative clause. *Der, die, das* are ousting *welcher, welche,
welches* in modern German, especially in the spoken language. The
four examples in the first paragraph above are, in German:

1 and 2. *Der Mann, der (welcher) alt war, trat vor.*

3 and 4. *Das Buch, das (welches) auf dem Tisch lag, war offen.*

The Relatives are declined as follows:

Singular

N.	der	die	das	welcher	welche	welches
A.	den	die	das	welchen	welche	welches
G.	DESSEN	DEREN	DESSEN	DESSEN	DEREN	DESSEN
D.	dem	der	dem	welchem	welcher	welchem

Plural

N.	die	welche
A.	die	welche
G.	DEREN	DEREN
D.	DENEN	welchen

NOTES.—In English we can leave out the Relative: The man I
met; the woman I know; the beer I am drinking. It cannot be
omitted in German: *der Mann, den ich traf; die Frau, die ich
kenne; das Bier, das ich trinke.*

The case of the Relative depends on the part it plays in the Relative clause, but its number and gender depend on those of the antecedent, as shown in the following examples: *Wo ist das Kind, mit
dem (welchem) ich spielte?* Where is the child with whom I used to
play? *Kennen Sie die Dame, der (welcher) ich die Blumen gab?*
Do you know the lady to whom I gave the flowers? *Das sind die
Leute, von denen (welchen) ich sprach,* those are the people of whom
I was speaking. *Das ist der Herr, dessen Sohn krank ist,* that is
the gentleman whose son is ill. *Hier wohnt die Frau, deren Sohn
mein Verlobter ist,* here lives the woman whose son is my fiancé.

If the Relative refers to an inanimate object and is governed by
a preposition, it may be replaced by *wo* (or *wor*, like *da* and *dar*)

fused with the preposition: *Das Buch, in dem (welchem) ich lese* or *Das Buch, worin ich lese*, the book in which I am reading. *Der Baum, von dem (welchem) ich spreche* or *Der Baum, wovon ich spreche*, the tree of which I am speaking.

Was is used as a Relative when the antecedent is an indefinite pronoun, a neuter adjective used as a noun, or a statement in a sentence: *Ich weiss alles, was Sie getan haben*, I know everything you have done; *Das ist das Beste, was man sagen kann*, that is the best that can be said; *Sein Freund starb, was ihn sehr betrübte*, his friend died, which greatly grieved him.

Here is a trick sentence to show the uses of *der, die, das* as a Demonstrative and Relative Pronoun: *Ich war mit der, die das sagte*, I was with her (the woman) who said that. *Der* is the Dat. Fem. of the Demonstrative, *die* is the Nom. Fem. of the Relative, and *das* the Acc. Neuter of the Demonstrative.

XIV. A. INTERROGATIVE ADJECTIVES AND PRONOUNS

The Adjectives are **welcher, welche, welches**, which? or what? as in: Which (what) book are you reading? *Welches Buch lesen Sie?*; and **was für ein?**, what sort of? as in: *Was für ein Hut ist das?* What sort of a hat is that?, and *Was für einen Hut haben Sie?* What sort of a hat have you?

Welcher, welche, welches is declined like *dieser*, and *was für ein* like *ein, eine, ein*, the *für* having no influence whatever on the case although normally *für* takes the Accusative. In the Plural the *ein* is dropped: *Was für Hüte sind das?* What sort of hats are those?

The Pronouns are *wer?*, who?, and *was?*, what?, as in *Wer singt so schön?* Who is singing so beautifully?, and *Was tut er jetzt?* What is he doing now? They are declined as follows:

N. wer?	who?	was? what?
A. wen?	whom?	was? what?
G. wessen?	whose?	(little used)
D. wem?	to whom?	(little used)

NOTES.—*Was?* is used mainly in the Nom. and Acc.; *Was ist auf den Tisch gefallen?* What has fallen on the table?; *Was wünschen Sie?* What do you want? When referring to inanimate objects and governed by a preposition, *wo* (or *wor*) fused with the preposition is used: *Womit schreiben Sie?* With what are you writing? *Woraus macht man Zigaretten?* What do you make cigarettes of?

Wer can be used as a " condensed " Relative: *Wer das tut, ist ein Narr*, he who does that is a fool.

B. INDEFINITE PRONOUNS

Mention must be made of **man**, one, like the French " on ": *Man spricht Deutsch*, one speaks German, German is spoken; **jedermann**, everybody; **jemand**, anybody, somebody; **niemand**, nobody. They are declined as follows:

Nom. **man**, Acc. **einen**, Gen. **eines**, Dat. **einem.**

Nom. **jedermann**, Acc. **jedermann**, Gan. **jedermanns**, Dat. **jedermann.**

Nom. **jemand**, Acc. **jemand(en)**, Gen. **jemandes**, Dat. **jemand-(em)**.

Niemand is declined like *jemand*, the (*en*) and (*em*) in the Acc. and Dat. being frequently met with. Examples: *Man sagt dass . . .*, it is said that: *Warum kann er an einen nicht schreiben?* Why can't he write to one?; *Sie glaubt einem nicht*, she doesn't believe one; *Das ist nicht jedermanns Sache*, that is not to everybody's taste (" not everybody's cup of tea " in modern parlance); *Es kommt jemand*, somebody's coming; *Es ist niemand da*, there's nobody there.

Etwas, something, frequently **was** in spoken German, is useful: *Ich habe etwas für Sie*, I've got something for you; *Geben Sie mir etwas zu essen, etwas Fleisch*, give me something to eat, some meat. The negative is *nichts*: *Ich habe nichts zu essen*, I have nothing to eat. *Etwas* and *nichts* with the Neuter Adjective are neat: *Gibt's etwas Neues?* Is there anything new?; *Nein, es gibt nichts Neues*, no, there's nothing new.

XV. PREPOSITIONS

1. Those governing the Accusative ONLY are:

bis, up to, till
durch, through, by
für, for
gegen, against, towards, about

ohne, without
um, around, at
wider, against, in opposition to

Examples:

1. *Er bleibt bis nächsten Donnerstag,* he remains till next Thursday.
2. *Er ging durch den Garten,* he went through the garden.
3. *Er wurde durch eine Kugel getötet,* he was killed by a bullet.
4. *Dieser Brief ist für mich,* this letter is for me.
5. *Gegen Ende Juli,* about the end of July.
6. *Sie hat etwas gegen mich,* she has something against me.
7. *Ohne meinen Bleistift kann ich nicht schreiben,* I can't write without my pencil.
8. *Wir sassen um den Tisch,* we sat round the table.
9. *Um jeden Preis,* at any price.
10. *Er arbeitet wider meinen Willen,* he works contrary to my desire.

2. Those governing the Dative ONLY are:

aus, out of, from
bei, at, near
mit, with
nach, after, according to

seit, since
von, of, from, by
zu, to, at

Examples:

1. *Aus dem Hause kam ein Kind,* a child came out of the house.
2. *Er wohnt bei seinem Onkel,* he lives with his uncle.
3. *Bei dieser Gelegenheit,* on this occasion.
4. *Ich schreibe mit einer Füllfeder,* I write with a fountain-pen.
5. *Wir gehen nach Hause, nach Berlin,* we are going home, to Berlin.
6. *Zehn Minuten nach seiner Abreise,* ten minutes after his departure.
7. *Nach meiner Meinung* or *meiner Meinung nach,* in my opinion.
8. *Ich bin seit einer Stunde hier,* I have been here an hour (literally, since an hour).
9. *Er wurde von seinen Feinden getötet,* he was killed by his enemies.
10. *Er ist ein Freund von mir,* he is a friend of mine.
11. *Sie ist nicht zu Hause,* she is not at home.
12. *Ich gehe zu Bett; zu meinem Vater,* I am going to bed; to my father.

3. The prepositions shown below govern both the Accusative and Dative: the Accusative when " motion towards " is expressed, and the Dative when " rest at " is meant. Thus *er geht in den Garten* means " He goes into the garden (from somewhere else)," but *er geht in dem Garten* means " He walks (about) in the garden." *Er schwimmt unter die Brücke* means " He swims (from somewhere else) under the bridge''; *Er schwimmt unter der Brücke* means " He swims (about) under the bridge." It it answers the question *wo?,* where?, the Dative is used: *Wo geht er? In dem Garten. Wo schwimmt er? Unter der Brücke.* If it answers the question *wohin?,* whither?, where to?, then the Accusative is used: *Wohin geht er? In dem Garten. Wohin schwimmt er? Unter die Brücke.*

an, at, to	in, in, into	unter, under, below
auf, on	neben, beside, near	vor, before, in front
hinter, behind	über, over, above	zwischen, between

Examples:

1. *Er ging an den Fluss*, he went to the river. *Er stand an der Tür*, he stood at the door.
2. *Er legte das Buch auf den Tisch*, he put the book on the table. *Das Buch lag auf dem Tisch*, the book lay (was) on the table.
3. *Die Katze kroch hinter den Ofen*, the cat crept behind the stove. *Die Katze schlief hinter dem Ofen*, the cat slept behind the stove.
4. *Ich stecke meine Feder in die Tasche*, I put (stick) my pen in my pocket. *Meine Feder steckt in der Tasche*, my pen is (sticking) in my pocket.
5. *Er setzte sich neben mich*, he seated himself (sat down) next to me. *Er sass neben mir*, he was sitting next to me.
6. *Der Vogel flog über das Haus*, the bird flew over the house. *Der Vogel schwebte über dem Hause*, the bird hovered over the house.
7. *Der Dieb schlüpfte unter das Bett*, the thief slipped under the bed. *Der Dieb blieb die ganze Nacht unter dem Bette*, the thief remained the whole night under the bed.
8. *Mein Pult steht vor dem Fenster*, my desk stands in front of the window. *Ich stellte mein Pult vor das Fenster*, I put my desk in front of the window.
9. *Das Flugzeug flog zwischen die hohen Berge*, the aeroplane flew between the high mountains. *Das Dorf liegt zwischen hohen Bergen*, the village lies between high mountains.

4. Prepositions taking the Genitive are:

anstatt or statt, instead of	während, during
trotz, in spite of	wegen, on account of

um...willen, for the sake of

together with **ausser-, inner-, ober-, unter-** compounded with **-halb**, meaning outside of, inside of, above, below, as *ausserhalb des Reiches*, outside of the Empire. **Trotz, während** and **wegen** are also occasionally found with the Dative.

Examples:

1. *Die Schwester sprach anstatt des Bruders*, the sister spoke instead of her brother.
2. *Ich kam wegen des schlechten Wetters spät an*, I arrived late on account of the bad weather.
3. *Trotz des Sturmes fuhr er nach dem Bahnhof*, in spite of the storm he drove to the station.
4. *Um Gottes willen helfen Sie mir!* For God's sake help me!

XVI. CONJUNCTIONS

There are two kinds of Conjunctions:

1. Co-ordinating, which join sentences (or words) of equal rank. They do not affect the word order, the verb remaining in its normal position. They are:

und, and	**oder,** or
aber, but	**entweder...oder,** either...or
sondern, but (after a negative)	**weder...noch,** neither...nor
allein, emphatic but, yet, however	**denn,** for (= because)
jedoch, emphatic but, yet, however	

Examples:

1. *Ich lese die Zeitung, und mein Vater macht einen Spaziergang,* I read the paper and my father takes a walk.

2. *Hans will nach Hause, aber ich möchte gern hier bleiben,* Jack wants to go home, but I should like to remain here.

3. *Er ist nicht alt, sondern er ist jung,* he is not old, but young.

4. *Er war mein Freund, allein (jedoch) ich konnte auf ihn nicht vertrauen,* he was my friend, but yet I could not trust him.

5. *Sie müssen nach Hause eilen, denn es ist sehr spät,* you must hurry home, for it is very late.

6. *Er muss arbeiten, oder sein Geschäft wird zugrunde gehen,* he must work or his business will be ruined.

7. *Entweder du gehst allein, oder du musst mit mir gehen,* either you go alone, or you will have to go with me.

8. *Weder er noch sein Vater haben schwarze Haare,* neither he nor his father has black hair.

2. Subordinating conjunctions which link a subordinate clause to a main sentence. These always throw the verb—i.e. the inflected verb agreeing with the subject of the subordinate clause—to the end and must always be preceded by a comma. They are:

als, when, as	**während,** while
wenn, if when(ever)	**weil,** because
wann, when (indirect question)	**bevor, ehe,** before
bis, until	**indem,** while
da, since, as (= because)	**seitdem,** since
dass, that	**nachdem,** after
damit, in order that	**sobald,** as soon as
ob, whether (indirect question)	**wo,** where (indirect question, or
obgleich, although	relative)

Examples:

1. *Er sprang auf, als ich in das Zimmer trat,* he jumped up when I entered the room. *Als* refers to an event at a past point of time only.

2. *Er sprang immer auf, wenn ich in das Zimmer trat,* he always used to jump up when(ever) I entered the room. *Wenn* is used for a repeated action.

3. *Er würde aufspringen, wenn ich in das Zimmer träte* (or *treten würde*), he would jump up if I entered (were to enter) the room. *Wenn* is also used when a condition is implied.

4. *Wissen Sie, wann er ankommen wird?* Do you know when he will arrive? *Wann* is interrogative only.

5. *Ich werde warten, bis der Briefträger den Briefkasten geleert hat,* I shall wait until the postman has cleared the letter-box.

6. *Da das Dienstmädchen krank ist, kann ich das Haus nicht verlassen,* as (since) the maid is ill I cannot leave the house.

7. *Ich weiss, dass der Zug eine Stunde Verspätung hat,* I know (that) the train is an hour late.

8. *Wir schreiben ihr, damit sie die Nachricht sofort bekommt* (or *bekomme,* the Subjunctive), we are writing to her in order that she gets (shall get) the news at once.

9. *Obgleich das Wetter heiss ist, trägt sie einen Mantel,* although the weather is hot, she wears a coat.

10. *Ich weiss nicht, ob er Tee oder Kaffee trinkt,* I don't know whether he takes tea or coffee.

11. *Bitte, warten Sie, bis ich meine Schuhe putzen lasse,* please wait until I get my boots polished.

12. *Mutter konnte keine Butter kaufen, weil der Laden leer war,* mother couldn't buy any butter because the shop was empty.

13. *Bevor ich das Haus verlasse, muss ich alles abschliessen,* before I leave the house, I must lock everything up.

14. *Indem ich den Kaffee koche, kannst du den Tisch decken,* while I am making the coffee, you can be laying the table.

15. *Seitdem ich an der Küste wohne, habe ich keine Erkältung gehabt,* since I have been living at the coast, I have not had a cold.

16. *Nachdem die Kinder ins Bett gegangen sind, ist alles still,* after the children have gone to bed, everything is quiet.

17. *Sobald Sie ankommen, müssen Sie mir schreiben,* as soon as you arrive you must write to me.

18. *Können Sie mir bitte sagen, wo das Postamt ist?* Can you please tell me where the post-office is?

XVII. THE VERB

Before setting out the conjugation of the verbs, we shall do well to discuss some important points.

1. The **Infinitive** ends in -en: *lieben*, to love; *machen*, to make; *sprechen*, to speak; but *sein*, to be. The Infin. is a verbal noun and when used as a pure noun it is Neuter and written with a capital letter: *Das Lernen kommt ihm schwer*, he finds learning difficult. The use of the Infin. with *zu* (= English " to ") frequently agrees with English usage: I can (must, will, may, etc.) go home, *ich kann (muss, will, darf, etc.) nach Hause gehen*; I wish to go home, *ich wünsche, nach Hause zu gehen*. The Infin. in a principal clause falls to the end of the sentence: *Ich muss morgen um 7 Uhr aufstehen*, I must get up at 7 tomorrow. In a subordinate sentence it falls next to the inflected verb: *weil ich morgen um 7 Uhr aufstehen muss*, because I must get up at 7 tomorrow.

The Infin. can be used as a sharp command: *Aufstehen!*, get up!; *Nicht rauchen!*, no smoking!; *Langsam fahren!*, drive slowly!

2. The **Present Participle** is both adjectival and verbal: *überraschende Nachrichten*, surprising news; *den Feind überraschend, gewannen wir die Schlacht*, surprising the enemy, we won the battle. It is formed by adding -d to the Infin.: *lieben, liebend*, loving; *machen, machend*, making; *sprechen, sprechend*, speaking; but *sein, seiend*, being. It is much less used in German than in English and cannot be used as in: I am loving, I was loving = *ich liebe, ich liebte. Am* with the Infin. can be used to express the idea of being in the act of doing something: *Ich bin am Arbeiten*, I am working.

3. English has a verbal noun in -ing, the **Gerund,** which is lacking in German and must be turned in various ways: Learning is difficult, *das Lernen ist schwer;* By reading too much you will harm your eyes, *indem Sie zu viel lesen, werden Sie sich den Augen schaden:* After saying this he stopped speaking, *nachdem er dies gesagt hatte, hörte er auf zu sprechen.*

4. The **Past Participle** is also both adjectival and verbal: *ein gebrochener Stuhl; Er hat den Stuhl gebrochen.* It is formed by prefixing ge- to the stem and adding -t in the case of Weak Verbs or -en (with vowel change) for Strong Verbs: *lieben, geliebt*, loved; *sprechen, gesprochen*, spoken; but *sein, gewesen*, been. If the verb ends in -ieven, as do those taken from a foreign language, no ge- is prefixed: *telephonieren, telephoniert*, telephoned. (See also Inseparable Verbs, p. 303.) The Past Part. can be used to give a sharp order: *Aufgestanden!*, stand up!, get up!

5. German has only two **Simple Tenses,** the Present and the Imperfect, all the others being Compound and formed by means of the Auxiliary Verbs *haben, sein,* and *werden.* (See par. 8 below.)

6. The **Present Indicative** is formed by adding -e, -(e)st, -(e)t, -en, -(e)t, -en to the stem: *lieb-en, ich liebe, du liebst, er liebt, wir lieben, ihr liebt, sie lieben,* I (you, etc.) love, am loving, do love. If the stem ends in -d or -t the e in brackets must be used: *du redest,*

er redet, ihr redet, you speak, etc.   If the stem ends in a sibilant the *-est* contracts to *-t :* du *reist,* not *du reisest ; du schiesst,* not *du schiessest.*

Strong Verbs with stem-vowel *a* modify it to *ä* in the 2nd and 3rd persons sing.: *fallen, du fällst, er fällt.*   If the stem-vowel is a short *e* it modifies to *i : sprechen, du sprichst, er spricht ;* long *e* (= *eh*) modifies to *ie : stehlen, du stiehlst, er stiehlt,* but there are exceptions, e.g. *nehmen, du nimmst, er nimmt.*

7. The **Imperfect,** or Past Indicative, is formed by adding *-te, -test, -te, -ten, -tet, -ten* to the stem of Weak Verbs ; if the stem ends in *-d* or *-t* an *e* must be inserted before the *t : ich liebte, ich redete ; du liebtest, du redetest,* etc.   Strong Verbs show the past by vowel change in the stem and by adding *-st* in the 2nd pers. sing. and *-en, -t, -en* in the plural : *singen : ich sang, du sangst, er sang, wir sangen, ihr sangt, sie sangen.*

8. The **Compound Tenses** are : the Perfect, I have loved ; the Pluperfect, I had loved ; the Future, I shall love ; the Conditional, I should love ; the Future Perfect, I shall have loved ; the Past Conditional, I should have loved.

In the case of Transitive and Reflexive Verbs the auxiliary *haben* is used to form the compound past tenses : *Ich habe (hatte) geliebt,* I have (had) loved.

With **Intransitive** Verbs indicating a change of position or state, and a few others, *sein* is the auxiliary.   You will find these verbs in the list of Strong Verbs on p. 124 marked with an asterisk.   Examples are : *sein, ich bin (war) gewesen ; werden, er ist(war) geworden ; kommen, wir sind (waren) gekommen ; bleiben, Sie sind (waren) ge-blieben.*

NOTE.—With verbs of motion like *reiten, schwimmen,* etc., *sein* is used if there is movement to a destination : *Ich bin nach Berlin geritten ; Wir sind nach dem Boote geschwommen.*   If only the manner of movement is referred to, *haben* is used : *Ich habe den ganzen Tag geritten ; Wir haben heute viel geschwommen.*   I rode the whole day ; we have swum a lot today.

Usage, however, varies with many verbs, the North preferring *haben* and the South *sein : ich habe* (or *bin*) *gestanden ; wir sind* (or *haben*) *gesessen.*   The North would also use *haben* in : *Wir haben nach dem Boote geschwommen.*   We swam to the boat.

The **Future** is formed by the Present of *werden* plus the Infin. of the verb : *ich werde lieben,* I shall love ; *du wirst lieben,* thou shalt love ; *er wird lieben,* he will love, etc.   In spoken German it is frequently replaced by the Present : *Ich bringe es sogleich,* I'll bring it at once.

The **Conditional** is formed by the Past Subjunctive of *werden* plus the Infin. of the verb : *ich würde lieben, du würdest lieben,* I should love, etc.

9. The **Subjunctive Mood,** which reports non-facts, wishes, desires, demands, conditions, probabilities, and is used to report state-ments not made by the speaker (Reported Speech), has two Simple Tenses, though they are not really tenses in the same way as the Indicative Mood deals with time.   In the Indicative, the Past

indicates remoteness in TIME ; in the Subjunctive, the Past indicates
remoteness of PROBABILITY : Indic. : The book was green ; Subj. :
Were the book green—which means that the book IS NOT green and
the probability of its greenness is very remote!

The Present Subj. is formed by adding to the stem *-e, -est, -e,
-en, -et, -en :* *ich liebe (singe), du liebest (singest), er liebe (singe),
wir lieben (singen), ihr liebet (singet), sie lieben (singen).*

The Imperfect Subj. of Weak Verbs has exactly the same form
as the Imperfect Indicative. In Strong Verbs it is formed by modi-
fying the vowel of the Imperfect Indicative and adding *-e, -(e)st,
-e, -en, -(e)t, -en.* *Singen, ich sänge, du säng(e)st, er sänge, wir sängen,
ihr säng(e)t, sie sängen,* (if) I were to sing, etc.

10. The **Imperative** is formed for both Weak Verbs and Strong
Verbs that do not modify in the Present Tense, by adding *-(e)* for the
2nd pers. sing. and *-t* for the plural, the polite form being the same
as the Indicative : *lieb(e) !, liebt !, lieben Sie !* (But : *Sei !, seid !,
seien Sie !*) Note that German requires an exclamation mark after
the Imperative and that the polite form requires the pronoun. The
2nd pers. sing. may be : *liebe !* or *lieb !* ; *singe !* or *sing !* It is also
found with an apostrophe : *lieb' !* In Strong Verbs which modify *e*
to *i* or *ie*, the modified form is used and there is no *-e* in the 2nd pers.
sing. :

> *sprechen : sprich !, sprecht !, sprechen Sie !*
> *geben : gib !, gebt !, geben Sie !*
> *nehmen : nimm !, nehmt !, nehmen Sie !*

XVIII. TABLES OF CONJUGATION OF THE VERB

A. THE AUXILIARIES HABEN, SEIN, AND WERDEN

Pres. Part. habend, seiend, werdend.   *Past Part.* gehabt, gewesen, geworden.

PRESENT

	Indic.	*Subj.*	*Indic.*	*Subj.*	*Indic.*	*Subj.*
ich	habe	habe	bin	sei	werde	werde
du	hast	habest	bist	seiest	wirst	werdest
er	hat	habe	ist	sei	wird	werde
wir	haben	haben	sind	seien	werden	werden
ihr	habt	habet	seid	seiet	werdet	werdet
sie	haben	haben	sind	seien	werden	werden

IMPERFECT

	hatte	hätte	war	wäre	wurde	würde
ich	hatte	hätte	war	wäre	wurde	würde
du	hattest	hättest	warst	wärest	wurdest	würdest
er	hatte	hätte	war	wäre	wurde	wurde
wir	hatten	hätten	waren	wären	wurden	würden
ihr	hattet	hättet	wart	wäret	wurdet	würdet
sie	hatten	hätten	waren	wären	wurden	würden

PERFECT INDIC.

ich habe gehabt	ich bin gewesen	ich bin geworden
etc.	etc.	etc.

PLUPERFECT INDIC.

ich hatte gehabt	ich war gewesen	ich war geworden
etc.	etc.	etc.

FUTURE INDIC.

ich werde haben	ich werde sein	ich werde werden
etc.	etc.	etc.

CONDITIONAL

ich würde haben	ich würde sein	ich würde werden
etc.	etc.	etc.

FUTURE PERFECT

ich werde gehabt haben, etc.	ich werde gewesen sein, etc.	ich werde geworden sein, etc.

PAST CONDITIONAL

ich würde gehabt haben, etc.	ich würde gewesen sein, etc.	ich würde geworden sein, etc.

IMPERATIVE

habe !	sei !	werde !
habt !	seid !	werdet !
haben Sie !	seien Sie !	werden Sie !

B. WEAK VERB **LIEBEN**, AND STRONG VERBS: **SINGEN; SPRECHEN**

Pres. Part. liebend, singend, sprechend.
Past Part. geliebt, gesungen, gesprochen.

PRESENT

	Indic.	*Subj.*	*Indic.*	*Subj.*	*Indic.*	*Subj.*
ich	liebe	liebe	singe	singe	spreche	spreche
du	liebst	liebest	singst	singest	sprichst	sprechest
er	liebt	liebe	singt	singe	spricht	spreche
wir	lieben	lieben	singen	singen	sprechen	sprechen
ihr	liebt	liebet	singt	singet	sprecht	sprechet
sie	lieben	lieben	singen	singen	sprechen	sprechen

IMPERFECT

	Indic.	*Subj.*	*Indic.*	*Subj.*	*Indic.*	*Subj.*
ich	liebte	liebte	sang	sänge	sprach	spräche
du	liebtest	liebtest	sangst	sängest	sprachst	sprächest
er	liebte	liebte	sang	sänge	sprach	spräche
wir	liebten	liebten	sangen	sängen	sprachen	sprächen
ihr	liebtet	liebtet	sangt	sänget	spracht	sprächet
sie	liebten	liebten	sangen	sängen	sprachen	sprächen

PERFECT INDIC.

| ich habe geliebt etc. | ich habe gesungen etc. | ich habe gesprochen etc. |

PLUPERFECT INDIC.

| ich hatte geliebt etc. | ich hatte gesungen etc. | ich hatte gesprochen etc. |

FUTURE

| ich werde lieben etc. | ich werde singen etc. | ich werde sprechen etc. |

CONDITIONAL

| ich würde lieben etc. | ich würde singen etc. | ich würde sprechen etc. |

FUTURE PERFECT

| ich werde geliebt haben, etc. | ich werde gesungen haben, etc. | ich werde gesprochen haben, etc. |

PAST CONDITIONAL

| ich würde geliebt haben, etc. | ich würde gesungen haben, etc. | ich würde gesprochen haben, etc. |

IMPERATIVE

lieb(e) !	sing(e) !	sprich !
lieb(e)t !	sing(e)t !	sprech(e)t !
lieben Sie !	singen Sie !	sprechen Sie !

It is usual to arrange the Strong Verbs in groups according to the vowel changes in the stem: *helfen, half, geholfen*, to help; *dreschen, drosch, gedroschen*, to thresh; *werfen, warf, geworfen*, to throw, etc. In order to save space we have given a list of the more common Strong Verbs with their parts on p. 124, those conjugated with *sein* being marked with an asterisk. This list includes the so-called Irregular Weak Verbs: *bringen, brachte, gebracht*, to bring; *nennen, nannte, genannt*, to name; *rennen, rannte, gerannt*, to run; *senden, sandte (sendete), gesandt (gesendet)*, to send; *wenden, wandte (wendete), gewandt (gewendet)*, to turn. You will be well advised to consult this list frequently and to learn the verbs by heart, ten at a time.

XIX. USE OF THE PERFECT AND IMPERFECT INDICATIVE

In English we say (a) I saw him yesterday, last week, last year, when I was in Paris, but (b) I have seen him today, this week, this year, since I came back from Paris. We use (a) the Imperfect when the action is cut off from the present, and (b) the Perfect when the action is linked up with the present. In both cases we have TIME in our mind.

German uses the Perfect when the present result of a past action is uppermost in the mind, or when the past action is an isolated one, not one of a connected series. Thus both (a) and (b) above—which are isolated actions—will be in the Perfect: *Ich habe ihn (gestern, heute) gesehen.* German will say *Kolumbus hat Amerika entdeckt,* Columbus discovered America, because the result of his discovery still exists and it is an isolated action. If we put it in a series of connected actions we use the Imperfect: *Kolumbus entdeckte im Jahre* 1492 *die Antilleninseln und hielt dieselben für Ostindien,* Columbus discovered the Antilles in 1492 and took them to be the East Indies. Hence the Imperfect is the tense used in narration and is the one most commonly met with in books. It is also used for actions related to each other: *Er schrieb, als ich eintrat,* he was writing when I entered; *Er blickte sofort auf, als er die Nachricht vernahm,* he at once looked up when he heard the news.

The situation is complicated by the fact that the Perfect is becoming more and more used in spoken German, especially in the South, so that it tends to oust out the Imperfect, so much so that one almost forgets that such a form as *schrieb* exists, as in daily life one hears and uses *hat geschrieben!*

XX. USE OF THE SUBJUNCTIVE

The Subjunctive is used to express wishes: *Es lebe der König?*
Long live the King!; *Gott bewahre!* God forbid!; *Ich wollte
(wünschte), er käme*, I wish he would come; concessions: *Sei es noch so
schwierig, ich tue es doch*, be it ever so difficult, I will do it; purpose:
Er arbeitet, damit er Geld verdiene (or the Indic. *verdient*), he works in
order that he may earn money; commands: *Er verlangt, dass das
Kind gehorche*, he demands that the child (shall) obey; in rejected
conditions, i.e. conditions which are contrary to fact: *Wäre das Buch
hier, so könnte ich lesen*, were the book here (but it is not), I should be
able to (could) read; *Wenn er das täte, bliebe ich nicht hier*, if he did
(should do) that, I should not stay here. The Past Tense is: *Wenn
er das getan hätte, so wäre ich nicht geblieben*, if he had done that I
should not have stayed.

In Indirect or Reported Speech the Subjunctive is used in order
to indicate that the reporter does not guarantee the factual truth of
what another says! In English, if I say "I am ill," you report my
statement as: "He said he was ill." In German "*Ich bin krank*"
is reported as: *Er sagte, er sei* (or *wäre*) *krank*. Either the Present
or Past Subjunctive may be used and *dass* may introduce the subordinate clause: *Er sagte, dass er krank sei* (*wäre*), but the omission of
dass is more usual. If the Subjunctive has the same form as the
Indicative then another form must be chosen which shows it to be
Subjunctive: "*Ich liebe sie*," "I love her" becomes in Reported
Speech: *Er sagte, er liebe sie*, and not *Er sagte, er liebte sie*, because
liebte is both Indicative and Subjunctive. "*Die Leute kommen spät an*"
is reported as: *Er sagte, die Leute kämen spät an*, and not: *Er sagte,
die Leute kommen spät an*, as *kommen* is both Indicative and Subjunctive.

If the Direct Speech is in a Past Tense, the Indirect uses the
Perfect or Pluperfect Subjunctive: "*Ich war krank*" or "*Ich bin
krank gewesen*" or "*Ich war krank gewesen*" all become when reported: *Er sagte, er sei* (*wäre*) *krank gewesen*.

If the Direct Speech contains an Imperative, this must be para-
phrased with *sollen* or *mögen*: "*Bleib hier, mein Kind!*" becomes
Er sagte, das Kind solle (*möge*) *hier bleiben*.

XXI. THE PASSIVE VOICE

It takes some effort for the student of German to grasp the Passive Voice and hence we will spend some time on it.

"The boy finds the key" is in the Active Voice because the subject "boy" does the action of "finding". "The key is found by the boy" is in the Passive Voice because the subject "key" suffers the action of "finding". In English we use the verb " to be " both for the Passive Auxiliary and for the Copulative verb, as in "The key which was lost is now found."

Consider the following examples. I go to a friend's house and see that his windows are shattered. He says: "My windows are shattered." Wheh I get home I say to my wife: "His windows were shattered." In both cases I describe the acutal state of the windows.

I call on another friend whose windows are whole. He says, looking at the whole windows: "My windows are shattered in every air-raid." I say to my wife: "His windows were shattered in every air-raid." I am not now describing the actual state of the windows, since they were whole, but am referring to an action which the windows have suffered. In English we use " to be " in describing the actual state of the windows and in referring to the action they suffered; German uses *sein* for the former, *werden* for the latter:

State (*sein*)	Action suffered—Passive (*werden*)
My windows are smashed.	My windows are smashed in every air-raid.
Meine Fenster sind zer-schmettert.	*Meine Fenster werden in jedem Luft-angriff zerschmettert.*
His windows were smashed.	His windows were smashed in every air-raid.
Seine Fenster waren zer-schmettert.	*Seine Fenster wurden in jedem Luft-angriff zerschmettert.*

We could replace the " are " and " were " in the Passive column by " get " and " got ": His windows get smashed in every air-raid. Which is Passive in: These goods are sold, you cannot buy them, and: These goods are sold at high prices? The German is: *Diese Waren sind verkauft, Sie können dieselben nicht kaufen,* and: *Diese Waren werden zu hohen Preisen verkauft.*

If the agent is a person the preposition used is *von : Er wurde von seinem Feinde getötet,* he was killed by his enemy; if a thing, *durch* is used : *Er wurde durch eine Kugel getötet,* he was killed by a bullet.

In English we can make either the Direct Object (the Accusative) or the Indirect Object (the Dative) the subject of the Passive sentence: "The book was given (to) the boy" and "The boy was given the book." In German only the Accusative can become the subject of the Passive, and hence verbs which govern the Dat. and the Gen. have a special form: He was given a book, *ihm wurde ein Buch gegeben* or *Es wurde ihm ein Buch gegeben.* The Active form is often met with : *Man gab ihm ein Buch,* one gave him a book ; *Man spricht Deutsch,* German is spoken; *man sagt,* it is said. (See also under " Impersonal Verbs," on p. 305.)

Werden is conjugated as on p. 296, but its Past Part. is *worden* instead of *geworden*. Here is a skeleton of the Passive of *lieben*.

Pres. **ich werde geliebt**	*Perf.* **ich bin geliebt worden**
I am loved	I have been loved
Imperf. **ich wurde geliebt**	*Pluperf.* **ich war geliebt worden**
I was loved	I had been loved
Fut. **ich werde geliebt werden**	*Cond.* **ich würde geliebt werden**
I shall be loved	I should be loved
Fut. Perf. **ich werde geliebt worden sein**	*Past Cond.* **ich würde geliebt worden sein**
I shall have been loved	I should have been loved

Imperative : **werde geliebt !   werdet geliebt !   werden Sie geliebt**
　　　　　　be (thou) loved　　　be (ye) loved　　　be (you) loved

XXII. A. SEPARABLE AND INSEPARABLE VERBS

Separable Verbs are made up of a prefix so loosely attached that it splits off from the mother verb under certain conditions. Inseparable Verbs are made up of a prefix which never splits off from the mother verb. Thus *abfahren*, to start (fare off), is Separable and behaves as follows: (1) *ich fahre morgen abend ab;* (2) *ich fuhr gestern abend ab;* (3) *ich bin gestern abgefahren;* (4) *ich werde nächste Woche abfahren;* (5) *ich wünsche morgen abzufahren;* (6) *ich kann nicht kommen, weil ich morgen abfahre;* (7) *fahre ab!, fahr(e)t ab!, fahren Sie ab!* Nos. 1 and 2 show the position in a principal clause with *ab* at the end; No. 3 shows the *ab* joined to the past participle from which it never breaks away; No. 4 shows the *ab* joined up to the Infin. from which it never breaks away but, as in No. 5, allows *zu* to link it up with the Infin.; No. 6 shows the *ab* fusing again with the mother verb when they both fall to the end of a Subordinate clause; No. 7 shows the Imperative.

The following are Separable particles : **ab,** off : *abbrechen,* to break off ; **an,** at, to : *ankommen,* to arrive ; **auf,** up, open : *aufspringen,* to jump up ; **aufmachen,** to open ; **aus,** out : *aussprechen,* to pronounce (speak out) ; **bei,** by, near : *beistehen,* to support (stand by) ; **bevor,** in front, ahead : *bevorstehen,* to impend, be imminent ; **ein,** into : *einreiben,* to rub in ; **empor,** up : *emporsteigen,* to rise up ; **fort,** forth, away : *fortgehen,* to go away ; **entgegen,** towards, against : *entgegenarbeiten,* to counteract (work against) ; **her,** motion towards the speaker : *herkommen,* to come hither ; **hin,** motion away from the speaker : *hingehen,* to go hence ; **nach,** after : *nachlassen,* to leave behind, bequeath ; **mit,** with : *mitkommen,* to accompany ; **vor,** before : *vorschlagen,* to propose (put before) ; **weg,** away : *weggehen,* to go away ; **zu,** towards : *zustreben,* to strive towards ; **zurück,** back : *zurückkommen,* to return ; **zusammen,** together : *zusammenwohnen,* to live together.

The Inseparable particles are never split off or separated by *zu* or *ge-* from the mother verb : *befahren,* to drive or navigate on : *ich befahre diese Strasse ; habe diese Strasse befahren ; will diese Strasse befahren ; hoffe, diese Strasse zu befahren.* They never form the past part. with *ge-*.

Note that the separable prefix is always accentuated : *ABfahren ;* the inseparable prefix never : *beFAHren.*

The inseparable prefixes are : **be-, ent-** (emp before *f*), **er-, ge-, ver-, wider-,** and **miss-.** Examples with the principal meanings of the prefixes are :

be- turns intransitive into transitive : *ich antworte auf Ihren Brief,* I reply to your letter or *ich beantworte Ihren Brief ; weinen,* to weep, *beweinen,* to lament, weep for. It also indicates intensive action : *besehen,* to examine.

ent- indicates a commencement : *entstehen,* to arise ; *entflammen,* to set alight, inflame ; taking off, away, reversal : *entaupten,* to behead ; *entfesseln,* to unchain ; *entehren,* to dishonour.

er- frequently indicates attainment to a state : *erkälten,* to chill ; *sich erkälten,* to catch a cold ; *ergrünen,* to grow green ; *erfahren,* to experience (to attain by " faring ").

ge- often is equivalent to our co-, com-, or con- meaning " together," as in congeal, *gefrieren* ; coagulate, *gerinnen*.

ver- has frequently a pejorative effect : *führen*, to lead, *verführen*, to mislead ; *sich versprechen*, to make a mistake in speaking ; *vergreifen*, to make a mistake in seizing ; *verlegen*, to misplace, also to transfer ; *verraten*, to betray. It also indicates change of state : *vergrössern*, to enlarge ; *verkohlen*, to char.

zer- means " to pieces " : *zerbrechen*, to break to pieces ; *zerbröckeln*, to crumble ; *zerblättern*, to strip of leaves.

miss- indicates failure as in English : *misslingen*, to fail, not to succeed ; *missverstehen*, to misunderstand. *Miss-*, unlike the other inseparable prefixes, is sometimes found with *zu* and *ge-* in the Infinitive and Past Part. as if it were separable : *miss-zuverstehen* ; *missgelaunt*, ill-humoured.

The prefixes **durch-, über-, unter-, um-,** and **wieder-** may be separable or inseparable. If the prefix is accentuated it is separable and both the prefix and the verb generally retain their original meaning. *ÜBERsetzen* means " to set over, to ferry across " : *Die Fähre setzte uns über*, the ferry carried us (ferried us) across ; *ist bereit, uns überzusetzen*, is ready to ferry us ; *hat uns übergesetzt*, has ferried us. *ÜberSETZEN* is inseparable and is used figuratively, i.e. " to set over from one language into another, to translate " : *Er übersetzte das Werk aus dem Deutschen ins Englische*, he translated the work from German into English ; *hat das Werk übersetzt*, has translated the work ; *wünscht, das Werk zu übersetzen*, wishes to translate the work.

Here are some typical examples :

UNTERlaufen : Ein Irrtum ist untergelaufen, an error has slipped *through*. *UnterLAUFEN : Er unterlief den Schlag*, he dodged the *blow* ; *Die Wunde ist mit Blut unterlaufen*, the wound is suffused with blood. *UMgehen : Die Räder gehen um*, the wheels turn round. *UmGEHEN : Ich umging die Regenpfütze*, I avoided the puddle. *WIEDERholen : Ich holte die Kinder wieder*, I fetched the children *back* ; *WiederHOLEN : Ich wiederholte den Befehl*, I repeated *the command*. *DURCHreisen : Ich reiste durch, ohne mich in Berlin aufzuhalten*, I travelled straight through without staying in Berlin. *DurchREISEN : Ich durchreiste ganz Deutschland*, I travelled about in the whole of Germany.

B. REFLEXIVE VERBS

There is no difficulty in the conjugation of Reflexive Verbs, but it should be remembered that the reflexive pronoun may be in the Dative Case. We give below the Present and Imperative of *sich erinnern*, to remember, and *sich schmeicheln*, to flatter oneself :

Present

ich erinnere mich	ich schmeichle mir
du erinnerst dich	du schmeichelst dir
er erinnert sich	er schmeichelt sich
sie erinnert sich	sie schmeichelt sich
es erinnert sich	es schmeichelt sich
wir erinnern uns	wir schmeicheln uns
ihr erinnert euch	ihr schmeichelt euch
sie erinnern sich	sie schmeicheln sich
Sie erinnern sich	Sie schmeicheln sich

Imperative

erinnere dich ! **schmeichle dir !**
erinnert euch ! **schmeichelt euch !**
erinnern Sie sich ! **schmeicheln Sie sich !**

The Perfect is : *ich habe mich erinnert ; ich habe mir geschmeichelt.*

C. IMPERSONAL VERBS

These verbs have a "sham" subject *es*, used only because we are accustomed to a verb having a subject of some sort, as in : It is raining, *es regnet*.

There is a large class in German, such as : *Es klopft*, there's a knock, somebody's knocking ; *Es klingelt*, there's a ring, somebody's ringing the bell ; *Es riecht hier nach Gas*, there's a smell of gas here.

Es gibt, there is, there are, is used in a general sense : *Es gibt viel Wasser in der See*, there is much water in the sea ; *Es gibt auch viele Fische darin*, there are also many fishes in it. In a particular sense *es ist, es sind* are used : *Es ist viel Wasser in diesem Glase*, there is much water in this glass ; *Es sind seltene Fische im Aquarium*, there are rare fishes in the aquarium. The *es* of *es ist, es sind* disappears if it does not stand at the beginning : *Frisches Wasser ist im Glase*. *Es gibt* governs an Acc. : *Es gibt keinen Mensch, der . . . ,* there is no man who...

There is a useful group concerned with the weather : *Es regnet*, it is raining ; *Es schneit*, it is snowing ; *Es donnert*, it is thundering ; *Es wird kalt*, it is getting cold, etc.

Some Impersonals require the Dat. : *Es gefällt mir*, it pleases me ; *Es geschieht mir*, it happens to me ; *Es gelingt mir*, I succeed ; *Es fehlt ihm an Mut*, he lacks courage.

German also uses a Passive Impersonal freely : *Es wird hier getanzt*, dancing goes on here (but *Hier wird getanzt*) *; Es wurde viel gelacht*, there was a great deal of laughing going on ; *Heute wird gebadet*, there's bathing today.

XXIII. THE MODAL AUXILIARIES

These are : **dürfen,** to be allowed (our " dare ") ; **können,** to be able (can) ; **mögen,** may, like ; **müssen,** to be obliged, must ; **sollen,** to be (morally) obliged, shall ; **wollen,** to be willing, will.

They are conjugated as follows :

PRESENT

	Indic.	Subj.	Indic.	Subj.	Indic.	Subj.
ich	darf	dürfe	kann	könne	mag	möge
du	darfst	dürfest	kannst	könnest	magst	mögest
er	darf	dürfe	kann	könne	mag	möge
wir	dürfen	dürfen	können	können	mögen	mögen
ihr	dürft	dürfet	könnt	könnet	mögt	möget
sie	dürfen	dürfen	können	können	mögen	mögen
ich	muss	müsse	soll	solle	will	wolle
du	musst	müssest	sollst	sollest	willst	wollest
er	muss	müsse	soll	solle	will	wolle
wir	müssen	müssen	sollen	sollen	wollen	wollen
ihr	müsst	müsset	sollt	sollet	wollt	wollet
sie	müssen	müssen	sollen	sollen	wollen	wollen

IMPERFECT

Indic. ich durfte konnte mochte musste solite wollte, etc.
Subj. ich dürfte könnte möchte müsste sollte wollte, etc.

The Present Participles are regularly formed by adding -*d* to the Infinitive, but they are little used.   The Past Participles are **gedurft, gekonnt, gemocht, gemusst, gesollt, gewollt,** but these are used only when—as rarely happens—there is no dependent Infinitive : *Ich habe es gekonnt,* I have been able (to do) it.   With a dependent Infinitive the Infinitive replaces the Past Part. : *Ich habe es tun können,* I have been able to do it.   In the Compound Tenses we shall therefore conjugate the verbs with a dependent Infinitive.

Perf. **ich habe sprechen dürfen, können,** etc.
Pluperf. **ich hatte sprechen dürfen,** etc.
Fut. **ich werde sprechen dürfen, können,** etc.
Fut. Perf. **ich werde haben sprechen dürfen,** etc.
Cond. **ich würde sprechen dürfen,** etc.
Past
  Cond. **ich würde haben sprechen dürfen** or (more usually)
      ich hätte sprechen dürfen
Imperative : Only *wollen* has one : *wolle l, wollt l, wollen Sie l*

Examples of the use of these verbs are :

dürfen : Man darf hier nicht rauchen, you may not (are not allowed to) smoke here.   *Drarf ich um noch eine Tasse Tee bitten?* May (might) I ask for another cup of tea? *Sie dürfen so etwas nicht sagen,* you shouldn't (mustn't) say such a thing. *Ich habe die ganze Zeit kein Wort sagen dürfen,* I couldn't (was not allowed to) say a word the whole time. *Das dürfte wohl whas ein,* that is very probably true.

können: *Ich kann es nicht sehen, weil ich keine Brille habe,* I can't see it
because I haven't any spectacles. *Wir können ihn jeden Augenblick
erwarten,* we can (may) expect him any moment. *Sie können nach
Hause gehen,* you can go home (there is nothing to stop you). Note the
difference between *konnte* and *könnte: Als ich in Berlin wohnte, konnte
ich mit Deutschen sprechen,* when I was in Berlin I could (was able to)
speak with Germans. *Wenn ich in Berlin wäre, könnte ich mit Deutschen
sprechen,* if I were in Berlin I could (should be able to) speak with
Germans. Note also: *Ich hätte ihn sehen können, wenn ich nicht zu
spät gekommen wäre,* I could have seen him (should have been able to
see him), if I had not come too late.

mögen: *Das mag die Wahrheit sein,* that may be the truth. *Was Sie auch
sagen mögen,* glaube ich Ihnen nicht, whatever you may say I don't
believe you. *Ich mag diesen Wein nicht,* I don't like this wine. *Ich
möchte ihn gern besuchen,* I should like to call on him. *Ich hätte das
Buch gern lesen mögen,* I should have liked to read the book (or in
incorrect but very usual English; I should like to have read the book).

müssen: *Das Kind muss seinem Vater gehorchen,* the child must obey his
father. *Er musste plötzlich abreisen,* he had to (was obliged to) go off
suddenly. *Wir haben einen hohen Preis bezahlen müssen,* we have had
to (or had to) pay a high price. *Er müsste schon angekommen sein,* he
must have already arrived, I think (the Subj. here indicating probability). *Sie hätten viel fleissiger arbeiten müssen,* you ought to have
worked much harder.

sollen: *Du sollst nicht töten,* thou shalt not kill. It is also used in the
meaning of " is said to ": *Der König soll krank sein,* the King is said to
be (reported to be) ill. *Man sollte dieses Bier kalt trinken,* you ought
to drink this beer cold. *Wenn es ihm misslingen sollte, würde ich es
bedauern,* if he should fail I should regret it. *Sie sollen ein kleines
Geschenk bekommen,* you shall get a small present. *Sie hätten das nicht
tun sollen,* you ought not to have done it.

wollen: *Wollen Sie mich begleiten?* Will you accompany me? *Er wollte
mir helfen,* he wanted (intended) to help me. *Wollen Sie Tee oder
Kaffee?* Do you want tea or coffee? *Er will den Brief nicht
geschrieben haben,* he claims not to have written the letter. *Wir wollen
mal sehen,* we'll see. *Ich hätte sie gern begleiten wollen,* I should have
liked to accompany her.

The dependent Infinitive of verbs of motion is frequently omitted:
Ich will nach Hause, I want to go home; *Er muss weg,* he must go
away.

The verbs *heissen,* to bid, order; *helfen,* to help; *hören,* to hear;
lassen, to let; *sehen,* to see, also use the Infinitive form instead of the
Past Part. when they have a dependent Infinitive: *Er hat mich
kommen heissen,* he bid me come; *Wir haben ihr umziehen helfen,*
we have helped her to move (her furniture); *Ich habe einen Brief
schreiben lassen,* I have had a letter written; *Ich habe mir das Haar
schneiden lassen,* I have had my hair cut; *Wir haben ihn spielen
sehen,* we have seen him play.

XXIV. A. VERBS WHICH GOVERN THE DATIVE AND GENITIVE

The following verbs govern the Dative: *befehlen*, to command; *begegnen*, to meet; *danken*, to thank; *dienen*, to serve; *drohen*, to threaten; *erlauben*, to allow; *fehlen*, to lack; *folgen*, to follow; *gefallen*, to please; *gehorchen*, to obey; *gelingen*, to succeed; *geschehen*, to happen; *glauben*, to believe; *gleichen*, to resemble; *gehören*, to belong; *gratulieren*, to congratulate; *genügen*, to suffice; *helfen*, to help; *schaden*, to harm; *schmeicheln*, to flatter; *trauen*, to trust; *widersprechen*, to contradict; *verzeihen*, to pardon, forgive; *ziemen*, to suit, become.

The Genitive is found with: *bedürfen*, to need; *sich bedienen*, to make use of; *sich bemächtigen*, to seize, take possession of; *sich erinnern*, to remember; *sich erfreuen*, to enjoy; *gedenken*, to remember; *sich schämen*, to be ashamed of; *spotten*, to mock.

The Genitive is, however, showing a tendency to fall out of use and to be replaced by a preposition: instead of *Ich erinnere mich meines Freundes*, it is more usual to say and write, *Ich erinnere mich an meinen Freund*, I remember my friend.

B. VERBS REQUIRING PREPOSITIONS

NOTE—In the following, Accusative is abbreviated to (A) and Dative to (D).

Verbs requiring **an**: *denken an* (A), to think of; *sich erinnern an* (A), to remember; *erkranken an* (D), to fall sick of; *sich gewöhnen an* (A), to get used to; *leiden an* (D), to suffer from; *schreiben an* (A), to write to; *sich wenden an* (A), to apply to; *zweifeln an* (D), to doubt.

Verbs requiring **auf**: *achten auf* (A), to pay heed to; *bestehen auf* (D) to insist on (but *bestehen aus* (D), to consist of); *eingehen auf* (A), to agree to; *folgen auf* (A), to follow (after); *sich freuen auf* (A), to look forward to; *warten auf* (A), to wait for; *zeigen auf* (A), to point at.

Verbs requiring **über**: *sich ärgern über* (A), to get angry at; *sich belaufen auf* (A), to amount to; *klagen über* (A), to complain of; *lachen über* (A), to laugh at; *spotten über* (A), to mock at; *urteilen über* (A), to judge of; *sich wundern über* (A), to be astonished at.

Verbs requiring **nach**: *schicken nach* (D), to send for; *sich sehnen nach* (D), to long for; *streben nach* (D), to strive for.

Verbs requiring **um**: *bitten um* (A), to ask for; *flehen um* (A), to implore; *sich kümmern um* (A), to worry about.

Verbs requiring **vor**: *sich fürchten vor* (D), to be frightened of; *sich hüten vor* (D), to be on one's guard against; *warnen vor* (D), to warn of.

XXV. WORD-ORDER

In German, word-order pivots on the finite verb, i.e. the inflected verb agreeing with the subject.

I. In principal clauses the normal order is: 1. subject; 2. finite verb; 3. all that comes within the scope of the verb: the objects, direct and indirect, the adverbs, and lastly those words closely linked with the finite verb, such as the Infinitive, Past Part., separable particle, predicative adjective.

Note that in German the subject cannot be separated by an adverb from its subject as in English, e.g. " I often seen him " is: *Ich sehe ihn oft.*

Here is a rather laboured example of this word-order: *Ich habe ihn gestern um 2 Uhr auf der Strasse mit grosser Freude gegrüsst,* I greeted him with great joy in the street yesterday at 2 o'clock.

First comes the subject *ich*; next the finite verb *habe*; next the pronoun object *ihn*; then the adverbs in the order of time, place, manner; lastly the Past Part. *gegrüsst.* Note the order of the adverbs: indefinite time first, definite time next, then place, then manner. Remember: TIME BEFORE PLACE. And note also: the FINITE VERB ALWAYS TAKES THE SECOND PLACE.

If we use a dependent Infinitive we get:

> *Ich werde ihn...morgen grüssen.*

If we have an Infinitive plus a Past Part.:

> *Ich werde ihn...gegrüsst haben,*

the Infinitive following the Past Part.

If we have a Past Part. of the same form as the Infinitive:

> *Ich habe ihn...grüssen müssen,*

the Past Part. *müssen* following the Infinitive.

II. We get Inverted Order if any word other than the subject begins the sentence, the subject being then switched directly behind the finite verb. All of the following are possible:

(*a*) *Ihn habe ich gestern...gegrüsst,* it was he whom I greeted.

(*b*) *Gestern um 2 Uhr habe ich...gegrüsst,* it was yesterday at 2 that I greeted him.

(*c*) *Auf der Strasse habe ich...gegrüsst,* it was in the street that...

(*d*) *Mit grosser Freude habe ich...gegrüsst,* it was with great joy that...

(*e*) *Gegrüsst habe ich ihn...,* I greeted him (i.e. I didn't pass him by).

As you see, putting a word or phrase in the first place brings it into prominence.

The subject may be an Interrogative: *Wer hat ihn gegrüsst?*; and this word-order may, with rising intonation, be used to ask a question: *Ich habe ihn gegrüsst?*   I have greeted him?

III. In questions the finite verb comes first : *Habe ich ihn gegrüsst?* It is also first in the Imperative : *Grüssen Sie ihn!* Greet him! and in exclamations : *War das doch schön!* Wasn't that lovely!

IV. In Subordinate clauses the finite verb falls to the end. (See pp. 286 and 291.)

V. When a verb takes an Acc. and a Dat., the Dat. comes first if the Acc. is a noun or any pronoun except the personal and reflexive :

> *Ich gab meinem Sohn ein schönes Buch.*
>
> *Ich gab ihm ein schönes Buch.*
>
> *Ich gab ihm jenes.* (I gave him that one.)

If the Acc. is a personal or reflexive pronoun, the Acc. precedes the Dat. :

Ich gab es ihm, I gave it him ; *Wir bringen sie Ihnen,* we bring you them ; *Er schenkte es ihr,* he made her a present of it ; *Das rechte Verständnis hat sich ihm eröffnet,* the proper understanding has revealed itself to him.

VI. A German adjective precedes the word it qualifies and so do its modifiers. This leads to long, involved concertina-like adjectival groups, especially with past and present participles :

In einem Artikel des eben geschlossenen Vertrags, in a clause of the treaty just concluded ; *Einen durch ganz Europa ausgebreiteten Briefwechsel sorgte er selbst,* he himself attended to a correspondence spread over the whole of Europe ; *Es gibt nur ein einheitliches, für alle Verben Konjugationssystem,* there is only one uniform system of conjugation valid for all verbs ; *Die zu wählende Form,* the form to be chosen (note that this Passive use of the Pres. Part. is common). Finally here is a nice long one such as Mark Twain described in *A Tramp Abroad* : *Das von mir mehr und mehr beim Unterricht in den Oberklassen und bei der Unterweisung von Lehrern in Fortbildungs-kursen empfundene Bedürfnis.* The first word *das* qualifies the last word *Bedürfnis* and all that is in between is one adjectival group! It means: The need felt more and more by me when teaching in upper forms and instructing teachers in Continuation Courses. These headache-giving and only by patience and ingenuity to be unravelled adjectival groups perhaps explain a certain woolliness in German thought and, on the other hand, their capacity for plodding on patiently to the end!

Nicht falls to the end of the sentence if it modifies the verb : *Ich zeigte ihm die Fahrkarte nicht,* I didn't show him, the ticket. Of course it comes just before the separable particle, the Past Part., or the dependent Infinitive : *Ich zeigte ihm die Fahrkarte nicht vor,* I didn't show (produce) the ticket (to the conductor) ; *Ich habe ihm die Fahrkarte nicht vorgezeigt ; Ich brauchte ihm die Fahrkarte nicht vorzuzeigen,* I didn't need to show him the ticket.

It stands immediately before the individual word or words it modifies : *Ich zeigte nicht ihm die Fahrkarte...,* I didn't show *him* the ticket (but somebody else) ; *Ich zeigte ihm nicht die Fahrkarte...,* I didn't show him *the ticket* (but something else).

XXVI. A. USE OF THE ARTICLES

The Definite Article is used:

1. With the days, months, seasons: *Am Montag; im Juli; im Winter.*

2. With Fem. names of countries: *in der Schweiz*, but not with neuters unless qualified: *England*, but *das alte England*.

3. With proper nouns if qualified: *der kleine Hans*, little Johnny.

4. With parts of the body if the reference is clear: *Der Bauer kam herein, den Hut in der Hand* (or *mit dem Hut in der Hand*), the farmer entered with his hat in his hand. Note *den Hut*, the Absolute Acc.

5. With nouns denoting a class: *Der Mensch ist sterblich*, man is mortal; abstract nouns: *der Geiz*, avarice; *die Chemie*, chemistry; names of materials: *das Eisen*, iron.

6. With the names of streets, squares, etc.: *Die Kipdorfstrasse liegt um die Ecke*, Kipdorf Street is round the corner.

7. The Definite Article is used where English uses the Indef.: *Das kostet zehn Mark das Pfund.*

8. The Article is omitted with *sein, werden, bleiben* if a trade or profession is referred to: *Er wird Kaufmann*, he is going to be a business man; *Ich bin Lehrer*, I am a teacher; *Er bleibt Soldat*, he remains a soldier.

9. The Indefinite Article is omitted before *hundert* and *tausend*: *hundert Mann*, a hundred men. Note the Sing, as also in: *fünf Glas Bier; drei Pfund Butter*, but with Fem. nouns the Plural: *sechs Flaschen Wein.* Note the omission of " of " in: *ein Glas Bier eine Flasche Wein; eine Tasse Tee*, an in *die Stadt Berlin*, the city of, Berlin; *die Universität Heidelberg.*

B. AGREEMENT

The finite verb agrees with its subject in number and person: *ich machE; er machT; die Kinder machEN*. In English collective nouns tend to take a plural verb: the Government have . . ., the police are . . .; England have won the Test, etc. In German they are singular and take the verb in the singular: *die Regierung hat . . .; die Polizei ist; England hat den Wettkampf gewonnen.*

If, however, a word of quantity or number is followed by a plural noun, the verb is often found in the plural: *eine Anzahl Leute war* or *waren . . .*, a number of people were; *eine Menge Wagen stehen* or *steht . . .*, a number of carriages stand. If two words combine to make one idea or are almost synonymous with each other or closely related, the verb may be in the singular: *Gleich und gleich gesellt sich gern*, birds of a feather flock together; *Alt und jung freut sich*, old and young rejoice; *Zwei und zwei sind (ist) vier.*

A noun in apposition is in the same case as the noun to which it refers: *am Montag, dem ersten September*, on Monday, the 1st Sept.; *Ich sprach mit Marie, der jüngsten Tochter meines Bruders*, I spoke to Mary, the youngest daughter of my brother.